"No greater calamity can happen to a people than to break utterly with its past."

The Right Honorable William E. Gladstone
Prime Minister of Great Britain
1868-1894

The Moffetts
of Leggygowan & the Land of Lincoln

David M. Moffett & Mark K. Windover

The Moffetts
of Leggygowan & the Land of Lincoln

Copyright, 2019
David M. Moffett & Mark K. Windover

Moffett map on the front cover created by Constance Brown.
Copyright, 2019, Constance Brown, Redstone Studios.

Print of Moffett map by Michael Suozzi, Suozzi Studios,
digital fine arts printer.

Photograph of Moffett map by Tim Nighswander,
IMAGING4ART, fine arts photographer.

Cover layout by Capri Porter.
Interior layout by Capri Porter
and Mark K. Windover.

Printed in the United States of America

ISBN: 978-1-7322-135-5-5

Published by Legacies & Memories
St. Augustine, Florida

www.LegaciesandMemoriesPublishing.com

Dedication

The completion of this story has been a dream of many family members for a number of years. The inspiration came to me about fifteen years ago when my Aunt Margaret Moffett Jones (my father's sister) handed me a two-page account of the family history recited at a family gathering on Christmas Day in 1900. It turned out the accounts of the family history were mostly factual and thus served as the foundation that lead to this book.

My curiosity with the Moffett family history began with the Christmas Day story of the Moffetts. Ever since my Aunt Margaret and I discussed the history of our Scottish clan, I became intrigued with the idea of retracing the steps of those immigrants that came before us. I wanted to know more. Where did they come from? How did they live? What were the political and economic issues of their time? Were they farmers or merchants? What were their religious beliefs? What kind of people would leave their beloved Scotland for Northern Ireland and then take a dangerous voyage to the United States? What happened in their search for freedom and economic independence as they traveled through Pennsylvania across the frontier to Kentucky and then finally on to Illinois? How did they live, survive, then ultimately prosper in such a new and difficult period in our nation's history? I wanted to bring to life the story of our ancestors in hopes of better understanding ourselves and "where we came from." Understanding people in context of their times helps us better understand who we are today.

My first step was to seek the services of a remarkable genealogist, Mark K. Windover, in Williamstown, Massachusetts. Mark's skills as a genealogist and his personal enthusiasm for the project heightened my own desire to complete this very complicated, and at times, overwhelmingly difficult attempt at finishing the Moffett story. Twelve years later and with Mark's hard work and tenacity, the story is complete and the story of this Moffett clan will be documented and known for all future generations. I am extremely proud of this wonderful story. It has been an experience I will always remember.

I wish to dedicate this book first to my Aunt Margaret. Her dedication to uncovering the history and her enthusiasm became my passion. I was challenged by her to learn more and share it with all the Moffetts who follow in our footsteps. Aunt Margaret was a wonderful aunt, mother and wife. She touched us all and she will always be remembered for her love, devotion and dedication to her family, community and church. We all miss her.

Finally, I wish to dedicate this book to my mother, Dorothy Moffett McCall. My life's successes are directly attributed to her dedication and devotion. She always encouraged us to look at the world with enthusiasm, curiosity and optimism – all good traits a true Scotsman possesses. Mom's continued support of me throughout all stages of my life has always been comforting and assuring. A comfort only a mother can provide. She was always a great example to me how to live one's life. For this I will always be grateful.

I hope all future generations of Moffetts will enjoy this story. Please pass it on to future generations. The story of the Moffetts' immigration to the U.S. in the late 1700s is just one of a million examples of a people's pursuit of freedom and a better life. Always be proud of your great heritage and remember where you have come from, and let it be a guide for where you are going.

David McKenzie Moffett
June 5, 2019

Contents

Acknowledgments

This book was twelve years in the making. The research effort was conducted continuously over the course of that time in the United States, Scotland and Northern Ireland by myself and the genealogists noted below. In addition, a number of Moffett family members provided insightful advice, unique exhibits, answers to my endless and intrusive questions, and thoughtful encouragement. All of which were welcomed and appreciated. I am so deeply appreciative for the support all these family members provided. I pray they find the final product, "The Moffetts of Leggygowan & the Land of Lincoln," to be an enjoyable and life-long treasure to remind us all of the rich heritage from which we come.

United States: Mark Windover, coauthor and genealogist, has worked on this project almost continuously for the entire time. His rich insight, persistence, advice and leadership were invaluable. All the historical setting backdrop was Mark's product, as well as the early years research on William Moffett1685 and son, James Moffett, and the family in America with unique focus on David, William and Thomas Moffett, the immigrants from Leggygowan. I will always be grateful to Mark and the publication of the first book, "The Moffetts of Lauder, Loughinisland, Leggygowan & the Land of Lincoln," and the revised book, "The Moffetts of Leggygowan & the Land of Lincoln."

Scottish Genealogists: The following genealogists conducted extensive research primarily to identify our oldest known ancestor, William Moffet, born in 1685 in Scotland. The bulk of their research focused on original public source documents and in many cases poring through private archives and collections of family papers throughout Scotland. I learned a great deal about Scotland, the rich history and the plight of the people of Scotland during the 17th and 18th centuries. It is in their research that I developed such a tremendous pride in my Scottish roots and will be forever grateful for their important and unique participation in making this book a reality.

Dr. Bruce Durie
Alison Farrer, Ayershire Genealogists
The Genealogists and Officers of Clan Moffat, UK and U.S.A.
The Moffat Museum,Moffat, Scotland
Ian Imchad of Ian Imchad Ancestry
Beverly and Hazel Crammond

Northern Ireland Genealogists: The bulk of the research effort by these distinguished and incredibly talented and resourceful genealogists was focused on the family in Leggygowan and Saintfield and sought to identify the connection to a William Moffet of Scotland. The expansive family information about this courageous and loving family is directly attributable to the efforts of these great researchers.

Ms. Beverly Brown,Belfast
Mr. Brian Watson, Family Ulster, Belfast
The Saintfield Heritage Society
PRONI
Ros Davies and her incredible website of everything County Down

Moffett Family members: Almost all of the Moffett-specific exhibits in this book are from the archives and personal collections of the Moffett family members listed below. All these family members descend from William1763 and branches thereof and hence their knowledge was directly relevant to this project. All had great familiarity with the family trees and earlier research efforts. This family is blessed to have generations of diligent record keepers. Without these records, it would have been impossible to catalogue and research this incredible story of what I deemed our Family Manifest Destiny. Their willingness to share their knowledge and exhibits has been so helpful to establish the story as revealed in this book. I want to express my sincere appreciation to all family members who answered my unfamiliar emails and phone calls and responded with their unique and gracious contribution. To you, I am eternally grateful and forever in your indebtedness.

Helen Moffett Russell: Helen has long since passed and although I never met her, I feel like she is with me every day on this project. As early as the 1960s, Helen devoted much of her spare time to our family genealogy. Researching, cataloguing, traveling and contacting family members are evident in every single document I pick up. She compiled hundreds of pictures, exhibits, family information sheets and original documents. She transposed original documents from the 1700s into lasting source materials for future generations to enjoy. Helen had a very sharp attention to detail and it's her clear analytical eye that dissected difficult documents into stories. She traveled to Leggygowan and knocked on doors to find long lost relatives. She sent letters and responded to anyone who would help her locate missing family members. I know this all to be true because in every document and picture, I see "HMR" at the top. We are all heavily indebted to Helen for all she did and the legacy she left behind. I only regret that I never meet her. But somehow, I feel she has guided me and many others in the preservation our family's story in history. We are so blessed to have had Helen Moffett Russell preserve our family history.

Jim Oldfield: I can't say enough about the contribution Jim has made to building the family history. He built an incredible family tree extending from John Bigham down to the current generation of Moffetts. We are all very indebted to Jim and can't express how appreciative I am of his lifetime of work on behalf of the family.

Susan Moffett: I found Susan several years ago in Indiana. She was very receptive and helpful to me by sharing her treasure chest of family documents all curated and catalogued in a digestible and understandable manner. Susan was so supportive and was always willing to help. Susan recently passed. We will all miss her. She made such a contribution. I am so sorry she didn't see the final product.

Cole Scott Moffett: I tracked down Cole several years ago and the search was extremely gratifying. I refer to Cole as the patriarch of the family since he descends from William's oldest son, James. He had tubs of family history sheets dating back to William of Scotland compiled by an aunt. Cole enthusiastically shared all his documents and responded to all cries for help. Again, we all benefit from a family of recordkeepers. Scott's involvement came at a very critical time and I am so appreciative of his very important help.

Francis Ruddick: Francis was one of the first persons to return my intrusive emails. Her significant family tree on Ancestry was very helpful in filling in a lot of missing names and dates. She was always encouraging and supportive despite my many requests for information and reminders. I will always remember her thoughtful encouragement and eagerness to help.

Laura Moffett Darby: One great benefit of this research was that I was able to locate all the descendants of John Bigham Moffett II (son of William Thomas Moffett). As Jim Oldfield once said, "We all wondered what happened to this branch of Moffetts." A second book, published in 2019, is entitled "John Bigham Moffett II and Descendants, the Southern Moffetts." This entire branch lived mainly in Georgia and Florida. Laura is one of the Southern Moffetts, just as the coauthor is as well. Laura was so helpful in helping me with establishing the identities of this branch. She responded quickly with requests for pictures and stories of this branch of the family. Book 2 on John Bigham Moffett is to a large extent the reflection of her efforts. I am extremely thankful to Laura for all her help and wisdom.

Kevin Kittilson: Another source of Moffett Family information came from Kevin. I found Kevin on the Internet and he quickly responded to my inquiry. His ties go back to Decatur and his knowledge and familiarity with family stories of Lincoln were very helpful. Always responsive and willingness to help, Kevin's insight on the DNA relationships also helped put people in perspective.

Kyle Moffit: Kyle was another early responder to my call for help. He too responded to my intrusive email for information about the Moffetts. Kyle has the distinction of being both a Moffitt and a Moffett. More research needs to be done to sort out the connection between these Moffitts and their source in Scotland. Kyle is extremely knowledgeable and always responded to inquiries about things Moffett.

Randy Moffett: Cousin to Laura and also very helpful early in the research aspect of the project. As a "Southern Moffett," Randy helped put many of pieces of the Hebert Rutherford Moffett branch of our family together, always checking in to volunteer to help in any way. I appreciate Randy's enthusiasm for this book and I know he always looked forward to reading it.

Peggy Moffett Jones Cobb: My direct cousin, Peggy, has been an enthusiastic supporter of this project from the beginning. In fact, it was her mother, my aunt, who was the family genealogist of our branch. It was Aunt Margaret who shared with me the reading of the family story of 1900. It was also her who tasked me with continuing the research further and passing on the story of the Moffetts. Some 20 years later, I hope I succeeded. Peggy has been invaluable in sharing the family archives of pictures, papers and forgotten stories. She climbed through all the abandoned closet shelves and drawers to find records and documents known only to her mother and forgotten by most. Peggy's sense of family pride and history has made her a kindred spirit in this effort, and her can-do attitude always came at the right time. She is a real joy to have as a cousin and it will be this experience that binds further our sense of family just as her mother, Margaret Moffett Jones, did.

Elizabeth (Liz) Perry: Elizabeth is a relative by marriage and resides in Crossgar, County Down. She is the only living relative to the early Moffetts in County Down that I have been able to locate. Our connection arose when Elizabeth heard about the Moffetts at a Saintfield Heritage Society meeting in 2018. We both shot off letters to each other and finally met on a trip to Saintfield in May, 2019. Elizabeth is a very engaging and delightful person who eagerly invited us to her home to see all her Moffett and Morrow family heirlooms and family records. We had such an enjoyable weekend spending time with Elizabeth. Of particular interest are four letters she has preserved dating back to the 1890s. All four letters were correspondence between her grandfather, Martin Perry, of Saintfield and William Z. Moffett of Minneapolis. William Z. descends from James Moffett, oldest son of William Moffett who immigrated to America in 1784. These letters are wonderful expressions of relatives seeking information about their family ties back in County Down. The family connection between the author and Liz Perry is as follows: Liz Perry's grandfather was Martin Perry. Martin Perry's grandmother was Jane Moffett, wife of Christopher Morrow. Jane Moffett was the granddaughter of James1720. What a joy it is to have a family connection in Saintfield. You couldn't ask for a more wonderful individual to share your kindred spirits than Liz Perry.

Finally, I would like to thank my family and especially my wife, Lori, for indulging me while I fill rooms with books and stacks of papers sprawled all over the house. The family describes this disease as an obsession of unknown proportions and consequences. How can someone be so fascinated with the dead, stomping through graveyards from Scotland to Tallahassee, Florida only to hear a shriek of joy by a turned-over gravestone? And more importantly, when does this stop, and have we run out of dead people yet? My answer has always been just one more look, one more book, one more Internet search, one more DNA test and one more dinner disturbed by my response of "what did you say" while I pondered a newly found piece of the family pie. I am forever grateful to have such a supportive family who manages a smile when I say, 'guess what else I learned today?'

David McKenzie Moffett

The Moffetts

of Leggygowan & the Land of Lincoln

1 — The Surname Moffat

Surnames are an ancient innovation, having been with us for millennia. The Christian New Testament makes references to surname-like devices at several points. The reference to St. Paul as Paul (Saul) of Tarsus is such a device. Even the Savior, for all his fame and the seeming uniqueness of his given name, was often tagged with the place-name reference, "Jesus of Nazareth."

Originally, surnames were not passed on from generation to generation, because they would lose their descriptive value in most cases. The change to the use of surnames as permanent family names occurred at different times in different countries. In England and the Scottish Lowlands, it happened very early – well before the emigrations to the Americas began.

There are several different types of surnames, classified by the nature of their derivation. All surnames were originally used to distinguish among persons with the same given (first) name. If there were three men named John in a village, it would be helpful to have a distinct second name to identify which one was being discussed. So surnames were in some ways descriptive of the person.

Some surnames are occupational, such as Baker, Taylor, Smith or Carter. Another group is referred to as patronymic, which are derived from the name of a person's father or other forebear. Examples of these, in English speaking lands, are Johnson, Thomson, Williams, and so on. In cultures where languages other than English are spoken, suffixes and prefixes distinctive to that language are used. Another group of surnames is one based on some personal characteristic, such as Long, Short, Brown, White, or Gross (meaning large). They may also relate to a specific spot where the person lived, such as Atwood, Hill, Lane, Ford, and so on.

The name Moffett is none of the above, but rather what is known as a place name, or locality surname. These names are taken from the name of the place where the person had lived – a town, village, settlement, province, etc. Some other examples of these would be London, Lancaster, Manchester, Kent and Berlin. Those names are all derived from places with whose names we are most probably familiar. Moffett however is one of the much larger group of place names of whose locality name might well have no idea – such as Ashby, Kipling, Tetlow, Cottingham, Kempton and Renton. Originally, these surnames usually included the preposition "of" or, in Norman French, "de". Persons who were given the name would therefore be called John of Kipling, James of Kent, Paul of Cottingham, and so on. Eventually, when surnames began to be retained as permanent family surnames, the preposition was dropped.

The surname Moffett is taken from the parish of Moffat in Scotland, which is situated in the former Scottish county of Dumfries.[1] No one is certain of its etymology, but the consensus is that the name comes from a Gaelic language description of the topography of the place. There are two elements, *magh*, meaning a plain, and *fada*, meaning long; i.e., a long plain.[2]

The earliest citation of the name as a surname dates from the year 1232, when a cleric named Nicholas de Mufet witnessed a charter by Walter, bishop of Glasgow; and his name appears again as the archdeacon of Theuidale in 1250-51. This same priest was elected bishop of Glasgow in 1268, but died in 1270. George F. Black also found records of the name bearing dates in 1296 (de Muffet and Moffet), 1303 (de Muffet), 1348 (de Moffat), and 1467 (de Moffethe).[3]

These locality surnames were useful only if used somewhere other than the place from which the person hailed. If someone lived in London all his life, it would not often make sense for Londoners to refer to him as Robert London. However, if he came to London from Manchester, the Londoners might well call him Robert Manchester. So while the surname Moffett was first used to refer to one of this family's ancestors, who was a native of the parish, probably few or none of the subsequent generations lived there.

One of the more confounding aspects of surnames is that so many of them can be found with a variety of spellings, particularly in historical records; and the older the record, the greater the variations may be. From the perspective of the twenty-first century in America, this is an unsettling aspect, but until the nineteenth century, there was very little desire or need to standardize spellings of any words, especially names. Anyone who has read documents or other writings which are 200 or more years old can attest to the large number of odd spellings in the text. Often, many words were not spelled according to today's standard spelling. Furthermore, the same word may have been spelled differently in different places in the same document. Even capitalization followed no very strict rules.[4]

Place names and surnames were certainly not exempt from the spelling vagaries of earlier centuries. This especially was true in such places as Scotland and Ireland, where the ruling class was often of a different native tongue than were the persons who had first applied a name to a person or place. There might be one obvious way to write Leggygowan or Moffett in Gaelic, but when written in English it might acquire a variety of spellings from different persons. The place in Dumfriesshire which today bears the standard spelling of Moffat has borne a variety of spellings, as have those persons who bear the place's name as a surname.

---

[1] See the map on page 11.

[2] Henry Harrison, *Surnames of the United Kingdom: A concise Etymological Dictionary* (Baltimore, 1969), vol. 2, p. 25.

[3] George F. Black, *The Surnames of Scotland* (Edinburgh, 1993), p. 604.

[4] Bill Bryson, *The Mother Tongue – English and How it Got That Way* (New York, 1900), Chapter 8.

While the name of that place is now standardized, the surname can commonly be found spelled Moffett, Moffet Maffet or Maffett, as well as other variations. In his discussion of the surname, George Black notes the following spellings: Moffat, Moffatt, Moffett, Meffatt, Meffet, de Mufet, Maffit, Moffit, Moffot, Muffett and Mwffett.[5]

In family history research, the variations in the spelling of surnames very commonly present themselves in various records. This will often be reflected in this work when discussing a person with the Moffett surname, but while citing the wording of original sources; otherwise, the current standard spelling used by this line of the family – Moffett – will be used. When referring to the parish in Dumfries, the now standard spelling of Moffat will be used.

Moffett Shield

Moffett

---

[5] Black, p. 604.

2 — The Story

The American story is one of immigrants. Even those noble souls whom we currently refer to as "Native" Americans, originated somewhere on the Eurasian landmass, and came to the Americas only recently in the history of homo sapiens. We Americans often speak of our nation as a melting pot, where the various peoples, from all corners of the world, have come (and continue to do so) usually looking for a better life. In most cases, within a generation, these people begin to adopt the language and culture of this place, albeit often with respect and fond attachment to at least a few of the traditions of their former homes.

A generation ago, the study of one's ancestry was a limited endeavor, pursued almost entirely by those whose forbears were among the first Europeans to come to this continent. Much of the popularity which this discipline then enjoyed was due to the desire to distance one's self from the more recent immigrants, and from persons of other races. Today, genealogy is a very different experience, shared by persons of every socio-economic class, and every race, religion, and national origin. It has become the tool of the whole of society as we all begin to feel cut off from who our family once was. Even as we all bear great pride in America, we are increasingly thrilled by the opportunity to learn what came before the American experience. Today, any Americans who want to know where and how their forbears lived can reasonably expect to be able to do so.

Of course, no family has made a clean break from their former home. All of us carry some cultural inheritance from the old countries, even as we have adopted so many new cultural aspects. Our families, our neighborhoods, and our nation are constantly reformed as the newest immigrants bring and give to us the best and the worst of their various cultures. The American story really is one of immigrants. Everything we are, and are about, is derived from those who came here.

To study a particular family then, it is essential to study more than just their names, dates of births, marriages and deaths. Every family's story must be wrapped in the culture of its former home, and we must observe how that family goes about radiating their old culture to the rest of us.

This is the story of a family line of Scots named Moffett. They were *Ulster Scots*. They originally lived in the Lowlands of Scotland. They and vast numbers of their countrymen emigrated, but not to America at first. In the seventeenth century they went to the northernmost of the ancient provinces of Ireland, where they spent from two to six generations. Ireland however, was not the melting pot that America would be, and there were numerous reasons why these Scots in Ulster struggled to preserve their distinct culture, and avoid being absorbed into that of the indigenous Irish or, to a lesser degree, that of the Episcopal Establishment. Even though they succeeded to a large degree, they were changed by their time in Ireland, and by the time many of these people emigrated for a second time, they had developed a culture which was distinct from that of either the Lowland Scots or the indigenous Irish.

When Ulster Scots left Ireland in the eighteenth century, they ventured to virtually every corner of the world. No such corner was the destination of more Ulster Scots than was North America. As with every ethnic and cultural group who has come here, their presence was felt when they arrived and forever after. While this is the story of a family of Ulster Scots named Moffett, it is also one tiny, essential piece of the story of America.

William Moffett's Lineage

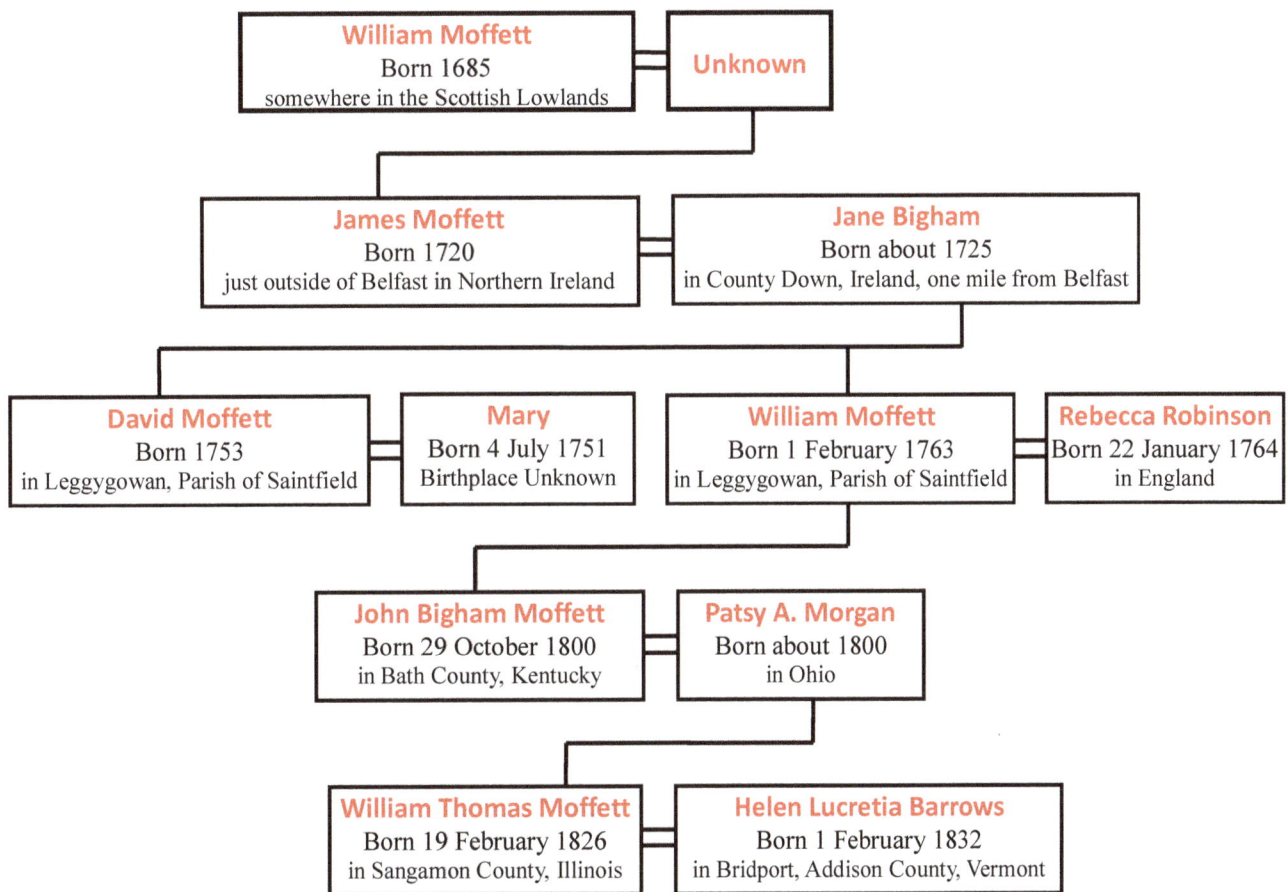

William Moffett
Born 1685
somewhere in the Scottish Lowlands

Unknown

James Moffett
Born 1720
just outside of Belfast in Northern Ireland

Jane Bigham
Born about 1725
in County Down, Ireland, one mile from Belfast

David Moffett
Born 1753
in Leggygowan, Parish of Saintfield

Mary
Born 4 July 1751
Birthplace Unknown

William Moffett
Born 1 February 1763
in Leggygowan, Parish of Saintfield

Rebecca Robinson
Born 22 January 1764
in England

John Bigham Moffett
Born 29 October 1800
in Bath County, Kentucky

Patsy A. Morgan
Born about 1800
in Ohio

William Thomas Moffett
Born 19 February 1826
in Sangamon County, Illinois

Helen Lucretia Barrows
Born 1 February 1832
in Bridport, Addison County, Vermont

3 – Origins of This Line of Moffetts

What we know of the story of this family begins somewhere in Scotland. They descend from one William Moffett who was born there in 1685. From him and his unknown spouse, a genealogical lineage can be identified down some eight generations to the co-author of this book, David McKenzie Moffett. This work attempts to provide significant specifics of family details of each of nine generations, and we are very fortunate that such details have been gathered, recorded and passed down to their descendants. With regard to the names, dates, residences and more of the lineage, very significant details of the first four generations etc. are available because of the efforts of one of the fifth – William Thomas Moffett (1826-1901).

Unfortunately, of this 1685-born William Moffett, we find little information. At this time, all we really know *for certain* is included in the first two sentences here above. There is no doubt that he was born in Scotland, but there appears to be very little in the way of surviving church records from the period in which he was born and would have been baptized. We don't know when, where or to whom he was married. Some have drawn various conclusions, but none have found hard evidence. In fact, it is quite unlikely that there is any record of the birth or baptism of William1685[6] because of the small number of such records which survive from the 1680s.

On the other hand, we do have a valuable collection of information and specific records pertaining to those generations which followed the first and which were gathered by William Thomas Moffett (1826-1901) – a lifetime resident of Illinois and a great-great-grandson of William1685 – and his uncle, 1787-born James Moffett who was born, married and died in Kentucky. From these two men we fortunately have learned much regarding those of the second and third generations.

History in general has given us a good bit of detail about the 1680s, `90s and early 1700s, in which period William1685 was born and raised. This period was filled with trial and upheaval in the British Isles, as was much of the 17th century. In the first half of that century, England suffered a bloody civil war, which ended with the execution of the monarch (Charles I), and a period where Oliver Cromwell and his army ruled the country along with the Parliament. After Cromwell died, the monarchy was restored in 1660 and the son of the executed king took the throne – Charles II. This solved very few problems.

---

[6]This book will usually refer to Moffett family members by their first name followed by his/her birth year – such as William1685 above. This clarifies which William, etc. is discussed.

To understand the upheavals in Scotland and in Ireland as well, one needs to be conversant regarding the three main religions to be encountered. What follows here is a brief discussion of the three and how they functioned in Britain. It is rather oversimplified, but for our purposes here it is sufficient.

We in America rarely even consider the concept of an established church. However, when the U.S. Constitution was written, and the Bill of Rights added, ours was alone on the planet in its abandonment of such establishment. In Britain, the existence of differing religions was not, by itself the cause of strife. Rather, it was the presence of an Established Church in each kingdom, given the added complication of the variety of religious practice which brought about the conflict.

The Roman Catholics were very largely absent from England and Scotland after the Reformation. They remained the overwhelming majority in Ireland. They of course were a church ruled by bishops, and the bishops were ruled by the Bishop of Rome – The Pope. From the time of the beginnings of the Plantation of Ulster, in the early seventeenth century, the Roman Catholic Church was not the established church in any of the three kingdoms of Great Britain – Ireland, England or Scotland.

The Presbyterian Church was a Calvinistic (Reformed) religion, and atop this philosophy they placed a form of church government which removed the episcopacy – the bishops. This rather universally alarmed the monarchs as the bishops were a part of a hierarchy which had its parallels in the nobility and various parts of the civil government. Conversely, those who favored a republican form of government, possibly even without monarchs, found the Presbyterian Church, as well as other reformed churches, to be most to their liking. The Presbyterian Church or kirk as Scots called it, became the established Church of Scotland, and was so when the migrations to Ireland from Scotland took place in the seventeenth century.

The other major group was the protestant Episcopalians. The Church of England – the Anglican Church – is very similar in structure, practice and beliefs to the Catholic Church, except that it does not recognize the supremacy of the Pope. There was of course a period in the seventeenth century when the Episcopal adherents in England lost power to the Puritans – the English version of a reformed church. However, after the death of Oliver Cromwell, and the restoration of the British monarchy, the Episcopal form reasserted itself.

In Ireland, there had been little or no experience with reformed churches or any expressed interest in that ilk. When the English extended their control over Ireland, they established a Church of Ireland, which was essentially an Anglican, Episcopal Church. Given Ireland's experience, the idea of a reformed or Presbyterian Church as the established one was not remotely considered. So as the seventeenth century was drawing to a close, in Ireland, we find the established Church of Ireland, which of course was most adversarial to Catholicism, and which was likewise significantly different from, and adversarial to, the Presbyterian Church of Scotland. Unfortunately for Ireland, the Catholics were quite numerous, and the Presbyterians had become the next largest group. The established church had fewer adherents than either of these other two, so most residents of Ireland were at odds with the established church. The resulting conflicts were numerous.

Consequently, the reign of Charles II (1661-1685) was dominated by an exceptional level of civil unrest, and in some cases these activities could rightly be called (at least minor) rebellions. The king dealt with it by acting as an absolute ruler – a despot. Among the many pockets of resistance to the king and his policies, the infamous Covenanters provided a violent, uncompromising effort to restore certain forms of church government to the Church of Scotland. The reaction from the crown was to tighten the grip on the Church, and outlaw even the conduct of Presbyterian worship services. Uprisings would then resume and be defeated; the king would issue clemency and relax the persecutions, but then the uprisings would resume, and so forth. As usually happened with religion-based struggles, each time the violence broke out, the atrocities carried out by both sides became more numerous and more despicable. By the dawn of the 1680s, the situation had become so horrible that the period became known as the "Killing Time".[7]

Charles II died in 1685, and the throne went to his brother, who simultaneously reigned as James VII of Scotland and James II of England. James was a Roman Catholic, as was his brother, but was unwise enough to lift the sanctions and persecutions against Catholics. Even at that, despite the national grumblings and fears, the proverbial lid remained on until 1688, when James's second wife bore a son and heir, who was christened in the Catholic faith. Numerous struggles ensued, mostly diplomatic and political, but in Ireland also military. In 1689 James was forced from the throne and replaced by his sister, Mary, and her Dutch husband, William of Orange. This "Glorious Revolution" returned a good measure of domestic peace and stability to Britain.[8]

The revolution concluded while William1685 was just a very few years old. Although this brought a decent degree of political peace and stability in Scotland, there was still reason for these Moffetts to be concerned. William's family were ardent Anglicans. For several of the early decades of the 1600s Scotland had established Presbyterianism as the country's national faith, but when Charles II rose to the monarchy in 1661, he forcefully established the Anglican religion as the official one. While this did result in the "Killing Time", William's parents, William himself and his children were no doubt all much more comfortable with the Anglican establishment.

The times continued to change however, and after the "Glorious Revolution" and the rise of William and Mary to the monarchy, they allowed the Scots to return to Presbyterianism as their national faith. The majority in Scotland had been the Presbyterians for some time, and the act by which Charles II changed the official faith brought on religious violence. William and Mary realized that and felt it best to let the majority rule on religion; but William1685's family may well have been greatly upset. Meanwhile, in Ireland, the Anglicans ruled, and it may be that this was the driving force – or at least one of more – which resulted in the movement of the family to that country.

---

[7] Stewart Ross, *Monarchs of Scotland* (New York, 1990), pp. 92-94. Also, Samuel Lewis, *A Topographical Dictionary of Scotland* (Baltimore, 1989), II, pp. 156-158.

[8] *idem.*, pp. 143-148

If that was not the case, the nearly immediate future provided a good deal more reason to move on from Scotland. In those last two decades of the 1600s farmers in that country dealt with progressively complex and difficult economic, agricultural and political factors, as well as significantly poor weather which was part of what is recalled as "The Little Ice Age". The grief peaked in a seven-year stretch beginning in the autumn of 1694, referred to as "Scotland's Seven Ill Years". The weather from that autumn and on through the following seven years featured cold, harsh winters as well as cold and wet summers.[9]   The grief became extreme in much of Scotland, and food shortages were widespread. In many areas virtually all the crops were lost.

However, Scotland suffered from not just the famine but three additional disasters during the 1690s: The Nine Years war with France from 1688 to 1697, causing the loss of an important trading market and disruption to coastal and North Sea shipping trade; the failure of the Company of Scotland and the abandonment of Darien – two disasters which resulted in the loss of one-sixth to one-quarter of the country's liquid capital; and the raising of foreign tariffs against Scottish goods, making exports difficult. All of this at a time when additional financial resources were necessary to purchase emergency grain supplies from abroad.[10]

This of course suggests another reason and timing for the movement of William1685 from his native land to Ulster. It may well have occurred sometime in 1695-1702 – the "Seven Ill Years". While there were significant movements of Scots to Ulster through that period and on to about 1720, most occurred in the 1690s, and especially in the latter half of that decade.

While the famines and other difficulties plagued Scotland, Ulster was for the most part spared from that. For example, in the 1690s, period leases were easily available in Ulster while economic prospects in Scotland were at their worst; and again, in Ireland the Anglican religion was that country's official one.

The only specific indication regarding the movement of William1685 to Ulster was in the family history presented by WilliamThomas1826 in the gathering at his home in the Illinois Township of Blue Mound in 1900. It indicates that the relocation took place when William1685 was "at an early age". That would seem to indicate that he was not yet an adult at the time of his relocation, but it would also seem possible that it was when he was a *young* adult. In any case, it almost surely tells us that he was married and living in Ulster when his son James was born in 1720.

Further concrete information about William1685 does not seem to exist, although future efforts may discover more. It should also be pointed out here that the family has long believed that there were other children born to James1720's parents, and that one of them was named William. Here again however, concrete evidence of that has to this date been elusive.

---

[9] E. Le Roy Ladurie, *Times of Feast, Times of Famine: A History of Climate since the year 1000* (London, 1972), 66.

[10] T. C. Smout, *Scottish Trade on the Eve of Union, 1660-1707* (Edinburgh, 1963), 245-253.

Despite that, a number of researchers feel that they know where William1685 was born, or at least where he was most likely born, and whom he married, and sometimes more. This author believes it is highly unlikely that any of those views can be correct. Of the church records of Scotland's parishes only a significant minority survive from the times at and before 1685. Dumfriesshire is a striking example of the problem. From early times, its percentage of the population who were Moffats (of any spelling variation) was greater than in any of the others, at least until the early 1800s. For 1685 and earlier years however, records of births, baptisms, marriages, etc. (church records) only survive for three of the shire's 40 or more parishes. How many William Moffetts born in Scotland at that time will never be known due to the very serious scarcity of the surviving records?

Here below is information about the areas of concentration of Moffett families. Overwhelmingly they resided in the lowlands. In the census of 1841 we see that the shires of Lanark, Dumfries and Midlothian still by far had greater percentages of Moffetts among the total population. In fact, the total of those three had considerably more than there were in all of the rest of the country's shires put together. Each of those *first three* had more than five times as many persons as Roxburgh – the *fourth* shire in order.

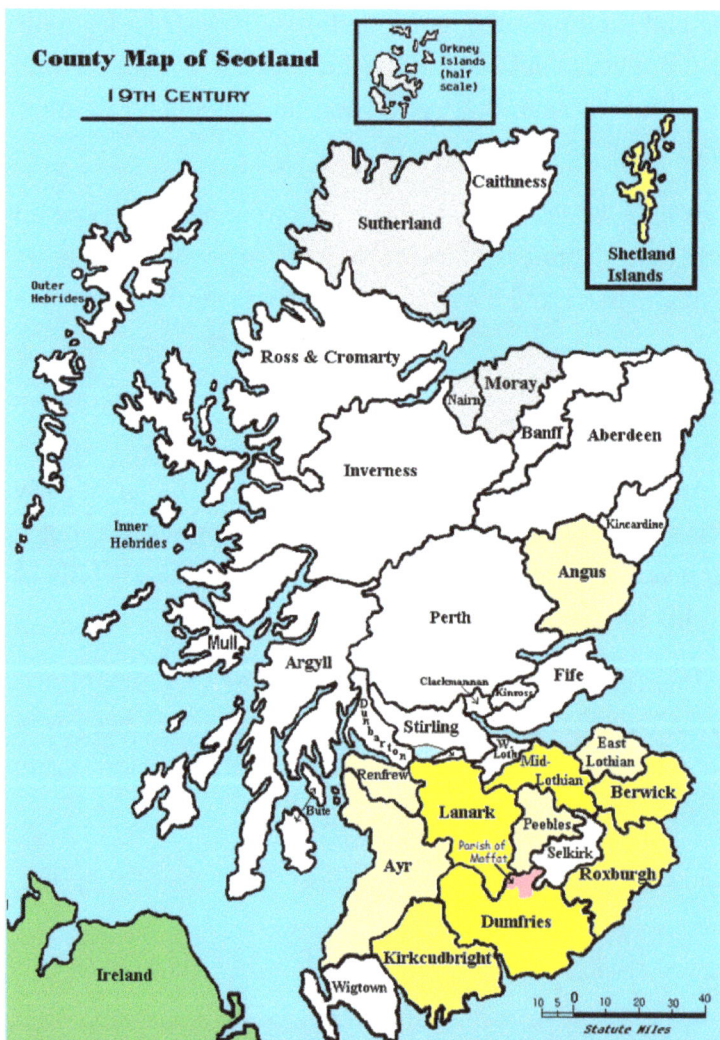

Populations of Moffetts
(all spellings)
in Scotland at the 1841 Census

1. Lanark – 838 / 838
2. Dumfries – 585 / 1423
3. Midlothian – 566 / 1989

4. Roxburgh – 126 / 2115
5. Berwick – 121 / 2236
6. Kirkcudbright – 106 / 2342
7. Shetland – 101 / 2443

8. Ayr – 95 / 2,538
9. Peebles – 90 / 2,628
10. Renfrew – 89 / 2,717
11. Angus – 62 / 2,779
12. East Lothian – 60 / 2,839

Total for the 3 brightest yellow – 1,989

Total for the 4 medium yellow – 454

Total for the 5 pale yellow – 396

Total for the 13th to the 29th white – 266

Total for the remaining 4 gray – 0

On the next three pages, note that these first three shires have the most Moffetts (any spelling) by far.

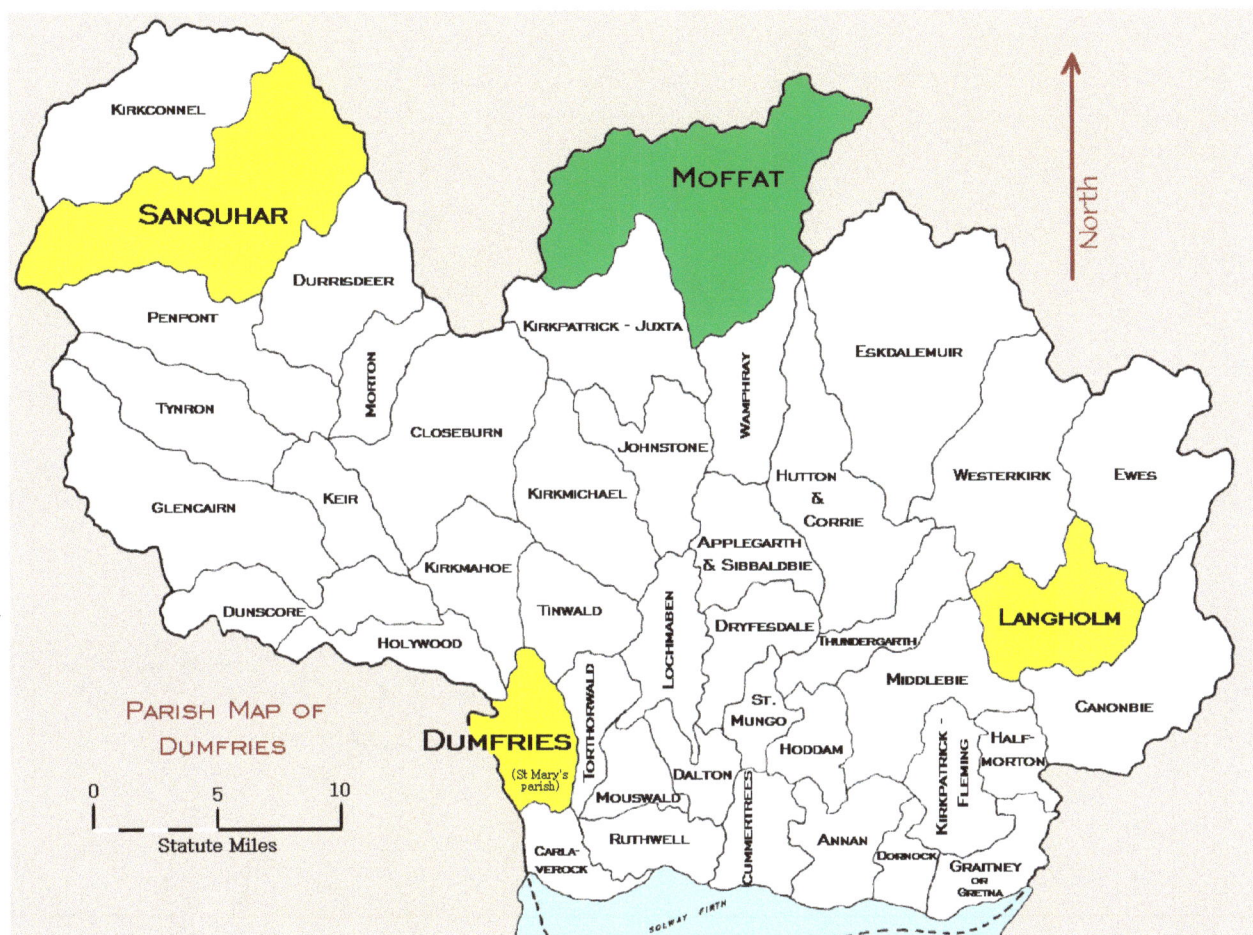

PARISH MAP OF DUMFRIES

Dumfriesshire – 1685

None of the forty-two Dumfriesshire parishes' church records survive for years before 1686, except for the three shaded yellow on the map above. As this is the shire which other research tells us it had the highest percentage of Moffetts (any spellings) it is almost certain that there were more William Moffetts born here in 1685. To the date of compilation of this volume in 2018, while some have concluded that they have found *the* William, the information so far uncovered has certainly not been conclusive.

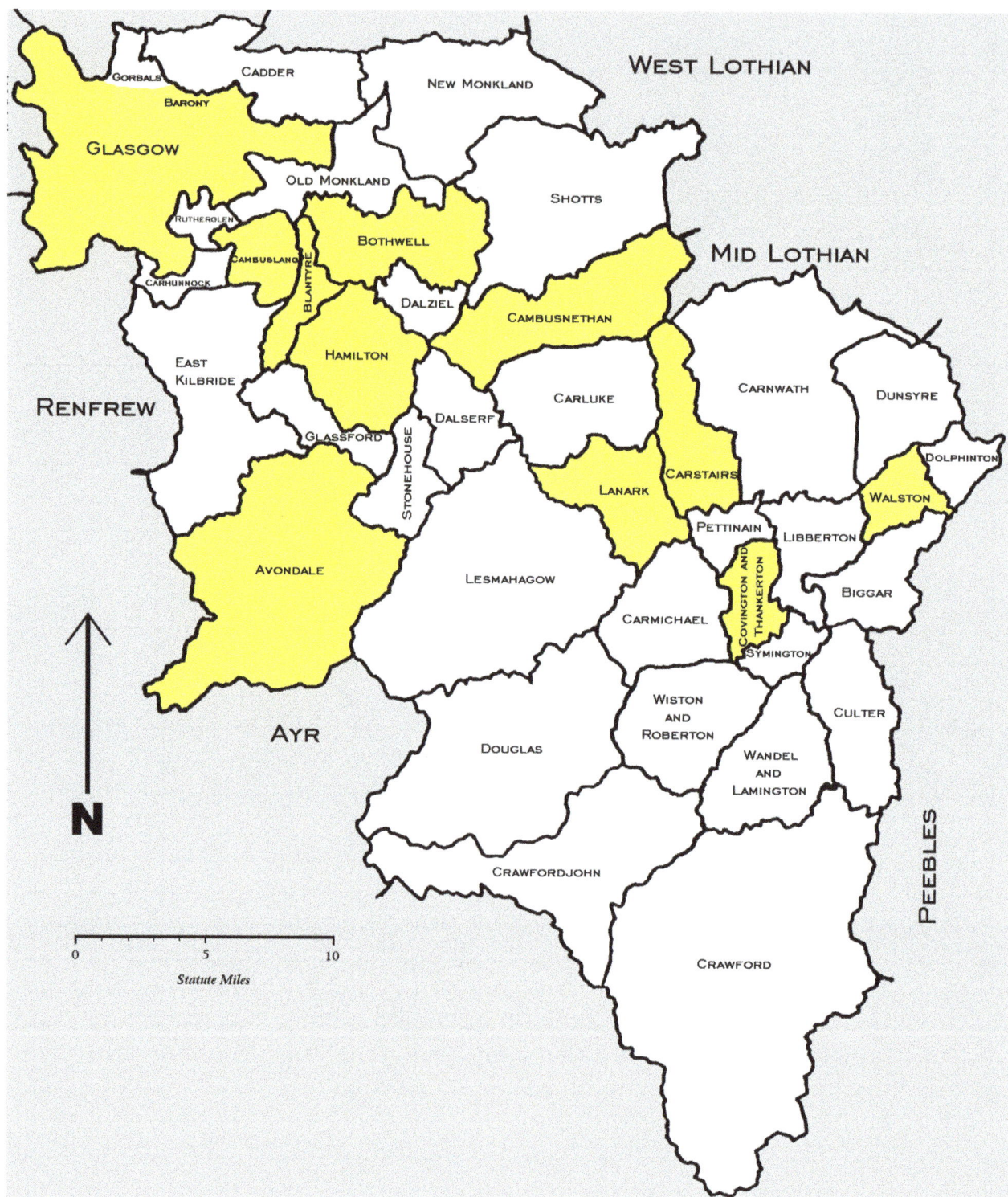

Lanarkshire – 1685

Here we have forty parishes, and only eleven survive from as early as 1685.

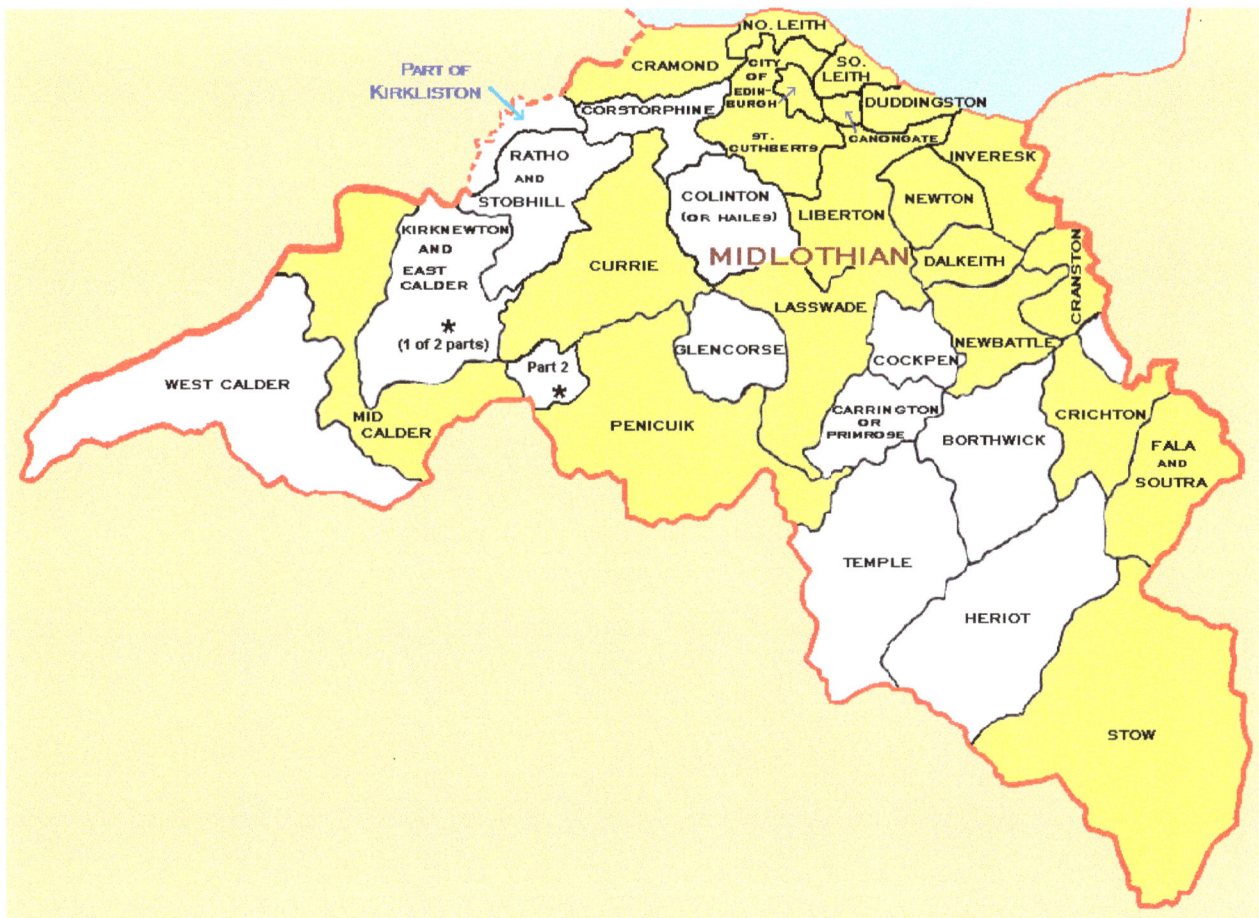

Midlothian – 1685

   This shire has the highest percentage of its parishes for which church records survive from 1685. Even so, twelve of the thirty-two have none for 1685 and earlier.

   In total then, of the 114 parishes in these three "full-of-Moffetts-shires", only 35 have any records from as early as 1685, and there are certainly several shires beside these big three who had Moffetts, including those named William, born at the "right time". Unless we locate hitherto unknown records which somehow specify that our James1720 *was* the son of a specific William, we will continue to be uncertain re the identity of the father.

14

4 – On to Ireland
The Moffetts Become Ulster Scots

It is quite reasonable to conclude that William1685 most likely left Scotland, very possibly with his parents and/or siblings and/or other relatives or close family friends. The events occurring in Scotland from the time of his birth to his arrival in Ulster suggest various likely times of his move, but the most logical conclusion would seem to be that it took place in the period from 1695-1702 – the period known as *The Seven Ill Years.* This was a time when migrations from Scotland to Ulster surged, for the third time since King James I of England (who was also James VI of Scotland) acceded to the English throne in 1603 and instigated the "Plantation of Ulster" migrations.[11]

During the Killing Time in Scotland, the civic situation in Ireland was by comparison blissfully peaceful. During the first years of the 1680s, large numbers of Scots left their homeland for Ulster. The flow was interrupted by the crises which resulted in the "Glorious Revolution". In Ireland that struggle between James VII and William and Mary was much more violent that it had been in England and Scotland.

The roots of the violence were in the Plantation. That scheme was an effort to populate Ireland with loyal Protestant subjects, who would not be so inclined to rebel against the English yoke as the Catholic Irish had been. Some came from England, but many more so from Scotland, partly because the Plantation's author, King James I, felt that as he was a Scot, the natives of the land of his birth would be yet more loyal than any others, and partly because the southwest of Scotland was so close to Ulster. So the Plantation brought into being the Ulster Scots, and their large numbers would make them a significant factor in whatever Ireland might become. It also was a perhaps inescapable disaster, waiting to happen.[12]

Time has shown of course, that the plan did not work as it was expected to. Rather than reduce the sources of conflict and rebellion, it increased them. Even today, the unfortunate innocent souls of Northern Ireland are living with the violent ant bigoted vestiges of the Plantation.

---

[11]James G. Leyburn, *The Scotch-Irish, A Social History* (Chapel Hill, 1962). This work provides for a good understanding of the phenomenon known as the Plantation of Ulster, and of the whole experience of the Ulster Scots in Ireland and North America.

[12]*idem.*

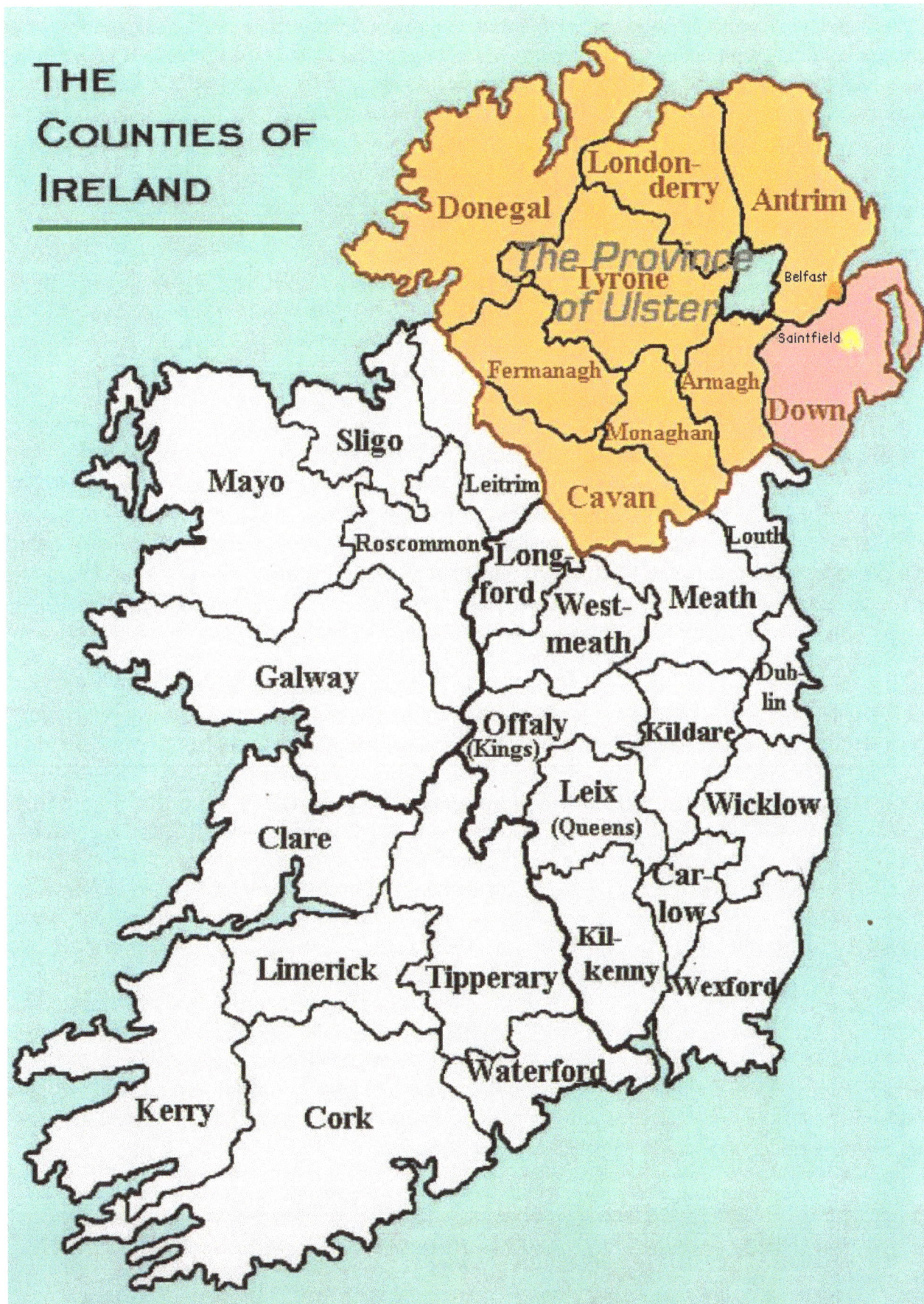

THE
COUNTIES OF
IRELAND

Donegal

London-
derry

Antrim

The Province
Tyrone
of Ulster

Belfast

Fermanagh

Saintfield

Armagh

Down

Monaghan

Sligo

Leitrim

Cavan

Mayo

Louth

Roscommon

Long-
ford

West-
meath

Meath

Galway

Offaly
(Kings)

Kildare

Dub-
lin

Leix
(Queens)

Wicklow

Clare

Car-
low

Kil-
kenny

Limerick

Tipperary

Wexford

Waterford

Kerry

Cork

When the English and Scots came to Ulster, the gentry and nobility who led and organized the settlements were given large tracts of land to occupy and farm. The lands had been seized by the crown, mostly without any compensation to the former residents or owners, on the promise that much of the land taken had been left vacant after the horrific warfare of the late 1590s (another bout of England versus Ireland). The settlers could hire workers, but regulations specified that they must hire fellow Protestants from Scotland or England, and not the indigenous, Catholic Irish. Often however, they did not find enough labor among the Scots and English and did have to resort to hiring the natives. What evolved was a large number of farms, owned and operated by various people whom the indigenous Irish saw to be interlopers. The natives were often now in the position of working as laborers on land they once had farmed themselves, or watching their former land being occupied and farmed by others while they themselves had to find some other means of support. All of this by foreign person on whose side (as the Catholics saw it) God was not!

As a consequence, there were numerous uprisings in the seventeenth century, and while they were representative of cultures clashing, the focus of both sides was the religious aspect, driving the intensity of the violence much higher than it might otherwise have been. In 1641, a particularly brutal rebellion left untold thousands dead, including many civilians, women, and children. First to be victimized were the Protestants who were caught off guard, and who had little or no immediate support from London because England was plunging into civil war. As the momentum swung back to the Protestants, they exercised bitter revenge in an attempt to at least repay the atrocities which had been heaped on them, and often to add one greater level of horror.

The seventeenth century was one of great instability in England, as we have discussed. Each time the instability grew significant, some Irish factions saw an opportunity to attempt a new rebellion. When the Catholic James VII was ousted in England, his natural ally in attempting to return to power was Catholic Ireland. James went to the Emerald Isle with an army consisting of French forces and joined them up with the forces in Ireland under his Catholic General Tyrconnel.

Initially, James's Catholic forces met with great success. Those Protestant Scots who had not already fled Ireland retreated to the north, burning and destroying everything they could not carry. Between this effort, and the initial efficiency of the Catholic forces, Ulster was a scene of significant desolation. Rather quickly, James and the Catholics had almost all of Ireland under their control.

There was one spot of resistance left – Londonderry – and the story of its ability to ultimately prevail is at the heart of the Protestant version of the saga of struggle and heartbreak of Ireland over the last four centuries.[13] As the Catholic/Jacobite[14] juggernaut continued to roll northward, and their own cities in Ulster were overrun, Protestant military men retreated northward and all funneled into Londonderry as a last refuge. That city lay under siege for 105 days, but somehow held out until supply ships arrived, at which time the forces within the city struck back at the Catholic forces and drove them off.

---

[13]Ian McBride, *The Siege of Derry in Ulster Protestant Mythology* (Dublin, 1997).

[14]Jacobites were the supporters of James, the name coming from the Latin form, Jacobus.

Parishes of County Down

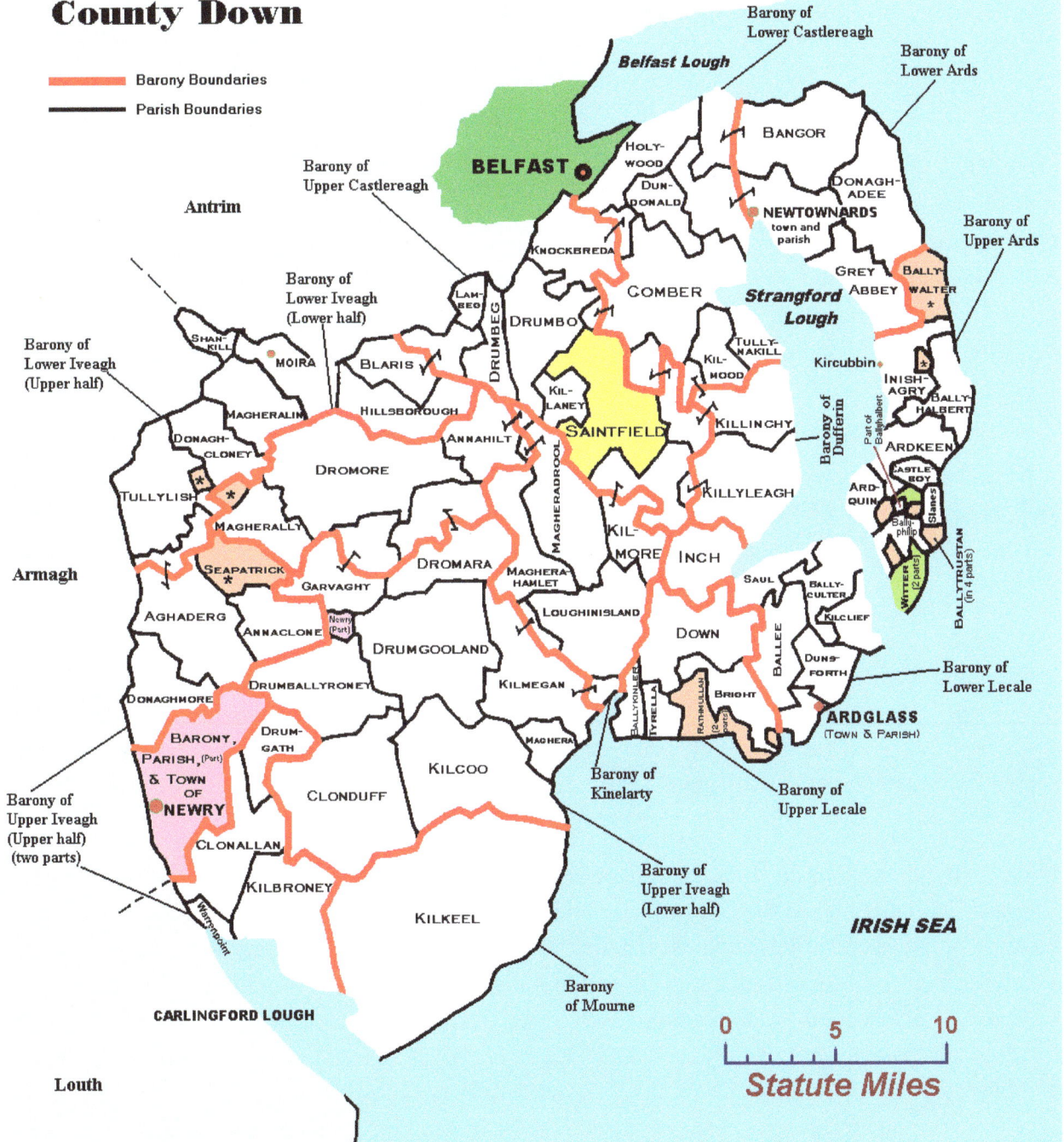

Barony Boundaries
Parish Boundaries

Antrim

Armagh

Louth

Barony of Upper Castlereagh

Barony of Lower Iveagh (Lower half)

Barony of Lower Iveagh (Upper half)

Barony of Upper Iveagh (Upper half) (two parts)

Barony of Lower Castlereagh

Barony of Lower Ards

Barony of Upper Ards

Barony of Dufferin

Barony of Lower Lecale

Barony of Kinelarty

Barony of Upper Lecale

Barony of Upper Iveagh (Lower half)

Barony of Mourne

Belfast Lough

Strangford Lough

IRISH SEA

CARLINGFORD LOUGH

BELFAST

NEWTOWNARDS town and parish

ARDGLASS (TOWN & PARISH)

BARONY, PARISH, (Port) & TOWN OF NEWRY

HOLY-WOOD
DUN-DONALD
BANGOR
DONAGH-ADEE
KNOCKBREDA
COMBER
GREY ABBEY
BALLY-WALTER
LAM-BEG
DRUMBEG
DRUMBO
TULLY-NAKILL
KIL-WOOD
Kircubbin
INISH-AGRY
BALLY-HALBERT
SHAN-KILL
MOIRA
BLARIS
KIL-LANEY
SAINTFIELD
KILLINCHY
Part of Ballyhalbert
ARDKEEN
MAGHERALIN
HILLSBOROUGH
ANNAHILT
MAGHERADROOL
CASTLE BOY
ARD-QUIN
Slanes
DONAGH-CLONEY
DROMORE
KILLYLEAGH
Bally-phillip
TULLYLISH
MAGHERALLY
KIL-MORE
INCH
SAUL
WITTER (2 parts)
BALLYTRUSTAN (in 4 parts)
SEAPATRICK
DROMARA
MAGHERA-HAMLET
BALLY-CULTER
AGHADERG
GARVAGHY
LOUGHINISLAND
DOWN
KILCLIEF
ANNACLONE
Newry (Port)
DRUMGOOLAND
BALLEE
DUNS-FORTH
DONAGHMORE
DRUMBALLYRONEY
KILMEGAN
BALLYKINLER
TYRELLA
BRIGHT
DRUM-GATH
RATHMULLAN (2nd)
NEWRY
CLONDUFF
KILCOO
MAGHERA
CLONALLAN
Warrenpoint
KILBRONEY
KILKEEL

0   5   10
Statute Miles

Note the very significant parish of Saintfield, shaded in yellow.
Other shading is to identify parishes with non-contiguous parts.

The other shoe dropped soon afterward when King William arrived in County Down with a well-trained force of ten thousand. Suddenly the whole success of James and the Catholics rested on whether they might be able to stand up to William's army. They could not. At the Boyne River, on the 11th of July, 1690, the armies met, and after two days William emerged triumphant[15.] For another year, the Catholics held on, hoping to gain a favorable settlement diplomatically, although they also held their military forces together well enough that they were not ultimately defeated until a year after the Boyne. In July of 1691, at Aughrim, the Catholics were handed so thorough a defeat that their morale plummeted and serious resistance to William was gone.[16]

The Catholics in Ulster were so reduced after this Williamite War, as the Irish call it, that the north of Ireland has ever since been a Protestant bastion. A civil security thus took hold, and after peace was established, the final flood of Scots headed west across the Irish Sea. A contemporary archbishop indicated that about fifty-thousand Scots came to Ulster in the 1690s. After about 1700, the stream slowed significantly. William1685 was probably among those who resettled in Ulster during that period. Their culture now would undergo alterations, as they joined the large contingent of Scots on Irish soil in Ulster.

The Ulster Scots – or Scotch-Irish – are a fascinating study. For the most part, they came from the Lowlands, the part of Scotland where social, agricultural and industrial progress all had a flourishing presence. Therefore, in each of these areas, they strongly tended to be more "advanced" than the indigenous Irish among whom they settled. They became accustomed to seeing themselves as innovators, which quickly became ingrained in their culture.

In one important sense, they were different from their Scottish brethren they left behind. They all were infused with some characteristic(s) which made it possible for them to surrender their known abode and lifestyle, and emigrate. No matter how many images they had conjured concerning their new lives, to some degree they surely were facing certain unknowns, and only certain members of our species seem to possess the willingness to face and embrace such a future.

Ulster was the only Irish province in which they settled in anything remotely like significant numbers. Partly this was due to its great proximity to the Scottish coast. It was also due to the terrible state in which Ulster lay at the end of the sixteenth century, following the 1595 uprising by a strong and fairly united group of Ulster chiefs and their clans. That revolt was initially so successful, despite the employment by England of a well-trained and disciplined army of twenty thousand, that a new commander was assigned – Lord Mountjoy – who significantly ratcheted up the brutality of the English assaults. His policy was not only to fight in the field, but between battles, to utilize his time and personnel to destroy all the houses, food and cattle he could find. Widespread starvation, homelessness, and indigence were the result, and the Irish rebellion evaporated just as Queen Elizabeth lay dying in 1603. Ulster was a wasted land, wanting for human occupation in large areas.

---

[15]*ibid*., pp. 128-131.

[16]R. F. Foster, *Modern Ireland, 1600-1972* (London, 1988), pp. 148-150.

The Battle of the Boyne, 1690, fought at the River Boyne in County Antrim. The army supporting the recently ousted British monarch, James II, met that of William of Orange who, along with James's sister, Mary, had replaced James on the British throne. It dealt a decisive blow to Irish hopes for a return of Catholic power, and any measure of independence from Britain.

There was the ever-present (in Ireland) religious factor too. The significant majority of Ulster Scots were Presbyterian[17]. In Ireland, they would find themselves in a country where the established church was not theirs, as it had been in Scotland. Even though the majority of Irish residents were Catholic, adherents to the Church of Ireland were even a smaller group than Presbyterians. Being dissenters gave them an essentially minority-like status. Because of their clan heritage, the Scots were never terribly fond of central governments which were not local and familial and the measures of control and discrimination they encountered from the Church of Ireland only reinforced this attitude. One might expect that the Scots in Ulster would see the established church as something of an ally for the Presbyterians in that both churches were Protestant, but to a large degree this was not the case. The Anglican Church of Ireland was no longer affiliated with Rome, and had undergone some modicum of reform, but was none the less a church of hierarchy, making Presbyterians uneasy. In many ways its forms were too similar to those of the Catholics.

---

[17]It is not certain whether William1685 and his parents and siblings were Presbyterian or Anglican. The earliest records of the family in Ireland show that William1685's son, James1720, was active in the Anglican Church in Saintfield and was praised by the church for his activity. However, it is very well known that large numbers of Scots who came to Ireland were soon afterward somewhat forced to join with the Anglicans.

By the middle of the second Christian millennium, the state of the Catholic Church in Scotland had deteriorated to a low which exceeded that of any other nation in Europe. Most Scots lived ever on the edge of disaster from plague, famine, or war. The Catholic Church meanwhile was staffed with clerics and others who were widely uneducated, and who enriched themselves at the further expense of their flocks. They had largely abandoned the works of Christianity in every real sense.

By the middle of the sixteenth century, the Reformation message arrived in Scotland in the person of John Knox, just as an independently spawned movement erupted to call the Catholic Church to account. With strong support of the nobility, Knox, his followers, and others who rose against Catholicism prevailed, and in 1560 the Scottish parliament put an end to the establishment of the Church of Rome, and in its place established the Presbyterian Church as the Kirk of Scotland.

Scots at all levels had become terribly disenchanted with the Roman establishment in their country. By contrast, the new Kirk was governed not by hierarchy, but in a limited democratic manner. Their ministers were possessed of excellent educations, and the Kirk immediately worked to bring basic education to all Scots. They toiled ceaselessly in their vineyards, resurrecting the Christian ideals, and lifting even the poorest of the poor to a place of self-respect and hope. Consequently, the Scottish nation was as enchanted by their Presbyterian Kirk as they had been disenchanted by the Episcopal forbear they overthrew. The Scots in Ulster therefore never rested easy under the thumb of the still (to them) rather Popish Church of Ireland.

As a result of all of these factors, the Ulster Scots developed a character unlike their indigenous Irish Gaelic cousins, and unlike their Anglican (in the civil and religious senses) cousins whose ascendancy ruled Ireland. It was also a character unlike their Scottish brothers and sisters whom they left behind on the eastern shores of the Irish Sea. They found themselves invited and coaxed to come to Ulster and establish a new life. By doing so they were assured they would do a great service to their King, James VI, and his kingdoms of Scotland, England, and Ireland.

When they arrived in Ireland, they found much opportunity, as advertised, but they found themselves unwelcome to the indigenous Irish, and treated shabbily by the English establishment which pleaded with them to come. As dissenters, they were often proscribed from many offices, and in this they fared no better than the Popish natives. When these natives saw fit to rise up and try to drive the Scots out, the English habitually were slow to provide protection – primarily because the revolts were usually staged precisely when the English were seriously preoccupied elsewhere.

The Ulster Scots therefore developed a remarkable self-reliance, which further enhanced their lasting disdain for government. They knew the value of education, which seemed a foreign concept to their Irish neighbors and to a lesser degree to their English overlords. The relative superiority of their agricultural methods over those of the Irish made them keenly aware of how important agricultural progress was. This was reinforced by the relative superiority of the agricultural methods brought by the English among them, and the Scots in Ireland became tinkerers and innovators, as frontier cultures seemingly always have.

Despite the setbacks, losses and ongoing problems, the Scots pressed on with their mission to settle Ulster, and convert it, not only politically and religiously, but economically, agriculturally and socially. We in twenty-first century America might describe them as "can do" folks. By the time they left for North America, they had a heritage of converting frontier into settled ground, and a culture of success, education, strict Christian discipline, and a self-reliance which might well be described as supreme. In the New World, they consequently proved to easily be the most effective frontiersmen of any white settlers. They and their descendants also were to be found among the leaders in nearly every facet of life[18].

Therefore, as the seventeenth century was turning to the eighteenth, these Moffetts came from somewhere in Scotland to the area of northeastern County Down or the southeast corner of County Antrim. Again, it seems most likely that William1685 made this relocation sometime in 1695-1702, in which case he was a teenager at the time. While it therefore is most likely that he made the move along with family, he also might have done so by himself, especially if his crossing took place in his later teens. Unfortunately, no one has yet found evidence to tell us with whom – if with anyone but himself – he made the move.

The records of Ireland are in general woefully inadequate to provide much success to genealogical research. It is fortunate that Moffett family members preserved the essentials of the family history from the time of William1685's settlement in Ireland. While some of the detail regarding him and his children are lacking, the available information about each successive generation is almost all well detailed.

Gathering evidence of an ancestor's place of settlement in Ireland has its quirks. The first division is that of the four provinces – Leinster (southeast), Munster (southwest), Connaught (northwest) and Ulster (northeast). Each province has a different number of counties – Ulster, where the Moffetts of this story ultimately settled, has nine. The counties are divided into parishes[19] on the one hand and baronies on the other[20]. The parishes may be all within one barony or in multiple baronies. On the map, in the waterway named Strangford Lough, just east of Saintfield, there is a small barony which contains only parts of only two parishes – Killinchy and Killyleagh. Most of the latter is in the Barony of Dufferin, and a small bit is in that of Upper Castlereagh. The largest segment of Killinchy is in Dufferin, but another part is in Upper Castlereagh, and two separate additional parts are both in the Barony of Lower Castlereagh.

Then, in every parish there are numerous subdivisions of land. These unique subdivisions are the townlands. Their sizes vary a good bit but obviously all are much smaller in acreage than the parish itself. Their existence is ancient, as is obvious from the almost entirely Gaelic names.

---

[18]Again, the discussion of the Ulster Scots and their character has been distilled from Leyburn.

[19]A "parish" in Ireland is the equivalent of what, in America, is said to be a "town", "locality", etc.

[20]The baronies' boundaries are red, while those of the parishes are black.

The map here shows the townlands in two parishes - Saintfield (white shading of townlands – except for Saintfield Parks, Leggygowan, and Drumaconnell West and East which are tan to highlight them) and the small, adjacent parish of Killaney (pink). This map illustrates the variety of numbers of townlands due to the variety of parishes' sizes. Unusually large parishes have several dozen townlands. Also note that the boundaries have virtually no straight lines – which is essentially universal in Ireland.

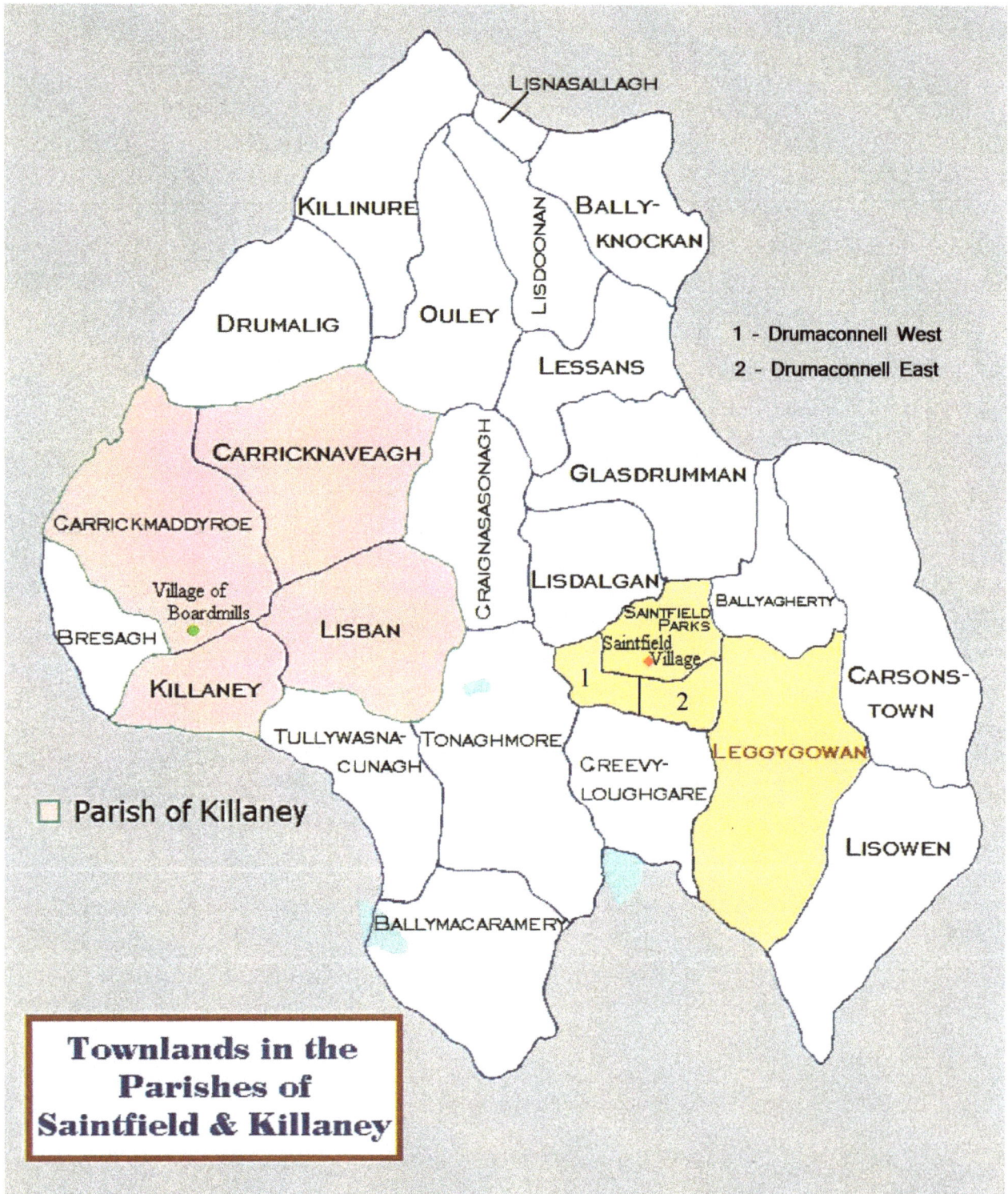

LISNASALLAGH

KILLINURE

BALLY-KNOCKAN

LISDOONAN

DRUMALIG

OULEY

LESSANS

1 - Drumaconnell West
2 - Drumaconnell East

CARRICKNAVEAGH

CRAIGNASASONAGH

GLASDRUMMAN

CARRICKMADDYROE

Village of Boardmills

LISDALGAN

BALLYAGHERTY

SAINTFIELD PARKS

Saintfield Village

BRESAGH

LISBAN

1

2

CARSONS-TOWN

KILLANEY

LEGGYGOWAN

TULLYWASNA-CUNAGH

TONAGHMORE

CREEVY-LOUGHGARE

LISOWEN

☐ Parish of Killaney

BALLYMACARAMERY

Townlands in the Parishes of Saintfield & Killaney

If in North America there is any significant similarity to townlands it might be our farms. Their variety of size matches up well and there is no government structure assigned to them. Its purpose appears to be no more than description of locality, such as we have for the names of streets for example. When first encountered, townlands are often a source of great confusion, as they appear on virtually no maps, and their names are mostly of Gaelic etymology. These names are often rather long, compound words, and the spellings given to them usually vary widely. They constitute a classic example of the way in which many spelling confusions originate. When maps were made and populations were recorded, the ruling class no longer consisted of indigenous, Gaelic speaking Irish, but was one of Anglophones. As a consequence, they were unfamiliar to the English ear, and spelled phonetically, as they sounded to each different individual. There were therefore no standardized spellings for any of these townlands, and the names which came to us from the Gaelic language were almost always spelled differently by different clerks, surveyors, attorneys and so on – which, to a degree, was common anyway until the mid-19th century.

Frequently, a researcher will find a record or tradition that indicates that the Irish immigrant to America haled from a particular place, and then in great frustration they are not able to determine where this place is, even if the reference included the correct county. Almost always, these are cases where the place of the person's origin is a townland name. In many cases the researcher may be unfamiliar with the fact that townlands exist. Even if they are aware of the townland system, as indicated above they do not appear on almost any maps, and certainly not on any published atlases, road maps, and the like. Even when one obtains a list of townlands in a particular county or even in a single parish, the spelling passed down is frequently different enough from the most commonly used modern spelling that researchers fail to, or are slow to, make the connection.

5 – The Second Generation Born in Ireland

Of the children who were born to William Moffett – aka William1685, the native of Scotland – the one from whom this American branch descends is James Moffett, born in 1720. In turn, his children were of the second generation of this line of Moffetts to have been born in Ireland. James1720 was born most probably in or near Saintfield, but perhaps near the northeast corner of County Down, and even possibly in the southeast corner of County Antrim – in or very near Belfast. At the latest, he had certainly settled in Saintfield by his mid to latter twenties. The earliest hard evidence of that is a record dated in 1748 which praises him for his active support of the community's Anglican (Episcopalian) Church of Ireland in Saintfield.

As for any siblings of James1720, there is reasonable certainty that there were some and descendants of William1685 widely believe there were. At least one has been identified – a male sibling named William, who very likely was older than James1720.

Of the second generation born in Ireland are the nine children born to James1720 and his wife Jane Bigham – five sons and four daughters. So far as we know, none of the daughters left Ireland.[21] Of the sons, three did so – David, William and Thomas.[22] James and Samuel remained in Ireland for life.

In eighteenth century Ireland, the lines between agriculture and manufacturing or trades were imprecise to say the least. A very good example of this effect was the grower of flax, who also worked a loom. Likewise, a family might raise sheep and weave the wool. Tradesmen such as masons, coopers, and the like were sometimes less likely to include agriculture in their personal economic plan, but this tendency was tempered by the size of the community, and the resulting market for the fruit of the trade. Here again, tradesmen who could not fully support the family from their trade would often in some way include agricultural activity, either on their own, or as hired help on a local farm. Hired help are of course always a considered part of the farmer's efforts, as there are times in the year when the work exceeds his ability to fully cope with it. In an area with only relatively small villages the tradesmen probably welcomed another source of income. While we don't know whether James1720 engaged in any money-making activities apart from agriculture, he must have done at least reasonably well. He had a descent quantity of land where he and his family lived in the Saintfield townland of Leggygowan to produce food from the ground, and enough to support animals to the extent that he did so.

---

[21]See the Family Group Sheet on page 26.

Moffett Lineage

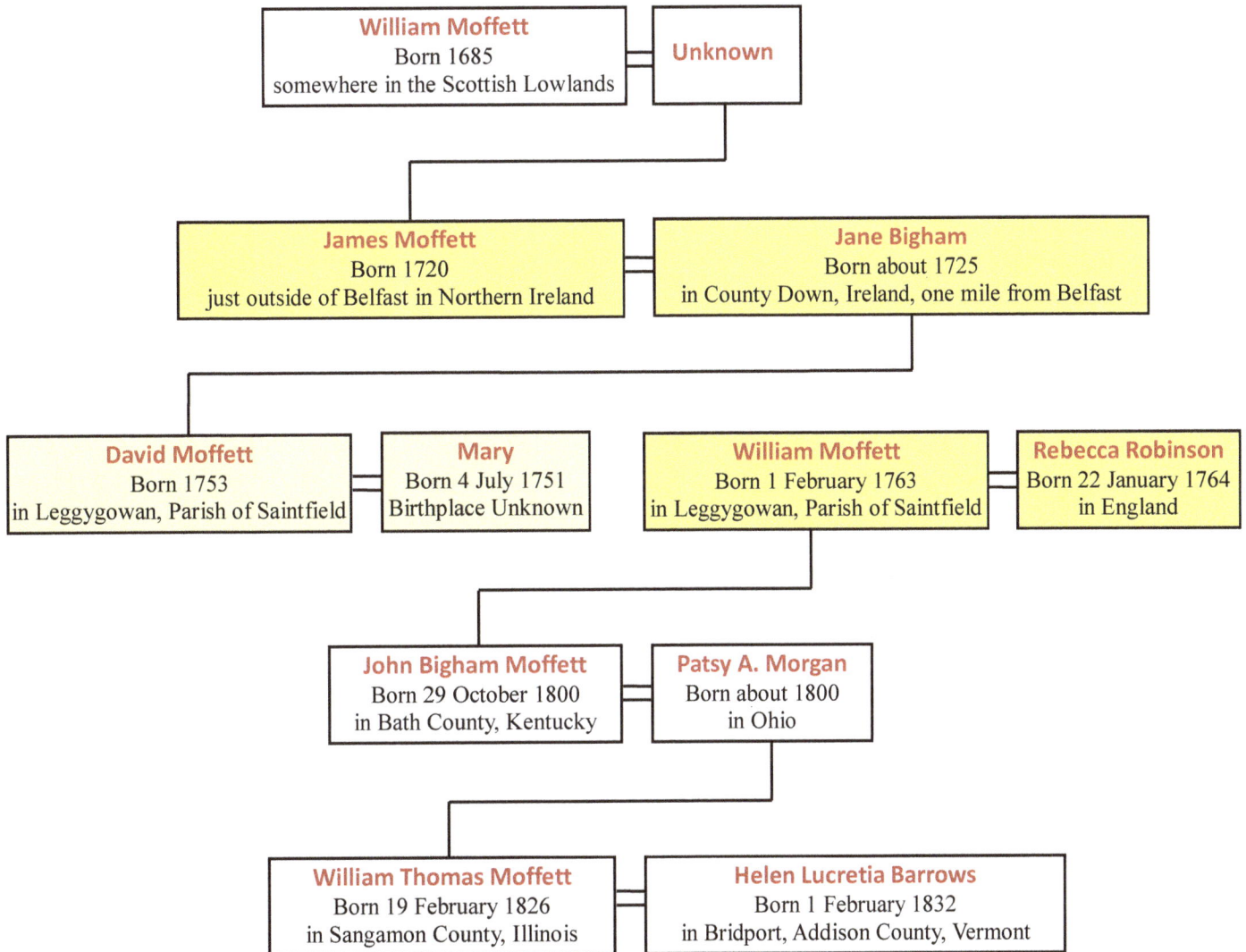

William Moffett
Born 1685
somewhere in the Scottish Lowlands

Unknown

James Moffett
Born 1720
just outside of Belfast in Northern Ireland

Jane Bigham
Born about 1725
in County Down, Ireland, one mile from Belfast

David Moffett
Born 1753
in Leggygowan, Parish of Saintfield

Mary
Born 4 July 1751
Birthplace Unknown

William Moffett
Born 1 February 1763
in Leggygowan, Parish of Saintfield

Rebecca Robinson
Born 22 January 1764
in England

John Bigham Moffett
Born 29 October 1800
in Bath County, Kentucky

Patsy A. Morgan
Born about 1800
in Ohio

William Thomas Moffett
Born 19 February 1826
in Sangamon County, Illinois

Helen Lucretia Barrows
Born 1 February 1832
in Bridport, Addison County, Vermont

James Moffett, who married Jane Bigham, (both shaded light yellow) was among the first generation of this line of Moffetts to be born in Ireland. Their children, including William (highlighted in yellow), belonged to the second generation born in Ireland. David Moffett – an older brother of the said William – and his wife Mary, are shaded in very light yellow. See the family group sheet on page 26 for details on all of the children of James and Jane.

Family Group Sheet – James Moffett and his Wife, Jane Bigham

Husband: James Moffett

Born: 1720	in: the northeast corner of Down or southeast corner of Antrim presumably where the bride's family resided, and supposedly a mile from Belfast
Married: 1748	
Died: 22 Jul 1789	in: Leggygowan, Parish of Saintfield, County Down, Ireland
Father: William Moffett	born in Scotland
Mother: Unknown	

Wife: Jane Bigham

Born: About 1725	
Died: 20 June 1789	

CHILDREN

1 M	Name: James Moffett Born: About 1750 Died: 19 April 1813 Married: About 1786 Spouse: Isabella McMullen	in: Leggygowan, Parish of Saintfield, County Down, Ireland in: Leggygowan, Parish of Saintfield, County Down, Ireland
2 M	Name: David Moffett Born: 1753 Died: 1810-1820 Married: probably about 1779 Spouse: Mary	in: Leggygowan, Parish of Saintfield, County Down, Ireland in: Westmoreland County, Pennsylvania
3 F	Name: Jennet Moffett Born: 1755 Married: Spouse: James Little	in: Leggygowan, Parish of Saintfield, County Down, Ireland
4 F	Name: Mary Moffett Born: 1758 Married: Spouse: John Thompson	in: Leggygowan, Parish of Saintfield, County Down, Ireland
5 F	Name: Elinor Moffett Born: 1760 Married: Spouse: George	in: Leggygowan, Parish of Saintfield, County Down, Ireland
6 M	Name: William Moffett Born: 1 February 1763 Died: 22 April 1826 Married: 4 February 1787 Spouse: Rebecca Robinson	in: Leggygowan, Parish of Saintfield, County Down, Ireland in: Bath County, Kentucky in: Dauphin County, Pennsylvania
7 M	Name: Samuel Moffett Born: 1765 Died: 1814 Married: 1785 Spouse: Isabel Strain	in: Leggygowan, Parish of Saintfield, County Down, Ireland in: Parish of Saintfield, County Down, Ireland
8 M	Name: Thomas Moffett Born: 1767 Died: 1793	in: Leggygowan, Parish of Saintfield, County Down, Ireland in: Lexington, Kentucky
9 F	Name: Jane Moffett Born: 1769 Married: Spouse: Robert Cole	in: Leggygowan, Parish of Saintfield, County Down, Ireland

The above children of James Moffett and Jane Bigham constituted the second generation of this line of Moffetts who were born in Ireland. The three who would emigrate to America are highlighted with color. William, from whom this line of Moffetts descends, is shaded in yellow. Thomas did not marry and died young, hence leaving no children. The fate of David was not known until recently – it was determined that he lived his last years in Westmoreland County, Pennsylvania and left generations of many offspring.

James1720 and his wife Jane had nine children born in the nineteen years from 1750 through 1769 – an average of slightly more than one child every two years. This would suggest that the couple had few if any early childhood deaths and that both had significantly good health through their childhood and young to middle adult lives. Their general health thereafter is not well known, except the occasion of their deaths which resulted from a small pox epidemic – Jane died on the 20th of June in 1789 and James passed away thirty-two days later.

Of those nine children, the three who came to America as young adults are those whom we know the most. By 1784 all three had emigrated. Subsequent information about the other six, for the most part, has only reached those of us in America today by way of late 18th century letters from those in Ireland. Of course, the letters include a good bit of personal greetings, expressions of care, hope and love, and questions about how things were going in the new world. They also included news about their lives in Saintfield and it was not always happy. The letters were being exchanged from the time the emigrants left, on into the early 1790s at least. Not long before the deaths of James1720 and his wife in 1789, the said James authored his will, and when he died and the offsprings learned its contents there was a deep divide among the family there. The will gave virtually all of the items of positive consequence to the oldest – James1750. A subsequent letter from Samuel included descriptions of his strong disappointment. More than anything else however, the letters expressed love and concern for the emigrants and the sadness of their separations.

We know the most about the three sons of James and Jane who removed to America. The oldest of these was David, born in 1753 in Leggygowan – where apparently all of his siblings were also born. As the family members living in the 20th and 21st centuries previously understood the flight to America, all three departed early in 1784, landed in Philadelphia, and soon relocated to Hanover Township, a dozen or so miles due east of Harrisburg in central Pennsylvania. Then after three years or so, William and Thomas headed for Kentucky and it was understood that David and his family resettled in Virginia. At some point thereafter, any communications with David ceased. If anyone tried to find him or contact him or his descendants, they focused on Virginia but never found him there.[22]

For all of the romantic ideas Americans cherish about the millions who came to these shores, seeing them as fleeing religious repression and the like, as with the Pilgrims of Plymouth Colony, historians agree that the majority of those who emigrated to America – from Ireland or anywhere else – came for mostly economic reasons. At first thought, it might well not seem obvious as to how this would be the case with these three Moffetts. In County Down, it would seem that the family was reasonably secure, and had some stature in the community. None the less, the family included nine children. In the latter years of the 18th century – in which period the parents of those nine died – it was not all that common for offsprings to receive relatively equal shares of the family's wealth upon the master's death. Of the nine in this case, four were females, those of which gender rarely received significant shares. Among the males, the bulk of the properties and money were most often left to the oldest; and that is how James1720 drew up his will.

_____

[22]See more of this in the next chapter.

It should therefore have been expected that James1750 – the oldest son – would receive most of the significant treasure. This may well explain why he did not remove to America as three of his four male siblings did. Again, James1720 and his wife died in 1789, by which time the three sons had departed for America, so they were left nothing. Samuel1765, the one male who remained and was not the oldest, was particularly upset with the very limited shares left to him, and his letters to his overseas brothers included substantial subscriptions of his disappointment and frustration.

The three sons who exited for America likely saw what was coming with regard to their lack of significant financial property gains but there were also other negatives which encouraged them to leave. Not surprisingly, the indigenous, Catholic, Gaelic Irish were thoroughly repressed and still keenly aware that their recent forbears had lost their lands and rights of virtually every kind to Protestant interlopers from England and to some degree Scotland. Rather than give up the fight and convert to the Church of Ireland, they saw the retention of their Catholicism as thoroughly entwined with the spirits of their nationalism, and the greater the repression, the greater became their attitudes.

The numerous Presbyterians, who had brought their religion with them – in Scotland, the Established Church was the Presbyterian – were often proscribed and repressed in much the same ways and to much the same degree as the indigenous Catholics. They felt that they had uprooted themselves, came to Ireland to make a better life, and successfully turned vacant and wasted land into productive and often prosperous farms. They felt that the government in London, which had so encouraged them to go to Ireland in the first place, had mostly turned its backs on them.

Ireland's trade was heavily regulated, which affected the Protestants (who were producing goods that could be exported) more than the Catholics (who generally were not). The Presbyterians saw themselves as the adversaries of both London and the indigenous Catholics, and at times they were an angry and defensive postured group. The land in Ireland, as we have discussed, was owned by a paltry few very wealthy landlords. The welfare of the tenants was usually tied to the attitudes of their particular landlord. The landlords owned these lands to make a profit, and the welfare of the tenants was almost always a secondary consideration. At times of economic change – which of course occurred fairly frequently through history – the result was usually the dispossession of many tenants, or a very marked change in the degree to which their arrangements with the landlord were favorable for them.

All of these points of friction, and some not described here, repeatedly touched the most sacred of points in human life. Religion, an opportunity to work and support a family, the presence or absence of human dignity, and more, all were the fields on which these battles were fought, and the ferocity of the fights was therefore understandably very intense. Set all of this in a land where crop failures, even famines at times, and war (usually with France and others of her Catholic allies) were frequent visitors; and the various conflicting groups bore long-held grudges, fired by monumental ethnic and religious bigotry.

The wonder is not that Ireland was usually in turmoil, but that things were not far worse than they were. It is probably true that the greater calamities were only avoided at the cost of the severe repression practiced by the few who constituted the economic, political, and religious establishments. Furthermore, the wonder is not that so many have emigrated from their homes in Ireland over the past two centuries, but that anyone is left there.[25]

When James Moffett and Jane Bigham were married in 1748 Ireland had been alternately turbulent and relatively peaceful since the youth of James's father. The island, now tied more tightly than ever to the fortunes of England, weathered the fallout from the War of Spanish Succession (1701-1713), Jacobite rebellions (1715, 1719, and the last gasp in 1745), a brief naval war with Spain (1739), and the War of Austrian Succession (1740-1748).

Each of these struggles had great impact while underway, and at their conclusions, with the expansion and contraction of English industry, and to a lesser extent that of Ireland. Furthermore, each of these wars was costly to London, and it was commonplace for England to make the tapping of the economies of her colonies (of which Ireland was certainly one) one significant part of dealing with her post-war debts. This usually came about through legislation which granted economic favor to English merchants, at the expense of others in the realm.

As Jane and James raised their family, the cycle continued. In 1756, England and France went to war with each other again, and the Prussians, Russians, and Austrians were part of the action. This war dragged on for seven years – we in North America refer to it as the French and Indian War – and had more direct impact on Ireland than previous conflagrations had.

France had always maintained a rather duplicitous relationship with what she saw to be England's involuntary subjects in the British Isles – the Scots and Irish. When France and England came to blows, the perennially rebellious elements in Ireland and Scotland became excited by the possibility of taking advantage of London's preoccupation with military events on the continent – and now on the North American continent as well. Always intrigued with the same possibility, France repeatedly considered the possibility of lending support to those rebellious elements.

The Castle at Carrickfergus, captured by a French landing force in 1760

In 1760, at the heart of the hostilities, the French actually landed a force on Irish soil, and captured Carrickfergus, near Belfast. While the invasion essentially went no further than that, London was terrified, and the Emerald Isle found many more British troops garrisoned on her soil. If nothing else, the frame of mind of Irishmen shifted more toward a feeling of being occupied by foreigners. Such a condition rarely bears only small fruit.

---

[25]Leyburn, chapters 10 and 11.

By the time the last children of James and Jane Moffett were being born, the disaffections in Ireland boiled over into violence, especially in Ulster, where a four- year-long outbreak known as the Ulster Land War reared its sinister head. The causes were economic. Large portions of Ulster leases were coming due in the late 1760s, and landlords found themselves with a seller's market. Rents to renew were hugely increased[26], and those who allowed their lease to lapse without renewing or vacating received heavy fines. Tithes – the obligatory payments to the established Church of Ireland, which were mandatory whether one was a member of that church or not – were raised. Large tracts of land were sold off to rich merchants who then became new rack-renters. The rent problems resulted in large numbers of tenants being removed by eviction – never an event which would improve political and social stability. Besides all of this, all those who were not members of the established church – the Church of Ireland, an Anglican, Episcopal Church – were prevented by the Test Act from holding any public office, as had been the case for decades.

The resultant uprisings began in 1770, and the "war" lasted for four years. The atrocities were carried out by secret societies which were bred from the discontent. The most prominent of these was the Hearts of Steel, or the Steel Boys. Their purpose "was to create a reign of terror that would deter new tenants from settling upon the vacant farms. Those who had the temerity to do so had their houses, stack-yards and turf stacks burned and their cattle houghed."[27]

As it happened, Saintfield was fully involved with this and later upheavals. Mr. Francis Price, who was essentially the lord of the manor of Saintfield, received several threatening letters, but apparently escaped the acts of violence which were frequently carried out. As the violence dragged on, the flow of emigration to America from Saintfield in particular began.

When peace was essentially restored after the Ulster Land War, it was not long before the great uprising in America took place – the Revolutionary War. For vast numbers of Irish citizens, many conditions which had so recently resulted in the Ulster Land War had not changed, and that uprising, which gave hope of bringing change, had for the most part been defeated. Shortly thereafter came news of the outbreak of war in America. As the resultant continued (and intensified) feeling of oppression at the hands of what they deemed a despotic monarchy and administration, large numbers of Irish natives felt a natural affinity for the rebels in North America. The language of the Revolution spread to Ireland and rang true in many ears. As the war progressed, news of it continued to spread the gospel of the Enlightenment's views of human rights and the responsibilities of governments.

---

[26]As mentioned previously, this was a frequent element of the story of Ireland's economy. The practice was referred to as rack-renting by the tenants, alluding to the old practice of torture on a rack.

[27]The Rev. David Stewart, *Historical Memoirs of First Saintfield Congregation (Tonaghneave) through Three Centuries, 1658-1958* (Belfast, 1958), pp. 38-39.

All of this was part of the reason David1753 was drawn to America. As things were going for the first year of the full-class war, many single young adult males in Ireland sympathized with the

American rebels, but the people of Ireland knew very well that the British Army and Navy were the most powerful such units in Europe and probably all of the world. Their own recent experiences of failure made them clearly aware that this military challenge to the British was quite a long-shot.

Consequently, while so many of the Irish wished the rebels in America well and good fortune, and may well have imagined that they would perhaps like to join the Americans in their struggle, they felt strongly that they knew better – until the autumn of 1777. At that time word began to arrive in Ireland that the American rebels had defeated a British Army and forced them to surrender!

No doubt, at first the response must have been to think the information bearers were mistaken, but of course they were not, and residents of Ireland were soon convinced. This of course was the victory at the battle (or more completely, the battles) of Saratoga. On-and-off battle between a growing number of American rebels and an army under the command of the British General, John Burgoyne, went on from the middle of September through that of October. On the 17th of the latter month, Burgoyne surrendered.

As a result, large numbers of young Irish male residents began to consider the notion of sailing to America, and perhaps doing what they could to assist the rebels' goal. Then, soon after the winter of 1777-78, large numbers began to leave the Emerald Isle for what was now called the United States of America by the rebels – or, as they called themselves, the "patriots". Records involving David Maffet (in other records spelled Maffat, Moffit, etc.) show that he had gone to America by 1779 and probably as early as early as `78.

Of course it would not be too exceptional for a family to be split over such a conflict. While we cannot be sure we know the minds of those who chose not to emigrate, the evidence does suggest that they opposed the efforts at reform, and supported the maintenance of the establishment as it was; or at the least, those who remained were basically too uneasy with the with the idea of significant change – a very common view for persons facing such choices. Older brother David however was very probably not uneasy and must have seen a chance for at least some better things in life, and/or maybe doing what he could to defeat the British. William and Thomas no doubt expected a better and probably more interesting life, and the facts that they left Ireland so soon after learning of the war's conclusion, and William's 21st birthday, tells us that they felt anxious to make the trip for a good while before leaving.

The influence of the American Revolution would have fallen on deaf ears in Ireland if there had not been numerous grievances, but numerous they were, and long standing. During and after the American Revolution, life back in Ireland was still troublesome for the majority. The Land War had changed nothing. In efforts to somehow continue the struggle, numbers of Irish of varying religious and ethnic backgrounds began to speak publicly of the application of the ideals of America in Ireland. The British government clearly felt this to be a seditious and subversive trend. Ultimately this would lead to the foundation of what was known as the United Irishmen. This group and a few allied ones soon were further encouraged by the influence of the French Revolution (1789). By the late 1790s their cause broke into violence, and they led an uprising. It failed.

Mathew Carey (1760-1839), born in Dublin and a voice for radical reform. He was driven from his homeland in 1784, going to Philadelphia. At about the same time, the Moffetts left Ireland for the same destination.

This post-Land-War development was new and very significant. The consistent resort to violence had repeatedly failed, without exception. Through the activity of their newest leaders, the disgruntled, disenfranchised and dispossessed reconsidered their approach, engaging political systems in Ireland. There arose significant new voices such as a young journalist named Mathew Carey, who aimed to accomplish change by debate and politics rather than violence. He rose to national attention as a result of his published sympathies to the ideas of the United Irishmen and others. Among other well remembered statements of his, in1783 he argued that all of the evils which had befallen Ireland came "from our blasting connection with Britain!" He loudly "demanded political democracy, religious equality, economic independence and cultural self-determination for Ireland. And when reforms were not forthcoming, he drew on the example of America to argue in 1784 for armed revolution."[29]

---

[28]All of this may well have been at least part of the reason David1753 was drawn to America. If so, we should wonder whether he served in any military unit in the war. Examining those records, it appears that he might have. There are of course documents which list those who served, a number of them identify a man named David Maffett who served in Pennsylvania, and at least one indicates that the individual was serving in or near Harrisburg.

[29]David A. Wilson, *United Irishmen, United States* (Ithaca, New York, 1998), pp. 17, 18.

Pretty strong talk! And Mr. Carey was by no means alone. On the other hand of course, not everyone in Ireland sympathized. Not surprisingly, many of those who saw the United Irishmen as dangerous were adherents to the Church of Ireland. They also tended to be those who were economically above the fray, who were of the middle class and higher, and who suffered little or none of the perceived injustices. They feared the loss of all they had gained. There were others too, but the members of the Established Church and those of property and the better classes were the primary opponents of these revolutionary thinkers.

It would seem that the exodus to America by Moffetts William1763 and Thomas1767 was likely driven by these rising signs of much greater turbulence soon to come. What then was their position in all of this? Were they revolutionary sympathizers, or were they frightened by them? Did they leave because of adherence to the causes of the United Irishmen or to escape the possibility of the group's victory?

Having relocated to America well before the end of the war, it would seem most likely that David1753 was enthused by the notion of the folks across the ocean in the British colonies breaking free from their master nation. The effort to overthrow the British started off poorly, and most who viewed the war from Europe saw no significant reason to expect an American victory. Then in September of 1777 the British army led by John Burgoyne was defeated and forced to surrender at Saratoga – a shocking event! The reactions in Europe and America were intense, and for the likes of David1753 this was very probably the news by which he began to seriously consider leaving Ireland for America. The one other such very significant defeat of the British army occurred in October of 1781, when Cornwallis was trapped by Washington at Yorktown, and cut off from escape by sea owing to the presence of the French navy. This second defeat of the British would also likely excite David's notion to head for America, but we know that he was already there at that time. It would thus seem most likely that he left for America not long after Burgoyne's defeat. Very possibly, he made the trip in the spring of 1778.

In the eighteenth century of course, everything moved slowly. To go from the surrender at Yorktown to the signing of a peace treaty took nearly two years. The treaty was signed September 3, 1783 in Paris. Over the next few months, the word spread across the European continent that the Americans were now independent.

On the other hand, being well educated persons, and bearing a natural caution which membership in the establishment will breed, while they no doubt held out quiet hope for a victory of some sort for the United Irishmen and their likes, that hope was very likely for a non-violent victory. However, simultaneous with the arrival of the news of America's success in gaining recognition of their independence, the storm clouds of probable violence in Ireland were growing darker. The rhetoric and political pressure had brought no change, except to further incite the advocates for change.[30]

---

[30]George Brown Tindall, *America, A Narrative History* (New York, 1984) vol. 1, pp. 227-229.

The Lisburn and Lambeg volunteers (potential rebels), assumed in the Market Square at Lisburn, on the boundary between counties Antrim and Down. The demonstration was in honor of the Convention of 1782. Scenes like this, duplicated around the country, signaled the very serious potential strength of this surge of Irish nationalism, which included very significant numbers of Protestants – especially Presbyterians and other dissenters – as well as Roman Catholics.

The Moffetts back in Saintfield must have been aware that victory – whether through political or military means – was hardly certain; and in participation in an effort to win, one might well result in their being charged with treason and cost them their lives. The American forces were successful however, and that allowed the parents of William and Thomas – now 21 and 17 years old – to grant them willingness to sail. Now, by removing to America, they could safely enjoy the hard-won liberties, and the happier circumstances they would afford.

The other two sons were old enough to join with the two who left, but chose not to, and none of the daughters left either. Consequently, they lived through such revolution as did come in 1798. The records show that they remained situated among esteemed classes there, and among the establishment. If they did harbor sympathies for the revolutionaries, they did not let it be known.

Of course it would not be too exceptional for a family to be split over such a conflict. We cannot be sure we know the minds of those who chose not to emigrate, but evidence suggests they opposed the efforts at reform, and supported the maintenance of the establishment; or at the least, those who remained were basically too uneasy with the with the idea of significant change – a very common view for persons facing such choices. Older brother David however was apparently not uneasy and must have seen a chance for at least some better things in life, maybe doing what he could to defeat the British. William and Thomas no doubt expected a better and probably more interesting life, and the fact that they left Ireland so soon after learning of the war's conclusion, and William's 21st birthday, tells us they felt anxious to make the trip for a good while before leaving.

There were plenty of differences between the family's lives in Scotland and Ireland, and that of religion was certainly at or near the top. It is most probable that Scotland born William1685 – the only identified member of that first generation of the Moffett lines discussed in this work – was initially born into a family of Presbyterians. When he settled in Ireland, he very likely was not yet married, he being a teenager or possibly even younger. He therefore most likely married in Ireland, at which time – likely very early in the 18th century – the established Church had become the Anglican religion – the *Church of Ireland*. Only in that faith could a couple be married. We know that William1685 was then a member of the Church of Ireland and his children were as well. For example, his son James1720 was a very active and well-respected member of the Church of Ireland congregation in Saintfield in the late 1740s, and he and his wife, Jane Bigham, were also married in the Anglican Church and all of their children were baptized in that faith as well.

In 1778, many laws which involved religious and statutory authorities were eliminated, and this is very likely what brought about – indeed allowed – the family's return to the Presbyterian faith. Family records and letters indicate that at the time James1720 died in 1789, he had relinquished his Church of Ireland membership and became a member of Saintfield's Presbyterian congregation. His sons James and Samuel had done the same. William1763 retained his association with the Anglican institutions in America. David1753 and his family apparently resumed the family's traditional affiliation with the Presbyterians, as the couple and at least one of their children were buried in a Presbyterian cemetery in South Huntingdon Township in Pennsylvania's Westmoreland County.

In any case, David had crossed the ocean, in 1778, never to return, and a few years later his two brothers had joined him. All three had "Gone to America".

6 — Gone to America

As the summer of 1777 wore on, George Washington's American army experienced significant defeats in quick succession of 23 days – at Brandywine on September 11, Paoli nine days later and Germantown on the 4th of October. For the American "Patriots" this was probably the point of the lowest hour in the Revolutionary War and a rather welcome relief for those in the newborn country who hoped for a return to accepted British rule. Many have wondered: Given those three disastrous beatings, with winter coming, if the battle at Saratoga which so promptly followed had not been so completely successful, would Washington have been able to convince his army to bear the misery of the winter at Valley Forge as they did? Would the war have been a failure?

As it happened of course, the American army in New York, led by generals Horatio Gates and Benedict Arnold, stunned the struggling infant nation – and much of the world – in mid-October of that year, forcing the surrender of General John Burgoyne's, British army. The Patriots and Many sympathizers beyond their border were handed a very

Surrender of the Generals - Burgoyne to Gates at Saratoga

significant change of view. Large numbers of young men in Ireland – especially Ulster Scots – were emboldened by the news and decided to go to America in order to perhaps do what they could to bring about independence for the thirteen colonies[31], and subsequently live in a country free of what they saw as many British negatives.

----

[31]Further north, the citizens of British origin had just recently gained control over the large French colony of Quebec, and apparently the British citizens in the adjacent areas north of the Niagara River and Lakes Erie and Ontario felt the need for considerable support from Great Britain and did not care to leave that empire.

The Winter at Valley Forge, 1777-78

David Maffet (as he and his family usually spelled his surname then, and whom we will mostly refer to as David1753), second son of James Maffet and Jane Bigham, was among those who first responded to the excitement of the defeat of Burgoyne and sometime rather soon after the winter of 1777-78 he arrived in the "State" – or "Colony" as the British still put it – of Pennsylvania. He was one among a rush of Ulster Scots who had suddenly felt the possibility that those thirteen colonies may well succeed in their effort to free themselves from British rule. Well into his twenties at that time, if his parents were worried or otherwise unhappy about it – as they may well have been – they were unable to keep him there in Ireland.

Some Maffet relatives were already in Pennsylvania when David arrived, and apparently he promptly went to their home, or somewhere very near it in the northern portion of Lancaster County. One William Maffet and his wife were residing there and had a son named James (this William being an older brother of James1720[32]) but apparently the couple had no other sons – or at least none who reached adulthood – and whether they had any daughters is unknown.

The family of William1715 – probable brother of James1720 – resided in what was then the north-central area of Lancaster County. In 1785 the northern half or so of Lancaster was set off as Dauphin County, and in 1813 the eastern part of Dauphin was set off as Lebanon County. More specifically they resided in that county's Hanover Township, which today is in three divisions in Dauphin County – East. West and South townships – and another part of East Township in Lebanon County. The Moffetts apparently resided in what became West Hanover Township.

─────────────────────

[32] The time of William's birth is not known, except that he was apparently older than James1720. Most agree that William was born sometime in the decade of 1710-19, and he is therefore usually referred to as William1715.

William1715 had one son, James Maffet, who served briefly with the militia. What appears to be the single surviving record pertaining to him reads in part, "Acquitted and referred to 5th Class". Initially he served in the 4th of the 8 classes in his militia company. The class numbers in these records are indications of some degree of quality service the individual can be expected to provide. The ratings may include measures of skill, physical ability, devotion, healthy, behavior, etc. The only one thing we know about James for certain is that he had died while still a young man, sometime after 1780 and almost surely before 1786. He may therefore have developed health problems from disease or injury. We cannot actually determine whether he ever actively engaged in battle.

It is highly likely that there was yet another sibling of William1715 and James1720 in the Moffett family, or possibly two, who resided for a time in the area of Northern Lancaster/Dauphin County. The records of men besides David1753, who served in what was the county's militia in the Revolutionary War, include additional Moffett men who were located in the very same area as David1753, in or very near Hanover Township[33]. The two were:

Thomas Maffit: The one record involving his activity indicates that he served in Lancaster's 9th Battalion in 1781. No doubt therefore he served in the same limited area of what shortly after the war became Dauphin County. It indicates that he had served "on a tour of Duty." Men who served in the militia did not often participate in "a tour of duty" but were only called into action when there was serious need for usually brief active service – usually no more than a few weeks, and often a good bit less if at all. They mostly lived with family and pursued their farming or other routine employment, but regularly joined in their unit's periodic military practice and might be called for services. The significant majority of militia men did not participate in a "tour of duty", and such service in the militia usually involved persons who were not greatly responsible for anyone but themselves. We can therefore assume that Thomas might well have been the youngest of these Moffett soldiers, not married, and those with whom he lived did not always seriously depend on his services.

William Maffet or Maffett or Maffit: Along with David1753, this man was the Maffet most frequently recorded as serving in the 6th and 9th militia battalions in Lancaster County, the two therefore obviously both serving in the same limited area and therefore surely residing near to or with each other. While David was serving as early as 1779 (or possibly '78), William was doing so by 1780, and both served at least as late as May of 1782. They therefore appear to have been the two in the family who were the most active in the militia. Like Thomas, William was neither a son of James1720 or William 1715, but apparently one whose father was yet at least a third son of William1685. We have no good indication pertaining to the name or names or age or ages, of these Thomas and William's father or fathers.

---

[33]More specifically, after the war Hanover Township was divided into three: East, West and South townships. Most or all of the Moffett men who were related to David1753 resided in what became West Hanover Township.

The above-mentioned Thomas and William – militia men in the Revolutionary War – apparently had departed Dauphin County sometime not long after the war ended as there were no Moffett households listed in the that county's federal censuses for 1790, 1800 or 1810. Unfortunately, it therefore may well not be possible to determine what became of either of these two men, who their parents were, or specifically when they or their family, or further ancestors, came to America. It would seem that any success in such a search would result from some degree of significantly good luck! On the other hand, it seems certain that they both do descend from a son or to Northern Ireland when he was a teenager or a bit younger. That they gathered together in the same spot in Pennsylvania, and that the given names were so consistent with those of each others' immediate families, it would be very difficult to argue to the contrary.

The war – specifically upon the stunning victory at Saratoga – drew David1753 to the continent to his west. This was certainly not only because he was anxious to fight, but first and foremost because of the rather stinging limits placed on the Scots who fled to Ulster by invitation of the British rulers in Ireland. Because of what the Scots saw as disrespect of their religious views, and other disregards they faced, many felt betrayed. They were invited because the English needed them, but their rewards were at best few and far between. What they saw of the goals of the American Revolution looked very much different and strongly suggested that a British defeat there would allow them opportunity which would be rewarded in kind. It would appear that when the war was over, William1763 apparently had determined that, like his older brother in America, he would have the opportunity to live a better life there than he likely would in Ulster. His younger brother Thomas1767, being yet only 17 years old, may have agreed strongly with William, but may also have been simply ready for excitement in a new land – and maybe both. For certain, the two sons of James1720 were quite anxious to join their brother and his family in America.

The war officially ended in the autumn of 1783, and as soon as the coming winter was over in 1784 they set sail. The pair landed at Philadelphia after almost three months at sea, and shortly thereafter were settled in Pennsylvania's Hanover Township with their brother and his family. They had "Gone to America".

7 — Arrival and Settlement

As already noted, David1753 Moffett left for America in 1778 to do what he could to aid the American rebels – or patriots as they called themselves – in their struggle to break free of the British government. Sometime in that year, after nearly three months at sea, he landed at Philadelphia.[34]

The eager young Scots-Irish men who fled their homes to engage the British in America hoped a victory would find them in a nation which would allow them to be full-blooded citizens. Their Scottish forbears had enthusiastically responded to the pleas of the British government, encouraging the Scots to take up the desolated lands of Ulster at the outset of the 17th century. When the Scots did so, they produced a great revival of persons, products, and support to the British. The Scots felt that they received little in the way of gratitude however. Their religion was not recognized as being fully worthy. If Scots married in the Presbyterian rather than the established Anglican Church, the marriage was not recognized by the government. Neither could Presbyterians serve in the government at any level. There were many other negatives as well and such limitations by the English/Anglican establishments persisted until the latest decades of the 18th century.

---

[34]By the time news of Saratoga arrived in Saintfield, it was seasonally too late to cross the Atlantic. He could have left in the spring, arriving in summer, but he may have held off until the news that the British had abandoned Philadelphia in June in which case he may not have arrived until autumn.

There was no more welcoming colony in North America than Pennsylvania, and most were not even nearly so. The establishment in New England for example was that of a reformed church, which was also the character of the Presbyterian adherents, but the New England Puritans' tolerance of others who were not strictly of that origin and faith was negligible at best.

From its years as New Amsterdam, New York has likely always been the most cosmopolitan of America's cities. However, beyond the city, the New York colony presented little in the way of an agreeable situation for the Ulster emigrants. The population was essentially Dutch and English, and largely confined to the valley of the Hudson River, and the lower portion of the Mohawk. Beyond these valleys, expansion to the west and north was thwarted by hostile indigenous people, as well as the extensive and hostile presence of the French to the north. Whatever the degree of welcome to Ulstermen who came to New York, their prospects for acquisition of significant quantities of inexpensive land were poor until after the Revolutionary War, late in the 18th century.

Maryland and Delaware were relatively welcoming, but they were small colonies, and there the prospects for expansion were adversely conditioned by the significant ridges of the Appalachians.

Ulster Scots, most of whom were Presbyterian, did not come to North America in significant numbers until about 1719 and later. By then the Church of England was the established church from Virginia southward and those colonies were initially saturated with a stoutly episcopal religion. As a consequence, the Scots-Irish often hesitated to attempt their settlement in those southerly colonies.

The result was that most came to Pennsylvania.[35] David1753's port of entry was and still is known as the City of Brotherly Love. The contrasts between Pennsylvania and the others are stunning regarding the 18th century variety of nations whose immigrants settled in that colony/state and their varieties of cultures and religions. This was the only state which fully welcomed any and all religions – something essentially absent from the entire world at the time. Whether or not those who wished to unite the colonies – and eventually to consider separation from Great Britain – consciously chose to promote Philadelphia as the ultimate gathering place to organize and produce unity and eventual independence, today we can certainly see its wisdom. The positives of varieties of thought, beliefs and ideas were consequently numerous and exceptional and have found their way into most of America, all of which has contributed mightily to her successes. Pennsylvania also had a good amount of land, little of which presented a danger from natives or French colonists. While the center of the state was traversed by the Appalachians, the lay of the land was such that, from central Pennsylvania, settlers could turn southward and southwesterly and find relatively easy access to the great valley west of the mountains. It quickly became obvious to the Ulster Scots and numerous others, that their best fortune would surely be found by landing in Pennsylvania.

---

[35]Occupation of Philadelphia began late in September of 1777. For multiple reasons, that move did not work well for the British, and they returned to New York in June of 1778 with about 3,000 loyalists. From that point on, the city was quite reasonably safe.

Upon arrival in the Keystone State[36], William1763 and Thomas1767 no doubt promptly found their way to Hanover Township – the part of which was soon to be West Hanover – and settled in with their brother and his wife and their (probably two) very young children. The group then remained together there for three years.

It was a time of significant social and political turmoil. The war for American Independence had just been won, and the institutions of government and society were struggling to return to normal. The economies of the various states were struggling to construct new systems, and the pain inflicted as a consequence was real and fairly extensive. The nearly nonexistent value of the Continental currency was legendary. The war had throttled much of what manufacturing and commerce existed, and the absences from their farms by the men who served as soldiers reduced agricultural output. The cities of New York and Philadelphia had been occupied by the British, and at the time resulted in significant flight of residents who favored the rebellion. Now, these cities were rebuilding their economies, as well as their social and political structures.

High Street in Philadelphia, near the end of the eighteenth century
The first Presbyterian Church is on the right, with white columns. If the Moffetts spent much time in this city, they might very well have worshiped in this church. It was razed in 1820 for a new building.

---

[36]A keystone is a central wedge in an arch that locks all other pieces of an arch in place. It is the part of an arch that all other parts depend upon. Pennsylvania's popular nickname refers to this necessary element.

In the midst of all of this the unfortunate families who had remained loyal to Britain were dispossessed of their property and viewed as peddlers of treason by the now fully established governments of the states. Large numbers of them fled the country, or were in the process of doing so, removing to Ontario, Quebec, New Brunswick and even back to the British Isles. A number of these families had occupied high stations in the political, economic, and social fabrics of the country, their departures leaving significant power vacuums in many areas and the struggle went on to fill these vacuums.

The economic crisis made life miserable for a large percentage of the population, and in a few areas, the hardships were compounded by new or higher taxes. With the prevailing view of their society being one of near anarchy, it was therefore not long before some groups resorted to force and violence to address their grievances.

In western Massachusetts there arose the most dramatic of the ensuing conflicts, led by Revolutionary War veteran Daniel Shays, who had served as a captain in the 5th Massachusetts Regiment. He participated in the battles of Bunker Hill, Saratoga, Ticonderoga and Stony Point, and was even rewarded a ceremonial sword by the Marquis de Lafayette. In the 1785 economic collapse, and subsequent years, farmers in his area of the state were suffering in excess, victims of the depression, compounded by high (and rising) taxes. Many went bankrupt, and their farms were being foreclosed. In 1786, Shays organized a small military force with the aim to stop the courts from meeting, so as also to stop them from issuing indictments against the numbers of farmers in arrears. The movement known as Shays' Rebellion, went on through the following winter, involving skirmishes and one small battle, but the rebels were routed in a serious battle early in 1787.[37]

Daniel Shays and his band of "rebels" confront government troops at Northampton, Massachusetts.

In another action, in Pennsylvania a disgruntled group of some eighty militia recruits gathered in Lancaster, marched to Philadelphia (where the congress then was housed), were joined by other units in that city, and the whole body then conducted a menacing and threatening demonstration outside Independence Hall, forcing the Congress to flee to New Jersey.[38] In Vermont, which was not yet a state but was claimed by New York, before the Revolution was ended Ethan Allen had effectively fought off the New Yorkers, and his territory became essentially independent.[39]

---

[37]Tindall, vol. 1, pp. 246-250.

[38]Michael A. Bellesiles, Revolutionary Outlaws (Charlottville, 1993), pp. 186-187.

[39]Tindall, vol. 1, pp. 258-281.

Upon the arrival of the two younger Moffetts at Philadelphia, the populace there and beyond was quickly progressing away from its initial jubilation and were wrestling with the realities of being cut loose from Britain. During all of this were the continued rise of economic recession, social and political upheaval, and the edge of a new rebellion. Conditions did not improve significantly until the 1789 establishment of a new government system laid out in the constitution created at the convention in Philadelphia in 1787. Following that critical step, the anarchy slackened when the governments and militia dealt sternly with the likes of Shays. A good deal of the social unrest began to settle down as the power and land vacated by Loyalists had been taken up by champions of the Patriot cause. The political weaknesses and turmoil faded when the beloved General George Washington assumed the leadership of the executive branch of the new United States government. From all of these kernels of stability grew a strengthened economy – eventually.

David, William and Thomas remained together in West Hanover for three years. Little is known about their activities in this period, but it is quite likely that they were taking on various employments, the specificity of which we also do not know, as they considered where in the country they each might settle. They were in that place because David had initially settled there; and he did so because it was apparently where his uncle William1715 had resided when David left home and his one known son – James – was still there in Hanover Township. At least two others of their Moffett relatives were also in the area during the war but there is no evidence indicating that either of them, or any others of their immediate family (or families) remained there for any significant time after peace arrived. To where they went has not been determined by the authors.

Annual records of adult males in communities in Pennsylvania survive from at least as early as 1783 – the end of the war. The lists involving Lancaster County in 1783, and Dauphin County from 1785 to `87, include the following Moffetts (actually in various spellings of course): 1783, David; 1785 and `86, David and William; and in 1787 Thomas is also included. After that none of them appear in Dauphin County. There also was one John Maffit listed as a "Freeman" (single adult male – not married) in 1788 in the Dauphin County township of Paxton, about 21 miles west-northwest of the area where David and his brothers lived in the mid-1780s. Efforts to determine anything about his family or his geographic origins have not been successful.

After the aforementioned three years in which David1753, William1763 and Thomas1767 all resided in West Hanover, the three relocated. Just prior to departure, on the 4th of February in 1787 in Harrisburg, William married Rebecca Robinson, whose family was no doubt situated among several Robinsons in West Hanover. That couple and Thomas ventured to the part of Virginia which shortly thereafter became Kentucky.

Apparently, the later descendants of William1763 Moffett somehow believed that when David1753 and his family left West Hanover, they settled in Virginia and that they died in that state. The family record, compiled and maintained by great-grandchildren of David's brother William, states that from the time of that parting, none of the family in Kentucky ever heard from David or his children again. In fact, he did not settle there at all, and we cannot be completely certain regarding the source of the confusion, but well experienced genealogists know too well that this is a classic example of time's proclivity to distort.

One reasonable possibility is that even before the Revolutionary War commenced and until 1784, what then became the southwestern corner of the state of Pennsylvania had been claimed by both that state and Virginia. Therefore until at least 1784, many persons would have referred to what became Westmoreland County as part of Virginia.

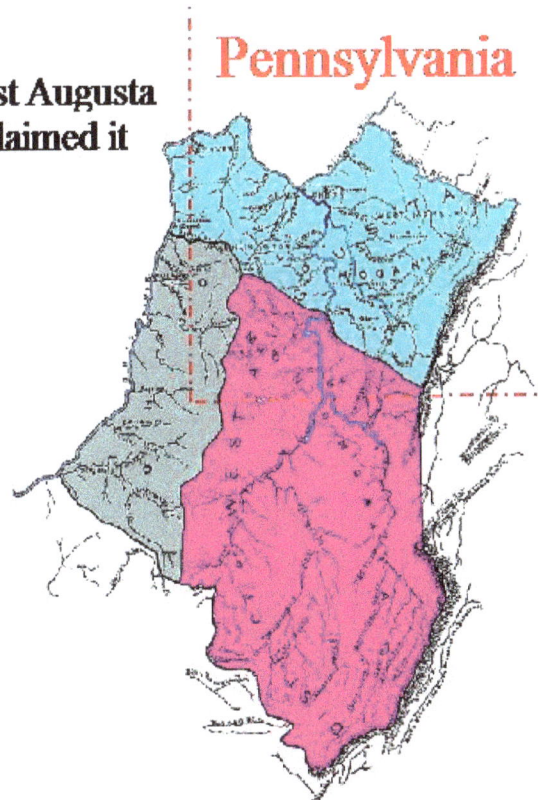

District of West Augusta as Virginia claimed it

Counties:

Ohio

Yohogania

Monongalia

Pennsylvania

When the war ended, the central government of the United States – such as it was – finally had things like this contest to consider and settle. In 1784 it was decided that Pennsylvania's southwestern corner would be what are shown here by the broken red lines, and the contested territory in that state included all or parts of Greene, Washington, Westmoreland, Fayette, Allegheny and Beaver counties. The remainder went to the Virginians.

The family did well know that David1753 expressed a desire to resettle in Virginia, but in fact the first place he located after leaving West Hanover in 1787 was the township of South Huntingdon in Pennsylvania's Westmoreland County. It was certainly known to most that, for at least a few years, the family remained there. Surviving letters from David to his siblings in Kentucky and from the family back in Ireland include references to the fact that David was living there in what had fully determined to be part of Pennsylvania.

No such letters were dated later than the first few years in the 1790s however. Therefore, from the time of the exchanges of the letters, through to the 20th and 21st centuries, it appears that some of David's descendants perhaps assumed that his family eventually did go to Virginia, while others may have not been aware of the letters written from Westmoreland County when Virginia was out of the contest for that section of Pennsylvania. The letters from David did include statements about his discontent with conditions of things there in South Huntingdon, and none of the letters indicated that he had decided to stay in South Huntingdon… that he no longer felt the need to go on to Virginia. These may have been at least a part of the confusion. For all we know however, the "Virginia" of which he spoke might well have really meant the southern area which became Westmoreland County – especially if all of his statements about removing to Virginia were made when he had not yet departed from West Hanover.

In any case, the family of David and Mary Maffet clearly lived in South Huntingdon Township from just before 1790 through a good part of the 1830s, and those who died there were no doubt buried in that cemetery. Mary was apparently the last to die there. Clearly their stones badly aged and all but Mary's are no longer there. In fact, although the cemetery was established at least a decade or two before 1800, virtually no stones cut and placed before the 1820s are to be found there now. They were made with stone which ultimately cracked, and which wore relatively quickly – as opposed to granite or quartzite for example. As can be seen on Mary's stone today, even those which survive in years before at least the middle of the nineteenth century are often difficult or nearly impossible to read.

One more thing: The federal census of 1800 tells us that the four females who were living in David1753's home at that time were all too young to be David1753's wife. From early letters, there is hard evidence that the woman he (first) married was named Mary, as is the aforementioned woman in the cemetery in Sewickley.

There would seem to be two possible conclusions: One is that David1753 had but one wife, who is the woman buried in that cemetery in Sewickley in 1836, and either she was away from home at the time the census taker visited or the census taker erred in recording the family's information; and the other is that the woman whom David1753 first married died not long before the 1800 census was taken, and he subsequently remarried another woman named Mary who was born in approximately the same period as the one who had died. What very much seems the *more* likely is that Mary was either absent from home or simply omitted when the census was taken, as opposed to the possibility that David1753 married two women named Mary who were born at about the same time; but of course, both scenarios are possible.

Here below is a photo of the tombstone of one Mary Moffett in the Sewickley Presbyterian Church Cemetery in the township of South Huntingdon, in which village David1753 resided for 20 to 30 years. It is virtually certain that this was his widow as the information on the stone is indeed compatible with the date of birth of the woman he married in about 1780. The stone tells us that Mary died 14 July 1836, aged 85 years and 14 days. She was therefore born on the fourth of July – before it was so special.

Text below is that which is engraved on the stone

In Memory of Mary Maffet Who Departed This Life July This 18th 1836 Aged 85 Years & 14 days

One can see that the stone is badly worn and difficult to read, especially in this photo which had to be taken with the sunlight at the back of the stone. It is just legible enough to make out all the lettering and numbers when viewing the stone in person. It is highly likely that there was a stone in this cemetery citing David1753, but it has no doubt been removed as the result of the face becoming totally unreadable and/or the stone having fallen over and cracked, etc. It is known that significant numbers of the earliest stones have met such a fate and notable spaces are to be seen in their areas.

We do know that there had been one other stone immediately adjacent to Mary's. Sometime in the first decade of the twenty-first century a gentleman named Darrel Trout went through the cemetery and listed all of the stones with whatever writing was on them that he could make out. The stone which was next to Mary's is no longer there. When Mr. Trout was compiling his information, it was there but had fallen against another stone, blocking a good bit of the writing space. What was still visible was only the following: *…Dee Maffett, died Aug 1, 1812 __? 9 mos 28d*

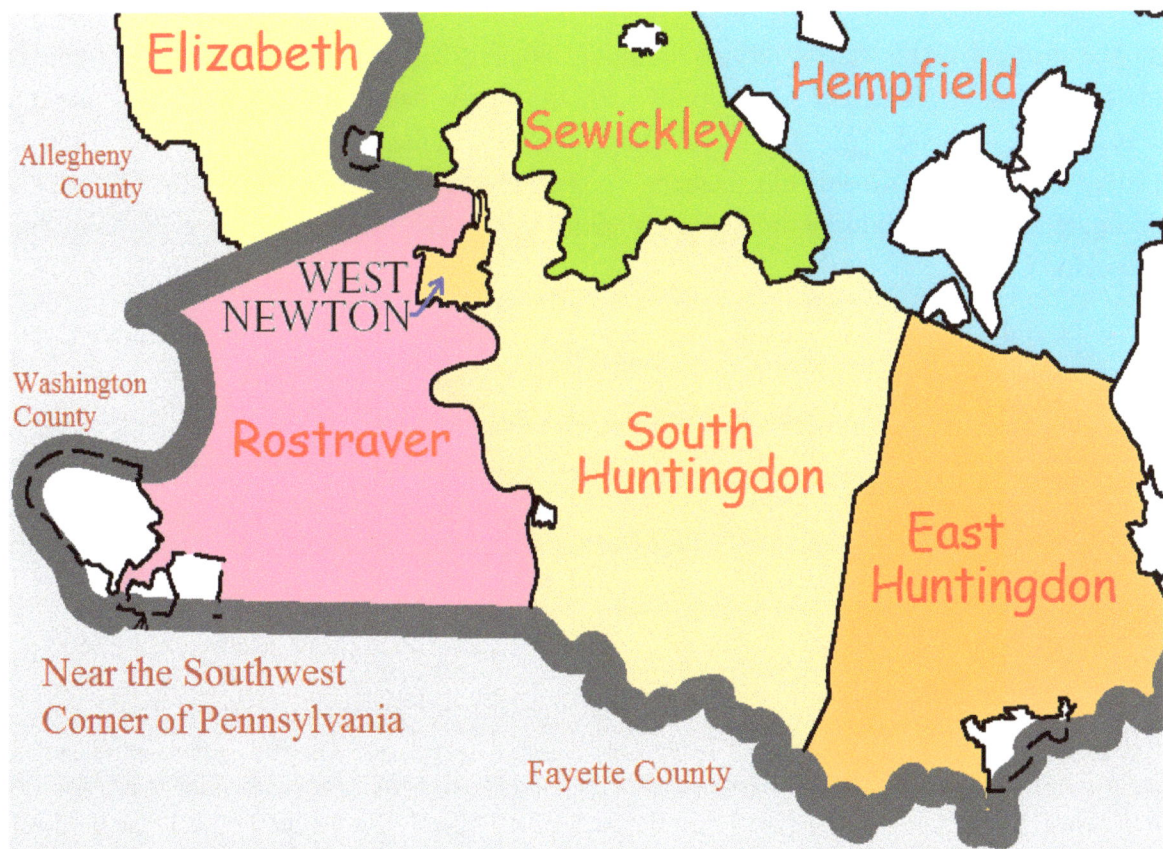

The descendants of David1753 are reasonably numerous, residing in or near western Pennsylvania, and very possibly well beyond that state. The authors have been unable to identify any of his daughters, and only two of his five sons – James1781 and David1800, the oldest and the youngest of the five. Of the three other males however, at least one appears to have died before reaching the age of ten years. As for the remaining two, they either also died young or departed to a considerable distance from south- western Westmoreland County while still barely an adult.

At the time of the 1810 census, James1781 was married, had fathered a son and daughter and set up his family's residence in Rostraver, a township adjacent to the west of his father's home in that of South Huntingdon. We know James's wife's given name was Sarah, but do not know her surname. The census records also identify two daughters of the couple. The older of the two, whose name and ultimate life story we do not know, was born in Rostraver in about 1809 or `10 and the 1830 census indicates that she was apparently still living at home and unmarried. The younger of the two was Sarah, born about 1823 and married James Brambley, a native of England. They had: Sarah Ann, born in May of 1850; Mary, born in about 1853; and James, born in about 1861.

Only the two youngest of the males have been identified, the first being James H., born in Pennsylvania about 1825. He first appears in the 1850 census residing in Westmoreland County's borough of West Newton. The household head was William L. Miller, a 30-year-old "Surgeon Dentist". Besides other Millers the last two entries for that household are two Maffetts – the aforementioned James1825 and a 13-year-old Kezia J. (or possibly **R**eziah).[40]

The successive U.S. census returns involving James1825 indicate that he married in the early to middle 1850s to one Margaret A. Cochran[41], and the couple had nine children, one of whom died before reaching adulthood. They and their children are listed in the censuses of 1860 and `70 residing in the Allegheny County township of Elizabeth. The census of 1880 tells us that James1825 had died[42], and Margaret and her children immediately removed to the adjacent Rostraver Township in Westmoreland County.

Of the eight children of James1825 who survived to adulthood, only two were males and neither of them ever married. We also know that David1800 and his wife had only three children, all of whom were daughters. As the 19th century progressed, the descendants of David1753 – mostly all being females, marrying and taking on different surnames – were less and less likely to have easily reconnected and/or to have been easily identified when searching for them. It is also pretty clear that the few male Moffett descendants of David1753 were geographically disconnected from those of William1763 and his descendants.

---

[40]The presence of this teenage girl in that household is the only bit of information which might suggest that James1825 may not be a son of James1781. The 1840 census of the latter's household includes no female child aged younger than 15 years, while Kezia would have been three years old at that time. Other evidence strongly confirms that James1825 *was* indeed a son of James1781. He died at his home in Elizabeth Township (Allegheny County), immediately adjacent to Rostraver, and his widow and children immediately removed to a home just two doors from that of the aforesaid Bramley family. She may have been a child of yet another Maffett – perhaps another son of David1753 – or may not have been a Maffett at all.

[41]Some sources indicate that her maiden surname was Curry.

[42]His tombstone indicates that he died in 1880, obviously before the census was taken.

Apart from James1825, the only other male child of James1781 who is to date known by name and had male offsprings is Carnie, born in about 1828 in Rostraver, Pennsylvania. In 1850, he is listed as a Rostraver household head with his wife Nancy Anne and a 5-month-old named Albert. About six years later, he and his family removed to Bloomfield in Davis County, Iowa where they still resided in 1860 and Carnie was employed as a carpenter. Ten years later, he had relocated to Vermillion, Ashland County, Ohio, and was reportedly a farmer. In that 1880 federal census (Carnie not enumerated) Nancy and the children – all seven of them – were still living in Vermillion; and in that census Nancy was labeled as a widow. She died there in 1895. It turns out that, wherever Carnie was in1880, he was not deceased, and in the 1900 census he was residing with his son, James William, but died a year later.

When the Civil War broke out, Carnie[42] was 33 years old, and in general the recruits were younger than that. In 1863 however, he was listed with men who were healthy enough to be considered for the draft, but there does not appear to be any record indicating that he ever served, even though the census of 1870 listed no children born to them in the period from 1860-65.[43]

This portion of a page includes the list of men from Ashland County, Ohio who had surnames beginning with the letter M – and not yet having served in the Civil War but were of an age and good health enough to serve if necessary. A search to determine how the two might be related was inconclusive.

_____

[43]By only a very small margin, this spelling – probably numbering nearly a dozen – happens to be the most frequently cited in the various records which include his name. In each of the federal censuses of 1850, `60, `70 and 1900, the name is spelled differently – Camie, Cannie, Carmie and Carmi – he not having been listed in the 1880 census.

The various censuses cited here indicate that the couple had these seven children in the approximate years stated: Albert, 1850; Mary E., 1857; Margaret Josephine, 1859; James W., 1866; Henry Bason, 1869; McClure, 1871; and Alice, 1873. The fifth and sixth children died before reaching adulthood, but all the others eventually married.

Carnie was absent from his family in 1880, but why was his wife labeled a widow? It would not seem that his absence from the census, and the entry in it which indicates that Nancy was a widow, were both census-taker errors. Whatever the cause, there is evidence that he left his family for a quite extended period of time. One obvious possibility is that the couple may have had an angry separation for personal reasons. Another would be that if he did in fact serve in the Civil War, he may well never had been the same person thereafter – a sad and painful result of service in the war for very great numbers of its soldiers! Of course, we find no record of his serving in the war, so it is unlikely that this was a source of his decision to depart.

In any case, Carnie certainly was absent for a long time. For example, in multiple census records pertaining to Alice – the couple's youngest child, born in 1873 – show that she did not know where her father had been born or lived. Despite that, he was still living in 1900 and at that time he resided with his son James's family in a township adjacent to Vermillion. It would seem very likely that he departed his family not long before or after Alice's birth, and probably did not return until after his wife's death in 1895. By 1880, he would likely have been absent for seven years, and his family therefore may well have declared that he had passed away. His death actually took place in 1901.

It is unfortunate that so many of the offsprings of both David1753 and his oldest son, James1781, apparently died or removed significant distances from South Huntingdon and Rostraver, etc. As a consequence, at the time of this compilation what lineages have been successfully traced to living, direct descendants of David1753 do not include persons who are from all-male lines, and so do not bear the Moffett surname. This of course makes it more difficult to locate those who are David1753's living descendants.

As mentioned previously, David1800 and his wife only had three children and they were all females – Mary, Nancy and Catherine. Therefore, if any of the three had any grandchildren, those children would not have carried the Moffett surname in any spelling. Given the time period when these three daughters would have married, no civil vital records survive to indicate the surname of a woman's husband in a marriage record. The search for a marriage in churches or other non-civil records is the best of the remaining opportunities but makes the effort much more difficult and perhaps impossible given that any records from congregations may well only have partial remains – if any – from the 19th and earlier centuries. In addition, the searcher may not know which congregation the individuals in question would have selected for the event. In this particular case, these three do not seem to be identifiable, so it seems likely that they married or died in the years from 1870-1900.

As spring was near in 1787, the newly married William and Rebecca Moffett, along with younger Moffett brother Thomas, departed from Pennsylvania to relocate in Virginia. Their plan was to settle in a part of that state which would soon be set off as a new one named Kentucky. Their path was no doubt along the contemporary routes of migration. For many decades, the Ulster scots had sailed to North America, most arriving at the port of Philadelphia. Early in the 18th century, they moved to the unsettled land in the interior of Pennsylvania and usually took up lands there. Penn's

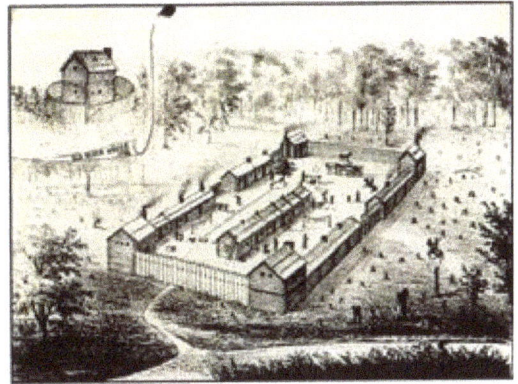

Fort Lexington, Kentucky, 1782

colony filled with the Ulster emigrants and many others from Germany and elsewhere, the focus of emigration turned from Central Pennsylvania south and southwest, down the great valley to the west of the front ranges of the Appalachians. The Ulstermen moved to the frontiers as a rule, their national character and culture leading them to the regions where they could maximize their sense of personal independence.

On the Trail in Kentucky

From Pennsylvania then, the migrants found the retreating edges of the frontier, and settled there, first in western Virginia.   From there migrants branched off to the west and others toward the south into the Carolinas, eventually following the frontier to the Gulf States, Tennessee, Kentucky, and the lands north of the Ohio and west of the Mississippi. Certain numbers of the First American-born generation of these pioneers then answered the restless call of the newest lands, and joined the European natives swelling the flow.

In 1787, when Thomas and William Moffett and William's wife set out from Pennsylvania, what became Kentucky was still a part of the state of Virginia. It was the newest frontier in the mid-Atlantic states. Only the far southwest corner was still held by indigenous people. Very few counties had yet been created there, and the arm of government had great difficulty reaching the many souls who had ventured so far from the more concentrated populations – a situation which the Ulster Scots saw as ideal.

The family record indicates that William, his wife, and Thomas went directly to what became Kentucky. There is no record of the specific path they took, but its general course can easily be deduced. In keeping with the migratory routes mentioned above, they would have left Harrisburg, and briefly traveled southward down the Susquehanna Valley, and then turned to the southwest until they came to an area just west of Baltimore. From there, a turn to the west would take them across the Potomac River, into Virginia, to the Shenandoah River Valley, and into the Great Valley. They were essentially on the highway to the frontier. Indeed, the route had been blazed by Daniel Boone and others, and had come to be known as the Wilderness Road. Their travel would then take them southward down the valley, through the present-day Virginia counties of Loudon, Warren, Shenandoah, Rockingham, Augusta, Rockbridge, Botetourt, Roanoke and Montgomery, to Fort Chiswell in present-day Wythe County.

The Appalachians in Kentucky

The Kentucky River in Estill County...
The Moffetts would have come down this very section of the stream.

The Moffetts would have taken one of two routes from here, and at this point, the trailblazers' work became much more appreciated. Both routes went from here to Castlewood in present day Russell County. At Castlewood the majority of the travelers would stay on the Wilderness Road, continue in a southwesterly direction, and pass through the Cumberland Gap, just about where the boundaries of the present-day states of Virginia, Tennessee and Kentucky all meet. Thence, turning north or northwest, it was a downhill effort to the major river systems. It is very possible that the Moffetts went this way.

On the other hand, it may have made more sense if they had turned to the northwest at Castlewood and followed what was known as the Kentucky Trace. From Castlewood, this route took them to Indian Creek, and then through the Pound Gap (present-day counties of Wise in Virginia and Letcher in Kentucky). Here the travelers would be right at the headwaters of the Kentucky River, which is certainly the river which, at some point, became the last leg of the Moffetts' trek.

As they went down the Kentucky River Valley, the family record indicates that they arrived at Boonesborough, Kentucky[44] in the early spring of 1787. This would have been the first settlement of significance which they had encountered since starting down the New River in Virginia. Presumably, they would have rested, obtained provisions and resumed their trek, initially settling somewhere near Lexington, Kentucky.

The tax records of Kentucky counties indicate that by 1790, William Moffett owned land in Fayette County[45]. Precisely where that land was is not known for certain, but it could not have been far from Lexington. In 1790, Fayette County approximately occupied the territories of present-day Fayette, Clark and Jessamine counties. No point within that area would have been more than about 16 miles from Lexington.

We know from family records that Thomas Moffett was living in or very near Lexington in 1793. Those records relate the details of the tragic accident which resulted in Thomas's untimely death "in the streets of Lexington."

> "*He was riding along on horseback, when two young sports contested in a horse race. Their horses were high strung and coming up behind Thomas ran against his horse. His horse jumped, and in consequence he was thrown off. He landed on a stump, striking his stomach, from the effects of which he lived but a short time.*"[46]

---

[44]The record actually says "Boonesville", but this is apparently an error. There is no populated place in Kentucky called Boonesville, and research in the United States Geological Survey (USGS)'s Geographic Names Information System (GNIS) indicates there has not been a place with that name in Kentucky in the past. There is a Boonesville in Greene County, Virginia, and the Moffetts may have passed near or through that village. However, in the manuscript, the following sentence is the last part of the description of the travel from Harrisburg to their new home in Kentucky: "They reached Boonesville in the early part of 1787." It hardly seems that the author of the manuscript would end the description of the travel with reference to a place in present-day Virginia only half way down the Shenandoah Valley.

There also is a Booneville in Kentucky, but it is situated in present-day Owsley County. While this town is situated on the South Fork of the Kentucky River, it is sixty to seventy miles upstream from where the Moffetts would have departed the river to head for the area of Lexington. On the other hand, Boonesborough was a frontier fort, and it makes perfect sense that arrival there would be a high point in the trip. Furthermore, Boonesborough is situated precisely at the point along the Kentucky where the family would have departed the river and is only about fifteen miles from Lexington.

[45]Charles B. Henemann, comp., *First Census of Kentucky, 1790* (Baltimore, 1981).

[46]"Moffett Family Narrative", 25 December 1900.

The yellow oval shows the approximate location of William and Rebecca Moffett's farm, and Springfield Presbyterian Church, in what became the southern edge of Bath County.

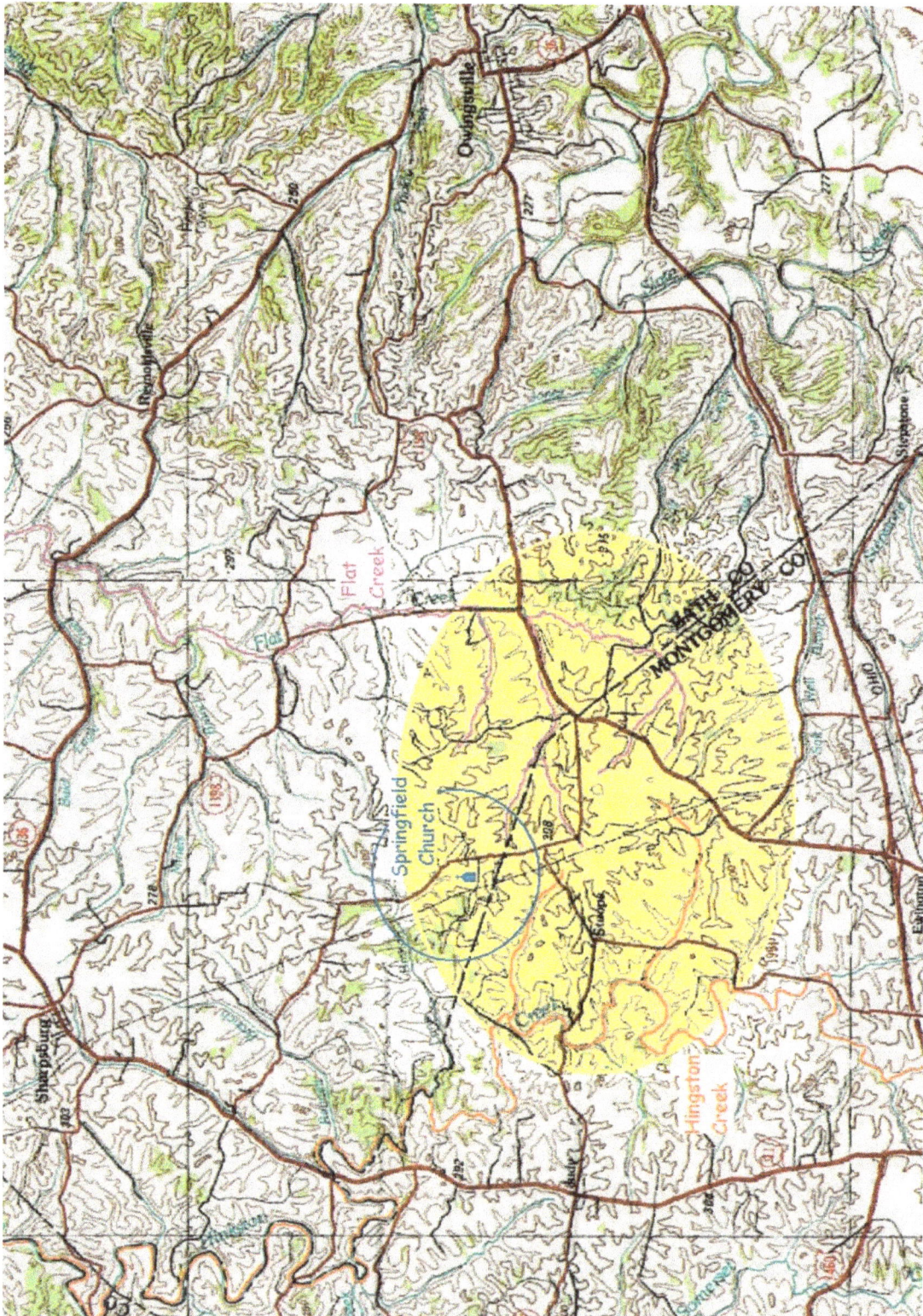

A small-scale topographical map, showing the area where the headwaters of the Hingston and Flat creeks meet, highlighted by the yellow oval, which corresponds to the same on the map above. The Moffetts' property would have been about in the middle of this oval. The location of the Springfield Church is shown, behind which building is the graveyard where William Moffett and his wife, Rebecca Robinson, are buried.

About the time Thomas died, William and Rebecca Moffett removed to land they had newly acquired some forty miles east of Lexington, in what was then part of Montgomery County. The name of William Moffett appears among the subscribers to a pair of petitions, respectively dated October 4, 1794 and Mary 17, 1795, for the services of Rev. Joseph Howe, from the congregation of the Springfield Presbyterian Church, whose church is located near the southern boundary of the present-day Bath County.[47] William's name appears on the Montgomery County tax list of 1797, the year for which the earliest of the county's lists survives. He held 100 acres of land on Hingston Creek.[48] In 1801, William Moffett purchased an additional 150 acres on Flat Creek from James McMillan and his wife Ellen.[49] The 1803 tax list indicates that he owned 250 acres. However, by 1811, the family held only 157 acres, most being the 150 acres on Flat Creek which had been purchased in 1801.[50]

Here the couple's wanderings came to an end. They lived the rest of their lives on this land, which became part of the County of Bath when created in 1811. William died there on Saturday, April 22, 1826, and Rebecca on a Sunday, July 2, 1843. The two were buried in the cemetery of the Springfield Presbyterian Church, in southern Bath County. While no gravestone survives over William's grave, that of Rebecca is marked with a stone which lists her dates of birth and death.[51]

The Moffett immigrants, born at Leggygowan in Ireland's County Down, had left their homeland for political and economic reasons, and risked losing their substantial social and economic status in the old country to start over in a land thousands of miles away, over a tempestuous ocean. In the 18th century sailing across the Atlantic was always an act of some risk and courage. Yet arrival on the new continent was only part of the journey. Leaving the American coastal plain as William did – a region of relative safety where the rule of civil law was established and traditional – he and Thomas pressed on, setting out for regions nearly devoid of government and civilization, full of risks and uncertainties. All of this to live on land they had never seen. If nothing else, the twosome was courageous, but they also must have had an abiding faith in the great republican experiment that was America – a new nation, whose system of government had no precedent, and whose fate no one knew.

---

[47]"Records of Reverend Joseph P. Howe", *USGenWeb Archives Project, Montgomery County, Kentucky*, January 2, 2006, 2petitin.txt, 3subscrb.txt, and 4subsrb.txt
<http://www.rootsweb.com/~usgenweb/ky/montgomery/toc.html>

[48]Commonweath of Kentucky. Montgomery County Tax Assessor. Tax List 1797.

[49]Commonweath of Kentucky. Montgomery County Court, Deed Book 2.

[50]Commonweath of Kentucky. Bath County Tax Assessor. Tax List, 1811.

[51]Kendel Culbertson, "Springfield Church Cemetery", *USGenWeb Archives Project, Bath County, Kentucky*, April 26, 2006. USGenWeb, May 5, 2006
<http://ftp.rootsweb.com/pub/usgenweb/ky/bath/cemeteries/>

8 — Living in the New, Young Country

Most Americans have been well versed in the images of the pioneers who settled the nation's wild lands. They have gained such acquaintance from school lessons and text books, "western" movies, museums, the rhetoric of prominent persons, and more. Even so, a full appreciation for the hardships these folks endured may not be possible for those of us living in long-settled American communities in the twenty-first century. Hardships there were however, most of which related to clearing the land, living in very rudimentary shelter, and surviving what was mostly subsistence farming for the first few years. We can be sure that the Moffetts had their share.

Still, in many ways the situation was certainly ripe for settlement. The western regions into which white Americans poured after the Revolutionary War, including the area which would become Kentucky, were essentially devoid of indigenous people, who had been bought out, escorted out, or driven out. Violent clashes with the Native Americans mostly preceded the arrival of serious settlers. Here in Kentucky in 1787, the native peoples had been pushed northward across the Ohio River.[70]

The new arrivals would have very fertile land on which to grow food and cash crops, trees and stone to raise buildings, a generally peaceful social environment, mostly good weather, and fellow settlers who had brought (or would soon bring) many important skills which most of them did not have – black-smithing, milling, improved preparation of lumber, river navigation, and more. Reasonably strong men, with the willingness and ability to work, could establish and own a significant farm in just a few years. If America was the land of opportunity, those opportunities' greatest nurseries were on the American frontier. The Kentucky River Valley in the late 18th century was certainly one of those nurseries.[71]

William Moffett was 24 years old when he arrived in Fayette County, Kentucky. The lands he worked when he first arrived, and the tract(s) he subsequently took up in what is now Bath County, were no doubt completely unimproved, and probably woodland for the most part. He and his family obviously worked very hard for much of his adult life to turn what had been a wilderness into good, productive, agricultural land.

---

[70]Alvin M. Josephy, Jr., *500 Nations, An Illustrated History of North American Indians* (New York, 1994), pp. 259-261.

[71]Richard A. Bartlett, *The New Country* (New York, 1974), pp. 175-188.

Corn grinding as it would have been accomplished in the late 18th and early 19th centuries. Horses were sometimes used for particularly large quantities, but many families only used this rudimentary system.

To those of us who reside in 21st century America, the contrasts between William's experience and the world we know are obviously very great. Mechanization was hardly a concept, much less an ongoing improvement. Plows were pulled by a horse (or ox) and pushed by a man. First shelters which were built by pioneers were made from logs, little hewn, and in some situations still bearing their bark. In the early nineteenth century, even the more permanent house which the family built after becoming established was not usually built with anything resembling modern lumber, for trimming the logs was still essentially accomplished at home with an axe. Milling was often accomplished at home too. Even when commercial mills were established, they were sparsely distributed, and because many families lived a good distance from the mill, it was often not worthwhile making the trip.

Of course, one of the factories in the cost/benefit analysis of traveling anywhere was the nature and conditions of the roads. Few of them, as such, existed in the first decade or two of William's life in Kentucky. What there were of trails and paths which passed for roads, were usually passable for horses. However, transporting larger quantities of goods overland often required a wagon, and in such case the roads were quite problematic. There were of course, no railroads until well after William died.[59] The only really efficient way to move goods was still by water. This situation was obviously a significant hindrance to progress. Procurement of any sort of finished goods, tools, clothing, paper, printing equipment – indeed, anything not found in nature – was rarely achieved by importation until significant progress was made in the quality of roads.

---

[54]*idem.*

Another striking fact of frontier life was the paucity of reliable communications. Newspapers were not part of the original landscape. Other communications were by word of mouth or letters, both of which present their own factors of unreliability. From the date when William Moffett and his family settled in Kentucky, it would yet be nearly five decades before the first instantaneous communication device – the telegraph – had been brought to a workable stage in the laboratory, and yet another decade before the first practical use of the device. Neither William Moffett nor his wife Rebecca would live to see a telegraph or telegram.

So it went. The list of significant differences between the life enjoyed by William and his family, and that of early 21st century Americans, is long, and of course a great deal of it involves technology. When William settled in Kentucky: It would be more than two decades before steam powered any commercial boats on the world's waters, and longer still before they would enable the birth of the railroads. It would be more than forty years before anyone began to have a comprehensive understanding of electricity, and only after that could it be considered as a possible tool in solving problems of human productivity.

Technology was not the whole story however. Politically, it would be several months before any state ratified the new constitution, almost two years before an American President was sworn in under that document, and more than four years before the "Bill of Rights" went into effect. It would be a generation before the requirement to own property was dropped from the qualifications to vote in America, and William's grandchildren would all be adults – some of them already deceased before men other than whites could vote. Before women could vote in all of the United States, William Moffett would be deceased for nearly a century, his wife for 77 years, and all but one of his daughters for more than 47 years.[55]

At the time William Moffett and Rebecca Robinson married and went to Kentucky, as difficult as communications were, there was not yet any United States Post Office Department and would not be for another five years. The U. S. Department of Agriculture would not exist for seventy-five years. It would be one-hundred-twenty-seven years before the institution of federal income tax and before American voters would directly elect members of the United States Senate.[61] No woman would serve in the Congress for one-hundred-thirty-one years, and no American Indian would be allowed United States citizenship for one-hundred-thirty-eight years.

Religion would change significantly too. Among other things, there would not be any very significant presence of Roman Catholicism, and no Mormons would appear, until after William Moffett and Rebecca Robinson died. No very significant presence of Judaism would arise until all of their grandchildren had long since lived and died. Moslem families in America were essentially unheard of before the twenty-first century.

------

[55]Tindall, vol. 1

[56]Until the passage of the XVII amendment to the Constitution, members of the US. Senate were chosen by state legislatures.

It would be five years after William Moffett settled in Kentucky before the New York Stock Exchange was established, or before the cornerstone would be laid for the White House, and another decade would pass before an American President resided in that mansion. Nearly two more decades would go by before the Congress would legislate the present design of the American flag.[57] William himself would die before there would be a dictionary produced by Noah Webster (1828), or before any popular reference would be made to the American mythical character of Uncle Sam (1852). William and his wife would not live to see the introduction of photography in the United States (1839), the development of the revolver (Colt's invention, 1836) or the safety pin (1849), the establishment of any national park (1872, Yellowstone) or professional baseball league (1876), or the appearance of the Tootsie Roll (1896). Cultural changes such as daylight savings time, Mother's Day, and the establishments of the Boy Scouts and Girl Scouts would not come forth until the twentieth century (1918, 1914, 1908, and 1912 respectively). The twentieth was also the century which would arrive before the first seeing-eye dog (1928) or neon sign (1915).[58]

The progress of labor was of course quite slow. A measure of this can be seen in the fact that, just two years before Rebecca Robinson Moffett died, the state of Massachusetts enacted legislation restricting the employment of children under the age of twelve. Hence forth, they could be required to work no longer than ten hours in a day!

While technology is certainly the most readily striking facet of change to embrace the generations of Moffetts in America, the state of health and medicine ius the particular element of technology which has had the most profound impact on society. Perhaps the most dramatic illustration of this lies in the history of American life expectancy, at the heart of which has been the rate of infant mortality. When the Moffetts settled in Kentucky, nearly one of every four children born in America did not live a single year. Childhood diseases ands a consequence, the life expectancy of a white male was about 35 years.[59]

---

[57]Prior to the Flag Act of 1818, when a new state joined the Union, both a star and a stripe were added to the flag, but that law permanently established the number of stripes at thirteen, and only a star was added for a new state.

[58]Sources for various stages of progress were: Larry Shapiro, *A Book of Days in American History* (New York, 1987); and Irving S. and Nell M. Kull, *A Chronological Encyclopedia of American History* (New York, 1969).

[59]See Appendix 4 for more detailed statistics regarding longevity and infant mortality.

It is difficult for twenty-first century Americans, especially those born after World War II, to imagine such a world. The cultural effects were certainly quite substantial. For generations, a very common American children's bedtime prayer included the line, "If I should die before I wake…." This plea was not hypothetical theology but based on widespread hard realities of life experiences. At this writing, the death of a child in America is so rare that families have very widely abandoned or revised the prayer, so as not to introduce children to unnecessary fears.[60]

Because the deaths of children were a foreseeable part of being a parent, American parents in the 19th and earlier centuries commonly made smaller emotional investments in their babies until they were a few months old and past the worst risks. Parents often delayed naming their newborns, sometimes for several months, and it was not uncommon for parents to receive fatalistic warnings from close friends and family, at the approach of each new birth, to not become too attached too early.[61]

While infant and child mortality, then as now, were more frequent among the poor and in areas of greater population density, no class or group escaped the tragic reach of disease. Indeed, poverty bred many ills to which persons of nearly any age or socio-economic status might well fall prey. Even though infants and children were susceptible to several life-threatening diseases to which adolescents and adults had obtained immunity, numerous other maladies were not subject to immunities obtained in childhood. Accidents and several epidemics especially stalked the population with little discrimination.

Epidemic disease even now effects large numbers of the human species, but has greatly diminished in twenty-first century industrialized nations. At the time the Moffetts settled in Kentucky however, the North American population was still frequently visited by epidemics of smallpox, perhaps the most deadly killer of the time. Tuberculosis was likewise a very common threat. To that could be added fairly frequent visitations of cholera, as well as typhoid, yellow fever, malaria, and many less frequent or less deadly illnesses, including influenza, scarlet and various fevers, diphtheria, pertussis, and others. Many of these were in fact essentially limited to urban areas, but many were not. For example, such mosquito borne ailments as yellow fever and malaria were certainly no strangers to rural areas.

Diseases did not always strike in epidemics. Numerous maladies which have nearly vanished from our experience were ongoing threads. The disease festering importance of impure water and milk, as well as various foods, was not well understood. Most urban settings especially lacked reliably clean drinking water. Antibiotics were of course unheard of.[62]

---

[60]Tim Chambers, "Bedtime Prayers", 19 September 2003, *Go Against the Flow, Live Differently*, 5 January 2006, <http://home.pcisys.net/~tbc/bedpryr.htm>

[61]Jack Larkin, *The Reshaping of Everyday Life 1790-1840* (New York: Harper Collins, 1988) 62-104.

[62]David Rosner, "Epidemics", 2006, *Answers.com*, <http://www.answers.com/topic/epidemics>

Additional threats to health and life were not always from disease. One of the more prominent threats to younger women was childbirth. It is difficult to obtain reliable statistics for years much before the twentieth century, but there is little doubt that by 1915, child birth mortality in America had diminished since the time of the Moffetts' arrival from Ireland. Even so, the mortality rate in that year was 60.8 per every 1,000 births, as opposed to a rate of 0.8 per 1,000 in 1997.

Fire was a common threat, because wood or coal stoves or open fire places heated people's homes and cooked their food, and the techniques and equipment for fighting fire were not well developed. As is the case today, accidents played a prominent role in both life and death, but perhaps excepting the modern factor of the automobile, their frequency was greater. In some areas, their preventability was greater, but in many others, because of the hazardous nature of life's essentials, preventability was far less. Riding (horses) accidents were pervasive, and a fall from a horse could often be fatal.[63] Felling trees, milling, and hunting were all sources of serious risk. As mechanization and industrialization were introduced, additional risks were manifest.

Weather was yet another factor which could wreak havoc in these pioneers' lives. Even in the 21st century, this great natural factor remains essentially uncontrolled by humankind. However, in the 18th and early 19th centuries, excesses in the weather were usually much more difficult to deal with. Weather forecasting and systems of warning for dangerous storms were non-existent. Tornadoes, floods, blizzards and extremes of heat and cold created excessive hardships across the whole area where the Moffetts had settled in Kentucky and Illinois.

The winter of 1830-1831 is a case in point. Those who lived in central Illinois at the time would forever more refer to it as "The Winter of the Deep Snow". To be able to claim a residency in Illinois which predated that bitter season invoked reverence from all who came afterward. Such a revered one came to be called a Snow Bird, and Old Settlers associations honored such pioneers with Snow Bird badges.[64]

The event was prolonged and intense. On Monday, December 20, 1830, a cold rain began in central Illinois. It continued until the day before Christmas, occasionally changing to sleet or snow, but then finally changed again to snow and accumulated to six inches. Suddenly, the storm changed character dramatically, conjuring a furious gale and heavy snow which quickly accumulated 3 feet in depth. The precipitation then changed to freezing rain, forming a very thick and hard crust. One veteran of the event later wrote that the icy crust was "nearly, but not quite, strong enough to bear a man". A resident of Logan County wrote that there the crust was "strong enough to bear the weight of team and sled."[65]

---

[63]The Moffetts knew this all too well. Refer back to page 54 and the recounting of the death of Thomas1767 Moffett, the immigrant.

[64]"The Deep Snow", *The Illinois Intelligencer*, January 28, 1968, published as part of the celebration of the Illinois Sesquicentennial.

[65]*idem.*

Here is a bison – a *large* animal.
This gives us a good idea as to how deep the snow was, and how much difficulty it caused.

On the heels of the precipitation came the classic clearing and cold, but intense beyond the experience of most if not all, with fierce winds. Dr. Julian M. Sturtevant, then a temporary resident of Jacksonville in Morgan County, immediately west of Sangamon County, wrote a detailed account of the whole episode. His wonder at the storm was all the more impressive considering that he was a young man, not quite 30 years old, and a native of Vermont. Any native of that state would have a clear idea of how difficult winters can be. One as old as Sturtevant would have lived   through northern New England's infamous "year without a summer" in 1816.[66]

---

[66]Howard S. Russell, *A Long Deep Furrow, Three Centuries of Farming in New England* (Hanover, New Hampshire, 1976), pp. 273-275. Besides the "year with no summer", 1816 was referred to by New Englanders as "the year with two winters", and "eighteen hundred and froze to death." The weather never progressed much beyond what is typical of early spring. Frosts killed vegetation every month of that disastrous year in many localities In Vermont, a foot of snow fell on June 8, and some sonow fell in both July and August as well. In western Massachusetts, plowed land was crusted with frost ¾ of an inch deep on June 7. Records show that ice formed in Maine on July 5 and August 5.

Dr. Sturtevant described how the wind "...came down from the northwest with extraordinary ferocity." He went on to write that, "...certainly for not less than two weeks, the mercury in the thermometer tube was not, on any one morning, higher than 12 degrees below zero. The wind was a steady, fierce gale from the northwest, day and night. The air was filled with flying snow, which blinded the eyes and almost stopped the breath of anyone who attempted to face it. No man could, for any considerable time, make his way on foot against it." The wind found the tiny openings in the walls of Sturtevant's log cabin and blew so much snow into it that the good doctor was forced to leave and take shelter in a partly finished building at the new Illinois College nearby.[67]

The weather remained intensely frozen, with high winds and blowing snow through January and February. Game and domesticated animals typically froze to death or were feasted on by wolves who found them hopelessly trapped in the deep, hard snow. Travelers and migrating pioneers were universally stranded, and often were fortunate to survive. The *Illinois Intelligencer* of February 26, 1831 included a report stating that "several travelers have perished nearby".[68] A Sangamon County history records the freezing deaths of two men: William Saxton of Lick Creek and Samuel Legg of Sugar Creek.[69]

---

[67]"The Deep Snow"

[68]*idem.*

[69]John Carroll Power, *History of the Early Settlers of Sangamon County* (Springfield, Illinois, 1876).

9 – The First Generation in America
John Bigham Moffett and His Generation

This chapter discusses the first family of children in this line of Moffetts who were born in America. These were the ten children of William Moffett, the immigrant from Ireland, and his wife Rebecca Robinson: John Bigham Moffett and his siblings. All were born in Kentucky, the earliest few while the family resided in Fayette County, and the rest on the farm in what became Bath County.

Half of the ten – James, Margaret Trimble, Jane Bigham, Mary (Polly), and Rebecca Robinson – remained in Kentucky all their lives. James, born in 1787, married Nancy Ratliff in 1811, they had twelve children, and he died at Sharpsburg in 1881. Margaret Trimble was born in 1789, married Edwin Young in 1812, they had at least four children, and she died in Bath County in 1835. Jane Bigham was born in 1791, married Samuel Crain in 1819 and they had five children; he died in Fleming County, Kentucky in 1830, and she there in 1861. Mary (Polly), born in 1792, was never married, but lived most of her adult life with her sister Jane Bigham Crain, and died in Bath County in 1873. Rebecca Robinson was born in 1799, was married to William Crain in 1826, they had eight children, and she died in Fleming County in 1855.

The other five children of William Moffett and Rebecca Robinson – William, Thomas, John Bigham, Elizabeth, and Willis Green – all moved on as young adults and died in other states. All five first settled in central Illinois in the 1820s, and three died there. One other went on to Missouri, and another to Minnesota. These Moffetts were nearly all members of the Cumberland Presbyterian Church. John Bigham Moffett and his children were especially zealous in this regard.[75]

The oldest of those who left Kentucky was William. Born in 1794 in Kentucky, he moved with his siblings to Sangamon County, Illinois in the 1820s. In 1827 he married Edith Kendall. They had twelve children, two of whom died before reaching adolescence. The first six were born in Illinois. Then, in about 1838, the family removed to Linn County, Missouri, where the remaining six were born. William and Edith died in that county in 1852 and 1876 respectively.

The next oldest child of William Moffett and Rebecca Robinson was Thomas, born in 1797, probably in what is now Bath County, Kentucky. Thomas was the only one of those five who came to Illinois who remained in Sangamon County virtually all of his life. He first found work there as a school teacher, and in any spare time he studied law. He settled in Springfield in November of 1826, and for many years he was a ruling elder in the Second Presbyterian Church there.[76]

---

[75] History of Macon County, Illinois (Philadelphia, 1880). Also see Appendix 5.

[76] John Carroll Power, Early Settlers of Sangamon County (Springfield Illinois, 1876).

Moffett Lineage

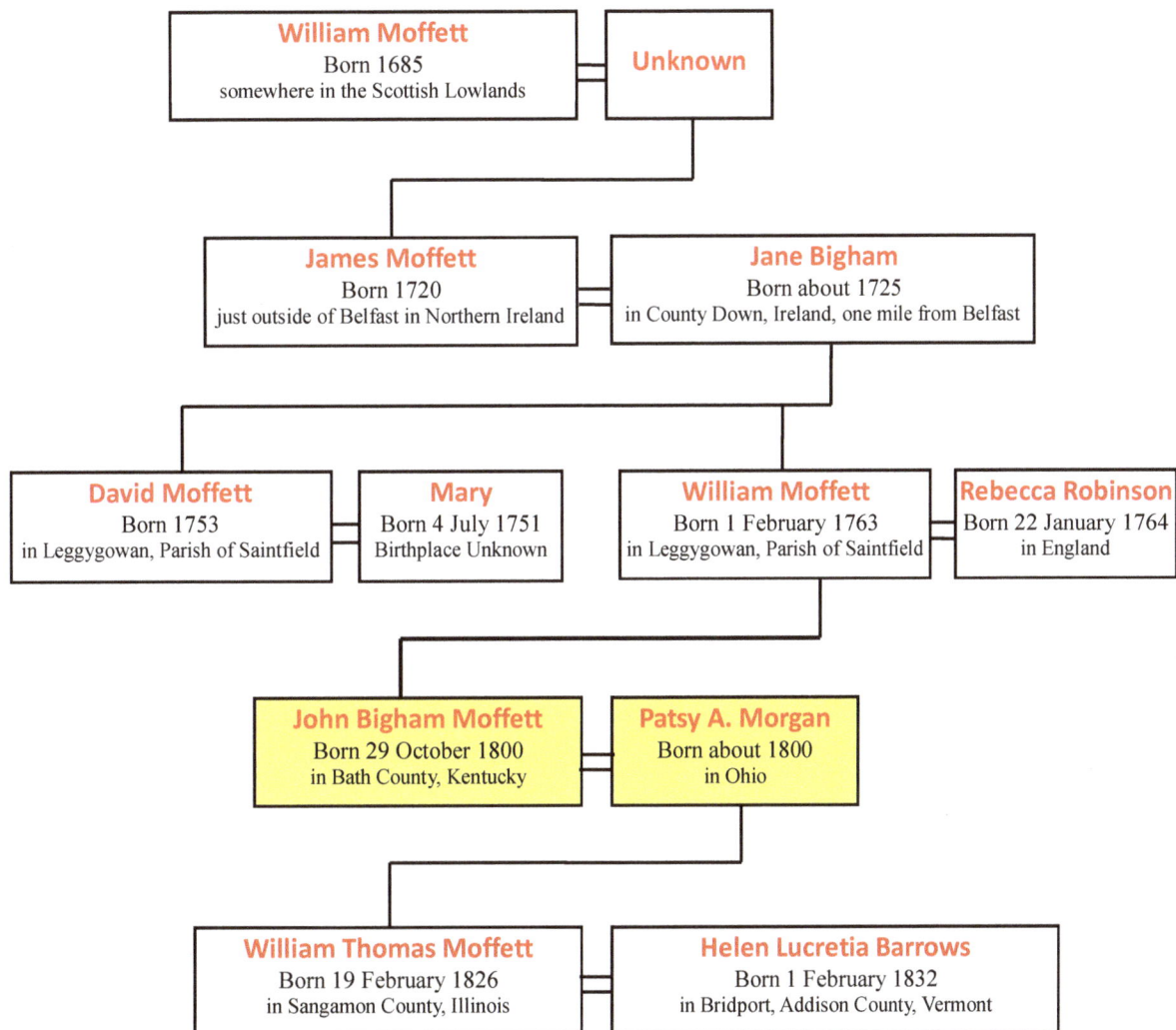

William Moffett
Born 1685
somewhere in the Scottish Lowlands

Unknown

James Moffett
Born 1720
just outside of Belfast in Northern Ireland

Jane Bigham
Born about 1725
in County Down, Ireland, one mile from Belfast

David Moffett
Born 1753
in Leggygowan, Parish of Saintfield

Mary
Born 4 July 1751
Birthplace Unknown

William Moffett
Born 1 February 1763
in Leggygowan, Parish of Saintfield

Rebecca Robinson
Born 22 January 1764
in England

John Bigham Moffett
Born 29 October 1800
in Bath County, Kentucky

Patsy A. Morgan
Born about 1800
in Ohio

William Thomas Moffett
Born 19 February 1826
in Sangamon County, Illinois

Helen Lucretia Barrows
Born 1 February 1832
in Bridport, Addison County, Vermont

Family Group Sheet – William Moffett and Rebecca Robinson

Husband: William Moffett	
Born: 01 Feb 1763	in: Leggygowan, Parish of Saintfield, County Down, Ireland
Married: 4 Feb 1787	in: Harrisburg, Dauphin County, Pennsylvania
Died: 22 Apr 1826	in: Bath County, Kentucky
Father: James Moffett	born in Ulster, Northern Ireland
Mother: Jane Bigham	born in England

Wife: Rebecca Robinson	
Born: 22 Jan 1764	in: Dauphin County, Pennsylvania
Died: 02 Jul 1843	in: Bath or Fleming County, Kentucky
Father: William Robinson	
Mother: Margaret Trimble	

CHILDREN

1 M	Name: James Moffett Born: 18 Oct 1787 Died: 25 Aug 1881 Married: 11 Apr 1811 Spouse: Nancy Ratliff	 in: Fayette County, Kentucky in: Sharpsburg, Bath County, Kentucky in: Bath County, Kentucky
2 F	Name: Margaret Trimble Moffett Born: 12 May 1789 Died: 25 Aug 1835 Married: 12 Jul 1812 Spouse: Edwin Young	 in: Fayette County, Kentucky in: Bath County Kentucky in: Bath County, Kentucky
3 F	Name: Jane Bigham Moffett Born: 2 Mar 1791 Died: 24 Dec 1861 Married: 25 Nov 1819 Spouse: Samuel Crain	 in: Fayette County, Kentucky in: Fleming County, Kentucky in: Bath County, Kentucky
4 F	Name: Mary Polly Moffett Born: 19 Dec 1792 Died: 28 Jun 1873	 in: Bath County, Kentucky in: Bath County, Kentucky
5 M	Name: William Moffett Born: 17 Nov 1794 Died: 19 Apr 1852 Married: 1 May 1827 Spouse: Edith Kendall	 in: probably Fayette County, Kentucky in: Linn County, Missouri in: Sangamon County, Illinois
6 M	Name: Thomas Moffett Born: 13 Apr 1797 Died: 19 Apr 1852 Married: 22 Jan 1829 Spouse: Eliza Ann Gatton Married: 7 Mar 1877 Spouse: Nancy Spencer Grider	 in: Fayette or Bath County, Kentucky in: Sangamon County, Kentucky in: Morgan County, Illinois in: Macon County, Illinois
7 F	Name: Rebecca Robinson Moffett Born: 25 Mar 1799 Died: 20 Mar 1855 Married: 21 Dec 1826 Spouse: William Crain	 in: Bath County, Kentucky in: Fleming County, Kentucky in: Bath County, Kentucky
8 M	Name: John Bigham Moffett Born: 29 Oct 1800 Died: 15 Sep 1862 Married: 26 Jul 1821 Spouse: Patsy A. Morgan Married: Spouse: Rebecca Robinson Married: Spouse: Nancy Spencer Grider	 in: Bath County, Kentucky in: Macon County, Kentucky in: Bath County, Kentucky in: Sangamon County, Illinois in: Schuyler County, Illinois
9 F	Name: Elizabeth Moffett Born: 29 Sep 1802 Died: Bet. 1880 - 1900 Married: 17 May 1831 Spouse: William Kendall	 in: Bath County, Kentucky in: Hancock County, Illinois in: Sangamon County, Illinois
10 M	Name: Willis Green Moffett Born: 9 Jun 1804 Died: 30 Jul 1875 Married: 4 Jan 1825 Spouse: Caroline Stone	 in: Bath County, Kentucky in: Hennepin County, Minnesota

After he was admitted to the bar, Thomas Moffett worked many years as an attorney, served two years as a county commissioner, and beginning in 1843 he was Judge of the Probate Court. In 1848, Thomas Moffett was also elected County Judge for four years. As a consequence of his legal and judicial services, Thomas Moffett was well acquainted with another Springfield attorney named Abraham Lincoln. (See Appendix 6 for more about Lincoln's interactions with the Moffetts.)

Within a decade of the arrival of the Moffetts in central Illinois, two military conflicts with indigenous people flared up in the region, and Thomas Moffett saw military service in both. The first, known as the Winnebago War, broke out in 1827. Throughout the 1820s, tensions grew between Native Americans of the Winnebago, Potawatomi, Sioux, Sauk, Fox, and other tribes on the one hand, and the whites in rapidly growing settlements on the other. A treaty was signed in 1825 at Prairie du Chien, but the tensions did not subside. In the spring of 1826, a family named Method was gathering maple syrup near the Yellow River in present day Iowa. They were attacked and murdered. Six members of the Winnebago tribe were arrested at Prairie du Chien and charged with the murders, but four of them were soon released.

Later in the year, the commander of federal troops at Fort Snelling, Minnesota ordered the garrison at Prairie du Chien's Fort Crawford to move to Fort Snelling. The two who had been retained in connection with the Method family murders were being held by the troops at Fort Crawford, and were therefore also moved to Fort Snelling. This left Prairie du Chien without any military defense. Unfortunately, when the story of the relocation of the Winnebago men reached the Native Americans, it was confounded, and it was understood that the men had been executed, not moved. Not surprisingly, tensions soared further.

On June 27, 1827, a Winnebago chief named Red Bird led a band of Winnebagos to Prarie du Chien to take revenge. They killed two men, and nearly succeeded in killing a one year old white child, then fled as the town began to gather forces to confront them. The tensions turned to a very high level of fear among white settlers throughout The region. The intensity rose yet again in early July when Red Bird's group attacked military supply coats on the Mississippi River, killing two whites, wounding four and losing seven Winnebago lives.

Thomas Moffett. 1797-

A brother of John Bigham Moffett, he was an attorney, probate judge, and county judge in Springfield, Illinois. He knew Abe Lincoln very well.

Other tribes joined forces with the Winnebagos as guerilla attacks continued through the summer. Settlers were killed along the lower Wisconsin River, and lead mines at Galena, Illinois were attacked. The response from various governors in the area was swift, as they attempted to put significant military forces in the field to deal with the raiders.[72]

As a part of the effort, on July 27, Illinois Governor Ninian Edwards wrote to the commander of a regiment located in Sangamon County, ordering him to raise 600 volunteers. These were raised, and among them was Thomas Moffett, who served as a sergeant in Captain Mitchell's Company, enlisting on July 25. The various federal troops, militia men, and volunteers were gathered at Fort Crawford on July 29 to make a show of force.[73] This was ultimately successful, as the force began to move up the Wisconsin River to the heart of the Native Americans' territories. On September 27, Red Bird, faced with open warfare with the whites' military forces, surrendered.[74]

The second outbreak of violence was known as the Black Hawk War. It evolved from ongoing senses of fear and resentment, focused on long conflict over territory. Black Hawk, a chief of the Sauk Nation, challenged the presence of large and increasing numbers of white settlers on land and he deemed to be rightfully that of his people. On April 6, Black Hawk and about 1,000 of his followers crossed the Mississippi River into Illinois, hoping to retake the lands in question. The governor of Illinois deemed this an invasion and mustered five brigades of militia. Thomas Moffett initially enrolled as a sergeant in Captain Saunders's Company of the second regiment, but soon was promoted to Captain, and commanded his own company in the fourth regiment, third brigade.[75]

Skirmishes and pursuits went on through May, June, and July. On the first and second of August decisive clashes at the junction of the Mississippi and Bad Axe rivers decimated Black Hawk's force, killing hundreds, and imprisoning most of the rest. Black Hawk had escaped with a few others but surrendered on August 27. On September 21, a peace treaty was signed.

[72]Frank E. Stevens, *The Black Hawk War* (Chicago, 1903).

[73]It would be another month before the force began to move toward strongholds of the indigenous forces. By that time, many of the volunteers, including Thomas Moffett, had been discharged on August 27, it having been judged that the forces gathered were more than enough to do the job.

[74]Francis Paul Prucha, *The Sword of the Republic, the United States Army on the Frontier,1783-1846* (New York, 1969), pp. 163-167

[75]Stevens, *The Black Hawk War.*

Thomas Moffett was married to Eliza Gatton in 1829 in Morgan County, Illinois. The couple had four sons and four daughters, none of whom ever married, and half of whom died early in childhood. The other four – two sons and two daughters – all died as young adults. The two sons who survived childhood both died during the Civil War years, but there is no indication that either of their deaths was a result of military service. The younger son, Thomas Gatton, was a clerk in the office of the Auditor of State four and a half years. Late in 1861 he enlisted with the Army, and was an officer with the 7th Illinois Infantry Regiment, but served only three months, and saw no combat, dying in Springfield on March 29, 1862, only 22 years of age. The older son, James William, an attorney, practiced law with his father for a few years, and died September 18, 1864, aged 34 years, never having served in the military at all. As for the remaining two daughters, Sarah Rebecca Moffett died in 1864 at the age of 27 years, and Jane Eliza died in March of 1858 at the age of 23 years. The mother, Eliza, died November 11, 1867, aged 57 years. The father, Thomas Moffett, died June 23, 1877 at the age of 80 years in Springfield.

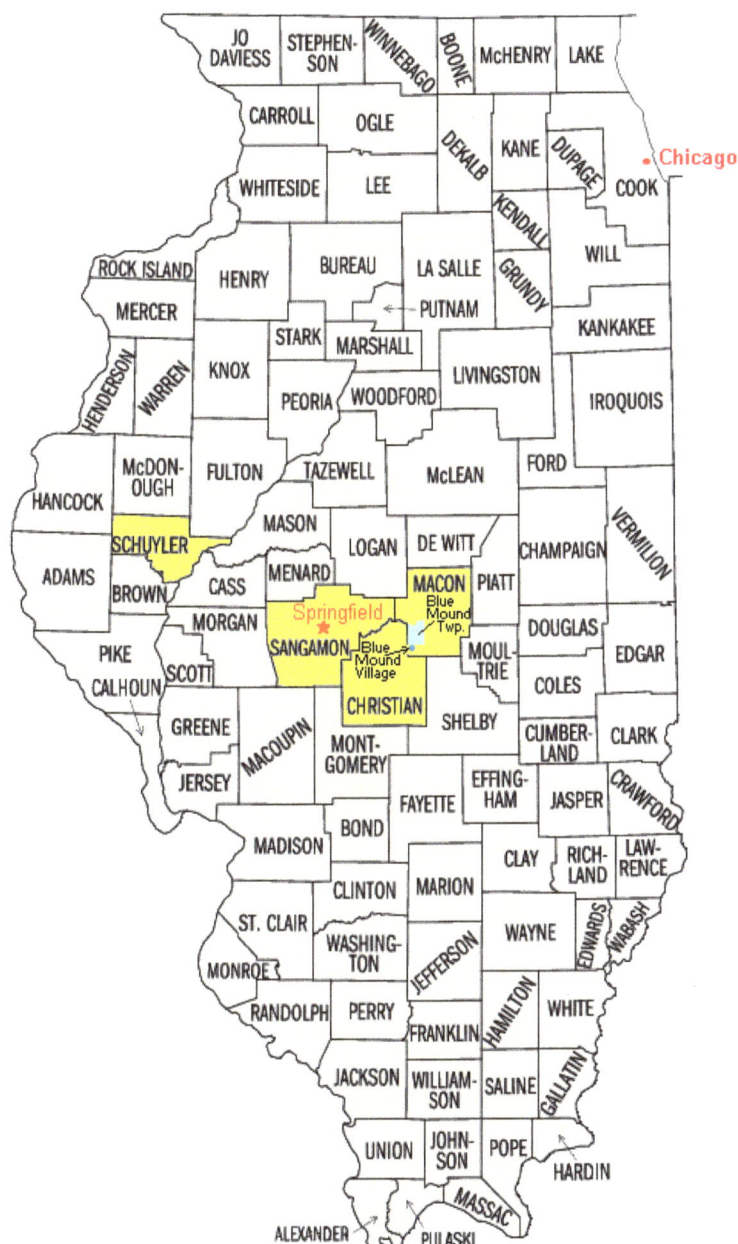

A map of the present-day counties in Illinois. Highlighted are the counties in which John Bigham Moffett (born in Kentucky in 1800) and his family lived – Sangamon, Schuyler, Christian, and Macon. Also shown are the locations of Blue Mound Township, Blue Mound Village, and the City of Springfield.

This family's poor longevity provides a stunning example of the radically different life expectancy of the 18th and early to middle 19th centuries from what has been experienced in America since the middle of the 20th. Despite the fact that the father lived to a ripe old age, and his wife to nearly 60 years, the life expectancy for the entire family of ten was a meager 22.9 years and the life expectancy for the eight children themselves was just 11.5 years!

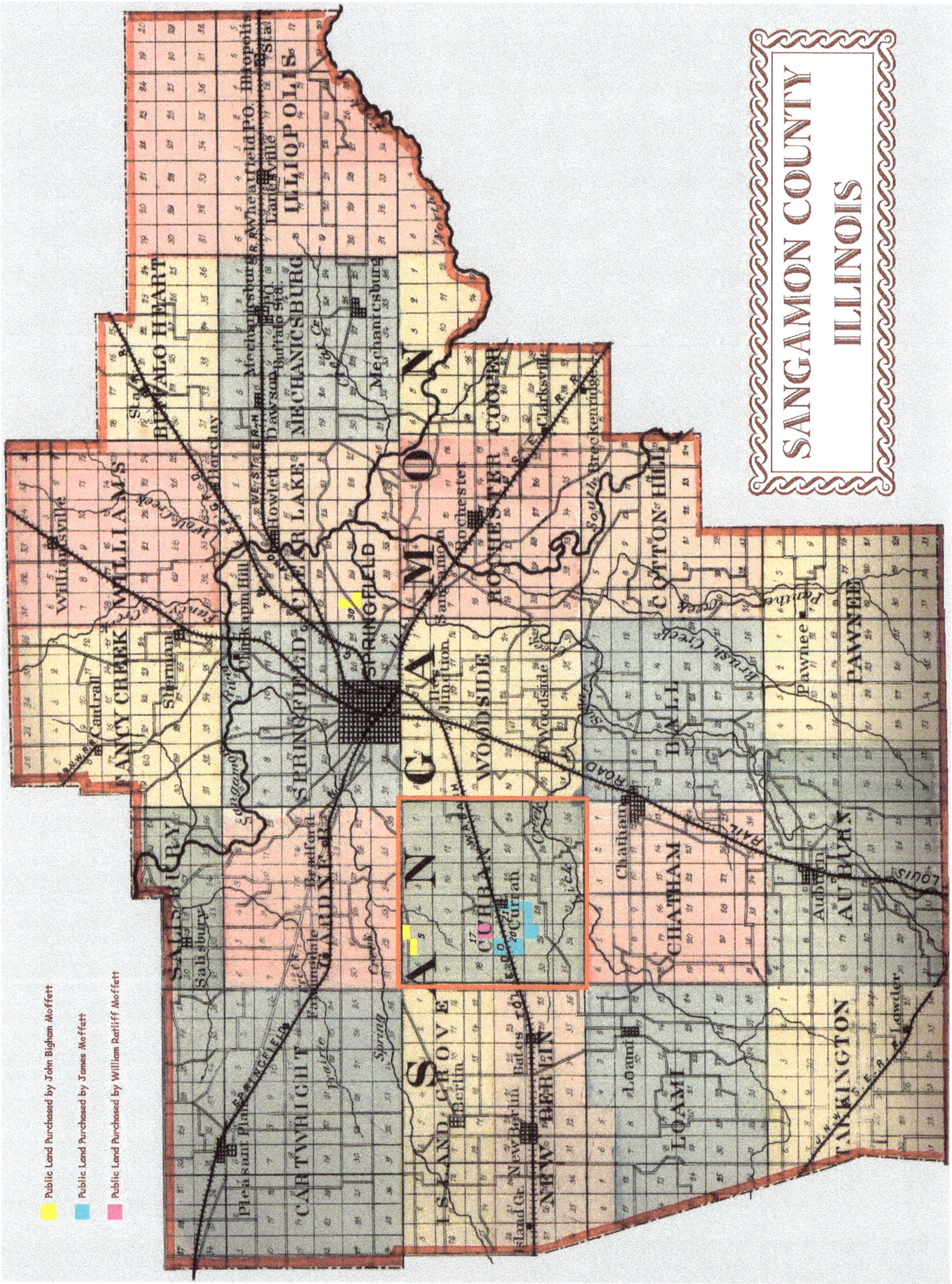
SANGAMON COUNTY
ILLINOIS
Public Land Purchased by John Bigham Moffett
Public Land Purchased by James Moffett
Public Land Purchased by William Ratliff Moffett
SANGAMON
SPRINGFIELD
WILLIAMS
FANCY CREEK
BUFFALO HEART
MECHANICSBURG
CLEAR LAKE
ILLIOPOLIS
COOPER
ROCHESTER
COTTON HILL
WOODSIDE
BALL
PAWNEE
CURRAN
CHATHAM
AUBURN
TAYLORVILLE
ISLAND GROVE
NEW BERLIN
LOAMI
CARTWRIGHT
GARDNER
SALISBURY
Springfield
Williamsville
Cantrall
Sherman
Chatham
Auburn
Pawnee
Rochester
Curran
Loami
Pleasant Plains
Salisbury
Mechanicsburg
Dawson
Howlett
Barclay
Clarksville
Breckenridge
Woodside
Berlin
Bates
New Berlin
Island Gr.
Lawder

SCHUYLER COUNTY
ILLINOIS

■ Public Land Purchased by Willis G. Moffett

The youngest daughter of William Moffett and Rebecca Robinson was Elizabeth, born in Bath County, Kentucky in 1802. She was married in 1831 in Sangamon County, Illinois to William Kendall, a native of Virginia. They had four children before William died in the mid to late 1840s. Elizabeth died late in the 19th century in Hancock County, Illinois.

The youngest son of William Moffett and Rebecca Robinson was Willis Green Moffett, born in Bath County, Kentucky in 1804. He married Caroline Stone in 1825 in Illinois, and they had at least six children.   They resided in Sangamon County until about the mid-1830s, then removing to Huntsville Township, Schuyler County, Illinois. In the 1850s, they removed to Hennepin County, Minnesota.[76]   Willis, a carpenter, died there in 1875, and Caroline in 1883.

Of the five sons of William Moffett and Rebecca Robinson, the one whose descendants this narrative continues to follow is *John Bigham Moffett*.   The first of these Moffetts to be born in the new 19th century, his birth took place in Montgomery County, Kentucky, very near what would become the line between Montgomery and Bath counties, on Wednesday, October 29, 1800. There he remained, on the family farm, through his childhood and adolescence.   During those years, the American economy grew and began to diversify. When John was 12 years old, the nation was drawn into its second war with Great Britain, and this had regionally varying effects on the economy, most of which, in Kentucky, were stimulating.[77]

What had been little more than wilderness with occasional settlements of pioneering white families when the Moffetts arrived in Kentucky, had become well settled lands, with farms and some loosely managed timberlands, and villages and some towns were springing up. Eventually growing to ten children, the Moffett family was a large one, as most were. With surrounding lands settled and the older sons taking up local farms from within and without the family, youngest sons frequently removed toward the retreating frontier, and/or turned to trades, industry, or commerce. John Bigham Moffett, as the eighth child of ten, and the second to youngest son, did embrace these alternatives. He was also known for his strengths of body and character, so it was little surprise that he sought out his own paths. He became a very talented artisan, no doubt apprenticing in carpentry while still a lad in his mid-teens.

Unfortunately, while the end of the War of 1812 brought a few years of continued expansion which spread to most parts of the country, in 1819, as John was settling into his journeyman years, the nation was struck by the first of its financial contractions, or depressions. The results were serious downturns in agriculture, trades, and manufacturing, and significant unemployment.   John faced difficult times, with no easy opportunity to return to agriculture, and poor prospects for his trade.[78]

---

[76]Moffetts from other branches of this extended family also settled in this area. Among them were a number of the children and grandchildren of James Moffett and Nancy Ratliff, who settled in Iowa County, Wisconsin, and later removed to Hennepin County, Minnesota.

[77]Donald R. Hickey, *The War of 1812, A Forgotten Conflict* (Chicago,1989), pp. 223-235.

[78]Murray N. Rothbard, *The Panic of 1819, Reactions and Policies* (New York, 1962).

In this case, as it would be throughout the century, young Americans in large number – especially those of Scotch-Irish heritage – saw a move to newer land as a chance at better prospects and rebirth. It was therefore a point of significant decision in John's life, and in those of the youngest of his siblings. On Thursday, July 26, 1821, John married Patsy A. Morgan in Bath County. Within weeks after his marriage, he and four siblings removed from Kentucky to the newly established county of Sangamon in the three-year-old state of Illinois. There, John was eventually employed as a wheel wright. By 1823, he had prospered enough in that trade to purchase a tract of 101.62 acres from the Public Domain along the northern boundary of the present-day Curran Township. Two years later, he purchased an 80-acre tract immediately west and south of his first purchase. Here, John and Patsy's children – two daughters and a son – were born.[79]

Family Group Sheet – John Bigham Moffett and His First Wife, Patsy A. Morgan

Husband: John Bigham Moffett

Born: 29 Oct 1800	in: Bath County, Kentucky
Married: 17 May 1827	in: Sangamon County, Illinois
Died: 15 Sep 1862	in: Macon County, Kentucky
Father: James Moffett	
Mother: Jane Bigham	
Other Spouses: Pollyana Taylor, Nancy Spencer Grider	

Wife: Patsey A. Morgan

Born: Abt. 1800	in: Ohio
Died: 28 Mar 1826	in: Sangamon County, Illinois

CHILDREN

1 F	Name: Rebecca Jane Moffett Born: 30 Jul 1822 Died: 22 Sep 1845 Married: 15 Jun 1841 Spouse: Lewis Robertson	in: Sangamon County, Illinois in: Illinois in: Sangamon County, Illinois
2 F	Name: Elizabeth Ann Moffett Born: 29 Jan 1824 Died: 01 Oct 1887 Married: 19 Mar 1846 Spouse: James Y. Taylor	in: Sangamon County, Illinois in: Madison, Madison County, Illinois in: Illinois
3 M	Name: William Thomas Moffett Born: 19 Feb 1826 Died: 12 Oct 1901 Married: 15 Oct 1856 Spouse: Helen Lucretia Barrows	in: Sangamon County, Illinois in: Rushville, Schuyler County, Illinois in: Macon County, Illinois

Rebecca Jane Moffett, the first child of John Bigham Moffett and Patsy Morgan, was born July 30, 1822 in Sangamon County. She married Lewis Robertson, a native of Kentucky, on June15, 1841. They had a son and a daughter, and Rebecca died September 22, 1845. Their son, John Lewis Robertson, married and raised a family in Marion County, Illinois, where his father, Lewis, died late in the 19th century. Lewis and Rebecca's daughter, Mary Elizabeth, married Addison C. Douglas, a physician and native of Ohio, and they had eight children. The Douglases resided in Illinois for many years, removing to Yellow Medicine County, Minnesota late in the 19th century.

---

[79]*History of Macon County, Illinois*, p.192.

Elizabeth Ann Moffett was the second child of John Bigham Moffett and Patsy Morgan. She was born in Sangamon County, Illinois January 29, 1824, and married James Y. Taylor in Illinois March 19, 1846. They had seven children: John B., Rebecca Louise, Mary Eliza, Thomas David, Charles Millard, Franklin Luther, and Nancy B. John B. and Thomas David died in their infancies. Mary Eliza was mute all her life, never married, and died in Macon County in 1889, aged 38 years. Rebecca Louise married John A. Barnes and had four children. Charles Millard was married briefly but was divorced and died in 1913. Franklin Luther married Mary A. Herbert, and they had a daughter and a son. It is believed that Nancy B. Taylor died, unmarried, as a young adult.

William Thomas Moffett was the third child, and only son, of John Bigham Moffett and Patsy Morgan, born in Sangamon County on Sunday, February 19, 1826. A mere five weeks later, Patsy died on Tuesday, March 28, 1826, probably from complications arising from childbirth. (More of William Thomas Moffett and his children will be found in Chapter 11.)

John Bigham Moffett, while blessed with growing economic prosperity, was not yet 26 years old, and was now left as a single parent with three children, all of whom were under the age of four years. He removed to Springfield, the county seat, presumably to take advantage of the presence of other family members there. It would be more than a year before his family situation stabilized, when he remarried, on Thursday, May 17, 1827, to Pollyana Taylor, daughter of David Sutton Taylor and Sarah Young. The first two of this couple's eleven children were born there in Springfield. In that city, John first worked as a cabinet maker, soon enlarging the scope of his work to include building construction and architectural design. Among others of his projects, he was the architect and builder of the first Sangamon County courthouse.[80]

In 1831, the family removed to Rushville, in Schuyler County, Illinois. Here, tragedy would strike again. Just six years after the death of John's first wife, John and Polly lost an infant daughter in 1832. In 1835, an infant son died. The grim reaper seemed never far from the doorstep.

At Rushville, John built and operated a saw and flouring mill, among other projects. It was the first such mill built in Illinois's War of 1812 Military District.[81] John's prosperity reflected that of his environment. The growth of Illinois and its economy was staggering. In 1821, when the Moffetts first came to Sangamon County, there were just 60,000 white settlers in all of Illinois. Just sixteen years later, in 1837, there were no fewer than 400,000 – an increase approaching 600%. In fact the figures for the new states west of the Appalachians were all similar. Ohio, Indiana, Missouri, and Tennessee all experienced frenetic expansion.[82]

---

[80]*idem.*

[81]That part of Illinois between the Illinois and Mississippi rivers, set aside for land grants to veterans of the War of 1812.

[82]Edward Morse Shepard, Martin Van Buren (Boston: 1888).

Family Group Sheet – John Bigham Moffett and His Second Wife, Pollyana Taylor

Husband: John Bigham Moffett

Born: 29 Oct 1800	in: Bath County, Kentucky
Married: 17 May 1827	in: Sangamon County, Illinois
Died: 15 Sep 1862	in: Macon County, Kentucky
Father: James Moffett	
Mother: Jane Bigham	

Wife: Polllyana Taylor

Born: 05 May 1809	in: Kentucky
Died: 21 Jan 1850	in: Christian County, Illinois
Father: David Sutton Taylor	
Mother: Sarah Young	

CHILDREN

#			
1 M	Name: David Sutton Moffett		
	Born: 14 Feb 1828	in: Sangamon County, Illinois	
	Died: 19 May 1868	in: Macon County, Illinois	
	Married: 19 May 1857	in: Macon County, Illinois	
	Spouse: Melissa M. Brockway		
2 F	Name: Sarah Taylor Moffett		
	Born: 23 Dec 1829	in: Sangamon County, Illinois	
	Died: 16 Feb 1854	in: Sangamon County, Illinois	
	Married: 28 Oct 1850	in: Christian County, Illinois	
	Spouse: Charles Fisher		
3 F	Name: Mary Eliza Moffett		
	Born: 15 Mar 1832	in: Rushville, Schuyler County, Illinois	
	Died: 28 Jun 1832	in: Rushville, Schuyler County, Illinois	
4 F	Name: Ann Eliza Moffett		
	Born: 29 May 1833	in: Rushville, Schuyler County, Illinois	
	Died: 08 Aug 1846	in: Christian County, Illinois	
5 F	Name: Robert Moffett		
	Born: 07 Dec 1835	in: Rushville, Schuyler County, Illinois	
	Died: Dec 1835	in: Rushville, Schuyler County, Illinois	
6 M	Name: John McDowell Moffett		
	Born: 14 Dec 1836	in: Rushville, Schuyler County, Illinois	
	Died: 14 Oct 1914	in: Boody, Macon County, Illinois	
	Married: 26 Jan 1860	in: Macon County, Illinois	
	Spouse: Elizabeth Jane McDonald		
7 M	Name: Rebecca Robinson Moffett		
	Born: 25 Mar 1799	in: Rushville, Schuyler County, Illinois	
	Died: 20 Mar 1855	in: Christian County, Illinois	
8 F	Name: Caroline Moffett		
	Born: 06 Aug 1842	in: Christian County, Illinois	
	Died: 06 Aug 1842	in: Christian County, Illinois	
9 F	Name: Louisa Catherine Moffett		
	Born: 12 Sep 1843	in: Christian County, Illinois	
	Died: 11 Jul 1845	in: Christian County, Illinois	
10 M	Name: Joseph Edwin Moffett		
	Born: 25 Sep 1845	in: Christian County, Illinois	
	Died: 13 Oct 1918	in: Chicago, Cook County, Illinois	
	Married: 25 Sep 1867	in: Macon County, Illinois	
	Spouse: Sarah M. Adams		
	Married: 13 May 1883	in: De Witt County, Illinois	
	Spouse: Nettie Hoyt		
	Married: 22 Jul 1886	in: De Witt County, Illinois	
	Spouse: Amanda Davis		
11 F	Name: Laura Amanda Moffett		
	Born: 10 Feb 1849	in: Christian County, Illinois	
	Died: Abt. 1867	in: Macon County, Illinois	
	Married: 29 Aug 1866	in: Blue Mound, Macon County, Illinois	
	Spouse: William Thomas Evans		

Indeed, the American economy as a whole grew at a healthy clip for most of the years after 1825. However, the dark underbelly of this expansion was acceleration of speculation, especially in lands, much of the land coming from the public domain at a fixed low price. During the Jackson administration, the evolution of American banking proceeded away from regulation, and toward wider and wider use of unsecured paper money, and it was this flimsy currency which provided an increasing share of the payments for the land speculation.

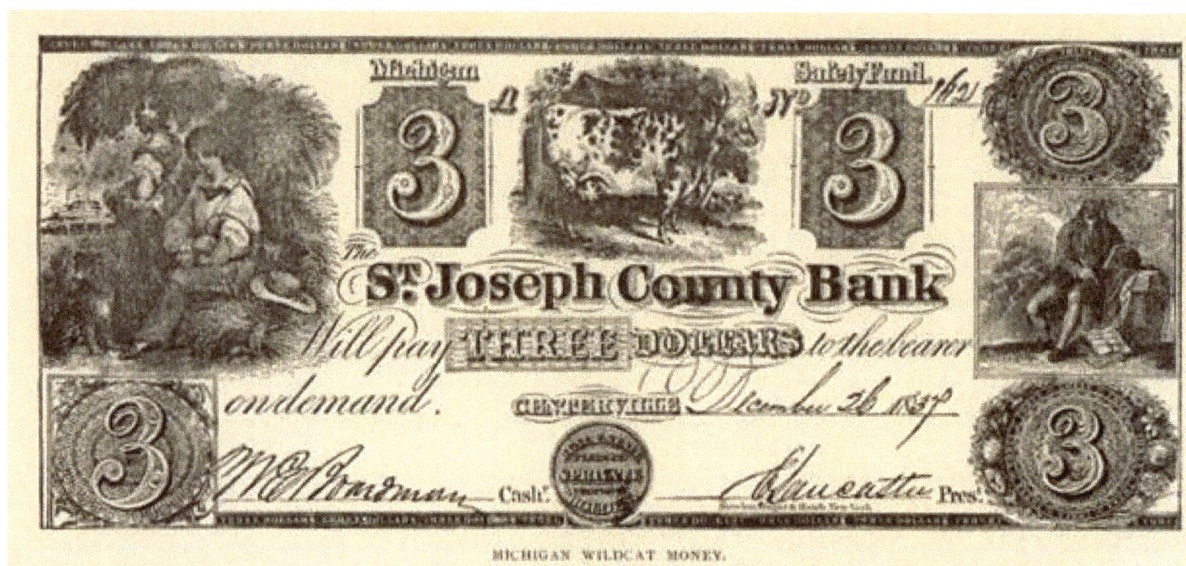

Paper money such as this, issued by the plethora of all but unregulated state and local "wildcat" banks, played an enormous role in the Panic of 1837 and the resulting economic depression.

Closely related to the increasingly wild speculation, the early and especially mid-1830s saw severe monetary inflation. The costs of all goods rose at incredible rates, including those of the most basic necessities. In March of 1835, the cost of a barrel of flour was $5.62, but a year later it was $7.75, and only another year later it hit $12.00. Pork rose from $10.00 per barrel in March of 1835 to $18.25 two years later; and within that same two-year span, the wholesale price per ton of coal shot up from $6.00 to $10.50. Those who did not produce their own food and/or fuel – which included the large majority of artisans such as John B. Moffett[83] – were faced with serious hardship and sometimes want, even if they were among the middle class. For the poor, the turn of financial events was an utter disaster.

The Moffetts in Illinois, having seen bad financial times at impressionable ages, became caught up in the speculation, particularly when inflation soared. Their doing so demonstrated that, while they were certainly not members of the American aristocracy, they were men and women of some means, still in a sort of middle class, as they had been in Ireland.

---

[83]While most artisans suffered extensively, John B. Moffett probably was able to cushion the blows because he owned a good amount of land and could have produced at least some of his food. However, there are no records which clearly tell us whether his immediate family's degree of want was great, small, or non-existent.

Certificate
No. 678.
61

1462.

The United States of America

To all to whom these presents shall come, Greeting:

Whereas, John B. Moffett, Sangamon County, has deposited in the General Land Office of the United States, a certificate of the Register of the Land Office at Springfield, Illinois whereby it appears that full payment has been made by the said John B. Moffett, according to the provision of the Act of Congress of the 24th of April, 1820, entitled "An act making further provision for the sale of the Public Lands," for the South half of the North East quarter of Section Five, in Township fifteen North of Range Six West, in the District of Lands offered for sale at Springfield, Illinois, containing Eighty acres.

according to the official plat of the survey of the said Lands, returned to the General Land Office by the Surveyor General, which said tract has been purchased by the said John B. Moffett.

NOW KNOW YE, That the **UNITED STATES OF AMERICA,** in consideration of the premises, and in conformity with the several acts of Congress, in such case made and provided, have Given and Granted, and, by these presents do give and grant, unto the said John B. Moffett, and to his heirs the said tract above described: To Have and to Hold the same, together with all the rights, privileges, immunities and appurtenances, of whatsoever nature thereto belonging, unto the said John B. Moffett, and to his heirs and assigns forever.

In testimony whereof, I, John Quincy Adams, **PRESIDENT OF THE UNITED STATES OF AMERICA,** have caused these letters to be made Patent, and the seal of the General Land Office to be hereunto affixed.

Given under my hand, at the City of Washington, the first day of May, in the year of our Lord, one thousand eight hundred and twenty Six, and of the Independence of the United States the _____

By the President, J. Q. A.

Moffett

Commissioner of the General Land Office.

1068991

Record of the first purchase of public land made by John Bigham Moffett. This purchase was made in 1826, just five weeks after the death of his first wife. The land is located near the northwest corner of what is now Curran Township in Sangamon County.

Historically, in times of rapid inflation, the poorest are left with nothing but despair, even as they work hard each day. Those with at least some disposable income however can make judicious investments, hoping to place their money where it will grow in excess of the rate of increase in the cost of the staples of life. In this case, in the mid-1830s in Illinois, the conventional wisdom would have been to make such an investment in public land. As Shepard described it,

> "The price of public lands was fixt by law at $1.25 an acre; and they were open to any purchaser, without the wholesome limits of acreage and the restraint to actual settlers which were afterward established. Here then was a commodity whose price to wholesale purchasers did not rise, and the very commodity by which so many fortunes had been made. In public lands, therefore, the fury of money-getting, the boastful confidence in the future of the country, reached their climax."[89]

In 1830, John B. Moffett purchased 80 acres from the public domain in Clear Creek Township,

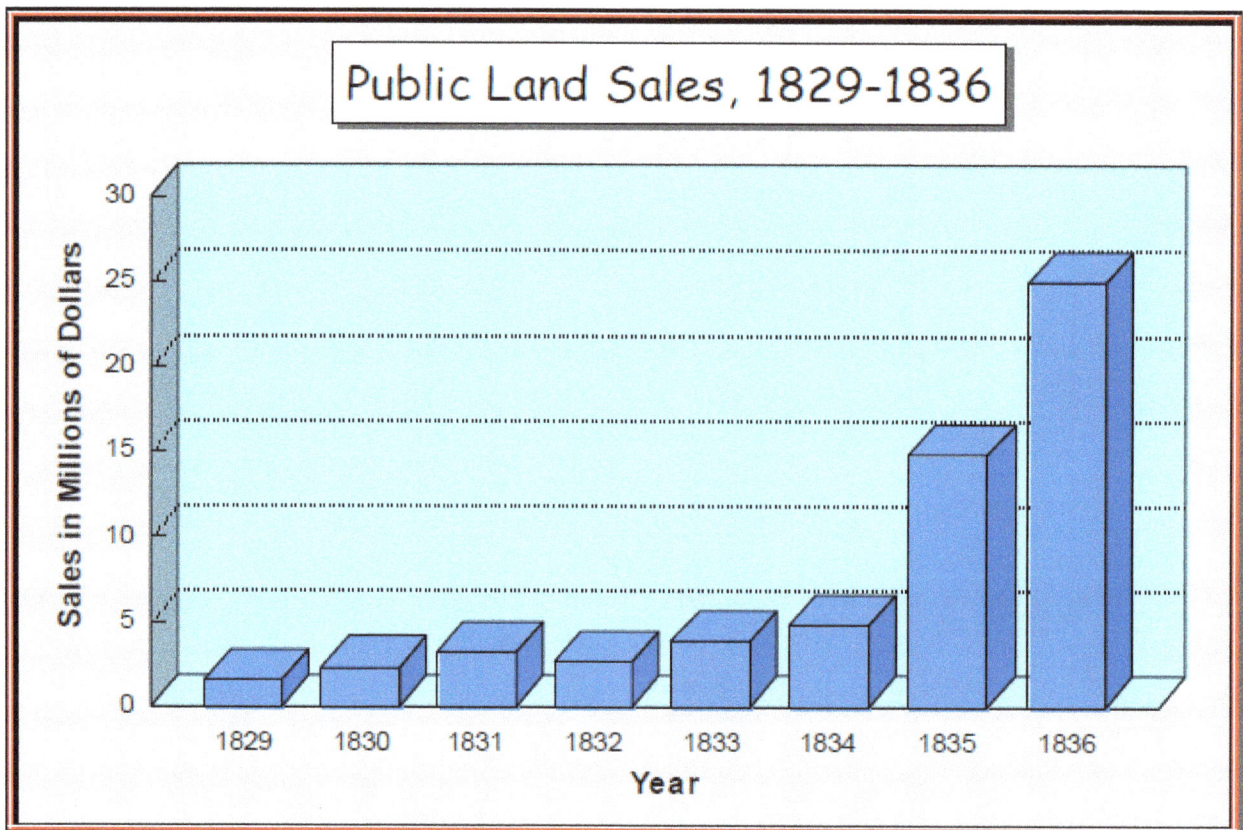

Public Land Sales, 1829-1836

Sangamon County. This probably was not an act of land speculation however, but rather more connected to his working in Springfield, as this property was only 2-3 miles from that town.

---

[84]Shepard, *Martin Van Buren*

When the painful inflationary spiral began in 1834, so too did the speculation in land experience an enormous surge. In 1835, in keeping with this national trend, the Moffett family's speculation spree began in earnest. In May and August, John Bigham Moffett purchased 40 acre parcels of land in Clear Creek Township, adjacent to his earlier purchase there. In June, Willis G. Moffett, the youngest of John B. Moffett's siblings, purchased three tracts of land in Schuyler County, totaling 347 acres, part of which would later become the little town of Huntsville.

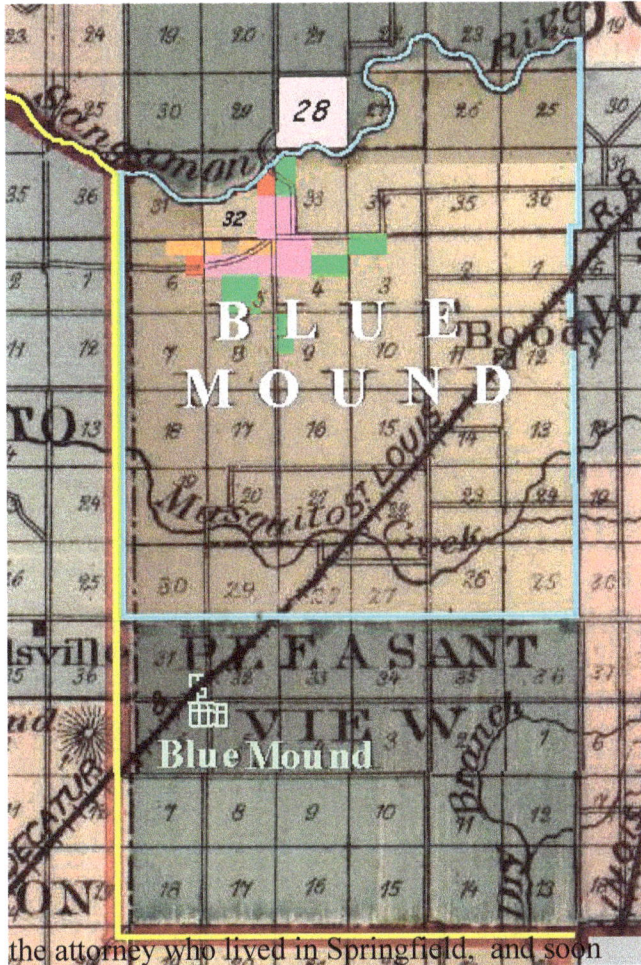

the attorney who lived in Springfield, and soon

In October of 1835, James Moffett, who was the oldest sibling of John Bigham Moffett, and who still resided in Bath County, Kentucky, purchased two parcels of land in Curran Township in Sangamon County, totaling 480 acres. At the same time, James's oldest son, William R. Moffett, who was now residing in tract adjacent to part of his father's purchase. Just two weeks later, James purchased 440 acres in four additional pieces of land in Curran Township, bringing his holdings to 920 acres.

Less than three months later, in January of 1836, the first of the family's purchases in Macon County were made. James Burch Moffett (another son of James and younger brother of William R.), who was living in Schuyler County, Illinois, purchased three tracts in Blue Mound Township, totaling 220 acres. John Bigham Moffett then bought five parcels in that township in February, which totaled 490 acres. In June of that year, Thomas Moffett, John B. Moffett's older brother would be well acquainted with Abraham Lincoln, joined the spree purchasing 248 Blue Mound Township acres in 3 parcels.

At this point, many sensed a looming disaster, and President Jackson issued his Specie Circular on July 11. This required any purchase of public land after August 15 to be made in specie – gold or silver – and not the increasingly worthless paper money. Among other effects, this dramatically slowed the speculation in public land.[85]

---

[85]Tindall, volume 1, p. 413

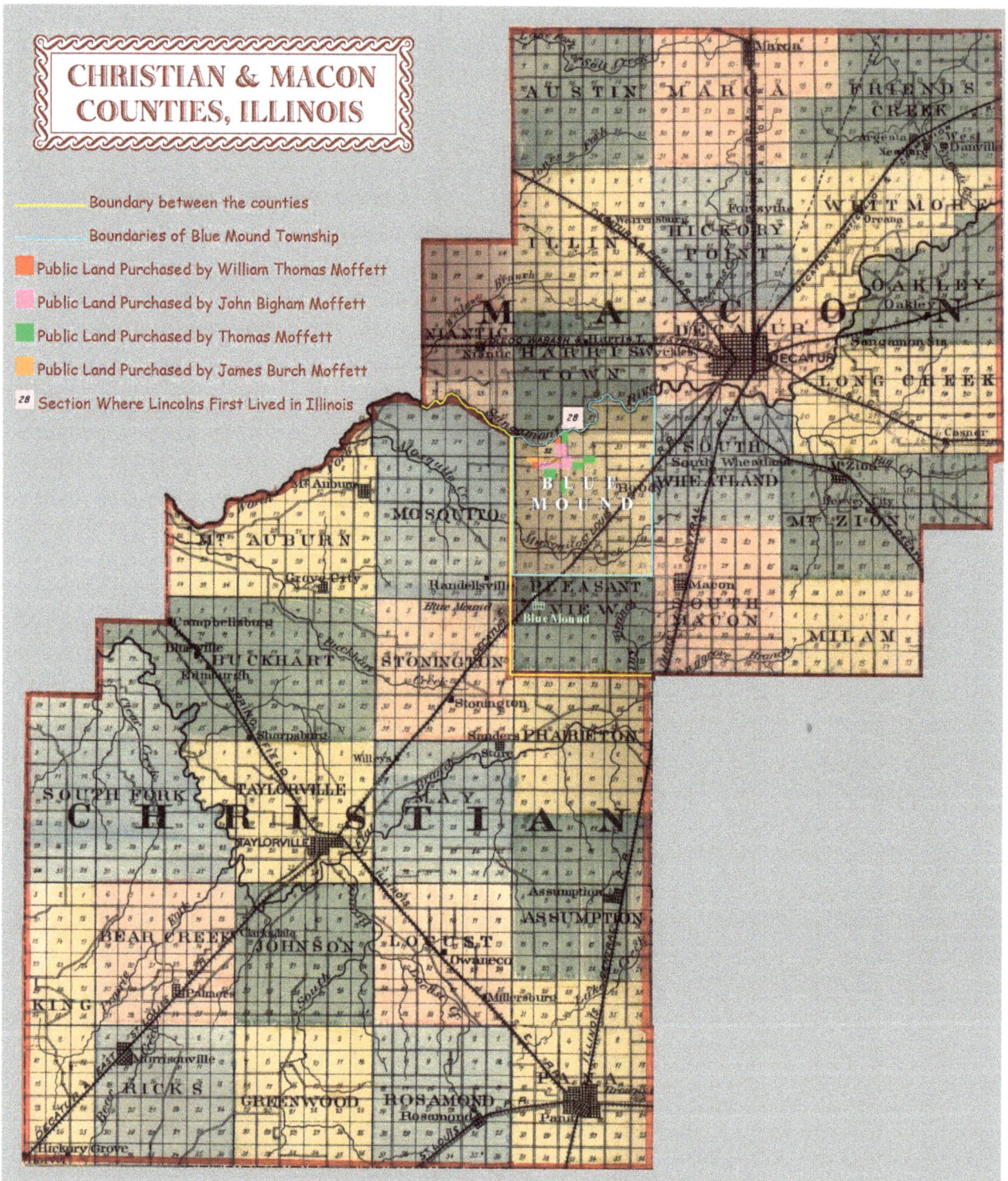

Note: In addition to indicating the locations of public lands purchased by the Moffetts, this map indicates the location of the section on which Abraham Lincoln and his parents first settled when they came to Illinois from Indiana in March of 1830. It is just across the North Fork of the Sangamon River from the Moffetts' holdings. The Lincolns left this place after only a year, removing to Coles County, Illinois. They had therefore left Macon County before the Moffetts purchased any of this land in Blue Mound Township.

Near the end of October, Thomas Moffett managed to assemble enough of the precious metals to purchase three more tracts in Blue Mound Township, totaling another 240 acres.[86] However, no further purchases were made by any of the family. In a period of just 17 months, these six Moffetts had purchased just over 2,700 acres of public land in three counties.

The monetary inflation was out of control by the end of 1836, and even though the economy was essentially still running at full speed, those with little or no disposable income were already in dire circumstances. Among the many signs of the deep unrest were the "flour riots" which broke out in several cities. Included was New York, where in February of 1837, despite bitter cold, some four thousand or more persons gathered in City Hall Park to hear speakers espouse various actions "to resist monopolists and extortioners". Things degenerated and some small packs of angry attendants followed impromptu orators around the outskirts of the crowd who particularly focused their anger on flour dealers. The crowds descended on flour warehouses bearing sticks, stones, and barrel staves, among other improvised weaponry. They ransacked and pilfered, until eventually being controlled by police after much damage had been done. Across the nation, thoughts and rhetoric harkened to the sparks which led to the French Revolution, barely more than a generation ago, as peasants rioted for bread.[87]

In the spring of 1837, the sharpest blow struck the American economy in the form of a severe financial panic, which quickly became the worst economic depression America had experienced to that date. Of this disaster, Milton Friedman has written,

"The banking panic of 1837 was followed by exceedingly disturbed economic conditions and a long contraction to 1843 that was interrupted only by a brief recovery from 1838 to 1839. This Great Depression is particularly interesting for our purposes. It is the only depression on record comparable in severity and scope to the Great Depression of the 1930's, and its monetary concomitants largely duplicate those of its later mate. In both, a substantial fraction of the banks in the United States went out of existence through suspension or merger – around one quarter in the earlier and over one-third in the later contraction – and the stock of money fell by about one-third. There is no other contraction that even closely approaches this dismal record."[88]

Many American artisans were so severely impacted that they left their trade within months of the breakdown. Others, especially those who had family support and/or farm land, struggled on as they could, adding farm work where they could.[89] John Bigham Moffett was among the latter group, as he did not assume operation of his own farm as his primary occupation until 1842.[90]

---

[86]The records of these last purchases by Thomas Moffett indicate that he was at that time a resident of Macon County, whereas in June he had still been residing in Sangamon. Apart from this reference there is no evidence that Thomas ever resided in Macon County, and indeed, by the time the 1840 census was taken, he was again in Springfield, the Sangamon County seat.

[87]Arthur M. Schlesinger, Jr., *The Age of Jackson* (Boston, 1989), pp. 217-220.

[88]Milton Friedman, quoted in "Panic of 1837," *Wikipedia*, June 26, 2006, Wikimedia Foundation, Inc., July 6, 2006 <http://en.wikipedia.org/wiki/Panic_of_1837>

[89]Shepard, Martin Van Buren

[90]*History of Macon County, Illinois* (Chicago, 1881), p. 570.

John B. Moffett

John Bigham Moffett, born in present-day Bath County, Kentucky, October 29, 1800, son of William Moffett & Rebecca Robinson, died September 15, 1862 – a carpenter, house and mill wright, architect and farmer.

John had been displaced from his trade by forces far beyond his control, and just at a time when a blossoming movement of labor unions and trade unions had been suddenly crushed by the depression. No doubt he experienced some degree of loss of morale and self-confidence. In addition, he now operated a farm, in which business he had little experience beyond his childhood contributions of labor to the family's agricultural enterprises in Kentucky. The evidence suggests that he, like so many other artisans of the period, was forced to borrow, sometimes heavily, to maintain any semblance of his non-agricultural enterprises. Then in February of 1842, the State Bank of Illinois collapsed, deepening the depression in the state, and while the national economy showed some recovery as early as 1843, that of Illinois suffered for another ten years.[92]   While he did struggle on, after the bank failure, John B. Moffett and his wife, Polly, removed to what is now Blue Mound Township in Macon County, and began to operate a farm on his land there. The last four of their children were born there.

Of the eleven children born to John Bigham Moffett and Pollyana Taylor, eight died very young and/or unmarried, and a ninth died when only forty years of age. Mary Eliza, the third child, was born in March of 1832, and died in June of that year. Ann Eliza, the fourth child, was born in 1833, and died in 1846. The fifth and eighth children, Robert and Caroline, died at birth, he in December of 1835, and she in August, 1842. The seventh child, James Milton, was born in August of 1839, but died before his 20th birthday, on June 1, 1859. Louisa Catharine, the ninth child, was born in September, 1843, and died in July of 1845.

The second child, Sarah Taylor Moffett, was born in December of 1829, and married Charles Fisher in October of 1850. They had two children, but Sarah died in February of 1854, at the still tender age of 24 years, and just three months after the birth of her second child. The youngest child, Laura Amanda, was born in February of 1849, and married William Evans in August of 1866, but it is believed that she died very shortly thereafter, leaving no children.[93]

The remaining three children of John Bigham Moffett and Pollyana Taylor fared relatively better in terms of their longevity. David Sutton Moffett, the oldest, was born February 14, 1828 in Sangamon County, Illinois. He married Melissa Brockway in Macon County, May 19, 1857. The couple had five children. Even this Moffett died before passing what might be called middle age, dying in his 41st year, May 19, 1868, and leaving his 27-year-old widow with children of ages 1-9 years. During the Civil War, David had served briefly as an officer in the Union Army. He is buried in Brown Cemetery, in Blue Mound Township, Macon County. His widow remarried in 1875 to Samuel P. Chesney, and removed to Jacksonville, in Morgan County, Illinois, where she died in 1912.

John McDowell Moffett, the sixth child of John and Pollyana, was born December 14, 1836 in Rushville, Schuyler County, Illinois. He married Elizabeth Jane McDonald in 1860 in Macon County, and they had eight children there. John died there October 14, 1914, and Elizabeth on January 18, 1923. Both are buried in Brown Cemetery.

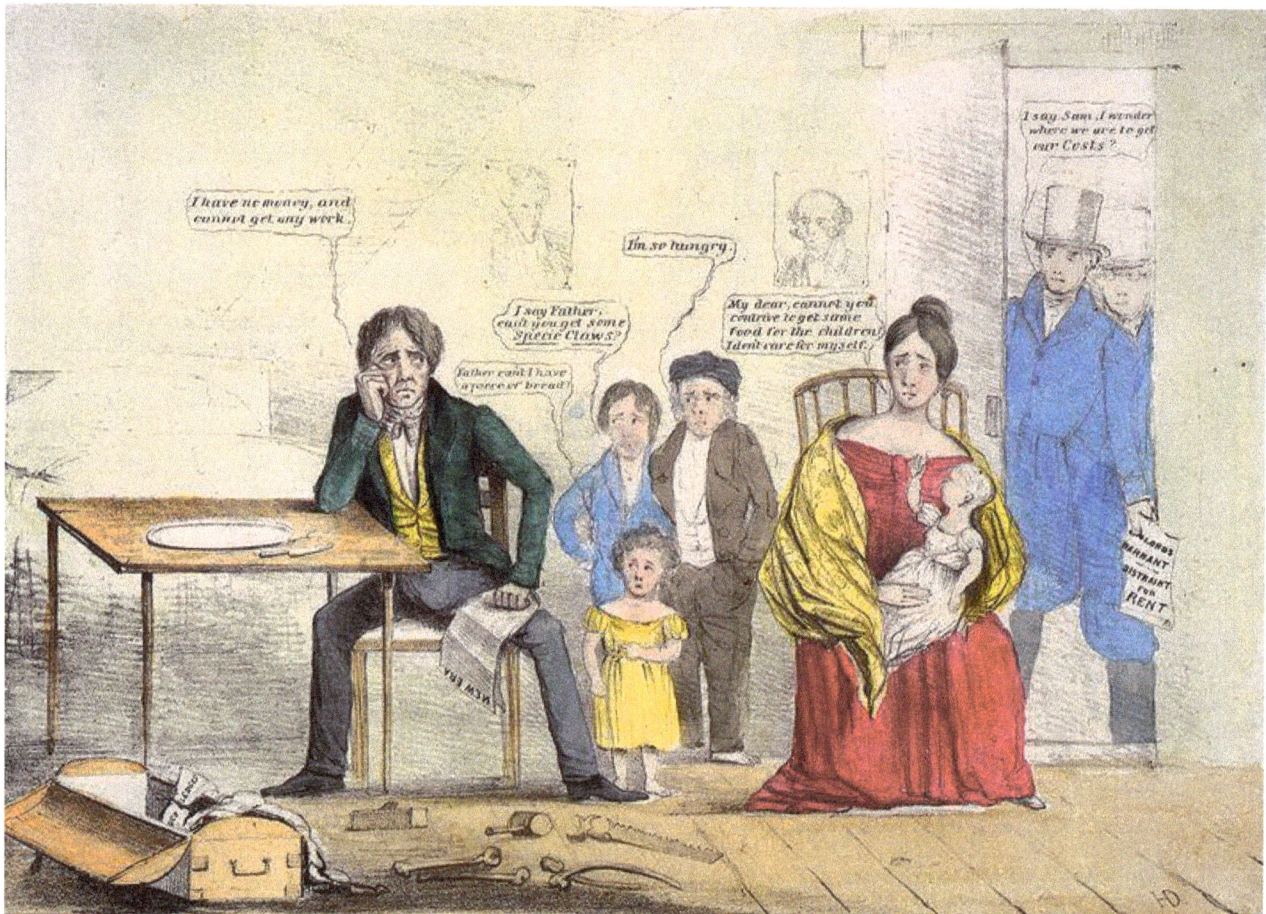

A contemporary cartoon, portraying the great sufferings of the artisans during the great depression of 1837-1843. The carpenter's face expresses his sense of great misfortune, as he says that he has no money, and can get no work. His tools lay in their box and on the floor, unused, and the platter on the table is empty. The point is also poignantly made that the suffering struck not just the men who were without work, but their wives and innocent children too. The little girl asks her father if she can't have just a piece of bread, and the oldest lad bemoans his intense state of hunger. The wife exhorts her husband to "contrive to get some food for the children", adding that she does not mean to ask any for her own self. At the door we see the well-dressed gentleman, bearing a warrant of eviction, explaining that he has no choice but to act, as he must recover his costs. While a depressingly accurate picture of the misfortunes of many at the time, the image was drawn by a pro-Whig cartoonist whose aim is to illustrate the terrible mistake he felt the tradesmen had made in bearing great allegiance to Andrew Jackson, his successor, Martin Van Buren, the Democratic party as a whole, and especially the increasingly radical wing of that party, known as Loco Focos. On the tradesman's knee is a copy of the *New Era*, a partisan, radical protrade-union paper, which first went to press just weeks before the bank panic struck. The two portraits on the wall are those of Jackson and Van Buren, and in his toolbox is a bound roll of papers marked, "Loco Foco Pledges".

Joseph Edwin Moffett was the tenth child of John Bigham Moffett and Pollyana Taylor. He was born September 25, 1845, in Christian County, Illinois. He saw military service in the Civil War,[93] and after the war he married Sarah M. Adams in Macon County on September 25, 1867. The family removed to Clinton in De Witt County, Illinois in the 1870s. Joseph and Sarah had two sons and a daughter, and Sarah died in Decatur, in Macon County, on May 24, 1882. Joseph remarried on May 13, 1883 to Nettie Hoyt in De Witt County, but she died on October 14, 1884 in De Witt County, leaving no children. Joseph then married a third time to Amanda Davis, on July 22, 1886 in De Witt County. Joseph and Amanda had one daughter, and lived at times in Clinton, and at times in Chicago. Joseph died at his home at 1551 Jonquil Terrace in Chicago on October 13, 1918, a victim of heart disease, from which he had suffered for some ten years.

Through the middle of the decade of the 1840s, John Bigham Moffett struggled to establish his farming business. After 1843, as the economy finally emerged from the depression, he also undertook what building jobs he could, usually in partnerships with others. Among other such tasks, he built the second school-house in Blue Mound Township. Court records show that his businesses were active, and at times contentious, for he appears as either the plaintiff or defendant in numerous cases.[94]

One such case came before the Circuit Court of Sangamon County in September of 1849 and appears to have been a particularly costly one for John B. Moffett. John had been a partner in business with Thomas Lewis and Willis Johnson, both of Springfield. When the partnership broke up, John felt he was unfairly compensated, and he hired the law firm of Abraham Lincoln and William Herndon to bring a suit against his former partners. A narrative of Lincoln's documents indicates that, pursuant to that case, on September 1, 1849, Abe Lincoln "writes John B. Moffett's affidavit."

The case was heard on the 12th of September. At stake was $2,377.41, all of which John B. Moffett sought to recover. The victory was only partial however, as the court allowed Mr. Lewis to retain $1,000.00. John Moffett appealed to the Illinois Supreme Court.

The appeal was heard in the Supreme Court on Wednesday and Thursday, January 16 and 17, 1850, Abraham Lincoln arguing the case for John Moffett. The appeal backfired. On Monday, the 21st of January, the court rendered its decision. Not only did they uphold the award of $1,000.00 to Mr. Lewis, but they also awarded him the $1,377.41 which the lower court had awarded to John B. Moffett.[95]

---

[93]See Appendix 7 for details of his military service.

[94]Records of the circuit courts of Macon and Sangamon counties.

[95]*The Papers of Abraham Lincoln, The Lincoln Log*, <http://www.stg.brown.edu/projects/lincoln>

Fate, as it can be, was especially cruel to John B. Moffett, for on the same day that the Supreme Court rendered this damaging decision, John's beloved second wife, Polly, died at her home in Blue Mound Township, at the age of 40 years. She was buried in Brown Cemetery.

John B. Moffett was still without the means to pay his attorneys. In March, the Sangamon County Circuit Court heard the case of Lincoln and Herndon vs. John B. Moffett, in which the attorneys sued for $150.00 in legal fees. The attorneys won the case, but John apparently still did not have the means to pay. A year later, they acquired land in settlement.[96]

John had meanwhile relocated to property in adjacent Christian County, in the area which became the townships of Mount Auburn and Mosquito.[97]   On Thursday, September 26, 1850, John Bigham Moffett married his third wife, forty-year-old Nancy Spencer Grider, a native of Warren County, Kentucky, daughter of Captain Henry Grider[98] and Elizabeth Smith, and the widow of Rev. Abner McDowell, of Rushville, a Cumberland Presbyterian minister. By neither of these marriages did Nancy bear children.

The legal troubles continued. After Polly (Taylor) Moffett died, her brother, John G. Taylor, who lived in Blue Mound Township, sued John B. Moffett and won a judgment of $167.27, which required the taking of some of John B. Moffett's Macon County land during November of 1852. Presumably, the suit was related to property to which the Taylor family felt it had a right, but of which Mr. Moffett had taken possession by virtue of his wife, Polly.

The family squabble went on however. Even as John B. Moffet's real estate was being seized for payment of the judgment, he was fighting an ongoing suit, also brought by John G. Taylor, calling for the "ejectment" (eviction) of John B. Moffett from land owned by the Taylors, which Moffett had leased, but which lease had expired.[99]

In the meantime, John B. Moffett's oldest son, William Thomas Moffett, had left Illinois for California in the wake of the discovery of gold, settling at Sacramento. He quickly perceived that mining the gold was unlikely to produce a sure profit for himself, and instead established a freighting business, providing for the badly needed exchange of goods for the increasingly large throngs of newcomers. At this he did make a tidy profit.

---

[96]*Idem.*

[97]United States Federal Census, 1850, Christian County, Illinois, District 22, page 155, dwelling 466, family 476. The specific present-day township was determined by nothing numerous families who were enumerated adjacent to the Moffett household in that 1850 census, and subsequently locating their whereabouts in the United States Federal Census of 1870, Christian County, Illinois.

[98]He served in the Revolutionary War, and was wounded in the disastrous Battle of Bluc Licks, Kentucky, August 19, 1782.

[99]*The Papers of Abraham Lincoln, The LincolnLog,* http://www.stg.brown.edu/projects/lincoln

Congressman Henry Grider
1796-1866[100]

John B. Moffett, with his fortunes sinking, sent urgent pleas to his son to return from the goldfields to assist in stabilizing the situation at home. After 18 months in California, William thus returned to Illinois, and with the considerable profits from his enterprises in the west, was able to clear his father's debts, and liens on his remaining real estate.[101]

---

[100]Henry Grider, brother of John Bigham Moffett's third wife, Nancy, was a member of the United States Congress from Bowling Green, Kentucky, serving five terms as Representative of that district. He was born in Garrard County, Kentucky, July 16, 1796, and was a veteran of military service in the War of 1812. He studied law and was admitted to the bar and commenced practice in Bowling Green, Kentucky. In the state legislature, he was elected to the Kentucky house of representatives in 1827 and 1831 and served in the state senate 1833-1837. He later was elected as a Whig to the Twenty-eighth and Twenty-ninth Congresses (March 4, 1843-March 3, 1847), as a Unionist to the Thirty-seventh and Thirty-eighth Congresses, and as a Democrat to the Thirty-ninth Congress and served therein until his death in Bowling Green, Ky., September 7, 1866. He is buried in Old College Street Cemetery, in Bowling Green. (*Biographical Directory of the United States Congress.*)

[101]*The Past and Present of the City of Decatur and Macon County, Illinois* (Chicago, 1903), pp 729-734.

The petition by William Thomas Moffett for probate of the will of his father, John Bigham Moffett, dated October 20, 1862. He states that his father died at his farm in Blue Mound Township, there in Macon County, on September 15, 1862. (This may well be an error. It seems likely that he actually died in Hennepin County, Minnesota, where he was living with his youngest son, Willis Green Moffett.) William signs with his usual "W. T. Moffett", and a finishing brief flourish of the pen.

With this, the family's lands in Blue Mound Township were freed, and John and his wife were able to return there. In the early 1850s, the family settled permanently just across the county line in Section 32 of Blue Mound Township, in Macon County. For the remainder of his life, he was engaged solely in agriculture and stock raising. Prosperity returned and remained.

Sometime between mid-1860 and early 1862, with his health failing, John Bigham Moffett essentially retired. He left Illinois, going to live with his youngest brother, Willis Green Moffett, a millwright in Richfield Township, near Minneapolis, in Hennepin County, Minnesota.[102] As he prepared his last will and testament, which he signed in Hennepin County on Wednesday, August 6, 1862, he described himself as "being of sound mind and memory but in feeble (sic) health."[103] In less than six weeks, he passed away on Monday, September 15, 1862. There is no record of his death in Illinois or Minnesota, but when his son, William Thomas Moffett petitioned the Macon County Probate Court to accept the will, he stated that his father died at his residence there in Macon County.[104] He is buried in Brown Cemetery, in Blue Mound Township, Macon County, Illinois.[105]

The provisions of the will of John B. Moffett shed some light on his status and thinking at the time of his death. He first of all made the standard provisions for payment of his debts, and for his burial, and directions for the layout of the cemetery plat. He then set down specific instructions regarding the disposition of much of his land, most of which was in Macon County, and some of which was in Missouri.[106]

---

[102]As his will shows, he was physically feeble, and presumably steadily failing. Why he chose to go to Minneapolis at that time is not clear. It may have been to seek the better medical care he felt he might find in a large city. He apparently chose Minneapolis over the nearer and larger city of Chicago because he would have a place to live with family members.

[103]See Appendix 9 for a complete transcript of the will of John Bigham Moffett.

[104]It would seem reasonable to question this. Given the state of John's health on August 6, and the trials which he would have faced in traveling back to his home, it would not be surprising if he remained in Minnesota. Also, in the record of the probate of John's will, a Justice of the Peace in Hennepin County, Minnesota, who interviewed two of the witnesses to the will, refers to "the last Will and Testament of John B. Moffett late of Henepin (sic) County, deceased".

[105]*Macon County, Illinois Cemetery Inscriptions* (Decatur, Illinois, 1968), vol. I, p. 21.

[106]These and all sebsequent descriptions of the text of the will in this chapter are taken from the official record of the will, *Will Book B*, pp. 134-141, Macon County Court, Macon County, Illinois.

To his widow, Nancy S. Moffett, he left his homestead farm in Macon County, which included 255.16 acres of land in section 5 in what later became Blue Mound Township. He also left her a life estate in 240 acres in sections 31 and 32 in that township. Furthermore, he left her horses, a cow, household and kitchen furniture, and over and above that, a share of his personal property equal to what the widow of an intestate would receive under Illinois law.[107] He made special provisions for his two youngest children, Joseph Edwin and Laura Amanda. At the time of his wife's death, the real estate John had left to his wife would go to these two, and he left specific instructions on how that real estate should be divided.

The fifth item in the will discusses the fact that John's son, William T. Moffett, had a deed giving him title to of conveyance to 160 acres of land, being the southeast quarter of section number 32 in what became Blue Mound Township. John points out that although John himself did not deed this property to William, "yet it was by him obtained through my means, and by my approbation...." At least part of this parcel was land which John had originally owned, so apparently this land was placed under some sort of lien and must be one of the parcels which William rescued when he came back from California, and in that process apparently the title to this land technically went to William. John obviously felt he had some understanding with William that the land would not have been there for William to have had not John originally procured it, and that John therefore had some "moral" claim to it. In any event, John goes on to relinquish any such claim, leaving that parcel as William's inheritance in his father's real estate.

With regard to John's son, David S. Moffett, there are curious instructions included in the will. John states that he had executed a deed of conveyance to David for 160 acres of land, being the west half of the southwest quarter and west half of the northwest quarter, of section 33 in what became Blue Mound Township. This was to be all of David's inheritance from John's real estate. He also left David two specific horses, a wagon, harnesses, one cow, and one calf.

At this point, John points out that the title for all this property left to David and that which he would subsequently describe as bequests to David's children, was to remain in the hands of John's executor, William T. Moffett. John goes on to specify the lands he leaves to David's children, reiterating that these lands should be held in trust by William T. Moffett until the children become of age. However, he further says that, "if my said Trustee shall think that at some time before the said children shall all become of age that the land would not be in Jeopardy in the possession of my son David S. Moffett (t)hen I hereby authorize and empower my trustee to convey the title to said real estate to my son David S. Moffett during his lifetime, and to his children at his Decease...."

---

[107]This is a curious reference. Clearly, whoever advised him as he composed this document, though doubtless an attorney, was not familiar with the probate laws of Illinois. This seems striking because John had a brother Thomas – who was a very able attorney in Illinois. Furthermore, at the 1860 census, one of the boarders in Willis Green Moffett's household was Thomas Moffett's son, James William Moffett, who was also an attorney. The suggestion is that John felt he did not have enough time to arrange consultation with these family members, which points to the gravity of whatever illness had seized him.

Nowhere in the will, or other probate documents, is there any explanation for the necessity of this trust. David had long since ceased to be a minor, was now married, and had children. However, there is some sense that David's level of responsibility was not what John thought it should be. One week to the day after John signed his will, David and William presented themselves to the officials who were forming the 115th Illinois Infantry, which would shortly join the Union Army's divisions known as the Army of Kentucky in the crucial battles for the border states, and David would be made an officer (1st lieutenant). This would not suggest a man of irresponsible nature. It is true that, after just six months of service, and very little in the way of active combat, David resigned for reasons of disability. However, it seems unlikely that he already bore that disability when he joined the 115th; rather, the disability was likely the result of exposure during the very severe winter of 1862-63.[108] Less than six years after the will was signed, David died. We do not know the cause of his death, or whether it had anything to do with his disability or his father's reservations about David's responsibility.

Ordinarily, a nineteenth century will would leave specific bequests to grandchildren if those children of the testator who were the parents of those grandchildren were deceased; or also if a grandchild was in some way special to the testator and/or the family. Further on, as we shall see, John B. Moffett's will does make such provisions for the children of John's deceased daughters, Rebecca (who had married Lewis Robertson) and Sarah (who had married Charles Fisher). However, immediately after the above discussion of assigning a trustee to the bequests left to David, John's will goes on to describe the specific lands to be left in trust for David's children: Eighty acres in section 33, and twenty acres in section 34, in what would become Blue Mound Township. The notion that John would leave a specific real estate bequest for David's children, even though David was still alive, and well enough to be accepted by the Union Army, does at least suggest that David's longevity was questionable.

The very next item in the will is a bequest to his son-in-law, Lewis Robertson, "for life remainder to his two children, John L. and Mary Elizabeth Robertson." Here again, John had already executed a deed to this effect, it being dated March 20, 1856, and the will states that this constitutes their portion of the estate. The land was 140 acres in section 5, in what would become Blue Mound Township.

John leaves bequests to his son-in-law and daughter, James Y. Taylor and Elizabeth Ann which, after the death of Elizabeth Ann, would be passed on to her children. There were three parcels of land, consisting of 113 acres in two parcels in section 4, and a 20-acre parcel in section 34, in what would become Blue Mound Township. Excepted and reserved from these bequests was a small rectangular parcel in section 4, 160 feet by 180 feet (approximately $^{66}/_{100}$ of an acre), which was to go to school district number 3.

Next, John discusses the fact that he had executed a deed of conveyance on March 20, 1856, to his son-in-law, Charles Fisher, giving him life title to 134 acres of land, which would pass on to the two of his children whose mother was John B. Moffett's daughter, Sarah, and this land was intended as John's bequest to those grandchildren.

---

[108]See further details of David's Civil War service in Appendix 7.

To his son, John McDowell Moffett, John left the west half of the southwest quarter of section 34, and the east half of the southeast quarter of section 33, in what would become Blue Mound Township. To this he added another twenty acres in section 34.

John then gives detailed instructions pertaining to the disposition of the remaining real estate. First of all, the executor could at his discretion sell of any of it which may be necessary to pay debts. What remained afterwards was to be divided among seven heirs: Lewis Robertson, Charles Fisher, James Y. Taylor and his wife, William T. Moffett, John McDowell Moffett, Joseph Edwin Moffett, and Laura Amanda Moffett. Note that David S. Moffett is not included in this residual clause.

In the closing John discusses miscellaneous items. The first is the sale of livestock, with directions for avoiding the sale of the animals at a less than desirable price. Second is the building and completion of a barn on his home farm, a plan for which John had laid out. He mentions that the land to be divided into the seven shares is situated in both Illinois and Missouri.

Finally, John appoints his son, William Thomas Moffett as the executor. He instructs that executor, "to faithfully execute its provisions", and, "to consult my Brother Thomas Moffett of Springfield Illinois in all matters in which legal advice may be desired and to pay him for such advice a reasonable compensation...." He signs the document with his full signature and seal, with the date of August 6, 1862.

From this we can see a man of great pride, one who had accumulated a very significant amount of land, and one who was perhaps unusually attentive to detail. He apparently had a hard time relinquishing control of what he deemed to be the important matters in life, and saw it necessary to extend that control from beyond the grave. He was obviously a very thoughtful man, giving very specific properties to each of his children or their heirs, and making sure to instruct his beloved wife (who was not the mother of any of his children) to care well for his youngest children who were still minors, and giving her specifics regarding the priorities of such care. His apparently special treatment of the bequests to David S. Moffett and his family notwithstanding, he appears to have left no hint of favoritism toward any of his children and/or grandchildren.

To this writer, John Bigham Moffett also appears to be a bit ahead of his time. In 1862, except in special cases, wives did not share ownership property with their spouse. Not surprisingly therefore, widows had small legal entitlements to their deceased husband's property. Typically, state laws provided that a widow should receive a one-third share of the property if a man died without leaving a will – her dower right. However, if an authentic will survived, the wife could possibly be given very little. Ordinarily, she was left with her bedroom furniture, kitchen utensils, and free access to come and go from the deceased man's home, so long as she lived, or until she remarried. Should she remarry, according to the large majority of nineteenth century wills, she may well go to her new husband's home with nothing more than her clothing and other most personal possessions.

In his will, John Bigham Moffett leaves a substantial bit of property to his widow. While she is alive, she clearly has control of the house, and the farm, and an additional 240 acres of land near the farm. Although her title to it is limited to her lifetime, in order that it would then pass on to the youngest children, he makes no mention of the eventuality of her remarriage. Despite all of his trials and tribulations, John Bigham Moffett left his wife and children well provided for. In part, he was able to do so because his family worked well together for their common good, whatever personal differences they may have had – a characteristic of frontier families who are successful. He was also able to do so because he clearly worked hard, exhibited remarkable self-reliance, and yet knew his limitations and did not hesitate to reach out when he needed help. It would seem that his was, in many of these senses, an exemplary life. The benefits of his efforts would be felt for generations.

There is also this postscript: John B. Moffett's widow, Nancy, remained in the Sangamon Valley, residing with various children of her late husband. However, at the time of John Bigham Moffett's death, his brother, Thomas, still resided in Springfield. Of Thomas's eight children, only two were still living, and both of them died in 1864, unmarried. Thomas and his wife, Eliza were left with no surviving children, and no grandchildren. When Eliza then died in 1867, Thomas was left with no immediate family. His siblings were also mostly deceased, and those few who still were living were residing at some distance.[109] After several years thus alone, John B. Moffett's widow, Nancy, married Thomas Moffett on Wednesday, March 7, 1877 in Macon County. They resided in Springfield. Ironically, little more than 15 weeks after their marriage, Thomas died in Springfield on Saturday, June 23, 1877. Nancy, once again widowed, returned to Blue Mound Township, where she spent the rest of her life with her step-son, William Thomas Moffett. She died there on Friday, March 11, 1892.

---

[109]Thomas's brother William had died in Missouri in 1852. The youngest brother, Willis, had removed to Wisconsin and Minnesota, and their sister, Elizabeth Kendall, lived more than 100 miles to the west of Springfield in Hancock County, Illinois. Their brother James and unmarried sister, Mary (Polly), still resided back in Kentucky.

10 — Intrigue in the Civil War

It is not hyperbole to assert that the American Civil War was the nation's greatist conflagration. Even considering the horrifc events of the Second World War died in the 1940s, America was not so deeply injured then as in the Civil War. Far more Americans died in the Civil War than in any other. Almost as many died in the Civil War as did in all the other American wars of the nineteenth century combined. More than 620,000 Union and Confederate soldiers perished before the war ended, in a country of 31 million. If the same percentage of the American population lost their lives in a war at the end of the twentieth century, the dead would number more than five million![109]

Noted Civil War historian, Shelby Foote points out that the calamitous numbers of deaths and maimings were not just a function of the fact that all the combatants were Americans. This war was decidedly more dangerous to the individual soldier than other American wars because, as Foote says, "The weapons were way ahead of the tactics." The weapons had increased frightfully in accuracy, speed of delivery, and devastating effect. Still, in order to mass their fire, tacticians massed their soldiers. As Foote further said, "So they lined up and marched up to an entrenched line and got blown away."[110]

Furthermore, the Civil War was the last war fought on our own soil. While there were incidents in the American Revolution and the War of 1812 in which enemy forces wrought destruction on our buildings and infrastructure, there had never been any experience to compare with such campaigns as Sherman's March from Atlanta to the Sea, in which the Union army of 62,000 men cut a 60-mile-wide scar across some of the most beautiful and productive territory in the Confederacy. They destroyed, "stores of provisions, standing crops and cattle, cotton-gins and mills, railways and bridges, in fact everything that could be useful to the Confederacy and much that was not."[111]

---

[109]Bruce Catton, *The American Heritage New History of the Civil War* (New York, 1996), pp. vi-vii.

[110]Geoffrey C. Ward, Ric Burns, and Ken Burns, *The Civil War: An Illustrated History* (New York, 1991), p. 265.

[111]Samuel Eliot Morison, Henry Steele Commager, and William E. Leuchtenburg, *The Growth of the American Republic* (New York, 1980), vol. I, pp. 702-703.

Following a battle at Savage Station, Virginia, June 29, 1862. One might be excused for assuming that this was just the doctor's waiting room, but there was not room in the available buildings and tents for all (or probably even for most) of the injured, great numbers of whom sat or lay on the bare ground awaiting attention. Some are being treated there in this photo. The principle difference between this scene and those which followed other battles is that, relatively speaking, this engagement was only a skirmish. The great number of much larger battles would have been followed by scenes of no less horror, but far greater scope.

Of course, it was not just the deaths, incredibly numerous as they were, which marked this war as unique. In similarly huge numbers, men who survived were greatly diminished. Limbs had been lost, other wounds rendered them partially to completely disabled, and the mental state of countless others -- whether physically diminished or not -- was forever altered for the worse. The survivors frequently returned to their families being changed men, and in a very real sense, those who had left for war did die, and other men returned in their places.

Besides being the war in which the greatest number of Americans died and were injured and mutilated, it was the war in which the largest percentage of the population actually participated. Thus the war's direct effects permeated nearly every American home. It would have been difficult to find a family in which no member was killed or wounded.

To many, while the scale is obviously a good deal smaller, the views of the destruction of Richmond are   so ghastly as to be evocative of Dresden in 1944 or even Hiroshima in 1945.

Modern societies do not consist of disconnected family or tribal groups. They form communities of multiple families and are heavily dependent upon them. Those families who were so fortunate as to lose no loved ones' lives in this great struggle, certainly had numerous friends and neighbors for whom tragedy struck directly. Companies of soldiers were usually raised by locality, so when a particular unit was overrun in battle and suffered enormous casualties, the town or county from which they hailed would likewise suffer a disproportionate human cost.

The suffering was great, even for the victors. Unlike other American wars, in this conflict both the victors and the defeated were all Americans. The defeated southern states, besides losing a larger portion of their population, had many significant parts of their short-lived country destroyed. Their infrastructure, their economy, and their social structure were all decimated.[117]

----

[112]Ward, Burns and Burns, pp. 264-273.

Such is the backdrop to the adult lives of the children of John Bigham Moffett – William Thomas Moffett and his siblings. William was born in 1826 and wed in 1856. His siblings were born from 1829-1849. Excepting the youngest (Laura), all were young adults, or in late adolescence, when the war was raging. Joseph Edwin was the next youngest, born in about 1846, and while he was in his mid-teens when the war broke out in 1861, before it ended, he was nearly 20 years old.

Few would argue that this struggle resulted from trivial matters. The mad dogs of war were loosed by Lincoln to save the Union – the great experiment in republican self-government; and by Davis to gain the southern states' independence, which they saw as the only way to preserve their self-determination, and their very way of life. It was not a coup carried out by one faction against another, not a power struggle between or among rival blocs, and not a dispute over possession of economically valuable territory. Most Americans deemed the stakes to be extremely high.

The roots of eventual secession, and the ensuing war, were long-standing, and deep. Since the foundation of white settlement in the Americas, the institution of slavery provided large portions of the necessary manpower, and generated tensions which ran through the whole of society. By the time the American colonies declared independence, the debate over slavery had become central and heated, but it was not addressed in any meaningful way then, nor for the next seventy-five years.

By the 1850s, while the children of John Bigham Moffett were growing and coming of age, the struggles over slavery and its abolition dominated political and civic life in every part of the country. Dramatic, polarizing events were scattered throughout the decade. To consider just a very few, we might look at the following four:

* The violent struggle over the status of slavery in Kansas

* A landmark decision by the U.S. Supreme Court in the case of one Dred Scott

* A financial panic in 1857

* The abolitionist raid on Harper's Ferry, Virginia

In January of 1854, Illinois Senator Stephen Douglas proposed a bill in the Congress to organize the unsettled regions of the Great Plains, which would be governed as the Territory of Nebraska. Regarding slavery, the details of the plan were in many ways inflammatory to all parties. They were drawn in this way to enhance the probability of success of Douglas's ultimate goals, which had nothing much to do with slavery, and everything to do with his involvement in land speculation, and the route which the proposed trans-continental railroad might take. The details of it all can be wearisome, but the key point was that the two states of Kansas and Nebraska might be carved from the territory. Nebraska was too far north to be considered a candidate for slavery. Kansas on the other hand would be immediately west of Missouri, a slave state. The Missouri Compromise (1820) had forbade the creation of new slave states north of 36O 30' north latitude, which provision would not allow slavery in the territory which would become Kansas. To make his self-interested bill appealing to southern members of the Congress, Douglas included in it the stipulation that the Missouri Compromise would not have effect regarding Kansas, and that the fate
of slavery there would be decided by popular sovereignty.

Richmond lies in desolate ruin after its fall to Union troops in 1865.

Union soldiers tear up the railroad lines in Atlanta after that city's capture.

The bill quickly created a stunning uproar among abolitionists and many other northerners who thought the Missouri Compromise to be inviolate. Despite that, and many other intrigues in the debate over its consideration, the Kansas-Nebraska bill was passed into law in May of 1854. What followed in Kansas was a disaster. Besides the many settlers who sought no one resolution of the slavery question over another, elements who presented themselves were radicals on each side of the debate. In March of 1855 elections were held for the territorial legislature, in which significant numbers, probably in the thousands, of Missouri pro-slavery men crossed the border and cast illegitimate ballots in favor of pro-slavery candidates. The legislature thus elected immediately wrote laws in favor of slavery. Abolitionists among the Kansans formed their own rump government, so that by 1856, the territory had two governments, but no legal one.

Meanwhile, organized abolitionist groups, especially in New England, sent hundreds of new settlers to Kansas to bolster the anti-slavery faction. Large numbers of them sat down at Lawrence, but their first settlement there was destroyed by pro-slavery agitators. In response, as more of the abolitionist migrants arrived, they were well armed. The inevitable result was repeated violent encounters between the groups of radicals on either side. Some have suggested that the first shots of the American Civil War were not fired on Fort Sumter; the first shots, they reasoned, were fired somewhere in Kansas, as were the second, third, fourth, fifth.... Throughout the country, the passionate were fully active, providing what they could for their proxies in this preview war.[113]

In the way of tribal feuding, the two factions escalated their violence. Among numerous other ghastly encounters, pro slavery elements entered the abolitionist stronghold town of Lawrence and destroyed the office and presses of the *Herald of Freedom* newspaper, burned the Free State Hotel, looted numerous businesses, and torched the residence of the abolitionist government's governor, Robinson. The response came a few days later, when a militant named John Brown and four of his sons joined with others and attacked the pro slavery community at Pottawatomie Creek, dragging five settlers from their homes and using excessive brutality to murder them. It would be months before peace could be restored.[119]

Charles Robinson
Abolitionist governor of
territorial Kansas

Dred Scott

A slave named Dred Scott, and his enslaved wife and two daughters, were taken by their master into the free state of Illinois, later into the unorganized territory north of the boundary assigned by the Missouri Compromise, and finally back into the slave state of Missouri. Scott sued for his family's freedom, as he had spent such periods as a resident of parts of the nation where slavery was forbidden. The case was brought to court in 1846, went from one court to an appellate court, and continued upwards, reaching the United States Supreme Court in 1856-57.

---

[113]Morison, Comager and Leuchtenburg, vol. I, pp. 584-590.

[114]Kenneth M. Stampp, America in 1857, A Nation on the Brink (New York, 1990), p. 146.

The Supreme Court, dominated by southerners, and whose Chief Justice was Roger B. Taney, an adversary to any limitations on slavery, rendered a stunning decision in March of 1857. They refused Scott's petition, partly on the grounds that, as a Negro, he was not a citizen of the United States and therefore could not bring suit. More importantly, in the process of the reasoning, the court deemed the Missouri Compromise to be unconstitutional, and essentially stated that all the territories were open to slavery.

The furor was instant and deafening through most quarters in the north. Its implications brought new vigor to the abolitionists, who opposed all slavery, and to the new Republican Party, whose adherents strongly opposed slavery in the territories, but did not feel that the U. S. Constitution allowed the abolition of slavery where it existed. The crisis continued to mount.[115]

Financial Panic

Through the 1850s, the relentless pressure to develop new lands continued. Perhaps the most prominent feature of this process was the ubiquitous presence of land speculation and speculators. While speculation was surely the main cause, it was not the only one, but it does make a simplified focus for a description of what ensued late in the summer of 1857. Twenty years after the nation's worst financial collapse (1837), the lessons of that disaster seemed long forgotten. Warnings came from many corners, but in August of 1857 the Ohio Life Insurance and Trust Company, one of the nation's most respected financial institutions, announced that it was suspending payment. Bank runs and bank failures quickly followed, and business failures shortly thereafter. While farmers were not immune to the pain, the real crises came in the cities and towns, where unemployment soared spectacularly. Again, tradesmen, mechanics, and employees of burgeoning industry were quickly without work or means.[121]   By 1859, a slow recovery was apparent, but the economy only really recovered with the onset of the Civil War.

Such intense unrest as is generated by economic contractions rarely operates in a vacuum. It colors already standing problems, usually aggravating them. The tensions between the northern and southern states were no exception. Economic tensions increased as the federal government attempted to correct things by, among other things, reducing tariffs, a step which decidedly favored the southern planters and only seemed likely to add to the woes of the northern industrialists.

---

[115]Ibid., pp. 82-109.

[116]Here John Bigham Moffett was cushioned greatly by his earlier decision to engage almost entirely in raising crops and livestock. He also had not engaged in the frantic speculation of the most recent years, unlike his predicament in 1837. He and his family were clearly able to ride out the disaster.

On another front, as usually happens in a time of economic pain, religious revival made a grand appearance, as people were convinced that they saw the punishing hand of God in such a disaster. In this case, the abolitionists added their own dimension to this response, as many of them had long warned that the terrible sin of slavery would not much longer be able to escape the inevitable wrath of the Almighty.[117]   Here of course, the invocation of religious interpretation continued to diminish the concept of adversaries in the simpler roles of folks who disagreed, but increasingly cast them as incarnations of evil, gravely heightening the level of the tensions.   Enter such characters as John Brown.

Harpers Ferry

John Brown, the fanatic who had led the retaliation on Pottawatomie Creek in Kansas, continued his penchant for violence after leaving that bloodied territory. He concocted a plan to raise a small military force, establish an independent abolitionist republic somewhere in the central and southern Appalachians, and from it to wage guerrilla war on slavery and slave owners. His force would consist of freed Negroes and militant whites.

John Brown, from an old daguerreotype. He was known to be a charismatic character, and the fierce and fearless determination can be seen in the penetrating stare of his eyes.

He began by seizing the federal armory at Harpers Ferry, Virginia, on the night of October 16, 1859. Leading a bi-racial force of eighteen men, they quickly took control of the building. In the process they also murdered the town's mayor and took five hostages from among the town's leading citizenry.

In the morning, the local militia surrounded the armory. Brown, his band, and his hostages barricaded themselves in the building and prepared for a siege. There were sporadic exchanges of gunfire.

The governor of Virginia called in the entire state militia and asked for further aid from the federal government. The news of the events rapidly spread throughout the country. As evening arrived on the 17th, so did a detail of marines, led by one Colonel Robert E. Lee. By now, all but Brown and four of his men were dead or incapacitated. The next day, the marines broke in to the armory and captured Brown and his gang.

_____

[122]Stampp, pp. 219-238.

Despite the widespread condemnation of the event by public officials, politicians, and newspapers throughout the north and south, southerners were greatly disturbed, and most seemed only to focus on the very well publicized lines written by Ralph Waldo Emerson:

"That new saint, than whom nothing purer or more brave was ever led by love of men into conflict and death ... will make the gallows glorious like the cross."

Brown and his accomplices were quickly (eight days after his capture) tried for murder, criminal conspiracy, and treason. His defense attorney tried to offer the plea of insanity, but Brown would have none of that. His demeanor throughout was one of righteous confidence, and he was convicted and hanged, becoming a great martyr to the abolitionist cause.[118]

Although it is not unwarranted to assume that no one imagined the carnage which would be wrought when the war came, the vision of an impending catastrophe was shared by more and more Americans as these and other riveting events arose through the 1850s.

Of course, while the root cause was slavery, the war itself was a struggle by the states which remained in the Union to force the rebel states to return – at least at the outset. Excited abolitionists expected emancipation to proceed swiftly after the war began. When it did not, leaders of the movement publicly put pressure on Lincoln to free the slaves promptly. However, the President repeatedly advised that preservation of the Union was his only concern. He pointed out that if he could restore the union by freeing the slaves he would do it; if he could preserve it by not freeing any slaves he would do it; and if he could preserve it by freeing some of the slaves but not others, then he would do that.

From American folklore to serious history studies, the Civil War has long been known and characterized as one in which brother fought against brother, and families' allegiances were split in many ways. The Moffetts were among those families who surely might have had conflicting interests in the matter. Some of them lived in slave states, and owned slaves, and others lived in free states and never owned slaves.[119] The two slave states in which some of them lived – Kentucky and Missouri – were loyal to the Union and did not secede.

In Illinois, the concept of split loyalties took on another dimension. It is not uncommon for us to have a very two-dimensional view of historic struggles. In the Civil War, we commonly assume that there were two sides, the Union and the Confederacy. We tend to think that residents in the northern states constituted one homogenous group, and those in the southern states constituted another. In fact, the picture was not nearly as simple as we generally suppose. No war is a simple, black and white picture, nor is it easily understood on any level.

---

[118]Morrison, Commager, and Leuchtenburg, vol. I, pp. 601-602.

[119]For a more thorough discussion of the various Moffett men, their residences, and their respective slave holdings, as well as a full discussion of their military services during the war, see Appendix 7.

By no means was every northern resident a Union supporter, an abolitionist at heart, and/or supportive of the war effort, nor did northerners universally welcome the Emancipation Proclamation. Neither were those who lived in the Confederacy uniformly in favor of slavery, vehemently opposed to abolition, happy to have separated from the Union, and/or very supportive of the war fought to maintain the independence of the Confederate States. Beyond this, we often forget about the border states which remained in the Union, but where slavery was legal. In those states, it was even more difficult to draw simple lines between distinct factions.

The American Civil War was more complex than many. While the notion of Unionism was widely popular in many of the northern states, it was not so in all of them. The numbers of citizens who supported both the Union and emancipation are uncertain, but there is plenty of evidence to the effect that large numbers of the northern state residents did not support both notions. Furthermore, while the prevalent notion in the northern states may have been sympathetic to the plight of the slaves, a large proportion of those who were active abolitionists were zealots, with a religious fervor. They saw no nuances in the issue, and they cared little for compromise. In a country in which compromise was what made things work, the abolitionists made even large numbers of northerners uncomfortable.

Beyond all of this, even before the fall of Fort Sumter, there were varying degrees of conviction that war was the way to settle these matters. As the violence began, as the level of the carnage shocked everyone on both sides, and as the Union forces failed to quickly snuff the rebellion, the reservations deepened and spread.

Illinois was a particularly complex society in this war. On the one hand, it was a free state, and slavery had not been legal there since statehood. Lincoln, whose election as President precipitated the secessions, had lived in Illinois since he was a boy. Even the eventual commander of the Union armies, U.S. Grant, hailed from Illinois. The white settlers in the northerly counties hailed mainly from the states north of the Ohio River and the Mason-Dixon Line.

On the other hand, Illinois shared borders with two slave states, Missouri and Kentucky. Many early white settlers in the central and southern counties had come to Illinois from states south of the Ohio and the Mason-Dixon. Most of these people or their families had owned slaves in the past, and many Illinois residents had family members who dwelt in slave states, if not in one or more of the states which seceded. As a consequence, the Land of Lincoln was by no means a society with one voice on any of the issues attendant upon secession and the war which ensued. Similar demographics created very similar diversity of opinion and interest in Indiana and Ohio as well.

Where then would the Moffetts of central Illinois stand? Theirs was a region filled with diverse opinions and passions. They themselves did not own slaves, but they had come there from the slave state of Kentucky, and their kinsmen there still held slaves. With no apparent exception however, they stood with the cause of Union. Four of them were engaged in military operations during the war, and all with Union forces.[120]

---

[120]Again, see Appendix 7 for more detail about specific Moffett men and their activity in the war.

A typical page from the 1850 U.S. Census of Macon County, Illinois, showing the very strong influence of the southern/slavery heritage. In the column where the birthplace of each individual is listed, orange stars highlight all of those who were born in a slave state. Of the forty-two persons listed on the page, eighteen were born in Virginia, Kentucky, or Mississippi. Of the twenty-four persons who were not born in a slave state, twenty-one are minors.

The most significant wrinkle in the fabric of Illinois during the Civil War was the large presence of citizens who either sympathized with the Confederacy or felt the preservation of the Union was not a cause for which a war was necessary. Generally, those who openly expressed these sentiments were Democrats. As the opposition party, they challenged what seemed to many to be the conventional wisdom, pointing out that the war was costly in financial and human terms, and as it dragged on into its second and third years, it was clear that the human cost far exceeded anyone's expectations. For many, their motivation had much to do with discrediting the Republican juggernaut which had swept the northern states in the election of 1860. For many others, they thought it unconscionable to allow the continuation of the slaughter which was the war. For yet many others, they had always sympathized with the causes of the southern states.[121]

For still many others, the economic environment resulting from the war was disastrous. With secession and the ensuing war, southern markets for Illinois grain evaporated, and the Mississippi River was closed to Union states. Grain prices dropped. This reopened the wound of the 1857 panic as many Midwestern banks based their paper money on Southern bonds. A good indicator of just how serious the matter became was the survivability of the banks in Illinois. On the eve of secession, there were 112 banks in the state, but only seventeen of them survived the secession and war.[122] Consequently, in Illinois, the war was widely unpopular from the viewpoint of the economy – always a very powerful molder of public opinion.

Still, in the initial period following secession, the natural rush of patriotic expression dampened the concerns. The belief was common that the war would be won, and won quickly. The opposition party bided its time. Gradually, public feeling began to swing toward their positions. The first major factor was the Union Army's lack of progress. There were occasional successes, such as the capture of Fort Donelson and Nashville in February of 1862, but they were relatively small. From the beginning, Union forces were humiliated in the more publicized engagements such as Bull Run.

The second factor was the human cost of the war. In April of 1862, the gruesome calamity of the Battle of Shiloh unfolded. The battle involved 63,000 Union troops, and 40,000 Confederates. The numbers of casualties in the two days of battle – those killed, wounded, missing or captured were staggering: 13,000 Union troops, and 11,000 Confederates. Americans on both sides were in disbelief at the numbers, and the enthusiasm ebbed.

The downward spiral of worsening news continued. The Union forces lost battles, or tactically won battles but failed to act upon their strategic advantage. In either case, the losses of life and limb battered the psyches of Americans nearly every day. As the Republicans and Unionists gradually grew less confident, the Democrats and those who wanted to see an immediate end to the war began to speak up.

---

[121] Frank L. Klement, *The Copperheads in the Middle West* (Chicago, 1960), pp. 1-39.

[122] Delores Archaimbault, and Terry A. Barnhart, "Illinois Copperheads and the American Civil War", *Illinois History Teacher*, vol. 3:1, 1996, p. 15.

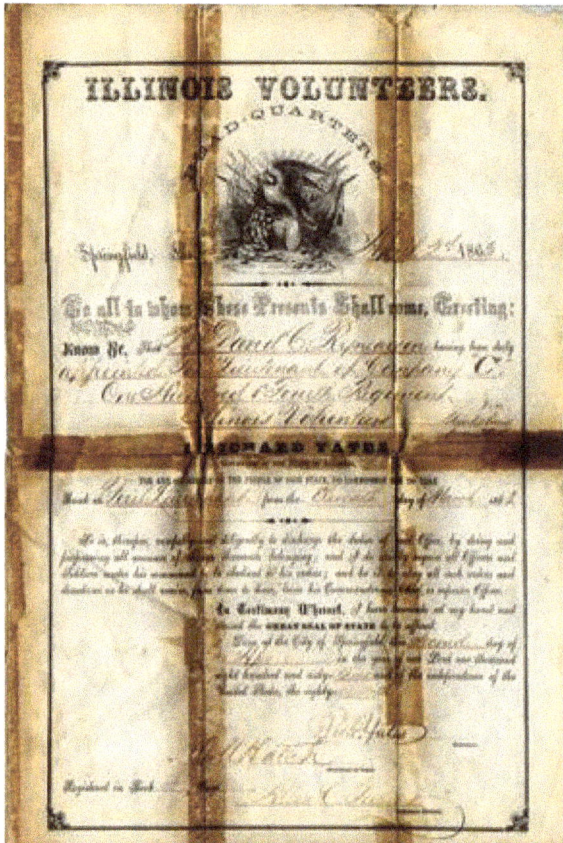

Draft notice signed by Illinois Governor Richard Yates in 1863. Ironically, the man is assigned to the 110th Illinois Volunteers.

The third and fourth factors in their favor now presented themselves: There was the talk of conscription in 1862, and at that time men were required to register; its implementation would not turn out to be necessary until 1863, and the Emancipation Proclamation, issued on January 1, 1863.[123] The two acts, delivered not from the Congress, but from the President's single authority, angered large numbers of northerners everywhere outside of New England. The draft was viewed as unconstitutional, and the Emancipation Proclamation likewise; and in both orders, whether or not they passed Constitutional muster, both soldiers and civilians found much fault. The draft flew in the face of the American tradition of volunteer forces. Furthermore, the draft could be dodged by providing a $300.00 payment in lieu of services, raising the specter of poor men fighting the rich men's war. As emancipation, apart from the abolitionists, northerners did not feel they were fighting a war for the black race, and the resentment Was great. The proclamation also seemed senseless to many as it did not actually free anyone – it did not apply to slaves in the loyal border states, and the main remaining slaves were without the jurisdiction where Lincoln could enforce it.[124]

The resistance to the war was becoming visible and audible, and in some cases disruptive of the peace and violent. Recruitment and enrolling officers were harassed verbally and physically. Mobs began to act: In Chicago in June of 1862, four hundred attacked four federal officials who had arrested two men who refused to give their names to the draft registrars.[125]

In a corollary to these constitutionally questionable moves, the Lincoln administration assumed other extraordinary powers: the suspension of habeas corpus, the arrest and detention of suspicious persons without bail or hearings, and the trial of some defendants in military courts. To the horror of many, some were even arrested and convicted of crimes based on their speech, expressing views that questioned the war's necessity and the like.

---

[123]Tindall, vol. I, pp. 626-646.

[124]Morison, Commager, and Leuchtenburg, pp.673-676.

[125]Wood Gray, *The Hidden Civil War, The Story of the Copperheads* (New York, 1942) pp. 137-138.

At the same time that emancipation was proclaimed, Lincoln announced that those who resisted the draft, discouraged enlistment, or were "guilty of any disloyal practice affording aid and comfort to rebels" would be subject to martial law, tried by court martial, and denied the writ of habeas corpus. Some 13,000 persons were ensnared by this action.[126]

With this background, the war went on, into 1862. In Illinois, as in Indiana and Ohio to a greater or lesser extent, the legislature was controlled by the Democrats. However, Governor Yates was a Republican. In 1860, Illinois voters had approved a constitutional convention, to bring the state's constitution up to date with the fast changing and fast-growing state.

The convention was held in 1862 under the control of the Democrats, and they were now emboldened by the souring atmosphere surrounding the war. They proceeded to carry out highly partisan activities. They took time to publicly investigate army purchases and appointments, hoping to cast shadows and doubts on the governor. They also wrote a constitution which removed military authority from the office of the governor, reduced the governor's term from four years to two, and for good measure carefully gerrymandered all the legislative and congressional districts.

The Democrats perhaps overplayed their hand. In June, the constitution was put to the voters who were in part disgusted by the partisanship displayed, and overwhelmingly rejected it. By this time, the Unionist public had developed epithets for the peace Democrats, but the one which stuck was "Copperheads." In part they developed the name from the habit the peace men had of wearing the head of a copper coin on their lapel, thus exhibiting the word "Liberty", and the female figurehead. In the adversarial press however, they were depicted as the deadly snakes by the same name.

The other part of the voters' backlash stemmed from the stream of charges leveled at the Democrats by the Republicans and the Republican-leaning press. Many were accused of membership in a secret political society called the Knights of the Golden Circle. The Springfield correspondent for the *Chicago Daily Tribune* made the charge public, and the newspaper made suggestions of treason. The Democrats denied the charges, and a bipartisan investigative committee found no basis for them, but rumors persisted.

The status of free speech and dissent in a democratic society during wartime has always been challenged by parties in power, and vehemently upheld by those in opposition and those who have preferred peace. It seems difficult to avoid ugliness in the debate as the specter of treason seems always inferred. The lines between treason and lawful free speech are not clearly delineated in the Constitution, and the debate about them rises anew with each wartime episode. While American society generally tolerates considerable criticism of those in power, many find it easy to suspect treasonous leanings, if not activities, among those who agitate for peace.

---

[126]Morison, Commager and Leuchtenburg, p. 674.

Our Legislature.

The dreaded institution at Springfield, called Legislature, has at last adjourned.

It failed to consumate its treasonable threats of asking a conference with the rebel states preparatory to her attempt to place Illinois in a state of anarchy worse than that of the border states.

Like the copperhead convention of last year, its whole system of gyremandering will be repudiated by the people. And we trust and pray, that our state may never again be disgraced by another legislature like the present.

We have but little thanks to the majority, for their delaying until June next their intended acts of treason, nor can we respect them any more if they there let their treasonable lights die then. It will only be because they will have learned that it will be an unhealthy undertaking for them. They have exhibited all the spirit of toryism, that is necessary to consign them and their resolutions of treason to eternal infamy.

Blistering editorial commentary in the *Decatur Gazette*, Wednesday, February 18, 1863, lambasting the "Copperheads" and the legislature they controlled, after the Governor suspended the bodies activity on a technicality. Note the use of words such as treason (twice), treasonable (twice), toryism, infamy, anarchy, and disgraced.

The tension was therefore well developed after the constitutional convention and the failure of the new constitution to pass with the voters. As autumn came, legislative and congressional elections provided more focus for the debate and further polarized the state. The general discomfort and defeatism which had spread through the Midwest enabled the Democrats to win majorities in both houses of the Illinois legislature. The battling continued into 1863 therefore, and the legislature did all it could to challenge the President and the Governor. The crafty Yates undid the legislature however by dissolving it. The state's constitution allowed for the governor to take this step should the legislature's two houses be unable to agree on adjournment. Thus deprived of their public podium, the laryngitis. With this action, Yates probably did more than any single person, in any single act, to thwart the juggernaut of Copperhead political activity in the Midwest.

Through all this period, the insidious rumors flew on both sides. Of special concern was the notion that numbers of the Copperheads were preparing various seditious actions. Many reports in 1862 indicated that they were arming and drilling, in order that they could resist the implementation of the draft, and there were other similar rumors from time to time.

With such reports in the air, and the memory of the insufferable violence in Kansas still alive and well, those who supported the Union and the war surely felt that preparation for such possibilities, and acute vigilance were the prudent courses to take. As a consequence, many counties many counties formed companies of home guards to deal with such eventualities, and also to do what they could in the way of intelligence regarding any plans for violence, or seditious or treasonous activities. In Sangamon County, where the numbers of visible he presence there of the legislature, three such companies were formed.

In Macon County, William Thomas Moffett, acting with a commission from Governor Yates, was active in the formation of the company which arose there, and was elected its captain[127]. There are few records of these companies, and none relating to the Macon County unit are apparently extant, but local histories, newspaper articles, and letters make reference to them. The essential mission of these companies was to maintain civil order if necessary, but they also frequently tracked down deserters, an occasional spy, or other perpetrators of what Lincoln had described as "any disloyal practice affording aid and comfort to rebels".

It was not necessarily a soft assignment:

"Opponents of the war often encouraged desertion, while the army's efforts to arrest deserters in southern Illinois sometimes met with civilian resistance. Deserters were concealed, and armed mobs often greeted their would-be captors. Mandatory enlistment under the Conscription Act of 1863 was extremely unpopular in Charleston, Jacksonville, and Vandalia. An armed mob drove Union officers in charge of enlistment from various parts of Fulton County in protest of the conscription law. The officers were actually attacked, and at least two fatal shootings were reported. Another mob at Olney threatened to burn the town if the local enrollment lists were not surrendered. In Union County, a guerrilla band assaulted Unionists and destroyed their property. Confederate sympathizers in southern Illinois sometimes practiced intimidation tactics, beating and shooting those who supported the Union war effort....

"It has been estimated that in a five-month period, eight hundred deserters were arrested in Perry, Saline, Jackson, and Williamson counties and two thousand for Illinois as a whole."[128]

As 1863 dawned, the Copperhead movement was strong; strong enough that, in Ohio, Indiana, and Illinois, Democrats took public stands which a year earlier might have seemed radical and dangerous. The Democrats of Illinois, in their state convention that year, adopted a resolution stating,

"That the further offensive prosecution of this war tends to subvert the Constitution and the government, and entail upon this nation all the disastrous consequences of misrule and anarchy. That we are in favor of peace upon the basis of a restoration of the Union, and for the accomplishment of which we propose a National Convention to settle upon terms of peace, which shall have in view the restoration of the Union as it was, and the securing by Constitutional amendments, such rights to the several States and the people thereof, as honor and justice demand."[129]

---

[127]*Past and Present of the City of Decatur and Macon County* (Chicago, 1903, pp. 729-734.

[128]Archambault and Barnhart, p. 16.

[129]Gray, p. 146.

Even in New England there were such rumblings. The Democrats in Connecticut nominated a peace candidate for governor, and their platform included the following:

"That while we denounce the heresy of secession, as undefended and unwarranted by the Constitution, we as confidently assert, that whatever may heretofore have been the opinion of our countrymen, the time has now arrived when all true lovers of the Constitution are ready to abandon the '*monstrous fallacy*' that the Union can be restored by the armed hand alone; and we are anxious to inaugurate such action, honorable alike to the contending sections, as will stop the ravages of war, avert universal bankruptcy, and unite all the States upon terms of equality as members of one Confederacy."[130]

Clement S. Vallandigham

In Ohio, former Congressman and leading peace Democrat Clement Vallandigham, who had been outspoken in his views, and had been tried and convicted by court martial, ultimately exiled, and was residing in Canada, was nominated for governor.   The whole affair of his arrest, treatment, and subsequent fate had enhanced his image greatly throughout the region.

As the summer of 1863 began, while the chances for success by the Copperheads had seemingly never looked better, the tide was about to turn. On the local levels in Illinois, the home guard units had installed a feeling that the Union supporters were in full charge. In early July then there came the news of the great battle at Gettysburg, where Lee was sent packing back to Virginia.   Immediately on the heels of that came the fall of Vicksburg and the highly strategic Union acquisition of full control of Mississippi River, cutting the Confederacy in two.

The effect was buoyant in the north. Defeatism, so recently a heavy fog obscuring the light of promised victory, was rapidly lifting. The opponents of the Copperheads seized upon the moment and took the offensive with relish. Repeated accusations of Copperhead treason coming from the pro-Union and pro-Republican newspapers were gaining effect. Suddenly such figures as Vallandigham were especially vulnerable. That Ohio candidate was frequently referred to by the Unionists as "a sympathizer with the rebels", and "a convicted traitor."   He was widely portrayed as a puppet of the Confederate government and compared to the likes of Judas Iscariot. His briefly high popularity was plummeting, and his contest in particular was keenly watched all over the Midwest, and the whole of the northern states. If he should win, the supporters of peace initiatives would find validation, and would gain significant influence; and should he lose, the tendency would be to validate the negative images with which he was portrayed. In the end, Vallandigham was decisively defeated, for by election day, the entire mood in the north had reverted to one of resignation to the war and hope for further success. The advocates of peace were marginalized. For the Republicans, "The political wind was again blowing in their direction, and they let out the sails to take advantage of it."[131]

---

[130]*idem.*

[131]Klement, pp. 129-133.

A contemporary political cartoon from the Harper's Weekly Magazine, indicating the sudden reverse of fortune felt by Copperheads after the events of 1863.

As the American Civil War came, all Americans were subject to the pain of loss, the terrible grief, the fear of further loss of loved ones, the economic and social disruptions. However, the war in the northern states did differ from place to place in important ways. The cozy Yankees in such areas as New England were surrounded by neighbors who had the unifying common belief that the war had been thrust upon them by a society with evil institutions, strange speech, and alien ways. They felt relatively little concern that agents of their enemy might be walking among them. There, the concerns were much more likely to be in the area of impatience with the administration's reluctance to strike significant blows against slavery.

By contrast, the Moffetts in the Land of Lincoln were involved in a very particular struggle during the Civil War, and one with which most Americans are never familiar. In their counties, the war was very present, and violence and betrayal in their midst was always a real possibility. For those years, they lived in a watchful and tense society. They believed that the enemy was among them, and of necessity, they took responsibility for dealing with that.

William Thomas Moffett was one who took this responsibility fully, and apparently was rewarded with a postwar status of respect and honor in his community. He found himself serving in public office at different levels, up to that of the Illinois State Senate. We really do not know much about the particulars of his company's activities, but his biographical sketches in local histories stress his grave concern over the preservation of the Union. His "personal acquaintance" with, and high admiration for Abraham Lincoln was a great influence. They also describe his service as captain of the home guard company in general terms, but clearly indicate his deep commitment to his task, and the high intensity with which he acted:

> "(He) rendered valiant service to the Union cause. He smote treason wherever he found it lurking in the rear of the Union army. Despising disloyalty to his government, he would tear the masks from the faces of those who sought to hide their treason and hold them up to public scorn and contempt."[132]

Two of William Thomas Moffett's brothers, and one first cousin, were active members of the Union Army. One of the brothers, David Sutton Moffett, resigned his commission as an officer after only six months owing to disability. Thomas Gatton Moffett, the cousin, was enlisted for only a three-month tour of duty early in the war, serving as adjutant on the company's staff. Joseph Edwin Moffett, just fifteen years old when Fort Sumter fell, joined the Union Army in the Spring of 1864, and was involved in some of the momentous campaigns of the war, including the capture of Atlanta, the March to the Sea with General Sherman, and the capture and surrender of the last significant Confederate Army.

Two other cousins in Kentucky also served in the Union Army: They were two brothers, Simeon Lewis Crain, and John Henry Crain, of Fleming County, Kentucky, sons of William Crain and Rebecca Robinson Moffett. Simeon served as a lieutenant and captain in a Kentucky cavalry unit, but died from disease, December 1, 1863. His younger brother was a hospital steward for a year with another Kentucky cavalry unit.[133]

---

[132]Past and Present of the City of Decatur and Macon County, pp. 732-733.

[133]Again, see Appendix 7 for details regarding the Moffett and Crain men and their service.

11 — William Thomas Moffett
A Full, Colorful and Productive Life [134]

William Thomas Moffett was born on Sunday, February 19, 1826, in a log hut in Sangamon County, on the Illinois prairie, about where the village of Curran would later rise. He was the third child of John Bigham Moffett, a wheel wright, and his first wife, Patsy A. Morgan. The birth apparently took its toll on his mother, and she died within less than six weeks, on Tuesday, March 28. His father, now the sole parent of three children, all under the age of four years, faced hardships hard to imagine from a modern perspective. As an infant, the outlook for William must have been particularly bleak.

There are no records which specifically detail how John Bigham Moffett dealt with the situation of his children, but it is very clear that

A rendering of the unsettled prairie in Central Illinois as it may have appeared in the 1820s.

he must have received the support of other adults in his family who were living in the area. Two of his brothers, William and Thomas, were both living in Sangamon County, but neither were married, and it seems highly unlikely that they were able to provide any significant support in the way of direct care for the three motherless youngsters. It seems more likely that his most immediate help came from his youngest brother, Willis, and/or his sister, Elizabeth, both of whom also lived in Sangamon County, Willis having married in 1825, but Elizabeth not marrying until 1831.

The children were well cared for, as all three survived childhood with good health. On Thursday, May 17, 1827, John Bigham Moffett was married to Pollyana Taylor, who was born in Kentucky May 5, 1809, the daughter of Sangamon County Judge David Sutton Taylor and his wife, Sarah Young. Pollyana would be the only mother William Thomas Moffett ever knew.

William and his family lived in the same area southwest of Springfield for the first ten years of his life. In the mid-1830s, the American economy was seized by a substantial inflationary spiral, and in 1836 the family moved to Springfield where his father attempted to establish a business as a cabinet maker.

---

[134]Much of the specific detail given in this chapter regarding the life of William Thomas Moffett is taken from Past and Present of Macon County (Chicago, 1903), pp. 729-734.

William Thomas Moffett

Helen Lucretia Barrows

Moffett Lineage

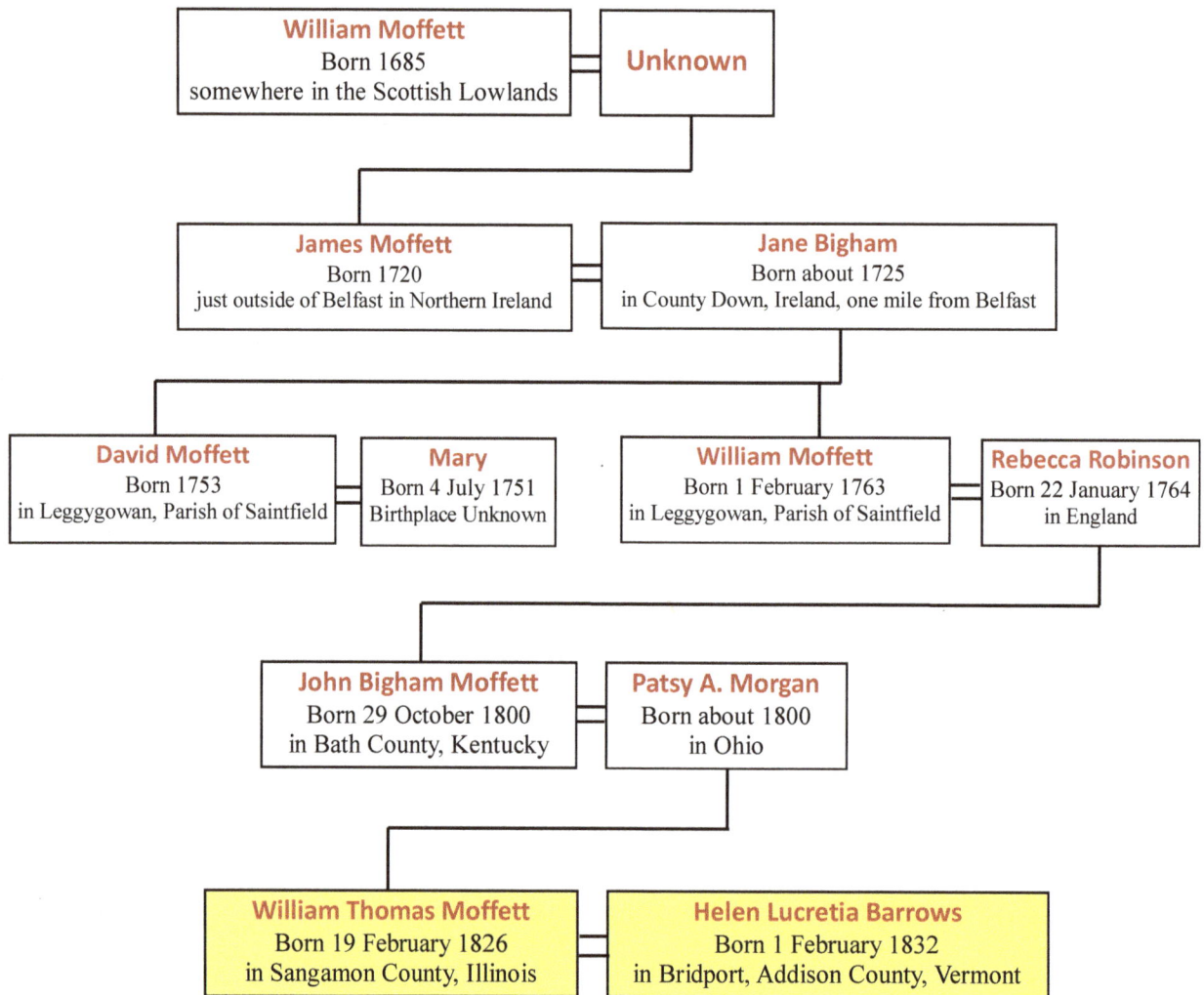

William Moffett
Born 1685
somewhere in the Scottish Lowlands

Unknown

James Moffett
Born 1720
just outside of Belfast in Northern Ireland

Jane Bigham
Born about 1725
in County Down, Ireland, one mile from Belfast

David Moffett
Born 1753
in Leggygowan, Parish of Saintfield

Mary
Born 4 July 1751
Birthplace Unknown

William Moffett
Born 1 February 1763
in Leggygowan, Parish of Saintfield

Rebecca Robinson
Born 22 January 1764
in England

John Bigham Moffett
Born 29 October 1800
in Bath County, Kentucky

Patsy A. Morgan
Born about 1800
in Ohio

William Thomas Moffett
Born 19 February 1826
in Sangamon County, Illinois

Helen Lucretia Barrows
Born 1 February 1832
in Bridport, Addison County, Vermont

It was not successful. In the spring of 1837, a disastrous financial panic struck, resulting in an economic depression which lasted for six years.[135]   About a year after the panic, there was a mild recovery underway in some places, and at this time, seizing on the positive economic signs, the family removed to Rushville in Schuyler County, Illinois. Here William's father built a steam powered flour mill and operated it briefly. By 1841 however, with the economy sagging badly again, that project was abandoned, and the family moved to land in Macon County which had been purchased during the rash of intense land speculation in the mid-1830's. Here they engaged in subsistence farming to produce the food and raw materials the family needed. William helped by working as a teacher for one term in 1843-44. As the economy finally recovered by the mid-1840s, the farm was operated to produce livestock as well as crops.

An agricultural flail, used to separate grain before the development of the thresher.

One might well say that William Thomas Moffett had a "tough life" as a child and young adult. As the oldest male, his labor was relied upon frequently. Even as a very young boy, his labor must have been essential to the family's economic success, and in those years, the prairies in and around Sangamon County were vastly unimproved, and notoriously unyielding to the plow. He labored with no mechanized equipment, plowing with a pair of oxen, and plows which were technologically quite poorly suited for working the prairie. Planting the grain was remarkably slow and laborious work. At the harvest, the earth's fruits were gathered with a flail. St. Louis and Chicago were the nearest markets of any importance. Until he was an adult, there were no railroads of consequence in central Illinois, making delivery of agricultural products to markets a tedious, weeks-long effort.

As had been the case in the life of his grandfather, who settled on unimproved land in Kentucky, William Thomas Moffett's youth was an existence on the frontier. Besides the mighty struggle to make a living, such a living included little in the way of frill or any consumer goods. There was little money, and little to buy. Barter was an economic staple. The 1903 Macon County local history paints an intense detail of life's routines, remarking that William, "wore clothing that was carded, spun, wove and made in his own home; he would hunt wolves, carry corn to the gristmill, fight prairie fires, attend corn huskings and house raisings, and experienced in all its rigors, what no pioneer escaped, the old time 'ague'". This last reference was to malaria, which was a frontier menace from the time of the first European settlement in North America, well into the nineteenth century. The disease was particularly virulent in the South and Midwest.[136]

---

[135]See pp. 74-81 for more information about this economic calamity.

[136]Frederick Merck, *The History of the Westward Movement* (New York, 1980), p. 183.

It was during his younger years that William began his life-long association with electoral politics. At the age of fourteen years, he was intrigued with the Presidential election campaign of 1840. This contest featured the incumbent President, Martin Van Buren, a Democrat of Jackson's branch of the party, and the man who had stitched together the widely successful modern party machine. He was opposed by William Henry Harrison, the nominee of the Whig Party, which had come together with the sole unifying characteristic of opposition to Jackson and his ilk.

Harrison was a man of good credentials, born in 1773 in Tidewater Virginia. His father, Benjamin Harrison, served in the Continental Congress, signed the Declaration of Independence, and was governor of Virginia. The younger Harrison had gained national attention from his early military service in 1811. As governor of the Indiana Territory, he led the militia against an Indian tribal confederacy. His forces were surprised in their sleep at Tippecanoe Creek, a tributary of the Wabash River, but they fought back, defeated the attackers and moved on to destroy their village. Two years later, he had become commander of U.S. forces in the Northwest during the War of 1812, repulsed a British-Indian invasionary force and pursued them into Ontario. His forces went on to defeat them in the battle at the Thames River in 1813, securing the Northwest region for the U.S.

Pro-Whig campaign medals, 1840, showing the likeness of "Maj. Gen. W. H. Harrison" on one side; inscribed above and below the legendary log cabin on the other side are the words, "The People's Choice", and "The Hero of Tippecanoe"

In the run up to the 1840 election, the actors at work favored Harrison over Henry Clay for the nomination, leaving Clay angry and distant from the campaign. Despite the blue hue of his blood, Harrison was portrayed in the 1840 campaign as a military hero, and a man who identified with the common folk, sporting a slogan which referred to his supposed preferences for hard cider and a log cabin. Still, the Clay stamp was on the party, and Old Tippecanoe embraced Clay's vision known as the "American System", including a recharterd national bank, higher tariffs to protect domestic products and federal aid internal improvements.

More than any other factor however, the direction of the electorate was determined by the deep economic depression under which the country had suffered since shortly after Van Buren took office. It was easy for the voters to accept the argument of the Whigs that the financial calamity was the inevitable result of years of Jacksonian policies. The urgency of the issue helped bring out a heavy vote. In addition, the two campaigns fought what is often termed the first modern Presidential campaign, with two well organized parties, using numerous speeches and demonstrations, and lots of printed media. The result was that 80.2 percent of the legally qualified voters cast ballots, a turn out figure which even at the dawn of the twenty-first century stands as the third highest voter participation of any of the Presidential elections in American history.[137]

[137]James M. McPherson and David Rubel, eds., *"To the Best of My Ability", The American Presidents* (New York, 2000), pp. 72-75.

As this election came upon the national scene, with intense feelings of the need for change, and well-orchestrated campaigning, it is not surprising that an impressionable-aged lad was caught up in the drama. William Thomas Moffett attended as many political gatherings as he could and worked for Harrison and the Whigs. The results of the election were doubtless electrifying for the young man, as Harrison won an Electoral College landslide, and the Whigs took solid control of both houses of the Congress.

A further sign that William Thomas Moffett would be a very active player on life's stage came with the discovery of gold in California in 1848. The actual discovery took place in January of 1848 near what is now Sacramento. At first the find was guarded in secrecy, and the news did not even reach San Francisco for two months. Beyond that, it was at first slow to spread. As the year went on, the rumors gradually seeped out of California and across the continent, but the further east they spread, the more widely they were greeted with skepticism. Perhaps in an effort to supply the promoters of Manifest Destiny with a sure-fire rush of American souls to the west coast, in December, President Polk addressed Congress and gave public confirmation that the rumors were apparently true – gold had indeed been discovered and was being mined in California. It worked, and rush was the right word. At the dawn of 1848, there were 14,000 U. S. citizens in California, but four years later, the population had grown by more than 250,000. It was a classical pipe dream of riches hysteria which seized Americans all across the country and many who came to North America from around the world.[138]

The Americans went to California either by sea or overland. Neither approach was quick, easy, a guarantee of success, or free from great risks. Early in the rush, those situated along the east coast tended to take to the sea, sailing south to Cape Horn, into the Pacific, and north to California; or they might sail south to the Isthmus of Panama,

A wagon train, headed west, such as those which carried emigrants to California during the Gold Rush.

disembark, cross that jungle strewn neck of land to the Pacific and wait (sometimes weeks or months) for a north-bound ship to take them to California. Those who would not travel by sea from the ports of the Atlantic or Gulf coasts found their way to St. Louis and St. Joseph in Missouri then faced a trek of another 2,000 miles over plains, mountains and deserts. Whether overland or by sea, under the best of circumstances, the trip itself took four months, which did not include the time necessary to organize, equip, and provision a party of emigrants. Delays might involve bad weather, a particularly treacherous stretch of landscape, difficulties with the indigenous people, and loss or failure of equipment, livestock, or vehicles. These might add a month, or two, or more to the trip.

---

[138]Clyde A. Milner II, Carol A. O'Connor, and Martha A. Sandweiss, eds., *The Oxford History of the American West* (New York, 1994), pp. 198-200.

Prior to 1848, there had not been a great deal of American settlement undertaken beyond the western borders of Missouri and Arkansas, or west of the eastern half of Texas. There were great pressures to expand further west, but to most, the possible rewards did not seem to justify the hardship, expense, and great risk. Yet some did undertake the great challenge. Some did so because they were more adventurous than most; some because they were ignorant of the difficulties they would face; and some, like the Mormons, because they were driven out of their homes and bore a religious fervor which called them to a promised land.

As a consequence, by the time the President confirmed the discovery of gold at the end of 1848, several trails had been blazed to the far west, and some of those who had succeeded in reaching the Pacific coast had published accounts of their trials. Any person who was reasonably thoughtful and prudent could read these accounts and obtain a good general idea of how such migrations should be approached.

Perhaps the most critical fact an emigrant to the far west needed to face was the importance of not undertaking such a trek alone. It was well understood that groups afforded all sorts of advantages – the larger the group the better. This provided for a larger accumulation of resources, and a greater variety of skills and experiences among the members of the party. Thus a person who was bedazzled by the dream of striking it rich quickly with California gold would seek out others with the same dream. This was the easiest part of the entire escapade, as the topic of the gold fields was the hottest one throughout the country. One could not avoid hearing of many others who were planning to make the trip.

CALIFORNIA

AND ITS

GOLD REGIONS;

WITH A

GEOGRAPHICAL AND TOPOGRAPHICAL

VIEW OF THE COUNTRY,

ITS MINERAL AND AGRICULTURAL RESOURCES.

PREPARED FROM

Official and other authentic Documents;

WITH

A MAP OF THE U. STATES AND CALIFORNIA,

SHOWING THE ROUTES OF

THE U. S. MAIL STEAM PACKETS TO CALIFORNIA,
ALSO THE VARIOUS OVERLAND ROUTES.

BY FAYETTE ROBINSON,
AUTHOR OF "MEXICO AND HER MILITARY CHIEFTAINS," ETC. ETC.

NEW YORK:
STRINGER & TOWNSEND, 222 BROADWAY.
1849.

Success depended heavily on the organizational abilities of members of any particular party of emigrants. Those whose strengths in this area were exceptional naturally rose to leadership. The best organizers had the most knowledge of those who had gone to the west ahead of them, and of what worked for them, and what had failed. They knew the advantages and disadvantages of the various routes. They knew the importance of traveling at the right time of the year, so as not to be trapped in the mountains as winter seized them. They also generally had creative abilities, were able to improve upon the successes of others, and to respond well to unforeseen circumstances.

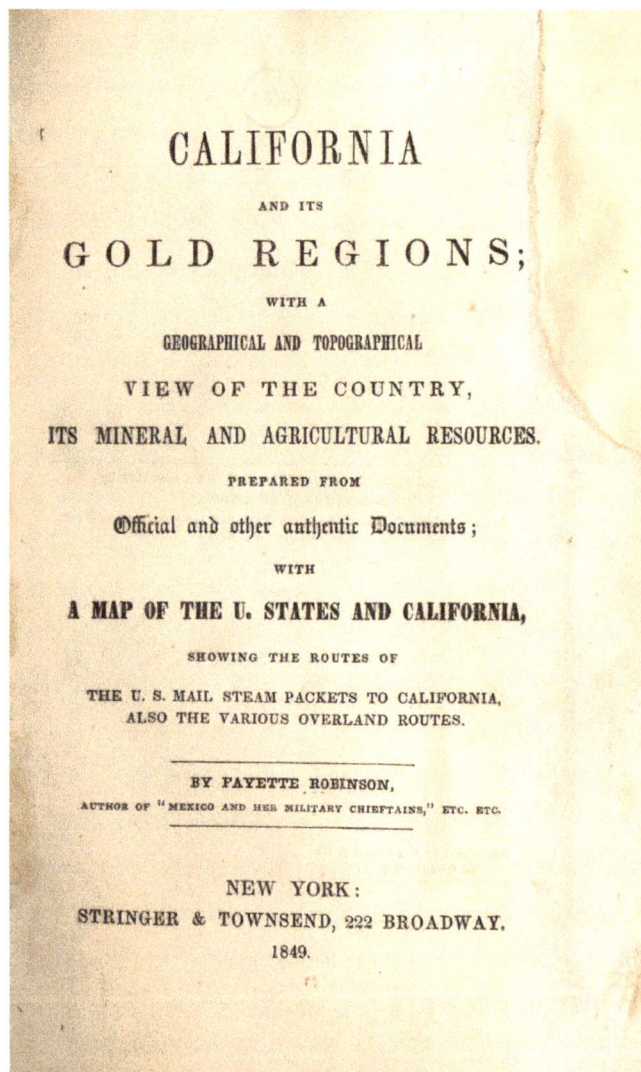

The migrants who rushed to the gold fields in 1849 were later consequently organized into thousands of these large groups. Then, as other groups in similar circumstances had done in North America since Europeans began to settle on this side of the Atlantic, very much in the manner of the Pilgrims with their Mayflower Compact, they adopted (usually in writing) detailed by-laws and rules by which the group would function. They chose leaders carefully. When they set out beyond the edge of the frontier, they were completely on their own. They immediately functioned as an independent community with their own government.[139]

In 1851, William Thomas Moffett responded to the call of the gold fields. We are told in local histories that he was a divisional leader in the overland wagon train with which he traveled to California. That he was chosen for such a position by his comrades indicates a widespread confidence in his abilities, despite his youth. (He would have been in his mid-20s.) That his party successfully reached their destination is a strong indication that such confidence was well placed, and that he and the others among them who assumed the responsibilities of leadership were quite talented.[140]

The details of his participation in this venture also give us a view of his business acumen and unusual common sense. We are told that he did engage in mining briefly when he arrived in California, but he very quickly abandoned it for commercial and mercantile projects. He could see how unlikely it was that any individual miner could significantly better his circumstances. On the other hand, he clearly saw that this massive new population needed food, raw materials, lumber, clothing, tools, and more, and that a large portion of the wealth being drawn from the ground must be directed to those entrepreneurs who met these needs.

William quickly experienced significant success with this approach to business in California. He intended to remain in there, but he had been there little more than a year when, in the fall of 1852, he received urgent pleas from his father to return to Illinois. Even the general return of prosperity had not brought solutions to the family's lingering debts and property liens. Before William's departure for the west, his father had already in fact been forced to abandon the farm in Macon County, and relocate to land near the northern boundary of Christian County, very near the village of Mount Auburn and near Mosquito Creek. His loyalty to his family was remarkable, and William liquidated his enterprises, and headed back to his childhood home. With winter close at hand, an overland return was no doubt not considered at all. He sailed south along the Pacific coast to the Isthmus of Panama, then trekked across that land neck to the Atlantic, then sailed to New Orleans, and returned up the Mississippi River to Illinois. He arrived early in 1853.

The significant amounts of cash William had earned from his enterprises in California were for the most part consumed in the process of paying remaining debts and legal settlements. Most, if not all of his father's endangered estate was preserved.

---

[139]Daniel J. Boorstin, *The Americans, The National Experience* (New York, 1965), pp. 51-89.

[140]Large numbers of these emigrants failed. A few turned back. Far more died en route from hunger, thirst, disease, depredation by natives, or accidents.

At this point William Thomas Moffett settled on a parcel of the family land in Macon County, in what later became Blue Mound Township, and made great effort to improve it. His father and brothers resumed the improvement of the family's other lands there. It appears that the painful experiences of their father in the building trades left the family convinced that farming in crops and livestock provided the best assurance of economic stability, and this was the primary occupation pursued by William and his generation.

In 1854, Erastus Wright[141] of Springfield wrote to his wife's cousin in Vermont – Helen Lucretia Barrows – who had recently (1852) graduated from Vermont's Castleton Seminary, inviting her to come to central Illinois. She had begun a career as a school teacher, but the laws of supply and demand generated much higher salaries for teachers in the Midwest than in the East. Wright pointed this out to her, she accepted the invitation, and late in 1854 she headed for Illinois.

The 1903 Macon County local history advises us that her arrival in Springfield was delayed for two weeks when the train on which she was traveling was overtaken by a fierce snowstorm and was marooned some forty miles south of Chicago. One can only imagine how the passengers must have dealt with this. It is quite unlikely that the spot where the train was stranded was in any settled place, with lodging, food, or other life necessities at hand. It very probably was a life-threatening situation. The fact that the train was unable to continue for two weeks indicates that the weather did not improve in the aftermath of the storm, but remained cold, preventing the melting of the snow for at least many days. Ultimately, she did succeed in reaching Springfield, and for the next year and a half she worked as a teacher in schools in Sangamon and Macon counties.

Helen Lucretia Barrows was born on a Wednesday, the first day of February, 1832 in Bridport, Vermont, the daughter of Josiah Barrows and his second wife, Susan R. Walker. Josiah Barrows' father, Isaac, came to Bridport from Windham County in northeastern Connecticut in about 1780. Bridport is situated on the shores of Lake Champlain, along the western boundary of Vermont, about half way between the state's northernmost and southernmost points. It is nestled along the lake in gently rolling hills, with the ridges of the Green Mountains to the east, and the peaks of the Adirondack Mountains to the west. Helen Lucretia Barrows frequently, and very fondly, spoke of the beauty of her home town and its surroundings.

The New England heritage of Helen Lucretia Barrows includes noteworthy individuals. Her father's mother, Catherine Mayo, was a descendant of John Mayo who came to the Plymouth Colony in about 1638, and in 1655 was installed as the first minister of the Boston church which would later be known as the Old North Church, and the belfry tower of which, 120 years after his installation, would serve as the signaling point from which Paul Revere was warned of movement of British troops out of Boston. Mayo also served jointly at that church for several years with Increase Mather, who may well have been the foremost leader of the Puritans in America.

---

[141]Erastus Wright was born in Bernardston, Massachusetts, in 1779. He settled in Springfield, Illinois in 1821. His many occupations included teacher, school superintendent, merchant, tax collector, pension agent, and land speculator. He became a very wealthy man in Illinois. He was perhaps best known as an early and very ardent abolitionist. His second wife was Lucy Barrows, who was Helen Lucretia Barrow's first cousin once removed.

General Artemas Ward, 1727 – 1800
First Commander-in-Chief of the American Revolution
From the portrait by Charles Willson Peale in Independence Hall

Another was General Artemas Ward, one of the important figures in the late colonial years, but especially in the Revolutionary War and early years of American independence.[142] He was a native of Shrewsbury, Massachusetts, was born there in 1727, and died there in 1800. He served as the first commander of American forces in the Revolutionary War, assuming the command on April 19, 1775, when the militia was called out in Massachusetts to respond to the movement of British troops to Lexington and Concord. The troops were driven back into Boston and besieged there. Two months later came the Battle of Bunker Hill. In July, General Washington, who had been appointed by the Continental Congress subsequent to the outbreak of military action in Massachusetts, arrived to assume the duties of commander in chief.

Artemas Ward had also served in the Massachusetts legislature both before and after the break with England, in his later years rising to the post of Speaker of the House of Representatives. was elected several times to the Continental Congress, beginning in 1779. He worked with Samuel Adams and Nathaniel Gorham on a special committee to deal with Loyalist activities in Hampshire County. After the Revolution, he served as a chief justice of the Court of Common Pleas in Worcester County. As a consequence of his office, at the time of the post-Revolutionary uprising by the followers of Daniel Shays (Shays' Rebellion), Ward was called upon to make a dramatic stand at the Worcester County court house, facing down a party of the rebels.

Yet another was Moses Simmons, one of the Separatist Pilgrims, who had arrived at the Plymouth Colony in the *Fortune*, on November 9, 1621. He had been born January 1, $16^{03}/_{04}$ in Leyden, in The Netherlands, where many of the Pilgrims first sought refuge from religious persecution they had suffered at home in England. He settled at Duxbury and died there in 1691. Sometime in 1855 Helen Lucretia Barrows made the acquaintance of William Thomas Moffett. The circumstances of their meeting are unknown, but it is clear that plans for their marriage were underway within months of their first encounter. In keeping with custom, they would be wed at the bride's ancestral home, in Bridport, Vermont. By the time they had courted, agreed to marry, planned, and arranged all the details, it was October of 1856. The ceremony took place on Wednesday, the fifteenth of that month. They would not be parted by death for forty-five years.

---

[142]On p. 733, the county history entitled *Past and Present of Macon County* (Chicago, 1903) says of Mrs. Helen L. Moffett that General Ward "was her great uncle."

William Thomas Moffett and Helen Lucretia Barrows had eight children, two of whom did not survive infancy. The remaining six (three sons and three daughters) lived well into the twentieth century, and five remained in central Illinois all of their lives. John Bigham Moffett, the third child, from whom this line of Moffetts continues its descent, lived in many parts of the United States, and died in Jacksonville, Florida.

Family Group Sheet – William Thomas Moffett and His Wife, Helen Lucretia Barrows

Husband: William Thomas Moffett		
	Born: 19 Feb 1826	in: Sangamon County, Illinois
	Married: 15 Oct 1856	in: Bridport, Addison County, Vermont
	Died: 11 Oct 1901	in: Blue Mound Township, Macon County, Illinois
	Father: John Bigham Moffett	
	Mother: Patsy A. Morgan	
Wife: Helen Lucretia Barrows		
	Born: 01 Feb 1832	in: Bridport, Addison County, Vermont
	Died: 02 Aug 1913	in: Blue Mound Township, Macon County, Illinois
	Father: Josiah Barrows	
	Mother: Susan R. Walker	
1 M	Name: Edward A. Moffett	
	Born: 11 Jul 1857	in: Blue Mound Township, Macon County, Illinois
	Died: 11 Jul 1857	in: Blue Mound Township, Macon County, Illinois
2 M	Name: Edward Raymond Moffett	
	Born: 11 Oct 1859	in: Macon County Illinois
	Died: 03 Sep 1926	in: Macon County Illinois
	Married: 27 Sep 1872	in: Macon County Illinois
	Spouse: Juliette A. Warrick	
3 M	Name: John Bigham Moffett	
	Born: 13 Jul 1861	in: Blue Mound Township, Macon County Illinois
	Died: 27 Jun 1926	in: Jacksonville, Duval County, Florida
	Married: 30 Mar 1887	in: Cimarron, Gray County, Kansas
	Spouse: Eva Ida Denny	
	Married: 1909	in: Tallahassee, Leon County, Florida
	Spouse: Susan A.	
4 M	Name: William David Moffett	
	Born: 24 Jan 1863	in: Macon County, Illinois
	Died: 18 Sep 1944	in: Decatur, Macon County, Illinois
	Married: 02 Feb 1894	in: Macon County, Illinois
	Spouse: Anna M. Cottle	
5 M	Name: Harry Josiah Moffett	
	Born: 05 Feb 1865	in: Macon County, Illinois
	Died: 21 Oct 1866	in: Macon County, Illinois
6 F	Name: Leonora Antoinette Moffett	
	Born: 18 Apr 1867	in: Blue Mound Township, Macon County, Illinois
	Died: 03 Apr 1952	in: Springfield, Sangamon County, Illinois
	Married: 10 Oct 1888	in: Macon County, Illinois
	Spouse: Edwin Preston Hall	
7 F	Name: Mary Helen Moffett	
	Born: 28 Dec 1868	in: Macon County, Illinois
	Died: 17 Aug 1921	in: Macon County, Illinois
	Married: 01 Sep 1887	in: Macon County, Illinois
	Spouse: Wright Edwin Allen	
8 F	Name: Elizabeth Ann Moffett	
	Born: 18 Nov 1871	in: Macon County, Illinois
	Died: 21 Jan 1954	in: Arcola, Douglas County, Illinois
	Married: 07 Apr 1894	in: Macon County, Illinois
	Spouse: William Newbitt Rugh	

Picture taken in the early to middle 1880s

Standing, left to right: Mary Helen, John Bigham, William David and Leonora Antoinette

Seated, left to right: Helen Lucretia (Mother), Edward Raymond, Elizabeth Ann, William Thomas (Father)

Picture taken very early in the 20th century
Men left to right: Edward Raymond Moffett, William David Moffett & John Bigham Moffetts
Women left to right: Leonora Antoinette Moffett, Mary Helen Moffett & Elizabeth Ann Moffett

An artist's conception of Wall Street in the 1857 Panic

The tragic year of 1857 followed soon on the heels of the marriage of William Thomas Moffett and Helen Lucretia Barrows. The couple's first child, Edward A., died at birth in July. It would be more than two years before they would be blessed with another.

Politically and economically, the mindset of the citizens of the United States rapidly changed in that year. At the outset, the country had, however temporarily, turned its attention from the conflicts of sectionalism and the slavery questions. The economy was booming, and all signs were positive. As the year progressed however, the Kansas question came back to everyone's mind, and the Dred Scot case was decided by the Supreme Court. These and other factors resurrected the fierce sectionalism. Then, as the summer passed, the economic clouds were found to be quickly gathering. In August, the economy began to unravel, and soon a severe panic was underway. On the first day of autumn, Robert C. Winthrop, whose family had been a force in New England politics, religion, and scholarship since his illustrious ancestor led the fleet of Puritans who established the Massachusetts Bay Colony in 1630, was moved to write that, "the world never seemed to me a less hopeful place than in this month of September, in the Year of our Lord 1857."[143]

---

[143]Stampp, p. 213, quoted from a letter from Robert C. Livingston to John H. Clifford, preserved in the *Winthrop Papers*.

Heavy language, and from a man who well understood the forces at work across the continent. In Macon County, Illinois, the fear was just as strong. The Moffett families there had struggled through the hardships of a major economic depression before, and its effects lingered for nearly twenty years. Having just finally fully recovered in 1853, now, less than four years later, they saw the national economy spiraling down again. In 1837 however, while the depression was more severe than what would develop now, there were no accompanying political storm clouds. Now however, the bitter sectional debate had reared its ugly head, and those on the fringes spoke even louder than ever, with threats of violent uprisings, and of secession – the breakup of the federal Union. The Moffetts now dealt with the rapid drops in prices of agricultural goods and the value of their land. This time around however, their debts were quite minimal, and they produced their own basic necessities, so they needed little or no cash. Even though they were not prospering, they were not sinking.

As alarming as the political situation was, the reaction of the moderate voices served as a reassurance that catastrophe was not likely at hand. It was a form of mass denial. Still, the new Republican Party, which had burst on the scene in the 1854 election and stunningly won a plurality of the seats in the U. S. House of Representatives, demonstrated that the climate had shifted, and many more voters were prepared to at least contain slavery than their elected officials had probably realized. The debate was being pushed off of dead center, and the slave holders felt themselves to be on the defensive – hence the discussion of secession.

William Thomas Moffett had abandoned his affiliation with the Whig Party and embraced the Republicans. It seems that his acquaintance with Abraham Lincoln and his admiration for the man and his philosophy had a good deal to do with Moffett's early attachment to Lincoln's party, but the Whigs were in rapid decline across the nation, and most Whigs would eventually join the Republicans whether or not they had any knowledge of Lincoln.

Then came the election of 1858. It would seem a certainty that, if William Thomas Moffett had not already become an activist for the Republicans, he would now do so. As we have seen, he had already been active politically since well before he could vote. In 1858, his home state of Illinois became the site of the central drama of the day. The state's Republican convention had nominated Abraham Lincoln for the U.S. Senate. His acceptance speech stands today as one of the most memorable in American history – the speech in which he declared that, "A house divided against itself cannot stand."[144]   The speech drew major attention across the country.

His opponent was one of the Democratic Party's brightest national stars, the incumbent Senator, Stephen A. Douglas – a northern Democrat, with enormous support in the South, and an eye on a run for the White House in 1860. Lincoln, on the other hand, was a virtual unknown outside of Illinois, and was not all that well known yet beyond Springfield, except to Republican activists, and those who had served with him in the state's legislature.

---

[144]McPherson and Rubel, pp. 118-120.

Lincoln therefore challenged the incumbent to a series of public debates. At first, Douglas refused, no doubt understanding that such debates would give his little-known opponent extensive exposure. He soon reconsidered however, apparently worrying that his refusal would be seen as a lack of confidence and/or fear of Lincoln's competence. The two campaigns then negotiated the details of the debates, agreeing that there would be one debate in each of the state's (nine) Congressional Districts, excepting those of Chicago and Springfield, as each candidate had delivered major speeches upon their nominations by their respective parties, which speeches were well publicized – Lincoln's in Springfield, and Douglas's in Chicago.

The Seven
Lincoln - Douglas Debates
in Illinois, 1858

1. **La Salle County**
   Saturday, August 21, Ottawa, 12,000 people

2. **Stephenson County**
   Friday, August 27, Freeport, 15,000 people

3. **Union County**
   Wednesday, September 15, Jonesboro, 1,400 people

4. **Coles County**
   Saturday, September 18, Charleston (Coles County Fairgrounds), 12,000 people

5. **Knox County**
   Thursday, October 7, Galesburg (Knox College), 20,000 people

6. **Adams County**
   Wednesday, October 13, Quincy, 12,000 people

7. **Madison County**
   Friday, October 15, Alton, 8,000

Macon County
Sangamon County

50 Miles

The omission of these two districts was likely insisted upon by Douglas. The Republicans were strongest in the northern part of the state and Chicago was there. Lincoln was personally strong in his home town of Springfield. Both of these venues therefore would likely draw crowds which were dominated by Lincoln supporters. Furthermore, as the state's largest city (Chicago) and capital city (Springfield), these were the two primary media outlets. Douglas very likely hoped that by omitting them, the press coverage of the debates would be greatly reduced.

Of course, Douglas was wrong. That the individual voters were riveted by the events is clear from the unexpectedly large crowds which turned out at six of the seven venues. All but two of them drew more than 10,000 persons, three drawing 12,000, one drawing 15,000, and in Knox County, 20,000 turned out for the debate which took place on the campus of Knox College.

The two gentlemen were articulate and quick on their feet. Because of their well-publicized opposing views on the central argument of the day, the press in Illinois naturally seized on the debates as a superior way to sell newspapers. The national press well understood that this race highlighted the new political alignment, in which the majority Democratic Party now essentially had the single opposition of the Republicans to deal with. These debates seemed to provide the nation with a primer on the two parties' relative positions. The texts of the debates were carried by newspapers across the country. Newspapers of the time being very highly partisan, those aligned with each side trumpeted the certainty that their man had easily won each debate.

Robert Marshall Root painting of Lincoln-Douglas debate at Charleston, Illinois, Saturday, September 18, 1858. It is likely that William Thomas Moffett was among the crowd there that day.

One can hardly imagine that this campaign passed without including a great deal of activity by William Thomas Moffett. It is not at all difficult to believe that he was activist enough to have been chosen as a delegate to the state's 1858 Republican convention in Springfield where the historic "house divided" speech was delivered. One would also conclude that he very probably was among the onlookers at some of the debate venues. If none other, he would surely have attended the session at Coles County Fairgrounds in Charleston on Saturday, September 18, that venue being just over 50 miles from his home as the crow flies.

Until 1913 and the passage of the seventeenth amendment to the United States Constitution, members of the United States Senate were not chosen directly by the voters, but by the legislatures in the various states. In Illinois, this process was undertaken by a joint session of the two houses of the legislature, voting as if they constituted one body. The vote was taken in January following a national election. In 1858, the people of Illinois elected a legislature whose total numbers of Democrats were slightly greater than those of the Republicans, and the new legislature re-elected Stephen Douglas as expected. None the less, historians have generally agreed that Lincoln drew his own victory from the national exposure he obtained by running against Douglas. Ironically, the 1860 election once again pitted the two Illinois figures against one another, but this time as candidates for the Presidency. For any such activist in Illinois as William Thomas Moffett, this must have been a heady time – especially so when Lincoln won the election in something of a rout of the votes in the Electoral College. 152 electoral votes were needed to win, and Lincoln garnered 180. His nearest competitor, John C. Breckinridge, the Southern Democratic candidate, won only 72, and John Bell, the Constitutional Union candidate just 39. Lincoln's old adversary, Stephen Douglas, the nominee of the regular Democratic Party, received a mere 12 electoral votes.[145] Historians have widely remarked that this election of 1860 was easily the most exciting and colorful campaign since 1840 – the election which had ignited Moffett's fascination with electoral politics.

The excitement must have dimmed quickly after the victory. As most had feared, the election of Lincoln left the southern states feeling that they had lost all control of the forces in Washington. Immediately after the result of Lincoln's victory was clear, the South Carolina legislature called a state convention, analogous to a constitutional convention. Little more than six weeks after the election, the convention was called to order on December 20, and unanimously voted for secession. The nation began to come apart, and the prospect of war loomed very large. The debate was much more heated in other southern states than it had been in South Carolina, and the votes to secede were anything but unanimous, but secede they did, one by one. By February, 1861, seven states had left the Union.[146]

The feeling among the majority in central Illinois had gone from jubilation in November to a sudden sobering in December, and slowly to a very grave concern by the end of January, in expectation of war. Economic recovery was still slow, and now the Mississippi was controlled by a hostile foreign country, and no longer an avenue for commerce for the people of Illinois. William Thomas Moffett, and his brothers and father, now engaging in agricultural production, would not have had markets in Dixie before the secessions, and so they were not directly affected by the incarnation of the Confederacy. In fact, the specter and arrival of war stimulated the northern economy in general, and from this point forward, the economic shadows essentially faded and vanished from Illinois and Macon County.[147]

---

[145]Kenneth W. Leish, ed., *The American Heritage Pictorial History of the Presidents of the United States* (New York, 1968), pp. 381-427.

[146]Morrison, Commager, and Leuchtenburg, pp. 604-607.

[147]Victor Hicken, *Illinois In the Civil War* (2nd edition, Urbana, 1991), pp. 34-50.

In mid-April of 1861, Fort Sumter fell, and the irrepressible conflict was underway. Soon thereafter, four more states seceded, and the Confederate States of America moved their capital from Montgomery Alabama to Richmond, highlighting Virginia's secession and hoping to bring Maryland out of the Union, which would isolate the District of Columbia from the rest of the United States. The new President called for 75,000 volunteers to deal with the military conflict and made it clear that it was his intention to follow through in forcing the departed states back into the Union. The reality of the impending calamity was rapidly coming into focus.

The Bombardment of Fort Sumter, April 13, 1861 (*Harpers Weekly*, April 27, 1861)

As the summer of 1861 approached, many folks in Union states primarily were concerned about the possibility of family members losing their life in combat, or about the negative economic effects they might have to endure. In the Confederacy, there were the added fears that failure to win their independence would result in the abolition of slavery, the attendant economic catastrophe, and the overall loss of their culture and way of life.

These were very weighty issues to be sure. William Thomas Moffett, being a political activist as he was, very likely saw beyond these basic factors. Large numbers of the population already knew how they felt about secession, preservation of the Union, slavery, and the new President. What they likely did not think about much were the serious advantages and disadvantages which the Union and Confederacy had, what the political stratagems were likely to be, and how much resolve lay in the hearts and minds of Americans of the North and the South. He would have had a clearer view than most of what the effects of the war would be, and of the further effects of victory by one side or the other.

He also would have seen that allegiances would not be uniformly decided within political jurisdictions. All around him there in central Illinois, there were those whose families' previous homes were in slave states – as were his own. Many of these neighbors sympathized with the South, would have brought slaves with them to Illinois if they could have, and felt strongly that states' rights were at least as important as – and usually more important than – Negroes' rights. As with the Moffetts, they often had relatives who were now citizens of the Confederate States of America, or who resided in the border slave states, which still clung precipitously to the Union. The northern portions of Illinois were primarily inhabited by Unionists, the southern portions were primarily populated by southern sympathizers, and the central portions were rather evenly divided.[148]

William Thomas Moffett would have foreseen that the resolve of the North would be critical to preserving the Union. He would have foreseen that, in his own state, that resolve would be endangered by its extensive southern sympathies. He would have foreseen that many of his neighbors in Illinois would show little support for the war effort, and in fact would be hostile to it. He would have foreseen that many loyal citizens there would none the less actively campaign against the war, and that many would carry their southern sympathies to the point of engaging in various subversive acts.

Moffett would further have seen that Illinois was not alone in this characterization. He would have known that Indiana and Ohio were directionally split from north to south in the same manner as Illinois. He would have known that Kentucky was sharply divided between Unionists and secessionists, and with his family connections there always in mind, he would have watched the news of the debate over secession there very attentively. Somehow of course, the Kentucky Unionists prevailed, but it was by no means anything like a foregone conclusion that they would.

As secession and political realignments progressed, he also knew that other "southern" states were rife with division. Virginia had seceded, and the Confederate capital moved there, but at the time of secession, a large number of the western counties refused to leave the Union, and instead left Virginia. He would have known that in Tennessee, the state was strongly pro-Unionist in the east, strongly pro-Confederacy or fairly split most of the rest of the counties in the state. He would have had a sense that the majority of the military activity would be on Confederate soil and in a few of the border states, and he very likely would have foreseen the guerrilla civil wars within the larger Civil War, which would develop in such places. He would rightly have foreseen the devastating effects which such situations would have on the civilian populace.[149]

---

[148]*Ibid.*, pp. 20-35.

[149]These guerilla wars were horrific in many spots. Two good histories of these are the following: Noel C. Fisher, *War at Every Door, Partisan Politics & Guerilla Violence in East Tennessee 1860-1869* (Chapel Hill, North Carolina, 1997); Thomas Goodrich, *Black Flag, Guerrilla Warfare on the Western Border, 1861-1865* (Bloomington, Indiana, 1995).

Of the coming pain, anguish, and in many cases desolation, William Thomas Moffett would therefore have had a clearer picture than most. His family and friends would have listened to and respected these views as he expressed them. It could not have been a hopeful time for the Moffetts, who must have found themselves at least somewhat depressed, and filled with pessimism. On the other hand, every description we have of William Thomas Moffett suggests that he would not likely have sunk to despair, even as things became worse.

Indeed, they did become worse – much worse than even the enlightened citizens such as Moffett could have foreseen. As described in chapter 10, the war went on much longer, and brought far more casualties, than anyone had imagined. Many thought perhaps the war would end before the dawn of 1862, but in fact, by that date the bloodbath had just begun. As the year progressed, the following *major* battles took place. Combined, the two sides suffered the number of casualties cited:

Date(s)	State	Action(s)	Combined Union & Confederate Casualties
January 19,	Kentucky,	battle of Mill Springs,	nearly **800**
February 12-15,	Tennessee,	battle, siege, and capture of Fort Donelson,	almost **19,000**
April 6 & 7,	Tennessee,	battle of Shiloh,	well over **23,000**
May 31 to June 1,	Virginia,	battle of Fair Oaks & Seven Pines,	more than **11,000**
June 25 to July 1,	Virginia,	Seven Days Battle, (six encounters)	more than **36,000**
August 28-30,	Virginia,	battles at Groveton and Gainesville, and the second battle of Manassas (2nd Bull Run),	more than **25,000**
September 14,	Maryland,	battle of South Mountain,	nearly **3,500**
September 17,	Maryland,	battle of Antietam,	more than **26,000**
October 3&4,	Mississippi,	battle of Corinth,	well over **11,000**
October 7 & 8,	Kentucky,	battle of Perryville,	more than **7,600**
December 11,	Virginia,	battle of Fredericksburg,	nearly **18,000**
December 31 to January 2, 1863,	Tennessee,	battle of Murfreesboro,	more than **26,000**

Brief Summary of Major Civil War Battles in 1862

The nation was stunned when the news broke of the capture of Fort Donelson. It was a decisive victory for the Union, and a serious setback for the Confederates, but the 19,000 casualties took away the nation's collective breath. The gruesome body count muted what might have been a needed boost for Union morale. Just weeks later came the news of Shiloh, where General Grant and his forces snatched victory from the jaws of defeat. Here the casualties were still more numerous however, and Washington was in an uproar. Finger-pointing was rampant, as loud voices called for retribution. The news changed virtually everyone's perceptions and brought anti-war critics out of the political woodwork. As the mind set was readjusting across the Union and Confederacy, and it seemed that things could not get worse, things did just that. General McClellan's "Peninsular Campaign", boastfully touted by the general as the great and noble mission to capture the Confederate capital (Richmond), went awry. In the "Seven Days Battle" of this campaign the effort slowly came apart and ultimately collapsed, and many of the Union troops found themselves hustling back to Washington to protect their capital from a brewing Rebel attack.[145]

---

[145]Morrison, Commager, and Leuchtenburg, pp. 651-657.

As the summer of 1862 came on, William Thomas Moffett would have well foreseen that to win the war, the South only needed to dispirit the North – to hold them off until the Yankees lost their will. On the other hand, the Union would need to regain control of all the seceding states by successful use of military force. At that moment, the signs were most discouraging. The 36,000 casualties in the Seven Days Battle brought a further sinking in morale – a collective social depression – across the Union states. There also arose the possibility that the Confederates might convince Britain (and/or other European countries) to enter the war in support of the Confederacy, and that would very likely further demoralize the Union, prolong the war, and possibly make ultimate victory impossible.

The staggering casualties and the lack of progress after more than a year of war made it clear that many more troops would be needed, and there was a great deal of discussion in Washington regarding the initiation of conscription. In Richmond, the Confederate Congress had already passed a bill authorizing a draft, just over a week after the calamity at Shiloh.[151] With his keen political sense, Moffett surely would have understood that a draft would be highly unpopular and would create further division among the populace. He would have had grave concern about his own state's support for the President and the war, as the Illinois legislature was under the control of the Democrats, with a large faction known as the "peace Democrats", or "Copperheads". The Democrats had already tried, and partially succeeded, in an effort to hamstring the Republican governor, Richard Yates. Moffett would have seen that should the Democrats continue their control, they could use the unrest which a draft would generate, in their efforts to further weaken the President's hand. He would have foreseen a further threatening of the climate for the elections of 1862 ... and 1864, should the war still be in progress then. Following an election in such an environment, the makeup of the Congress and legislatures, and the party affiliation of the various governors, could well see a reduced presence of Republicans, having a devastating effect on the effort to restore the Union.[152]

Still, Moffett held to his principles and continued his support for the President and the effort to save the Union. It was clear that more needed to be done, and that the war would not end very soon. It was also clear that many more able-bodied men would, sooner or later, as volunteers or as draftees, find themselves in military service.

---

[151]Ward, Burns, and Burns, pp. 128-129.

[152]See Chapter 10 for more details concerning the Copperheads and the peace movement. The Democrats suffered a political setback in the summer of 1862, when voters rejected a new, highly partisan and politically rigged constitution for the state of Illinois, which had been drawn up by a June convention which was under the complete control of the Democrats. However, the 1862 election kept the Illinois legislature in the hands of the Democrats, who continued with, and were emboldened in their efforts to hamstring the Republican governor's efforts to provide troops and other support for the war. Fortunately for Lincoln, who would have, at the very least, been politically weakened and humiliated had his own state pulled the political and military rug out from under him, the adept political moves of Governor shut down the legislature on a legal technicality.

New units were being formed in Illinois and across the Midwest. In August, a unit was being formed at Camp Butler in Springfield, and it would be known as the 115th Illinois Infantry Regiment. William Thomas Moffett and his brother, David S. Moffett, went to Camp Butler and enlisted.

David S. Moffett remained with the 115th for about seven months. The winter of 1862-63 was uncommonly brutally cold, and some 200 men of that unit died or were permanently disabled from exposure while marching and on scouting expeditions. David was one of those disabled, and he was discharged on March 25, 1863. He returned home, no doubt a hero in the eyes of many there. However, he only lived another five years.

As the Civil War geared up, and dragged on, scenes like this were common at ferry points along major rivers. Here new Union army volunteers are marching south to join with active units. Units were generally organized locally, mustered and received initial training there, then traveled together to join their assigned active army units in the field. The point on the Ohio River which is pictured here is the very one where David S. Moffett and the rest of the 115th Illinois Regiment crossed from Cincinnati on October 6, 1862, en route to their assignment in Kentucky. This particular scene recalls the crossing by an Ohio unit.

The fate of William Thomas Moffett was different. When he had only just accomplished his enlistment, he reluctantly withdrew it. Somber and compelling news had come to him from Minnesota, where his recently retired father had gone to live with the father's youngest brother. The health of William's father was gravely deteriorating, and it seemed that his death was near. As the oldest son, William had always assumed a good deal of responsibility for the family's estate. The father had composed a will and named William as the executor. He apparently was the only one of the sons who commanded the respect among his siblings which would be required to settle and preserve the estate with a minimum of controversy.

Mid-September of 1862 must have been a trying time for William Thomas Moffett. On a Saturday, the 13th of the month, his younger brother, David Sutton Moffett, mustered with the 115th Illinois Infantry and departed for the war. The parting was surely difficult, not knowing whether either would see the other again. Two days later, their father died. John Bigham Moffett was 62 years old. His third wife, Nancy, to whom he had been married for twelve years, survived him. Of the fourteen children born to him by his two wives, only four sons and two daughters survived. Besides William and David, the surviving sons were John McDowell Moffett, now 25 years old, married, and the father of one son; and Joseph Edwin Moffett, now just ten days shy of his 17th birthday, still single, and living with his step-mother. His surviving daughters were Elizabeth Ann, the wife of James Y. Taylor, and mother of six children, four of whom were still living; and Laura Amanda Moffett, aged 13 years.

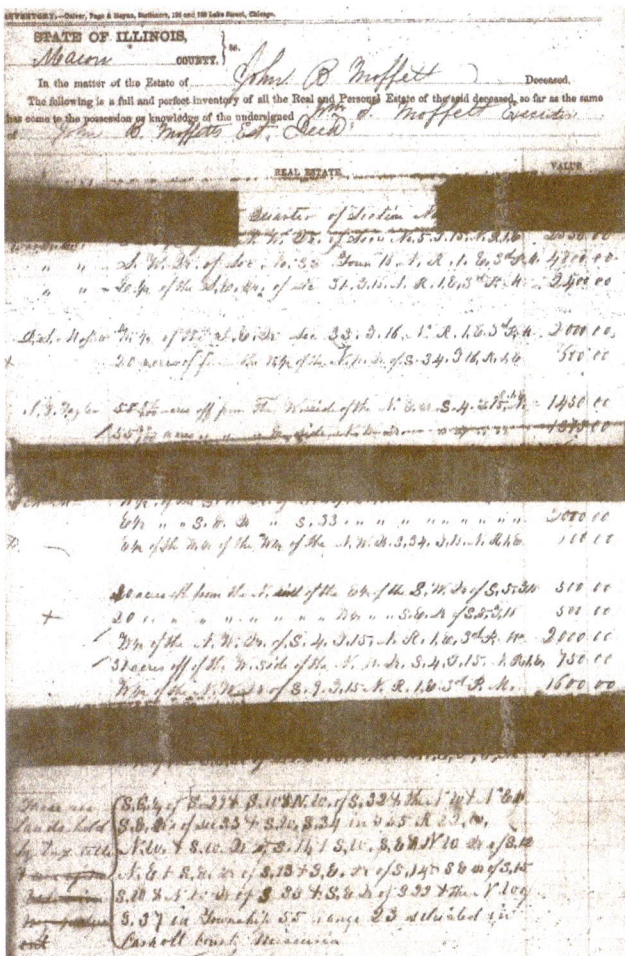

Real Estate inventory from the probate file of John Bigham Moffett, showing some twenty parcels of land in Macon County, and six more in Carroll County, Missouri. The dark, horizontal bands are from cellophane tape, applied to hold the crumbling document together.

The ensuing months were filled with challenges. While daily following the news from the military front, for personal, local, and national interests, William Thomas Moffett operated his farm, and dealt with the family matters. The estate was large, and probate needed to be settled. The war went on, and as detailed in chapter 10, the Midwest in general, and Illinois in particular, were home to a very large number of Copperheads. Generally, Democrats, they opposed going to war to force the seceding states to rejoin the Union. Lincoln repeatedly called for restoration of the Union by military force to preserve the American style of government[153], asserting that it would be lost if states had the option to leave the Union. The Copperheads disagreed with this theory, feeling that the two nations could coexist peacefully without inducing the death of our government style, and that negotiation might eventually bring the Confederate states back into the Union. Furthermore, they felt strongly that the dreadful cost in human life was not at all warranted by the situation.

---

[153]A society in which individual liberty was of foremost sanctity, as were the concepts of the republican form of government – government by freely elected representatives of the people.

Even in a free society, with constitutional guarantees of free speech, and under the best of circumstances, those who oppose a war in which the nation has become involved are often suspect. Their loyalty and patriotism is often questioned, and they become subject to charges of cowardice, espionage, or treason. While there is little evidence to show that most Copperheads were guilty of any of these vices, there were none the less those who did more than speak out, and this cast a dark shadow over all of them. Some actively engaged in very questionable behavior, such as encouraging desertion from the Union forces, or using violence to prohibit conscription officials from doing their job. These activities, and others of similar cast, made it easy for the suspicious war supporters to generate believable (though often false) rumors alleging much more widespread treasonous behavior by Copperheads.

In this atmosphere, there was deeply felt concern. The feeling of the "enemy" and his agents being among them certainly made Union loyalists angry and very uncomfortable. Many – William Thomas Moffett included – had family members in military service and recoiled at the thought of their neighbors somehow abetting the armies which might kill or maim their loved one. Of still greater concern was the possibility of seeing the horror of nearby Kansas and Missouri replayed in and around their own homes. In those states, the war had brought opposing factions to vigilante violence against one another, and the consequences were horrifying. Many locales saw a complete breakdown in civil order.[154]

In Missouri "home guard" militia units were formed to deal with the civil disorder, and similar units were formed in Illinois as a preventative measure. Illinois Governor Richard Yates issued a commission to William Thomas Moffett, probably late in 1862 or early in 1863, when the tide of Copperhead popularity was rising. This instrument authorized Moffett to raise and command such a home guard in his vicinity in Macon County. He did so and bore the rank of captain. There are no extant records of this unit, but no doubt it was a challenging task, requiring leadership, and professionalism of Moffett.

Early in the spring of 1863, William Thomas Moffett's brother, David Sutton Moffett, returned from the army, permanently disabled. His wife and children no doubt needed the assistance of family members, and William no doubt would have played a leading and organizing part in those efforts. When David died in 1868, leaving his widow with four young children, the necessity of such activity became all the greater.

Around Christmas time in 1863, from Kentucky came the news of the death of William Thomas Moffett's cousin, Union Army Captain Simeon Lewis Crain had perished at Nashville on the first of December. Undaunted, on February 1, 1864, Joseph Edwin Moffett, the youngest brother of William Thomas Moffett, now eighteen years of age, enlisted in the 116th Illinois Infantry. Near the end of March, he was mustered in, and from then until he was discharged in August of 1865, he and his unit were involved in considerable combat. (See Appendix 7 for particulars.) Every news story detailing another of the fierce battles which would have involved the younger Moffett must have added new stresses to William's growing portfolio of problems.

---

[154]See Goodrich.

1858

1865

Abraham Lincoln, well acquainted with William Thomas Moffett and his father, and a friend of William's uncle, Thomas Moffett, served as sixteenth President of the United States. His time in office was nearly all coincidental with the fighting of the U.S. Civil War. The stress of serving in the Presidency during this war clearly aged Lincoln very quickly. The above photos of Lincoln were taken in the years shown. They show how terribly the man had aged in just seven years.

The Civil War concluded in the spring of 1865, and the nation's glee was turned to sorrow almost immediately with the assassination death of President Lincoln. The Moffetts no doubt felt more pain than most Americans, having had the privilege of personally knowing the fallen leader.

From the perspective of the Moffetts' personal family losses, while David Sutton Moffett may have ultimately died as a result of his military service, Joseph Edwin Moffett returned safely home, and lived another 53 years. He married Sarah Adams in Macon County in 1867, and they had three children – Harry, Jessie, and Mabel. He was widowed in 1882 but remarried to Nellie Hoyt in 1883 in De Witt County, Illinois. Nellie lived just seventeen months. His final marriage was to Amanda Davis in 1886 in De Witt County, and they had one daughter, Gertrude. Joseph died in 1918 in Chicago, and Amanda survived him.

Cousin John Henry Crain of Kentucky also returned home safely from his service in the war. Shortly afterwards he married and operated a livery business in Fleming County. In about 1875 he removed to Brown County, Ohio, but died there a year later. He left his wife, Mary, and four daughters – Mary, Maggie, Lizzie, and Rebecca.

Decatur Republican.

HAMSHER & MOSSER, Editors

B. K. HAMSHER. | J. R. MOSSER.

DECATUR :

THURSDAY, OCT. 6th, 1870.

Largest Paper—Largest Circulation.

Republican Nominations.

FOR STATE TREASURER,
GEN. ERASTUS N. BATES,
OF MARION COUNTY.

FOR STATE SUPERINTENDENT OF
PUBLIC INSTRUCTION,
HON. NEWTON BATEMAN,
OF SANGAMON COUNTY.

FOR PENITENTIARY COMMISSION-
ERS,
(LONG TERM,)
ELMER A. WASHBURN,
OF MADISON COUNTY.
(SHORT TERM,)
CASPAR BUTZ,
OF COOK COUNTY.

FOR CONGRESSMAN-AT-LARGE,
GEN. JOHN A. LOGAN,
OF JACKSON COUNTY.

FOR CONGRESS—VIITH DISTRICT
GEN. JESSE H MOORE,
OF MACON COUNTY.

FOR SENATOR—XTH DISTRICT,
MICHAEL DONAHUE,
OF DEWITT COUNTY.

FOR REPRESENTATIVES—44th DIS.,
JASON ROGERS,
OF MAROA,
W. T. MOFFETT,
OF BLUE MOUND.

FOR SHERIFF,
GEORGE M. WOOD,
OF DECATUR.

FOR CORONER,
MICHAEL Y. GIVLER,
OF DECATUR.

After the war, the events on the national stage receded to their more normal levels in local and personal importance. Not that there was nothing happening in America. In 1868, for the first time, an American President was impeached (Andrew Johnson). In 1869, the railroads geared up and completed a transcontinental connection. Reconstruction of the South turned out to be a tedious and messy business. The telephone came into use in the 1870s and '80's, and in many other ways, life in America was changing and becoming more complex.

In October of 1866, tragedy struck William and Helen's family. Harry Josiah Moffett, the youngest of their four surviving children, died on Sunday, the 21st day of the month. He would not have reached his second birthday until the following February. He was the second and last of the couple's eight children to die in childhood. No others of the children would pass away until 1921. The last of the family, Elizabeth Ann, the wife of William Nesbitt Rugh, died on Thursday, January 21, 1954, at the age of 82 years, in Arcola, Douglas County, Illinois.

For those who resided in the victorious northern states, the post-Civil-War era was mostly a time marked by prosperity. It appears that, for the most part, the Moffetts had now left their family financial and legal complications behind. William Thomas Moffett's farm, dealing in produce and livestock, was prospering and well enough staffed to allow him more time to participate in civic and political affairs.

William had first run for elective office in 1860, even as the Civil War was underway. He was elected the representative from Blue Mound Township on the Macon County Board of Supervisors for the year 1861. He did not serve in that post again until a six year stretch from 1864 through 1869. He also served several one-year terms in various later years, the last being in 1894.

It appears that his greatest political energy was devoted to service in the Illinois General Assembly – the state's legislature. In 1870, he was nominated by the Republicans as one of their two candidates for two seats, both of which would represent the 44th district in the House of Representatives.

Official Vote of Macon County, Nov. 8th, 1870.

TOWNSHIPS	CON. AT LARGE		STATE TREASURER		SUP'T PUB. INS.		PENITENTIARY COMMISSIONERS				CONGRESS-MAN		STATE SENATOR		REPRESENTATIVES				SHERIFF		CORONER	
	John A. Logan	Wm. B. Anderson	Erastus N. Bates	Charles Ridgley	Newton Bateman	Charles Fanse	Elmer Washburn	Casper Butz	Francis T. Sherman	Thomas Redmond	Jesse H. Moore	A. J. Hunter	Michael Donahue	Wm. H. North	Jason Rogers	Wm. T. Moffett	Wm. E. Nelson	John B. Carey	George M. Wood	George Goodman	M. Y. Givler	Henry Hummell
Decatur—1st District																						
" 2d "																						
" 3d "																						
" 4th																						
Macon																						
Whitmore																						
Maroa																						
Niantic																						
Wheatland																						
Blue Mound																						
Harristown																						
Mt. Zion																						
Hickory																						
Long Creek																						
Pleasant View																						
Milam																						
Oakley																						
Friends Creek																						
Austin																						
Illini																						
Total	1867	1778	1665	1772	1802	1710	1570	1770	1872	1768	1786	1827	1850	1914	1780 48%	1853 50.6%	1963 53.5%	1619 44.7%	1590	1591	1812	1695

Republicans in Roman; Democrats in Italic.

From the *Decatur Republican* newspaper, page 1, November 17, 1870

His fellow Republican on the ticket was Jason Rogers of Maroa (a village in the township of the same name, about thirteen miles north of Decatur in Macon County). The two Democrats in the race were William E. Nelson and John B. Carey. Voters were presented with the four names, from which they could choose no more than two. The winners therefore might be two Republicans, or two Democrats, or one of each. In a real sense, Moffett was competing not only with the Democrats, but with his fellow Republican.

From Moffett's perspective, it was a close race. Nelson was the top vote getter, with 1,953 votes. Moffett garnered 1,853 votes – 100 votes (or 2 % of the total cast) behind Nelson, but only 73 ahead of Rogers who was third. Carey was a relatively distant fourth with just 1,619. So the district elected one Democrat and the Republican Moffett.

can state platform of last fall.

An item of interest to your readers is contained in a bill offered by Mr. Moffett in the House last Friday, which provides for the purchase by the state of the Niantic mastodon. The bill fixes the price to be paid at $500. The committee to which

Paragraph from a long column by a news correspondent in Springfield, regarding the activities in the legislature. *Decatur Republican*, Thursday, February 9, 1871, page 4.

While in the legislature, William Thomas Moffett was clearly active. He was mentioned in numerous newspaper articles regarding his support for, or opposition to, various bills, most of which were of a routine and mundane nature. However, the first such mention of his activities there was neither mundane nor routine. Apparently a preservationist, he filed a bill which would have the State of Illinois purchase the remains of a mastodon, which had been found in Macon County in September of 1870, about six and one-half miles northwest of William Thomas Moffett's farmhouse. See page 136 for a Decatur news story about the find.

Moffett served as a representative in the legislature for four years, stepping down with the beginning of the 29th legislature in 1875. The next year he ran for a seat on the Illinois State Board of Equalization[160] and was elected to a four-year term in that office. This election campaign involved a much larger district than his races for the House of Representatives. The Board consisted of one member from each U.S. Congressional district.

---

[160]The Illinois State Board of Equalization, created in 1867, consisted of nineteen members at the time William Thomas Moffett was elected to it, each member representing one of the state's Congressional districts. The board equalized property tax assessments between counties, increasing or decreasing the total assessment in each county, provided the aggregate assessment in the State is not decreased, and limiting any increase of the same to one per scent. The board also assessed the capital stock of incorporated companies and also railroad property.

Decatur Republican.

HAMSHER & MOSSER, Editors

B. K. HAMSHER. | J. R. MOSSER

DECATUR:

THURSDAY, SEPT. 15th, 1870.

Largest Paper—Largest Circulation.

Republican Nominations.

FOR STATE TREASURER,

GEN. ERASTUS N. BATES,
OF MARION COUNTY.

FOR STATE SUPERINTENDENT OF PUBLIC INSTRUCTION,

HON. NEWTON BATEMAN,
OF SANGAMON COUNTY.

FOR PENITENTIARY COMMISSIONERS,

(WM. H. REED,)

ELMER A. WASHBURN,
OF MADISON COUNTY.

THE NIANTIC MASTODON.

DECATUR, ILL., Sept. 14, 1870.

EDITORS REPUBLICAN: Yesterday morning I, in company with my wife and little daughter Blanche, Dr. Ira N. Barnes and wife, Dr. Chenoweth, Gen. I. C. Pugh and others, visited the tomb of a mastodon, accidentally discovered the other day on the farm of Mr. Correll, situated in Macon county, two miles west, and half a mile south, of Niantic. We started about eight o'clock, and after a brisk ride of two hours through long lanes and between great fields of huge corn, at the end of fourteen miles we halted, about midway between Niantic and Illiopolis, in sight of the T., W. & W. R. R. Hitching our horses to a fence we walked a hundred yards or so across a meadow to a small marsh, or bog, where quite a number of men, under the supervision of Jacob Gross and Mr. Correll, were engaged in exhuming the bones of some monster which has now no living representative, nor has it had for unknown ages.— Stepping to the brink of the well where it was discovered, and looking down only four or five feet, we could see the bed where the body of this monster had reposed undisturbed for perhaps thousands of years.

Leaving the workmen and walking a few steps across the bog, we were permitted to examine the bones that had been exhumed during the morning. Among this group were part of the shoulder blade and fore leg, (these were taken out while we were standing by the workmen), one spinous process, the left under jaw with the teeth, several upper jaw teeth with portions of the jaw bone adhering, one large tusk, and fragments of bones too numerous to mention. I should think the fore leg would measure something over thirty inches in circumference. The spinous process is about eighteen or twenty inches in length, and in circumference about equal to that of a man's arm with the flesh on. The under jaw is huge in proportion. I do not know its length, nor will I attempt to give it, but I should think it had a circumference of at least thirty-six inches, measuring round the molar teeth, which are still set in the jaw. The teeth, on their upper surface, are between three and four inches broad, seven or eight inches long, and eight or ten inches in depth. The upper jaw teeth are still larger than these and are firmly set in the bone, only fragments of which have been found up to this time. The tusks, two in number, are of magnificent proportions, being full nine feet in length and two feet in circumference at their base; they taper beautifully from the base to the apex, and curve gracefully upward, forming nearly a semi-circle. One of these tusks is a splendid specimen. Prof. Worthen, the State Geologist, said he never saw a finer one. The other, we fear, is too badly damaged to ever assume anything like its original form and beauty.

Having now examined everything and given some advice about where to dig for the other parts of the skeleton, (which, by the way, was bad advice, for the labor was mostly fruitless,) we accepted the kind invitation of Mr. Correll to visit his home, about half a mile distant. His house is situated on an elevation overlooking all the surrounding country. The view from this place, in almost any direction, is enchanting. Here we spent a very pleasant social hour with Mr. Correll and his most estimable wife, whom we found to be a great grand-daughter of the venerable Peter Cartwright, a man of daring deeds and imperishable honor, known by everybody in all this land. Many thanks to Mrs. Correll for the most sumptuous dinner she, with her own hands, served up for us. We all partook and were greatly refreshed.

With Mrs. Correll added to our company we re-visited the scene of our morning's investigations, all anxious to witness further developments; but the great quantity of mud, water and quicksand to be removed, made it necessarily uncertain when other parts of the skeleton, more deeply sunken, would be reached; but enough has already been exhumed to invest the place with unusual interest. Here is food for the naturalist, geologist, antiquarian, and all classes of scientific men. We were fully paid for our visit. It is worth a ride of fifty miles to see one of the tusks; but few persons ever saw such a sight.

With reluctance we left this place of wonder for our homes, which we reached just in time to escape a shower of rain.

E. W. MOORE.

The author of this piece, Enoch W. Morre, was a physician who resided in Decatur Township.

RESIGNED.—W. T. Moffett, member of the state board of equalization from the fourteenth congressional district, tendered his resignation to the governor yesterday, and it was accepted. Moffett is senator elect from this district.

The Decatur Daily Review, Vol. VI, #119
Thursday, January 9, 1879.

In the fall of 1878, William Thomas Moffett successfully ran for a seat from the 29th District in the Illinois State Senate. He therefore resigned his seat on the Equalization Board on January 8, 1879 and entered the Senate. His State Senate term was for four years. He did not run for reelection in 1882.

It is intriguing to imagine William Thomas Moffett campaigning, as he must have done many times. We can conclude that he was a talented speaker, for as a candidate, this was easily the most important talent. Through the nineteenth century, and into the twentieth, American political figures had to face the people and speak well in order to make an impression. Before the appearance of the electronic media, the necessity of this talent can hardly be overemphasized. The candidate would move from neighborhood to neighborhood, town to town, and arrange a meeting where he could speak in an effort to convince the listeners to vote for him. In rural areas, where suitable meeting buildings were not readily available, the speaker would commonly find a large stump in a clearing, and stand on the stump to more easily be seen by what crowd might be assembled. Consequently, these became known as stump speeches, and eventually all candidates' speeches bore the name, regardless of the facilities.[156] (It still is in use in the first decade of the twenty-first century.)

Often, the candidate had one chance to impress any single voter. The powers of his oratory and sound reasoning were crucial. The esteemed historian Gilman Ostrander writes of this:

"Oratory was a lawyerly skill that boasted a tradition as venerable as the law itself, extending from Demosthenes to Daniel Webster. From medieval universities to nineteenth-century liberal arts colleges, orations remained an essential part of higher education, and forensic eloquence remained the mark of a cultivated man. Patrick Henry rose to the head of the Virginia bar chiefly on the basis of his forensic ability, being admittedly unqualified for practice so far as his technical knowledge of the law was concerned. The Olympian prestige and appeal of oratory in the ages of Patrick Henry and Daniel Webster is hard to appreciate in our present age of mass media, but in med-nineteenth century America, Emerson observed that 'The highest bribes of society are all at the feet of the successful orator. . . . All other fame must hush before his. He is the true potentate.'"(p. 104) [157]

---

[156]Douglas Harper, "S", *Online Etymology*, page 45, 2001, February 6, 2007 <http://www.etymonline.com/index.php?l=s&p=45>

[157]Gilman Ostrander, *Republic of Letters: The American Intellectual Community, 1775-1865* (Madison, Wisconsin, 1999), p. 104.

"Stump Speaking" painted by George Caleb Bingham in 1854. Through the nineteenth century, and into the twentieth, this was the heart of political campaigns in the times before the electronic media. Presumably the phrase refers to the early years when a speaker, in rural areas, would stand on a large tree stump to be seen above the crowd. The phrase, and its variation "Stump Speeches", are still with us in the twenty-first century's second decade and are especially descriptive of "live" appearances" of political candidates. We can be sure that the likes of William Thomas Moffett, his acquaintance Abraham Lincoln, and virtually every so oriented person who attempted to succeed to political service experienced this sort of campaigning in the 19th century. The famous picture here below is descriptive of another of Abraham Lincoln's seven major "stump speech" debates with Steven A. Douglas. (See the prior one on page 132.)

In general, William Thomas Moffett was obviously highly respected in his community. His service in the political arena and as commander of the Macon County Home Guard unit could not help but earn him some enemies however. Take for example the piece of political invective shown here to the right. The composer of this piece was apparently trying to cast Mr. Moffett as a shirker from military duty. It is not clear whether he thought ill of those who served in the home guard or was ignorant of Moffett's service.

> IN our state senate the other day, Senator Callon, who was a union officer in the late war, proposed an amendment to the Grant retirement resolution to the effect that all the private soldiers be retired on half pay. Senator Moffett offered an amendment to assess the cost of the war on those who took no part in it. This amendment was promptly accepted by Maj. Callon. What was Senator Moffett's rank in the late war.

Moffett's civic service was not limited to the political sphere. He was the first president of the Macon County Farmers' Institute. He was very active in the Cumberland Presbyterian Church, he was among the most generous contributors to the congregation, and he was a frequent attendee at its synod and general assembly meetings. He also served for several years as a member of the board of directors of James Milliken University (Decatur, Illinois).

"Mr. Moffett was a successful farmer and business man. His commodious home and large farm attest his thrift and enterprise."[158] So relates the published county history, and it is obvious that this was true. Still, he had economic struggles to surmount, as anyone did. In 1873, the nation was hit with an economic depression, which affected just about everyone in some way. It was to be the longest depression the country had seen to that point, even eclipsing the duration of that which followed the Panic of 1837. While the 1873 collapse saw immense losses among the moneyed interests, the greatest pain was to be suffered by workers, miners, and farmers. More than a million people were unemployed. It would be six years before recovery took a sure hold.[159]

For Moffett, the pain would have been from the falling prices of the livestock and crops he produced. It does not appear that he had a great deal of debt however, and he was blessed with the additional income from his elected offices for the last years of the depression. There were some eight years of relative prosperity which began in 1879, but for those (such as Moffett) whose livelihood lay in the agricultural sector, economic woes returned in 1887, when that sector was hit with a long, drawn-out depression. It was not until 1893 that additional weaknesses and failures brought the depression to the rest of America, as a classic panic ensued. As normally occurs in American history, the political landscape was as radically impacted as that of the economy.[160]

---

[148]*Past and Present of Macon County*, p. 733.

[149]William S. McFeely, *Grant, A Biography* (New York, 1981), pp. 392-393.

[150]The Democrats had slowly gained strength through the late 1870s and the 1880s, and had now held a strong majority in the House of Representatives. From 1885-1889, for the first time since before the Civil War the country's President was a Democrat, in the person of Grover Cleveland. As a result of the election of 1892, the Democratic party had gained control of both houses of Congress for the first time since the Civil War, and had returned Garfield to office. In 1894, in a dramatic reversal, the despair of the economy brought about the return of Republicans to power in both houses. In 1896, the recovery was still so weak that the Democratic party lost still more ground in Congress, and a Republican was again elected to the White House.

Early in 1901, William Thomas Moffett became ill, and the diagnosis conveyed the fatal nature of the disease. He managed to remain active for only a brief time, but lingered in life until Friday, October 11, 1903, the forty-fourth birthday of his oldest surviving son, Edward Raymond Moffett. He died at his home in Blue Mound Township. He was survived by his wife, and by three sons and three daughters: Edward Raymond Moffett of Blue Mound Township, then aged 44 years; John Bigham Moffett, then aged 42 years; William David; Leonora Antoinette of Springfield, Illinois, wife of Edwin Preston Hall, then aged 36 years; Mary Helen of Illini, Macon County, Illinois, wife of Wright Edwin Allen, then aged 34 years; Elizabeth Ann of Blue Mound Township, wife of William Nesbitt Rugh, then aged 32 years. He also left twenty grandchildren. He was buried in Brown Cemetery, in Blue Mound Township, in Macon County, scarcely a mile from his long-time home.

Helen Lucretia (Barrows) Moffett lived almost ten years after her husband's death. She largely resided in the same home in Blue Mound Township. On Thursday, July 17, 1913, the family held a festive reunion in Macon County, at the home of her daughter, Mary Allen in Harristown.   Nearly forty family members attended, including all six of her surviving children. In the spring of 1913, Helen had been in failing health, and it was decided that, at least for the summer, she would go to reside with the Allens.   It was against the backdrop of this failing health that the reunion was organized.

Helen had gradually grown restless in living away from her longtime home in nearby Blue Mound Township, and she expressed the desire to return there in the fall. She never did. She died at the Allens' home on Saturday, August 2, 1913, little more than two weeks after the festive reunion. She too was buried in Brown Cemetery.

IE DECATUR REVI

ALL HER CHILDREN HERE FOR REUNION

Mrs. Helen L. Moffett's Family Gathers At Harristown.

All six children of Mrs. Helen L. Moffett are expected to be present at the reunion of the Moffett family Thursday at the home of E. Wright Allen at Harristown. They are Mrs. E. Wright Allen, Mrs. E. P. Hall of Mechanicsburg, Mrs. W. M. Rugh of Argenta, J. B. Moffett of Tallahassee, Fla., W. D. Moffett of Boody and E. R. Moffett of Decatur. J. B. Moffett of Florida, his wife and two children have already arrived for the reunion.

Mrs. Helen L. Moffett is eighty-one years old. She is with her daughter, Mrs. Allen, this summer.

About thirty-five people altogether are expected to attend the reunion. It is probable there will be something in the way of entertainment though nothing definite has been arranged.

William Thomas Moffett was an extraordinary man. As a human being, he surely had his share of shortcomings, but it is difficult to find reference to anyone having remembered any of them.

He was born on the frontier, the son of a man who was also born on the frontier. Descended from the enterprising Moffetts of Scotland, he was the grandson of one who fled the caustic religious atmosphere and growing political tumult in Ireland and settled on the American frontier. He never knew his biological mother. He grew up in a place and time where the best schooling was not available, and yet, like the American President with whom he was acquainted, he was a skilled and enthusiastic politician, respected leader and an exceptional orator. He also must have borne an appropriate measure of self-confidence.

He showed an adventurous streak in his nature when he joined the California gold rush. He pulled his father and siblings out of the jaws of economic failure, and succeeded in business himself, despite many trials. He was remembered as one who served, as he was active in all manner of political, civic and religious affairs. Despite his many successes, he is described as one who did not preach about life but endeavored (and usually succeeded) to teach by example. Neither did his successes produce the least ostentation in his ways or his material holdings. He was remembered as one who escaped the too common human failing of hypocrisy. He was well known to be hospitable and generous. Most of all, he was remembered as one who strived to help those who experienced misfortune or distress of any sort.

The Homestead of William Thomas Moffett, in section 32, in Blue Mound Township, Macon County Illinois, late 19th century.

Note the various fashions and technologies of the day. There are three hitching posts in front of the house, and a set of steps for boarding a carriage (also called a surry or buggy). The carriage in the picture is very upscale in design. Likewise, the wagon in the foreground is beautifully decorated. The barn is a food size with three stories, and sports a decorative cupola. The house appears to have a cellar foundation, two above ground stories, and apparently separate chimneys for the kitchen and main central stoves. The yard has a variety of coniferous and deciduous trees planted with nice spacing, and a vine of some sort has climbed the front of the house almost all the way to the crest of the roof. Both the house and barn have lightning rods. The shadows on the ground suggest that we are looking west, in which case, the line of trees in the background, behind and to the west of the house, are perhaps a wind-break to protect the house and barn from the sometimes fierce prairie winds.

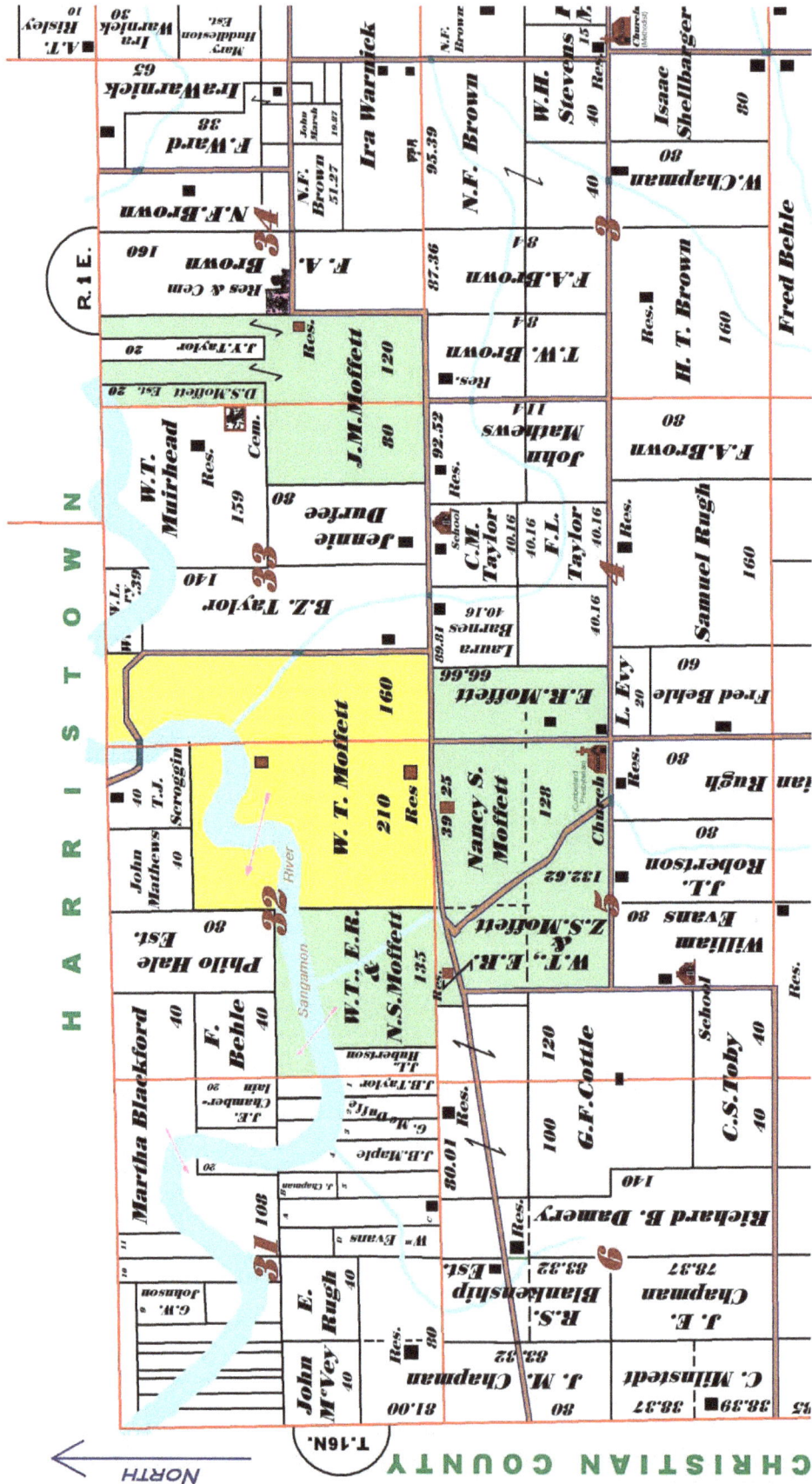

1891 map of the northwestern corner of Blue Mound Township, Macon County, Illinois
The farm owned and operated by William Thomas Moffett is shaded yellow. Other Moffett owned property is shaded in green.

The Moffetts
of Leggygowan & the Land of Lincoln

Appendixes

Appendix 1
The Moffett Family Narrative
Delivered at Christmas, 1900

THE MOFFETT FAMILY

CHRISTMAS, 1900

At the home of Honorable W. T. Moffett, in Blue Mound Township, on Christmas Day, a family reunion was held at which the following historical sketch of the family was read by Attorney John B. Moffett of this city (Decatur, Illinois). It will prove interesting to the many friends of the family.

"Somewhere in the lowlands of Scotland, in the year 1685 was born William Moffatt, our oldest known lineal ancestor. At an early age he moved across the Channel to the north of Ireland, where to him and his Scotch wife were born a number of children among whom was James Moffet, our great, great grandfather.

James was born near Legagowen in 1720, was married at the age of 28, begat the following children: James, born in 1750; David, born in 1753; Jennet, born in 1756; Mary, born in 1758; William, born in 1763; Samuel, born in 1765; Thomas, born in 1767.

William, born in 1763, was our great grandfather. He was possessed of remarkable energy and independence of character. When a very young man, he left his father's home and moved to Dublin, where he learned the silk-weaver's trade. He became an expert in the business, but on account of failing health, he returned home to rest. He soon tired of his father's farm and was tired of his native land. He longed for religious liberty and for civil freedom. The oppression of Ireland was at its height. Large and frequent tax levies were imposed upon its people. Industrial slavery was practically the condition there. America offered opportunity. He decided to embrace it. So in the spring of 1784, when but 21 years of age, our great grandsire, accompanied by his brothers David and Thomas, and David's family, started for America.

It was a perilous journey. There was much sickness on board the ship. The weather was stormy. After a voyage of three months, they landed at Philadelphia.

In Pennsylvania, they resided for 3 years. While there David obtained
a patent of some land in western Virginia. It was here that William
married Rebecca Robinson. While here in Harrisburg, occurred a family
event. It was with reference to the spelling of the surname. The
original way of spelling the name has been changed several times.
William (the Scotchman) spelled it "Moffat" in Scotland. But in some
unaccountable way when he entered Ireland, the name became "Maffet" as
our great grandfather James spelled it, and "Moffet", "Moffitt", and
"Moffatt" as his brothers spelled it. I have in my possession copies of
several letters written by brothers in Ireland to brothers in this
country in which they invariably spell the surname "Moffet", both in
their signatures and in their addresses. But before leaving Pennsylvania,
the brothers here changed the spelling of the name from "Maffet" to
"Moffett" in accordance with the Scotch intonation of the name. Whether
done by a decree of the court, or by common consent of the three brothers
here, I am not informed. But this much I am certain. Ever after our Great
grandfather and all succeeding him, spelled the name "Moffett", which is
the proper spelling of it now.

In 1787 David parted with his brothers in Pennsylvania, and with his
family departed for his lands in the "old Dominion". What became of
him afterward, I am not advised; neither do I know of a single
descendant of his. It occasions surprise and regret that the oldest
of the 3 brothers who came to this country and the only one who
brought a family with him, should be so completely and suddenly lost
upon the record of our family history; and that in the mazes of
subsequent time not a trace of a descendant can be found.

After David's departure William and Thomas moved to Kentucky. They
reached Boonesville[1] in the early part of 1787. Six years later
Thomas was killed in the streets of Lexington at the age of 26.
It happened in this wise: He was riding along on horseback, when two
young sports contested in a horse race. Their horses were high strung
and coming up behind Thomas ran against his horse. His horse jumped,
and in consequence he was thrown off. He landed on a stump, striking
his stomach, from the effects of which he lived but a short time.
Thomas was never married. He was the youngest of his father's family.
At the age of 17, he crossed the Atlantic with his older brothers. He
had the courage at early age to do what those of mature years would
quail before. A mere boy, he bid a lasting farewell to his parents
and native land, passed from under parental roof out onto a stormy
ocean and was borne more than 2000 miles away over its bosom to a land
full of peril. As we contemplate the heroism, the pluck, the
fortitude that animated such a boy, we might well wish he had been
spared to enjoy the reward to which such sacrifice entitled him.

---

[1]This should be Boonesborough. See footnote 49 on page 51 of the main text.

William continued to live in Kentucky until his death in 1826. He founded the Kentucky stock of Moffetts: Ten children were born to him; among whom was our grandfather John B. Moffett. Grandfather was born about 100 years ago in Bath County, Kentucky. In 1821 he moved to Sangamon County, Illinois. Ten years later he moved to Rushville, Ill. And about 1841 moved to Macon County, Ill. where he lived until his death in 1861.[2] He was three times married. By his first marriage with Patsy A. Morgan, three children were born, among them our father who alone survived, and he is now within the shadow of the three-fourths century mark.

I regard Grandfather as a typical Moffett as compared with his ancestors. He was full six feet in height and well proportioned and was endowed with an excellent mind. Whether as a miller or wheelwright, a farmer, or carpenter, he was a success. He inherited the characteristics of the Scotch. In religion a Presbyterian. Honest policies and principles in business were to him as inexorable as the ten commandments. He sometimes overreached in calculations, was at times oppressed and doubtless discouraged, but in no instance did these things swerve him from his moorings of integrity. He possessed a strong character, as a builder not alone of houses, but of society. Without seeking public favors he was a molder of public opinion in his community, and this without intending it. He was stern in his devotion to progress and equally stern in his antipathy to vice. He knew the value of schools and churches in a new country, and he organized them. Crude were the conveniences then for teaching and worship, but here are those organizations still with better buildings and better equipment. In brief he was one of a few who possessed not only a strong arm, but a strong heart, seemed to be singled out by providence to blaze the way through forest and unknown fields that a broader and better civilization may follow in the fullness of time.

----

[2]Probate records, and his tombstone, indicate the year of his death to be 1862.

Appendix 2
The Parish and Town of Moffat in Dumfriesshire

The name – Moffat (the most common spelling in Scotland), Moffett, and several other variations – applies not only to persons, but also to places. In Scotland's Dumfriesshire, where very numerous persons bore the surname, at some point a parish and a town in it were christened with it. Situated on the upper banks of the River Annan, the area includes lovely hills and lowlands. The ocean's closeness provides relatively mild weather for the latitude – never what most in America would call "hot", nor what would be called deep freezes.

Until late in the 11th century, many Scots spoke Gaelic, primarily in the east and north of the country, while those in the southwestern portion were utilizing what became English. Those persons who eventually bore the Moffat surname and resided in the Dumfriesshire parish of that name were in an area where neither Gaelic nor English was predominant. There is no hard evidence to indicate which language

This map shows the shire (county) boundaries as they were before 1974.

the Moffats favored, but the surname/place-name originated from Scottish Gaelic – *Am Magh Fada*. In English, these words mean *the Long Plain*, which probably indicates that it was first a place name and later applied as a surname to a clan.

It may or may not be the case that the clansmen were mostly Gaelic speakers. Excepting in the Highlands, Gaelic disappeared by the 17th century. The Highlands culture then became rather different from that of the rest of Scotland. The division of the languages remained for some time, but beginning early in the nineteenth century, Gaelic steadily declined and today is spoken by only about 1 percent of Scots. In the area which bore the Moffat place-name the very highly dominant language has been English for at least the last seven or eight centuries. While there are no detailed records of exactly when the clan was established and bore the Moffat surname, it is clear to historians that it was certainly no later than the middle of our present Christian millennium.[1]

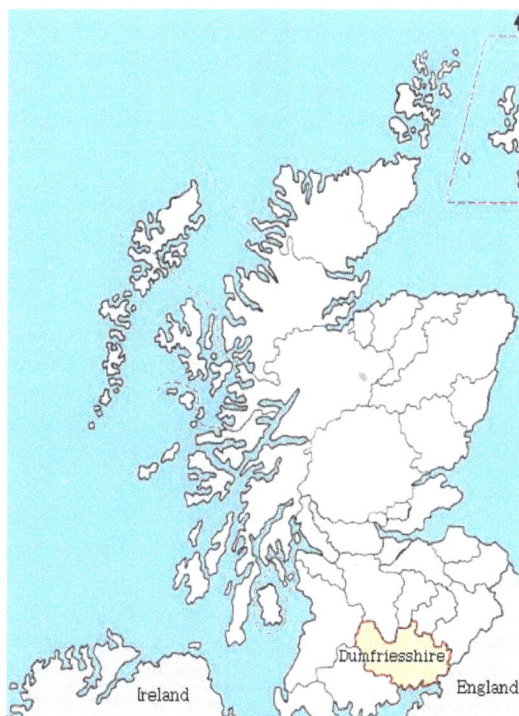

---

[1]*History of Moffat*, Chapter 1, W. Robertson Turnbull, 1871.

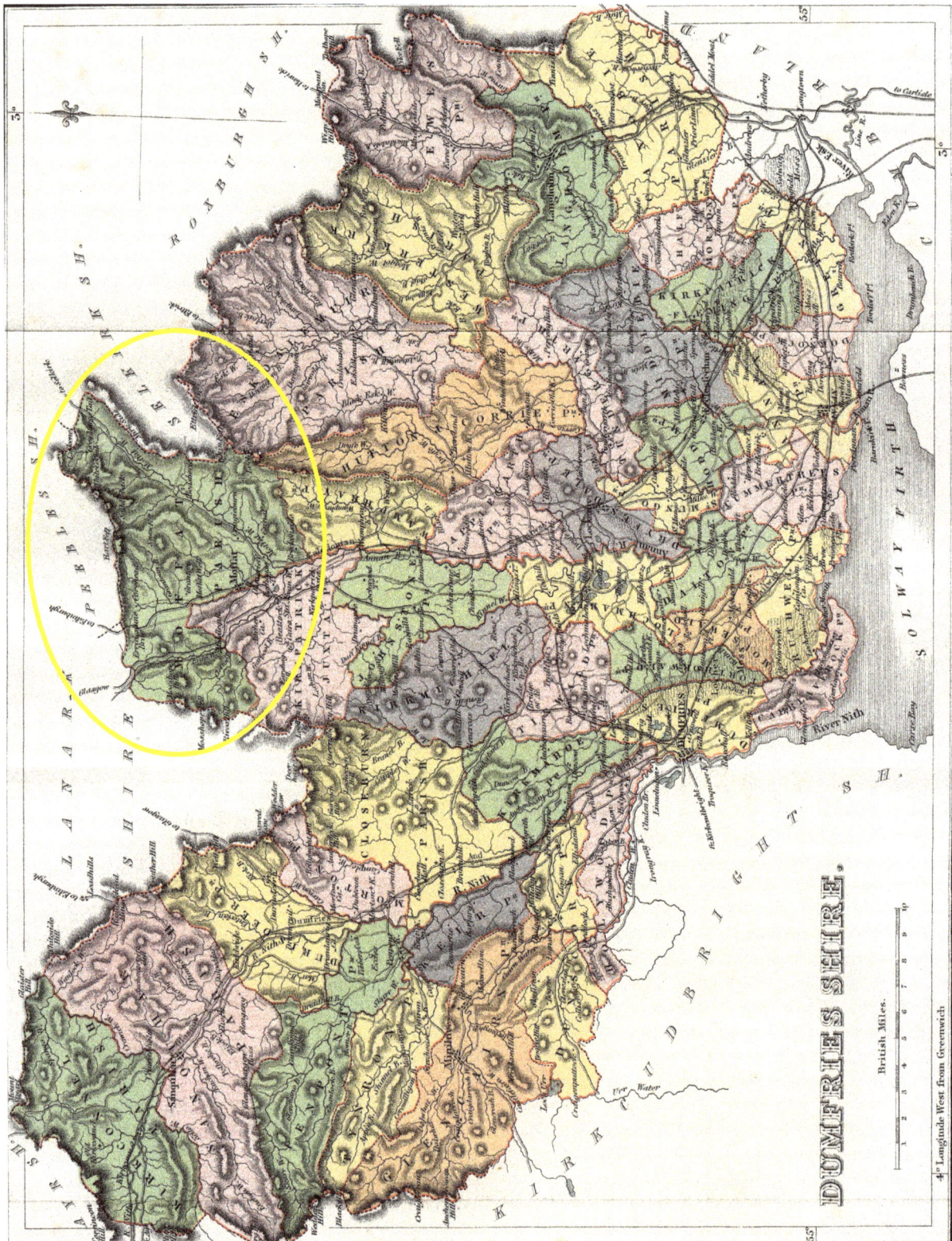

This map of Dumfriesshire shows the numerous parishes, having a background color different from that of any adjacent other parish. The Parish of Moffat is shaded green and circled in yellow. It is situated along the northern border of Dumfriesshire in Scotland, adjacent to the shires of Lanark, Peebles and Selkirk.

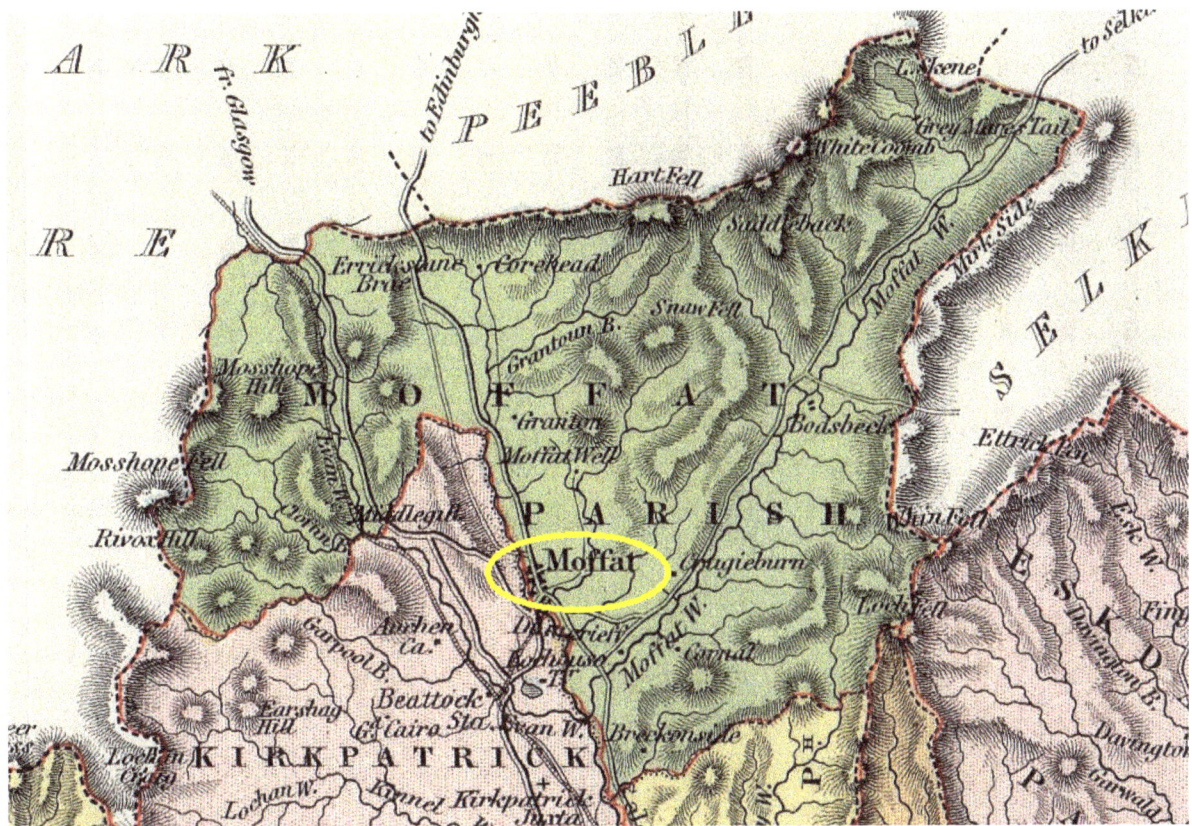

Here are map close-ups of the parish and town of Moffat.

From 1633 Moffat began to grow from a small village into a popular spa town. The sulfurous and saline waters of Moffat Spa were believed to have healing properties, specifically curative for skin conditions, gout, rheumatism and stomach complaints. In 1730 these were complemented by the addition of iron springs. During the Victorian era the high demand led to the water being piped down from the well to a tank and then on to a specially built bath house in the town center (now the Town Hall). The old well was refurbished in the mid-1990s and is still accessible by vehicle and foot. The water smells strongly of sulphur, with deposits on the walls and well itself. At the grand reopening of the well, people visiting it were encouraged to drink a glass of it. When the water was first piped into town for the baths, it was pumped uphill to a tank in the appropriately named Tank Wood, before traveling back downhill to the bath house.

----

[2]The above paragraph, and the information on pages 159 and 162-165 are predominantly taken from Wikipedia.

From 1633 Moffat began to grow from a small village into a popular spa town. The sulfurous and saline waters of Moffat Spa were believed to have healing properties, specifically curative for skin conditions, gout, rheumatism and stomach complaints. In 1730 these were complemented by the addition of iron springs. During the Victorian era the high demand led to the water being piped down from the well to a tank and then on to a specially built bath house in the town center (now the Town Hall), seen here to the right). The old well was refurbished in the mid-1990s and is still accessible by vehicle and foot. The water smells strongly of sulphur, with deposits on the walls and well itself. At the grand reopening of the well, people visiting it were encouraged to drink a glass of it. When the water was first piped into town for the baths, it was pumped uphill to a tank in the appropriately named Tank Wood, before traveling back downhill to the bath house.

Moffat was a notable market in the wool trade, and this is commemorated with a statue of a ram in the town's marketplace which was presented to the town in 1875 by William Colvin, a local businessman. The ram's ears are missing, as they have been since it was first presented.

Air Chief Marshal Hugh Dowding, commander of RAF Fighter Command during the Battle of Britain, was born in Moffat in 1882, and there is now a memorial to Dowding in Station Park. The town also has a recreation park with a boating pond and a memorial to Dowding.

Here below are a few more notable natives of Moffat:

— Dorothy Emily Stevenson (1892-1973) author and cousin to Robert Louis Stevenson.
— *William Carruthers* - botanist
— *James D. Murray* - mathematical biologist
— *James B Niven* and James Fraser - Scottish international footballers (soccer players to us yanks).
— *Danny Bhoy* - Indian-Scottish comedian.
— *Ivor Robson* - the official starter for the Open golf tournament since 1975.
— *Ellen or Helen Hyslop* - was said to have had a daughter, Helen or Ellen Armstrong, fathered by the poet Robert Burns. The gravestone of the mother and her daughter is to be found in the old cemetery. Unusually for Victorian memorials, the name of the father is not recorded on the stone. Ellen died aged 87 and her daughter lived until the age of 98.
— *William Dickson LL.D.* (1751-1823) - was secretary to the Governor of Barbados for 13 years. There he witnessed slaves being brutally treated. From January to March 1792 he toured Scotland from Kirkcudbright to Nairn presenting evidence of the evils of the slave trade. This evidence was summarized in 'An abstract of the evidence delivered before a select committee of the House of Commons'. He wrote a book titled *Mitigation of Slavery* on the subject.

Common multi-residence housing in the Town of Moffat

A cemetery in the Town of Moffat.
Hopefully, there are records which
can advise who is buried where.

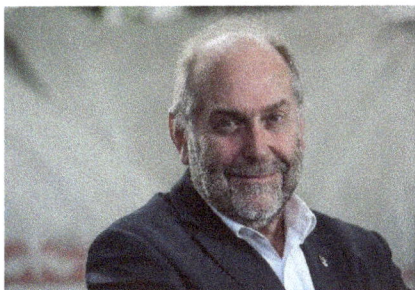

Alastair Moffat, Scottish award
winning writer and journalist

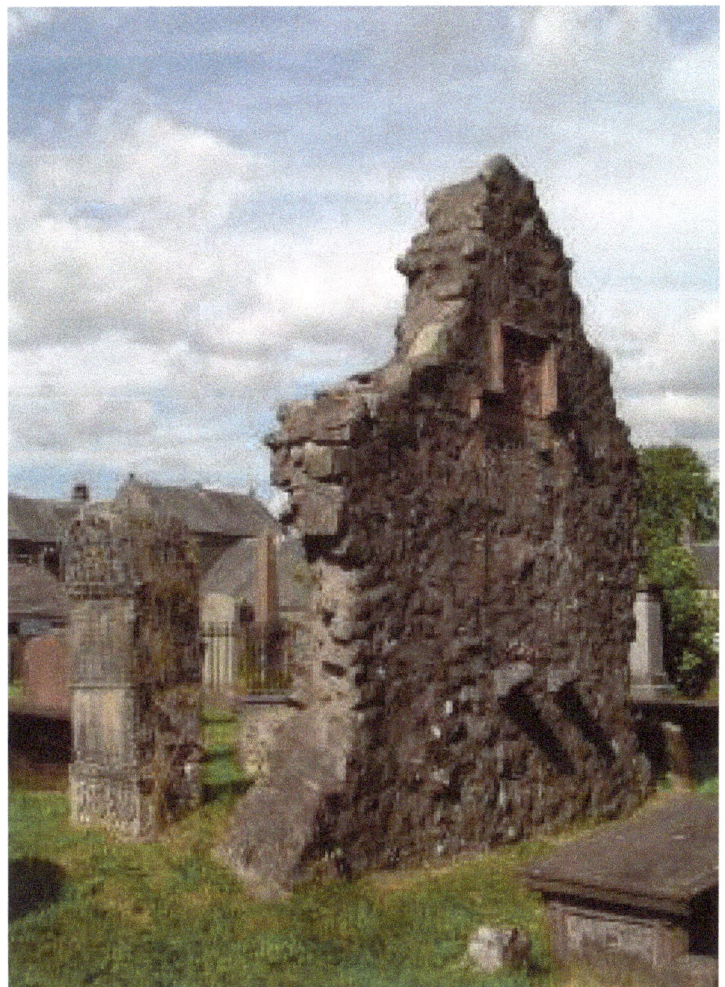

Ruins of a very old Church in the Town of Moffat

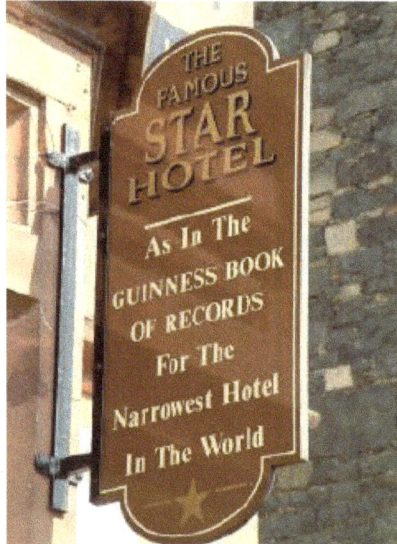

(No more information necessary)

The Gray Mare's Tail Waterfall in the Moffat Hills, near the Town of Moffat

The Town of Moffat viewed from the hills

An earlier image – the Town of Moffat from Coates Hill

These folks are even more famous/infamous:

Robert Burns: Scotland's national poet - often came for the waters and frequented the local bars. His favorite hangout was the Black Bull Inn & Hotel, established in 1568 and still in business. Burns inscribed a window there.

The infamous murderer and alleged grave robber *William Hare* may have stayed in the Black Bull Hotel during his escape to Ireland after tCoturning King's evidence against William Burke, (*Main article West Port murders*).

Dr Buck Ruxton: In 1935, the remains of the victims of the this man – the Lancaster murderer – were found in a stream near The Devil's Beef Tub. A landmark case in legal history, it was the first in which the murderer was successfully convicted using the type of highly sophisticated forensic techniques which are taken for granted in the 21st century. The bridge at the top is still used to this day - near the very top it is a switchback that is not quite wide enough for two vehicles to pass on. The area is colloquially known as "Ruxton's Dump". The bridge from which Ruxton threw the parceled remains has been straightened and widened; Gardenholme Linn, the deep wooded defile into which the packages were thrown is on the east side of the road (A701).

Samuel Wallace: Victoria Cross recipient, died in the town.

John Loudon McAdam (1756-1836): Scottish engineer and road-builder, was born in Ayrshire, but he died in Moffat and is buried there.

Merlin the Wizard: Throughout the western section of The Way – a well-known hiking trail in the hills around Moffat and north into Tweedsmuir – it is reputed that Merlin was frequently to be seen walking the "magical hills". It is to the north in Tweedsmuir at the join of the Tweed and the Drumelzier Burn that Merlin is said to be buried.

John Graham of Claverhouse (1648 - 89) – *Viscount Dundee* – *"Bonnie Dundee"*: Resulting from the reign of Charles I there was an attempt to suppress the Presbyterian style of religion and this led to opposition by those who were known as Covenanters. They were especially strong in the Moffat area and Southwest of Scotland.

Graham was sent by the Scottish Parliament to put down the Covenanters and he was posted to Moffat, setting up his lodgings at the Black Bull Inn. This was a bloody time and anyone found to have taken part in the "blanket preachings" was under threat of severe punishment. This fight was finally won by the Covenanters in 1688, but Claverhouse remained loyal to the Jacobite cause. In a different location and in 1689 Claverhouse lead the Jacobites at Killiecrankie and although they won Claverhouse was mortally wounded. Claverhouse was known by several names, the title 'Bonnie Dundee' is thought to have come from Sir Walter Scott's writings.

Sport and Recreation

Golf: Located high on Coats Hill overlooking the town, the Moffat Golf Club was founded in 1884 and twenty years later Ben Sayers of North Berwick was invited to design the present 18-hole course. It is some 670 feet above sea level and commands splendid views in all directions. He successfully incorporated all the natural undulations and hazards into his 1904 layout, combining deceptive approach shots with subtle greens. Referred to as the Jewel in the South, the 18-hole golf course is one of the most attractive, varied and interesting inland courses in the country. On many of the holes, there is nothing to be seen except the natural beauty of sky and hills. The 390-yard eighth hole is considered the most difficult on the golf course with a fairway in two sections. A deceptively sloping green adds to the challenge. That's followed by the course's signature hole. The 125-yard ninth hole is featured in Britain's 100 Extraordinary Golf Holes. An intimidating par-3, the ground rises - gently at first - before developing into a towering rock face. The saucer-shaped green is only a few yards over the top. The picture below is of the fairway on the 14th hole and the lovely distant hills. The green is just around the corner to the right and out of view.

Rugby: Moffat RFC caters for all ages from 6–80 years. The 1st XV plays in the Scottish Rugby Union league structure. They are also known as "The Rams" after the statue in the High Street. The ground wholly owned by the club is situated at The Holm, Selkirk Road.

Football (Soccer to Americans): Moffat's main football club is Upper Annandale F.C., who represent the town in the South of Scotland Football League.

Hiking etc.: A 53-mile (85 km) long-distance walking route called <u>Annandale Way</u> – often simply The Way – running through <u>Annandale</u> (from the source of the River Annan to the sea) was opened in September 2009. The route passes very close to the town of Moffat, and a diversion from it into the town adds very little in distance. The nearby <u>Moffat Hills</u> offer many walking routes, and the town itself is the closest base for access to these hills.

Historical Interest

Much has been written about Moffat over the years and two books in particular give an interesting insight into how Moffat became the popular tourist town it is today.

For instance, according to *Graham's Social Life of Scotland in the Eighteenth Century*: "In spring there meet round the little wells of Moffat a throng in their gayest and brightest from society in town and country, sipping their sulphur waters and discussing their pleasant gossip ... city clergy, men of letters, country gentlemen and ladies of fashion and the diseased and decrepit of the poorest rank, who had toilsomely travelled from far-off districts to taste the magic waters."

More recently, local historian Emilio Dicerbo, in his *Memories of Moffat* book tells that: "In the seventeenth century, Moffat's transformation from a poor 'Brigadoon'-like village to the beginning of a popular Spa town occurred". The sulphurous waters of Moffat Spa were believed to have healing properties and as more and more people flocked to Moffat, the "healing waters" were piped from the well to the "Baths Hall" (now the Town Hall).

The demands of those early visitors led to the building of a number of hotels. A Georgian exterior can be seen at the Annandale Arms Hotel on High Street.

Later, in 1878, the Moffat Hydropathic Hotel that epitomized the Spa Heritage of Moffat was built. Sadly, it was destroyed by fire in 1921. In its heyday this palatial hotel contained over three hundred bedrooms, an elegantly furnished drawing room and luxurious lounge. The spacious dining room seated three hundred diners in lavish surroundings.

Finally, a fascinating piece of information was reproduced in the local Moffat News: In 1837, Moffat residents were described as 'particularly clean and decent'. The Statistical Account of the year also revealed that:

"Their language is among the best samples of English to be found in any Scottish village." (Some Gaelic was still to be found even this far south.) ... and "There is hardly any smuggling or poaching and low and gross acts of immorality are seldom heard of in Moffat."

The Account also revealed that: Curling, bowling and billiards were popular sports - A subscription and circulating library operated locally - There were 2 daily newspapers - No houses were uninhabited. In addition, Moffat supported 50 weavers, 6 shoemakers, 6 tailors, 8 merchants, 1 watchmaker, 2 bakers, 5 masons, 6 wrights and 1 surgeon.

The town attracts many tourists all year round, both as visitors and as walkers in the surrounding hills. Notable buildings include the Annandale Arms Hotel and Restaurant which recently was awarded 4 stars by Food Review Scotland as well as The Real Food Award by Scottish Hotel Awards 2009.

Shops include the Moffat Toffee Shop and The Edinburgh Woolen Mill, while its restaurants and cafes include The Bombay Cuisine, Claudio's, Arietes, The Rumblin' Tum, The Balmoral and the Buccleuch Arms Hotel and Restaurant. The Buccleuch has also been awarded Gold in VisitScotland's Green Tourism Business Scheme.

There is an official Camping and Caravanning Club campsite (for tents, caravans and motor homes) that is open all year since March 13, 2008. This is situated next to the Hammerlands Centre – a combination garden centre, gift shop, restaurant, fish farm and children's play area with farmyard animals.

Northeast of Moffat is the Grey Mare's Tail waterfall. This "hanging-valley" waterfall is 60 meters high and lies within a nature reserve.

Education

There are currently 301 pupils taught at the Moffat Academy where pupils of Nursery, Primary and Secondary school age are taught. It was in its former location in the north of the town since 1834, but in February 2010 the school moved to a new site in the south-east of the town on Jeff Brown Drive.

———————————

Given that the parish and town of Moffat are in Scotland,
it shouldn't be a surprise that this picture is associated with "Moffat Travel Information".

A view of High Street – the "main drag" – in the Town of Moffat in the late 1930s
The building on the right with the clock tower is the jail. Note the exceptional width of the street!

Some eighty (or so) years later
Here is a very recent view of a part of the street. The building with the clock tower is now named the "Old Jail". We clearly see a good bit more vehicles and there is plenty of space for cars to drive in both directions. They are parked perpendicular to the traffic in the middle of the street among the row of well-spaced trees in the center as well as along the sidewalks.

These two black and white images are probably from the `20s, and the lower may be even a bit earlier. The top photo includes only four cars, and the lower none. It is interesting that this main street's layout is very wide. Whether or not the folks who set it up were anticipating a serious need for such an arrangement we don't know, but it surely turned out to have been a good idea.

This was a community with extensive movement of people travelling up and down on the main road to England. It was made a burgh in 1648 but it was not until the 18th century that it became more popular as a Spa Town. The Town Hall was the location of the sulphur spring baths and Moffat was regarded as the "Cheltenham of Scotland". Moffat has attracted many associated with the Scottish Enlightenment, such as David Hume, James Boswell and James MacPherson. The latter launched the Ossian Fragments while staying in the Moffat House Hotel.

The town's main street is reputed to be the broadest in Scotland and it is home to the famous Colvin's fountain surmounted by the Ram. Also, of note is Moffat House designed by John Adam and built for the Earl of Hopetoun.

In the town of Moffat, a large bronze statue of an anatomically deficient ram proudly surveys the town's central marketplace from his vantage point atop a sandstone fountain. Reputedly, it has more ghosts than it has ears, which would probably make it the world's only haunted, earless effigy of a sheep.

The powerful-looking bronze ram sculpture and drinking fountain were commissioned in 1875 by a local businessman William Colvin as a gift to his native town to commemorate its long association with sheep farming and the wool trade. The artist chosen to undertake the work was a prolific and celebrated Victorian Scottish sculptor named William Brodie, whose most famous work is the statue of a faithful dog, Greyfriars Bobby in Edinburgh.

According to legend, at the unveiling of the statue, a local farmer exclaimed, "It has nae lugs!" which, in English, translates to "It has no ears!" He was right. The otherwise perfect sculpture is totally lacking ears. If the legend were to be believed, the sculptor, Brodie, was so embarrassed at his mistake that he returned to his room in the Annadale Arms Hotel, within sight of the newly revealed sculpture, and hanged himself. The legend says he haunts the hotel corridors to this day, perhaps searching for the lugs. Fortunately for Brodie, and unfortunately for fans of ghost stories, this popular myth has no basis in truth at all, as embarrassed or not, Brodie died at home in Edinburgh six years after the unveiling.

The statue's other alleged spirit presence is that of Colvin who, 19th-century plumbing notwithstanding, is accused of making the tapping noises emanating from the fountain. Unlikely legends aside, the statue is an instantly recognizable symbol of the town, a poignant monument to the area's ties to the wool trade and an impressive sculpture by a much-celebrated artist.[3]

---

[3]The primary source of this information re the ram is Wikipedia.

The Black Bull Inn & Hotel in the Town of Moffat was established in 1568.
Among the famous frequent visitors was Robert Burns,
Scotland's national poet, who once inscribed a window there.

Among the other persons of note who spent significant time at the Black Bull was one John Graham of Claverhouse, Viscount Dundee, shown here.   In the building there is a large sign which reads as here below:

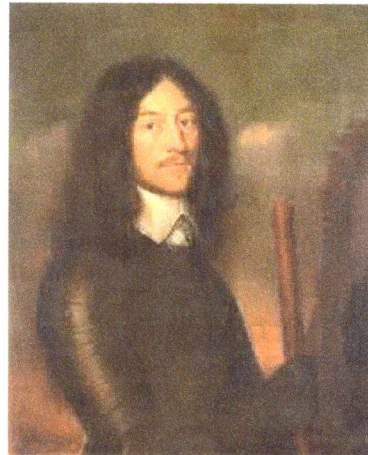

GRAHAM of CLAVERHOUSE made the 'BLACK BULL'
at Moffat his Headquarters from 1683-1685. When he Held the
King's Commission to suppress the Religious Rebels of the South West.
His Ruthless Methods earned him the title of 'Bloody Clavers'
and these Troubled Years the name of {THE KILLING TIME}

Here we see a Town of Moffat specialty: The sheep races!
A group of sheep are selected and dressed up with a white cover. Each animal bears a cute stuffed doll, most of whom fail to remain in position. As one can see here in the background, this draws a good crowd. For some reason, in the autumn of 2018 the shire and town governments decided to forbid further such races.

The Moffat Museum: Founded in the 1970s by a group of energetic Moffat people who wanted to preserve their local heritage for subsequent generations, the Museum was housed in an old Bakehouse until a big modernization project in 2012/13. Then the purchase of an adjoining property enabled the Museum to expand into the additional space. Innovative new projects were embarked upon and the Museum was able to attract loans from the Museum of Scotland and to offer services to local schools and groups. One exciting new exhibit is a working model of the busy Moffat railway station as it was in the 1950s. Admission is free. *www.moffatmuseum.co.uk*

The Moffat Woolen[4] Mill: This is the largest retail shop in Moffat, serving the local community and tourists alike. For two centuries wool has been a dominant business in the town. As part of the Edinburgh Woolen Mill brand, this mill is well renowned for their quality Scottish Knitwear and embrace the Scottish heritage and flavor throughout. At the Mill one can find a variety of goods. Clothing is of course the most prominent, but one can also find Scottish food and produce (Salmon, Haggis, Shortbread, etc.), an impressive selection of whisky and a large collection of Scottish trinkets and memorabilia – the traditional and the unusual. *www.ewm.co.uk*

Moffat Toffee: This goodies shop has a reputation far and wide for the unique and popular taste of its famous product. The recipe is a closely guarded family secret created by the passionate Janet Cook Johnstone and has been around since the late 1800's! The shop itself will have kids drooling and adults delving into their inner child with probably one of the largest selections of confectionery in Scotland if not the UK. You can expect to find old fashioned sweets, handmade chocolates, sugar free range, shortbread, biscuits, fudge, tablet and other up market confectionery. *www.moffattoffeeshop.com*

Such views of sheep in the parish of Moffat and throughout southern Scotland are seemingly everywhere.
On the other hand, it is not at all common to see this many sheep, none of whom are chewing grass.

Finally, one more view of the lovely Moffat hills – and plenty of sheep.

Appendix 3
The Dual Dating System
The Gregorian and Julian Calendars

The execution of the British monarch, Charles I, is usually recorded as having taken place on 30 January 1649 (NS), or 30 January 164⁸/₉, but in contemporary British documents it is recorded as having taken place on 30 January 1648. The parenthetical NS represents the designation, "New Style", which infers that which is he fact, that there was also an "Old Style" (OS). The entry of the year as 164k indicates that the date was 1648 in the old style, and 1649 in the new style. These notations are generally referred to as the dual dating system.

The cause of all this confusion lies in the tale of two calendars. One, called the Julian Calendar, dates from the days of the Roman Empire, and was named for Julius Caesar. The second, known as the Gregorian Calendar, was instituted in 1582, and named for Gregory XIII, then the Roman Pontiff. The Julian calendar was a solar-based system, developed when the scholars of the time knew that the length of one year was365¼ days. That was a very close approximation of the correct number, but it was imprecise. Although the actual difference is only about 11 minutes per year, which amounts to about 18 hours in 100 years, and in 1,000 years it

Julius Caesar

Pope Gregory XIII

amounts to about 7½ days.[1] As a consequence, by Pope Gregory's time, the actual vernal equinox (first day of spring)[2] had moved from the 21st of March to the 11th of that month. Problems had also developed with the assignment of a date for Easter. Because the date was related to the Jewish Feast of Passover, and the Jewish Calendar is a lunar one, that lunar calendar was used by the Church in Rome to fix the Easter date. This calendar had also grown conspicuously out of sync.[3]

---

[1]New York Public Library, *Desk Reference* (New York, 1998), p. 12.

[2]This was a relatively simple, astronomically observable event.

[3] "Gregorian Calendar", October 7, 2006, *Wikipedia*, December 5, 2006
<http://en.wikipedia.org/wiki/Gregorian_calendar>.

Perhaps the most significant fact about the Julian Calendar, for genealogists, historians, and others who conduct research with the help of old documents dated before 1752, is that the first day of a new year was deemed to be March 25. Accordingly, March was deemed to be the first month of the year, and February was the twelfth.[4] Under this system, the 24th day of March in the year 1466, would be followed by the 25th of March in the year 1467. Furthermore, the Latin numbers embedded in the names of the months from September through December were accurate – they were indeed the seventh through the tenth months.

Pope Gregory instituted the development of a new solar-based calendar system, in which there were three areas of change:

JULIAN 1582	October				Gregorian 1582	
Sun	Mon	Tues	Wed	Thurs	Fri	Sat
	1	2	3	4	15	16
17	18	19	20	21	22	23
24	25	26	27	28	29	30
31						

◆First, the calendar of 1582 was devoid of ten days which would normally have been included. The October day bearing the number 4 was followed by a day numbered 15. This returned the vernal equinox to the proper date.

◆Second, to insure that the calendar would not be in error in the future, three out of every four centennial years (i.e., years numbers ending in '00) would not be leap years. Only century years whose numbers were divisible by 400 (i.e., 1600, 2000, etc.) would be leap years.

◆Third, the first day of a new year would hence forth be January 1. January would be the first month of the year, and December the twelfth month.

September 1752						
Su	M	Tu	W	Th	F	Sa
-	-	1	2	14	15	16
17	18	19	20	21	22	23
24	25	26	27	28	29	30

If every country had dutifully agreed to implement the Pope's calendar at the same time, things would be smoother for historians, but they did not. By the time the British established colonies in North America, most other European countries had indeed made the change, but the British still had not. In fact, they did not make the change until 1752. By that time the vernal equinox had drifted back another day, so that when the new system was implemented, the British needed to drop eleven days from the calendar, which they did by eliminating the days between September 2 and September 14.[5]

The most significant problem which all of this creates for the historian and genealogist is the uncertainty of the year in which some events occurred. Keeping an accurate record of dates and timelines is a critical part of the effort to confirm that the information a researcher gathers is correct. These calendar inconsistencies can be a pitfall.

---

[4]Donald Lines Jacobus, "Genealogy and Chronology", Genealogical Research: Methods and Sources, vol. I (Washington, D.C., 1960), Chapter 4. vol. I (Washington, D.C., 1960), Chapter 4.

[5]"Gregorian Calendar".

Consider this example: A man dies in a particular parish in Scotland, and a record of his burial is made in the parish register at the time, indicating he was buried on February 7, 1708. The same parish register also indicates that his child was born April 22, 1709 and baptized 5 days later. Isn't something amiss?   In fact, the only thing amiss in that situation is that the poor fellow did not live to witness the birth of his child. The birth took place just two months and 15 days after the man died. At the time of these events, the first day of 1709 was the day which followed March 24, 1708.

Another example: A New Hampshire man writes his will on July 31, 1676. The colonial records include the will and show that it was presented for probate on January 8, 1676. Contrary to appearances, it is likely that neither of these dates is incorrect. The man composed his will in the fifth month of 1676, died, and then his will was presented in court in the eleventh month of 1676. The question one might well raise concerns what one is to do when a source simply says that an event took place on February 27, 1721. What was the "actual" year in which the event occurred? Was this one month before March 27, 1722? Was it two months after December 27, 1720?

When a researcher verifies the date of an event which took place between January 1 and March 24 inclusive, and it took place in the British Empire before the year 1752, but after 1582 , and then includes it in the results of his/her research, one of two methods of notation is used to demonstrate to the reader exactly what the situation was. One method is to use the abbreviation O.S. or N.S., which respectively refer to "Old Style" and "New Style". Old Style refers to the Julian Calendar – the system in which the first day of the new year was March 25. New Style refers to the Gregorian Calendar, in which January 1 is the first day of the new year. The entry would be written in such a way as this: John Browne, born January 28, baptized February 3, 1698, O.S.

The other method, referred to as dual dating, or "double dating", has nothing to do with two couples sharing an evening out at a movie. It is a notation which essentially writes the date with both years noted. The full old-style year is written, and then a back-slash is entered, followed by the last one or two numbers of the new style year. The above entry would, in this method, be written thus: John Browne, born January 28, baptized February 3, $16^{98}/_{99}$ ... or $169^8/_9$. With this method, one can see that the source was aware of the calendar situation, evaluated the matter, and understood that the event occurred in the year 1698 under the old system, which would have been 1699 in places which used the new system.

One other problem sometimes presented for researchers stems from the ten or eleven days omitted from the calendar when the change to the new system was made. George Washington's birthday provides the most frequently discussed example of this problem. On the day he was born, the calendar of the time read February 11, 1731. That was Old Style, of course. Compilers of the almanacs of the time began recognizing his birthday when he had gained fame as the commander of American forces. They adjusted the date to the New Style, adding the eleven days which had been skipped over in 1752 when the calendar system was changed, and adjusting the year, so that the date generally recognized when Washington was President was February 22, 1732.[6]

---

[6]Tobias Lear (Secretary to President Washington), "A Letter of Response to Col. Clement Biddle", Today in History: February 22, The Library of Congress/American Memory, December 3, 2006 <http://memory.loc.gov/ammem/today/feb22.html>.

As a rule however, the eleven day adjustment is rarely applied when modern historians and genealogists discuss the date of an event which occurred between 1582 and 1752. It was a bit more common in the eighteenth century, when many people were still living who were alive at the time of the transition in 1752. Subsequent to that however, it is generally much simpler to use the date as it was entered in the record, while using the dual dating system as necessary would make it clear to all what the facts are.

One additional snarl to the combat over the Julian vs. Gregorian calendars: In the late 1590s, Scotland's King was George VI. When the Gregorian calendar was established in 1582, the Scots remained with England and Ireland in retaining the Julian calendar, but King George later decided it would be a good idea to at least join the numerous other European countries with January 1 as the beginning of the calendar year. Consequently, the 31st of December 1599 was – in Scotland – followed by January 1, 1600. Three years later the Queen of England and Ireland died, and George became their monarch as well although there being identified as George I. The new king intended to reset the date of the first of the year in his additional territories but especially in England the people there would have no part of that! Consequently, Scotland continued with January 1 while Ireland and England went on with March 25 as the beginning of their year. Until 1752 however, the Scots did not remove ten days from the calendar as Pope Gregory had done, nor did they assume the additional Gregorian omission of the 29th of February in the years ending in "00" (which again excepted the years divisible by 400).[7]

---

[7]In fact there were many other variations regarding countries' calendars. For examples, these countries finally assumed the Gregorian calendar in the following years: Prussia 1610, Japan 1873, Bulgaria 1916, Estonia and Russia 1918, Greece 1923, Turkey 1927 and China 1929. Sweden and Finland had what we might call a double leap year in 1712. Two days were added to February, creating February 30, 1712, because the leap year in 1700 was dropped and their calendars were not synchronized with any other calendar. By adding the extra day in 1712 they were back on the Julian calendar, and subsequently both countries introduced the Gregorian in 1753.

Appendix 4
Statistics Relating to Life Expectancy and Infant Mortality
in Eighteenth and Nineteenth Century America

T he states of health and medicine are the particular elements of technology which had the most profound impact on society. Perhaps the most dramatic illustration of this lies in the history of American life expectancy, at the heart of which has been the rate of infant mortality. Depending upon the specific year and region, 20 to 25 percent or more of the babies died before their first birthday.[1] When the Moffetts settled in Kentucky, the U.S. average life expectancy was still only about 35 years.[2] By 1850, data shows that things had not changed much, for the life expectancy of white males was still only 38.3 years, and of white females 40.5 years. By 1900 white males could only expect to live to the age of 48.23 years, and white females to 51.08 years. Of course, for non-whites the numbers were significantly lower. Even by 1900, non-white males and females only had life expectancies of 32.54 years and 35.04 years respectively. These low numbers are attributable to many factors, but primarily to poor sanitation, inferior nutrition, and most especially to very significant rates of maternal and infant mortality.

This last point is made clear by the breakdown of life expectancy by age. That a newborn white male, whose birth took place in 1850, could only expect to live to the age of 38.3 years, but a white male who, in 1850, had already survived the first ten years of life, could expect to live to the age of 58 years. A white male who was aged 50 years in 1850 could expect to live to the age of 71. years.[4]

---

[1]Gary Walton, "A Brief History of Human Progress", 2004, *Is Capitalism Good for the Poor?*, Foundation for Teaching Economics, January 2006, <http://www.fte.org/capitalism/introduction/index.php>.

[2]Robert N. Butler, M.D., *The Wonderful World of Longevity*, 1 October 2001, International Longevity Center – USA, 2004 <http://www.ilcusa.org/wonder2001.pdf#search='18th%20U.S.

[3]"Graphing Changes in Life Expectancy", *Positively Aging, Unit 5, Our Aging World*, The University of Texas Health Science Center at San Antonio, 2005, <http://teachhealthk-12.uthscsa.edu/pa/pa05/0502.htm>

[4]"Life Expectancy by Age, 1850-2003", *Infoplease*. ©000-2005 Pearson Education, publishing as Infoplease, 23 January 2006, <http;//www.infoplease.com/ipa/A0005140.htm1#5142>.

Clearly, the infant mortality rates – per 1000 live births, deaths in the first twelve months of life – made a huge difference in the overall life expectancy, as did the rates of mortality for children who were not infants, although to a lesser degree. The above reference to Walton's assertion concerning eighteenth-century infant mortality is given in percentage – j20 to 25 percent or more – because the numbers were so high. In the format used for modern rates, this is a staggering 200 to 250 per thousand. Still, in the year 1850, well after William Moffett and Rebecca Robinson had died, and their grandchildren were all adults, the rate for white infants was 217.4 – essentially no better than it had been one-hundred-fifty years earlier.

In 1880, the rate was still 214.8, but at about that time it began to drop consistently. Even so, by 1900 – three generations after the birth of John Bigham Moffett I – the rate was 120.1. It was down to about two-thirds that rate by 1920, and by 1940 it was just a little less than one-third the 1900 rate.[5] By vivid contrast, in the year 2000, the average infant mortality rate for all races in America was down to 6.9 per thousand.[6]

---

[5]"Fertility and Mortality: Infant Mortality Rate", *The Reader's Companion to American History*, Houghton Mifflin Company, 2006, <http://college.hmco.com/history/readerscomp/rcah/html/ah_009701_fertilityand.htm>.

[6]"Infant Mortality Rates, 1950-2002", *Infoplease*. ©2000-2005 Pearson Education, publishing as Infoplease, 23 January 2006, <http://www.infoplease.com/ipa/A0779935.html>.

Appendix 5
The Cumberland Presbyterian Church

Replica of the log house where the
Cumberland Presbyterian Church was founded in 1810

On February 4, 1810 in the log cabin home (near what later became the town of Burns, Dickson County Tennessee) of Rev. Samuel McAdow he together with Rev. Finis Ewing, and Rev. Samuel King organized the Cumberland Presbyterian Church. The divisions which led to the formation of the Cumberland Presbyterian Church can be traced back to the First Great Awakening. Presbyterians split between the Old Sid (mainly congregations of Scottish and Scotch-Irish extraction), who favored a doctrinally-oriented church with a highly educated ministry; and a New Side (mainly English extraction) who put greater emphasis on the revivalistic techniques championed by the Great Awakening. The formal split between Old Side and New Side only lasted from 1741 to 1758, but the two orientations remained present in the reunified church and would come to the fore again during the Second Great Awakening.

At the beginning of the nineteenth century, Presbyterians on the frontier suffered from a shortage of educated clergy willing to move to the frontier. At the same time, Methodists and Baptists were sending preachers with little or no formal training into frontier regions, and were very successful in organizing Methodist and Baptist congregations. In this situation, Cumberland Presbytery in Kentucky began ordaining men without the required educational background, drawing on New Side precedents.

This practice created significant friction between supporters of the Old and New Sides. These were greatly exaggerated when Cumberland Presbytery allowed ministers to offer a qualified assent to the Westminster Confession. They were only required to swear assent to the Confession "so far as they deemed it agreeable to the Word of God." Old Sider sympathizers in the Kentucky Synod (which had oversight over Cumberland Presbytery) sought to discipline Cumberland Presbytery. Consequently, Presbytery and synod were involved in a protracted dispute, which touched upon the nature of ecclesiastical jurisdiction. Ultimately, Kentucky Synod decided to dissolve Cumberland Presbytery and expel a number of its ministers.

The denomination was made up of members of the Presbyterian Church and others in the area left abandoned when Kentucky Synod dissolved the original Cumberland Presbytery and expelled many of its ministers. A replica of Rev. Samuel McAdow's cabin now stands where the three founded the church, and a sandstone chapel commemorating the event has been erected nearby. These two buildings are two of the main attractions in the surrounding Montgomery Bell State Park. An outgrowth of "The Great Revival of 1800", also called the "Second Great Awakening", the new denomination arose to minister to the spiritual needs of a pioneer people who turned from the doctrine of predestination to embrace the "Whosoever Will" gospel of the new church. "Cumberland" came from the area's name (the Cumberland River Valley); "Presbyterian" described the form of government.

By 1900, the Cumberland Presbyterian Church was the third largest Presbyterian or reformed body in the United States.

In 1889, Cumberland Presbyterians were the first Presbyterian body to ordain a woman as a minister – Louisa Mariah Layman Woosley. Perhaps more importantly, Cumberland Presbyterians were the first body in the entire Reformed tradition to recognize the validity of clergy women.

In 1906, the Presbyterian Church (USA) proposed reunification with the CPC in the wake of revisions they had made to the Westminster Confession of Fait in 1903. As a result, a large number of Cumberland congregations re-entered the PC(USA) and those who remained in the Cumberland Presbyterian Church felt antagonistic towards the PC(USA).

The Cumberland Presbyterian Church maintains a four-year liberal arts college, Bethel College, in McKenzie, Carroll County, Tennessee, and a seminary, Memphis Theological Seminary, in Memphis, Tennessee. The Cumberland Presbyterian Center, also located in Memphis, Tennessee, houses other church boards and agencies. Many Cumberland Presbyterians have been attracted back into larger Presbyterian denominations over the years. There is a separate polity for some black Cumberland Presbyterians, the Cumberland Presbyterian Church in America, but relations between the two groups have for the most part been very cordial, and many of its ministers have trained at Memphis Theological Seminary.

Cumberland Presbyterian Congregations can be found all over the United States as well as in several foreign countries (Japan, Hong Kong, Columbia, etc.) but are primarily located in the American South and West.

Appendix 6
The Moffetts and Abraham Lincoln
References to the Moffetts in Lincoln's Papers

There were numerous interactions between the Moffetts of central Illinois and the man who would become the sixteenth – and perhaps most revered – American President. One of the dozens of ongoing projects undertaken by Brown University's Scholarly Technology Group is *The Lincoln Log*, a fascinating timeline of Lincoln documents, drawn primarily from *The Papers of Abraham Lincoln*. The latter, in turn, is a project of the Illinois Historic Preservation Agency and the Abraham Lincoln Presidential Library and Museum, and is cosponsored by the University of Illinois at Springfield. Here is assembled a substantial list of the documents from these sources which connect the sixteenth President with the Moffetts. At the end of each abstract there information regarding the source, printed in green. These include record books (Record), photocopies of original documents (Photocopy), *The Collected Works of Abraham Lincoln*(CW)[1], and other mostly self explanatory citations.

Monday, October 3, 1836 – Springfield, IL
Sangamon County Circuit court opens fall term. Judge Stephen T. Logan presides. Among lawyers present are **Lincoln**, Stuart, Henry E. Dummer, Dan Stone, George Forquer, Samuel H. Treat, Cyrus Walker, Josephus Hewett, Edward D. Baker, and Thomas **Moffett**. Record.

Friday, April 21, 1837 – Springfield, IL
Lincoln acknowledges before Justice of Peace Thomas **Moffett** quit claim deed he gave Hewett & Baker yesterday. Deed Book K, 616.

---

[1]Basler, Roy P., Marion Dolores Pratt, and Lloyd A. Dunlap, eds., The Collected Works of Abraham Lincoln, 9 vols. Springfield, IL: Abraham Lincoln Association; New Brunswick, NJ: Rutgers University Press, 1953

Notes of a Survey Made for David Hart[1]

1836

A part of the West half of the South East quarter of Section 13 in Township 17 North of Range 7 West of the 3rd Principal Meridian and bounded as follows (viz) Beginning at the South East corner of said half quarter. Thence West, with the Southern boundary line, 10 chains and 7 links. Thence North 12 chains & 40 links to the centre of the channel of Rock creek. Thence down Rock creek with it's meanderings to the place where the line dividing the East & West halves of the above named quarter, crosses the same. Thence South with said dividing line to the beginning. Containing 12 acres and 48 hundredths of an acre, more or less.

[Henry E. Huntington Library, San Marino, California.]

[1]In a deposition taken before Thomas Moffett, September 2, 1837, in the case of Elijah Houghton v. Heirs of David Hart, Lincoln said that he had surveyed this tract for David Hart in the fall of 1834, and that Hart had sold the same to Houghton. Lincoln's endorsement on the verso of the document reads "Houghton. Notes for a 12 acre tract," which suggests that the document may have been made from the record in preparation for Houghton's suit against the heirs of Hart, no deed having been executed by Hart.

Saturday, September 2, 1837 – Springfield, IL
Justice of the peace, Thomas **Moffett**, takes the depositions of **Lincoln** and Isaac Gogdal concerning the transfer of a 12.48 acre parcel **Lincoln** surveyed in November 1834. **Lincoln** writes and signs his own deposition and testifies that he surveyed the land for Hart and understood that Hart would transfer it to Houghton. Stuart & Lincoln file the deposition as evidence on behalf of their client, Elijah Houghton, inn Houghton v. Hart et al.   Record: Herndon-Weik Collection, Library of Congress, Washington, DC.

Tuesday, September 5, 1837 – Springfield, IL
Stuart and **Lincoln** are attorneys in Rice v. Lindsay, a case before justice of the peace Thomas **Moffett**. **Moffett** continues the case until the following Tuesday. Stuart & **Lincoln** fee book.

Tuesday, September 12, 1837 – Springfield, IL
Lincoln is one of attorneys in Rice v. Lindsay, a case before justice of the peace Thomas **Moffett**. Stuart & **Lincoln** fee book.

Wednesday, December 6, 1837 – Springfield, IL
Stuart & **Lincoln** are notified by Samuel H. Treat, attorney for complainant in Foster v. Cassidy, that John Calhoun's deposition will be taken December 22, 1837, in Thomas **Moffett**'s office. Record.

Friday, December 22, 1837 – Springfield, IL
Stuart or **Lincoln** probably are in the Thomas **Moffett**'s office during the deposition of John Calhoun in Foster v. Cassidy. The complainant deposed Calhoun and Stuart & **Lincoln** represent the defendant. Record.

Thursday, September 20, 1838 – Springfield, IL
Lincoln writes, signs and files declaration for Silas Harlan, plaintiff, in Sangamon Circuit Court in Harlan v. **Moffett & Moffett**, assumpsit. **Lincoln** writes and signs declaration in Judy v. Manary & Cassity. Herndon-Weik Collection, Library of Congress, Washington, DC.

Lincoln is listed as attorney in Bell v. Mitchell in Tazewell court but case is probably handled by Farnam, Frisby, and D. Stewart, also retained. Record.

Saturday, October 6, 1838 – Springfield, IL
Lincoln writes two bonds for costs in Orendorf et al. v. Stringfield et al. Photocopy.

As complainants' attorney he witnesses deposition of James Adams and Levi Cantrall, witnesses in Orendorf v. Stringfield, at Thomas **Moffett**'s office. Record.

Monday, October 15, 1838 – Springfield, IL
Stuart & **Lincoln** get aggregate damages of $1,637.02 in six default cases: Durley v. Mitts & Ball; Ellis & Vaughn v. Maxey; Trotter v. Phelps; Harlan v. **Moffett & Moffett**; Van Bergen v. Neale; Simpson v. Coffman. They get jury verdict for $15 in Dingman v. Derrin, and $74.15 in Kincaid v. Powers. They file defendant's plea in May v. Weber, Ruckle & Co. Record.

Saturday, July 20, 1839 – Springfield, IL
Stuart & **Lincoln** lose Orendorf et al. v. Stringfield et al. when complainant's bill is dismissed. Three lawyers, Douglas, Stuart and A. Campbell serve on jury which awards damages in Lee & Brady v. Crawford. Thomas **Moffett** is appointed to settle Darling v. Norred & Baker, in which Stuart & **Lincoln** represent defendants. Record.

Thursday, August 29, 1839 – Springfield, IL
Stuart & **Lincoln** file notice that on September 11, 1839 they will take depositions of two witnesses, in Thomas **Moffett**'s office, for use in Orendorf et al. v. Stringfield et al. Record.

Saturday, November 2, 1839 – Springfield, IL
John T. Stuart leaves to take seat in Congress. **Lincoln** signalizes his partner's departure for Washington by entering in firm's book, "Commencement of **Lincoln**'s Administration." Stuart & **Lincoln** fee book.

He does preliminary paper work in two Sangamon Circuit Court cases, writing and signing "Stuart & **Lincoln**" to declaration in Calvin Kendall v. Willis G. **Moffett**, and declaration and praecipe in Henry Kendall v. James F. Hardin & John R. Reagor. Herndon-Weik Collection, Library of Congress, Washington, DC.

He writes to William Doughty of Tremont, where he left his coat. He asks Doughty, keeper of Franklin Tavern, to buy length of coarse domestic (for which **Lincoln** will pay), wrap it around coat, tie in bundle with enclosed addressed card showing, "and hand the bundle to the Stage driver on his trip towards Springfield." Abraham **Lincoln** to William Doughty, 2 November 1839, CW, 1:154.

Thursday, November 28, 1839 – Springfield, IL
Lincoln gets judgment in two cases, Kendall v. **Moffett** for $157.90, and Atwood & Jones v. Douglas & Wright for $568.22. Stockton v. Tolly, suit for damages to cook stove, is dismissed at plaintiff's cost. **Lincoln** appears for defendant. He files answer as guardian in Levica Davenport, adm. of Marshal Davenport v. William Davenport et al. Record.

In Rhoda Hart v. John Sackett et al., he writes answer of Antrim Campbell, guardian, and decree of court approving sale of land. Herndon-Weik Collection, Library of Congress, Washington, DC.

Saturday, November 30, 1839 – Springfield, IL
Lincoln has two cases called. He moves to dismiss Lockwood v. Wernwag and agrees to three months stay of execution in Kendall v. **Moffett**. He writes bill of exceptions for Nathaniel Hay, plaintiff, in Hay v. Lasswell & Mock. He earns $5 for services as commissioner in Huston v. Bogue, on making report. [On March 25, 1840, **Lincoln** took Dendall v. **Moffett** execution to Schuyler County, but nothing was realized for want of bidders. Docket D.]   Record; Herndon-Weik Collection, Library of Congress, Washington, DC.

Wednesday, March 25, 1840 – Springfield, IL
Clerk of Sangamon Circuit Court gives **Lincoln** execution in Kendall v. **Moffett**, directed to sheriff of Schuyler County. Execution Docked D.

(See November 30, 1839.)

Saturday, June 12, 1841 – Springfield, IL

Lincoln takes four notes from Josiah Francis of Athens in settlement of two judgments against Francis in court of Thomas **Moffett**, Sangamon County justice of the peace. [See also November 17, 1845.] Receipt to Josiah N. Francis, 12 June 1841, CW, 1:254.

[Page 251]

Receipt to Josiah N. Francis[1]

June 12th, 1841 -

This may certify that I have this day received of Josiah Francis four notes, hereafter described, upon the following conditions that I am to keep them forty days unless the makers or any of them call and pay, and at the end of that time or any time afterwards am to return them or so many of them as remain unpaid, when said Francis may demand them of me at my office; and any money I may receive upon sd notes is to be applied to one or the other or both of two judgements obtained against sd Francis in one case & against him and others in the other, before Thomas Moffett a Justice of the Peace of Sangamon county. The constable who has the executions in those cases, if they will expire before the said forty days, may return them and take out new, & if they will not expire, he may suspend acting upon them for that length of time.

The notes are as follows - - -
1 on Wesley Eads for, $73.58
1 on William Boyd ds for, 34.06
1 on William Ramsay for, 20.00
1 on Bondurant & Primm for, 12.37.
A. Lincoln

All responsibility of A. Lincoln on this receipt is discharged by receipt & application of money & by return of notes.

Nov. 17, 1845   *Josiah Francis*

---

[1]Handwritten document, owned by Mrs. Logan Hay, Springfield, Illinois.

[2]See letter to Thomas Bohannon, August 7, 1839, n. 3, supra

Wednesday, April 27, 1842 – Springfield, IL

Document Drawn for Joseph Torrey and F. L. King
to William Butler and Thomas Moffett[1]

April 27, 1842

Whereas William Butler and Thomas Moffett are sureties on a certain promissory note for the sum of three hundred

dollars with twelve per cent interest from date until paid payable to P. C. Latham three weeks after date, and bearing date Sept. 22, 1839 to which note Joseph Torr[e]y & Co. are principals, and of which firm I am a member, and

have assumed to pay said note. Now therefore to secure said Butler and Moffett from paying said note or any part thereof I transfer all book accounts due to me to them; and for this same purpose I assign to [them the?] notes of which the following is a list, towit. **[Here is omitted a list of seventy-three debtors with the amount due from each of them].**

And for the same purpose I transfer to said Moffett and Butler a judgement in the Sangamon circuit court in favour of said Joseph Torr[e]y & Co against Folsom Dorset, for the sum of $636.21 cents rendered Nov. 17, 1841.

Said accounts, notes, and judgement, are to be in the custody and control of Turner R. King as the mutual agent of the parties who is to collect the money due thereon as fast as possible, and apply the

[Page 287]
same to the payment of the note first, mentioned, and to return the overplus if any to me.

In testimony whereof I hereunto set my hand this 27th day of April 1842.

F. L. King
By T. R. King

[Illinois State Historical Library, Springfield, Illinois]

[1]Document in Lincoln's hand excepting signatures.

Lincoln draws up agreement between F. L. King, Thomas **Moffett**, and William Butler for paying debts of J. Torrey & Co. Document Drawn for Joseph Torrey and F. L. King to William Butler and Thomas **Moffett**, 27 April 1842, CW, 1:286-87.

Tuesday, July 12, 1842 – Springfield, IL
B. S. Edwards appears for plaintiff and **Lincoln** for defendant in Mason v. Park (SC), appeal from Richland County,. Plaintiff is ruled to file abstracts by tomorrow and case submitted without argument. Record.

Logan & Lincoln give notice they will take deposition of William Porter on July 22, 1842, in office of Justice of Peace Thomas **Moffett**. Photocopy.

Lincoln writes and files, for complainant, notice to take deposition in Wagoner v. Porter et al. He writes and signs bond for security in Blaine, Tompkins & Barrett v. J. D. Allen & Co. Photocopy.

Friday, July 22, 1842 – Springfield, IL
Lincoln is present at taking of deposition of William Porter in office of Thomas **Moffett**. Logan & **Lincoln** are solicitors for defendant in Wagoner v. Porter et al., where deposition is to be used as evidence. Record.

Lincoln fills out summons form in Miller v. Freeman & Freeman. Thomas **Moffett** signs. Photocopy.

Lincoln buys $7.37 worth of merchandise. Irwin Ledger

Wednesday, July 5, 1843 – Springfield, IL
Lincoln takes depositions of three witnesses, at Thomas **Moffett**'s office, in Jackson v. Applegate. Photocopy.

Monday, July 10 1843 – Springfield, IL
Lincoln, Iankiewicz, and Purple continue their investigation of state house accounts until Friday. Logan & **Lincoln**, as attorneys for Seth M. Tinsley, take deposition of Thomas P. Pettus at office of Thomas **Moffett** Photocopy.

Wednesday, April 23, 1845 - Bloomington, IL
Logan & Lincoln collect from Thomas **Moffett** $10 as fee for services rendered Justus Hinkle, deceased. Photocopy.
deceased

[Mrs. **Lincoln**'s hired girl buys yard of "Lawn" (sheer cloth) for 50

Saturday, September 1, 1849 – Springfield, IL

In Graham v. Busher, **Lincoln** & Herndon lose an appeal from a justice of the peace court when the court finds for defendant. **Lincoln** & Herndon represent the defendant in an assumpsit case, Branson v. Stipp. They negotiate a settlement to the case with the plaintiff's attorneys. Please are filed in three other cases. Record.

In **Moffett** v. Lewis and Johnson, a case to resolve accounting differences between former business partners, **Lincoln** writes John B. **Moffet**'s affidavit. Herndon-Weik Collection, Library of Congress, Washington, DC.

Wednesday, September 12, 1849 – Springfield, IL

Lincoln & Herndon represent the complainants in Webster & Huntington v. French et al. Three defendants default. Four defendants file demurrers which the court sustained. In Moffett v. Lewis & Johnson, in which **Lincoln** & Herndon represent the complainant, the court permits them to file a bill of exceptions for appeal to the Illinois Supreme Court. Preparing for the appeal, **Lincoln** writes the exhibits he filed from evidence during the trial, and a memorandum of process by which decision was reached. Then he writes court decree and order granting appeal. In Watson v. Sangamon and Morgan Railroad the court refers the case to arbitrators. Record; Herndon- Weik Collection, Library of Congress, Washington, DC.

At his office, **Lincoln** talks to George D. Berry, from Christian County, who wishes to sue John S. Cagle for trespass. **Lincoln** writes declaration alleging that Cagle caused Berry's daughter Elizabeth to bear illegitimate child and be sick for nine months. **Lincoln** & Herndon ask $1,000 damages, asking clerk of Christian County to file declaration and subpoena eight witnesses. Record. Clayton, John M., U.S. Secretary of State.

Lincoln writes two patronage letters. He recommends Hart Fellows of Schuyler County for Oregon appointment to Secretary of State Claton. He tells Elisha Embree of Indiana that he has already made a recommendation for secretary of Oregon Territory. Abraham **Lincoln** to John M. Clayton, 12 September1849, CW, 2:62; Abraham **Lincoln** to Elisha Embree, 12 September 1949, CW, 2:63.

Wednesday, January 16, 1850 – Springfield, IL

Before the Illinois Supreme Court, **Lincoln** concludes argument for plaintiffs in Webster & Huntington v. French et al. (See January 19, 1850.) Stuart, representing the appellant, commences argument in **Moffett** v. Lewis & Johnson. He is followed by Conkling for appellees. Lincoln represents John B. **Moffett**, one of the appellees. Record.

Thursday, January 17, 1850 – Springfield, IL
Lincoln continues argument on behalf of appellees in **Moffett** v. Lewis & Johnson. Logan concludes arguments in the case on behalf of the appellant. The case involves the right of business partner, Lewis, to compensation for selling patent rights to a churn. At trial, the Sangamon County Circuit Court awarded Lewis $1,000 and ordered him to turn over $1,377.41 to another business partner, **Moffett**. Lewis appealed the case to the Illinois Supreme Court. Record.

Tuesday, March 5, 1850 – Springfield, IL
Lincoln writes, signs and files declaration and praecipe in Lincoln & Herndon v. **Moffett**, a Sangamon County Circuit Court case. He writes a praecipe in Nave for use of Matheny v. McCormack, in which he represents the plaintiff Levi Nave. Herndon-Weik Collection, Library of Congress, Washington, DC.

Wednesday, March 20, 1850 – Springfield, IL
Five **Lincoln** & Herndon cases come before Circuit Court. In one they are awarded judgment of $90; two are dismissed; pleas are filed in fourth. In fifth case – Lincoln & Herndon v. **Moffett** – they sue for fee of $150 for legal services. By agreement they are awarded $75 and costs. Record; William H. Townsend, **Lincoln** the Litigant (Boston: Houghton Mifflin, 1925), 19-20.

Monday, March 24, 1851 – Springfield, IL
Enyart v. McAtee, chancery case continued from April 1, 1850 is tried without jury in Circuit Court. **Lincoln**, Herndon & Ferguson represent complainant. Court takes case under advisement. People v. McHenry, recognizance to keep peace, is dismissed. In Watson & **Moffett** v. Gardner et al., Logan, **Lincoln** & Herndon, for complainants, argue defendants' motion to overrule their deposition. Record.

Lincoln and Herndon acquire land as settlement of judgment won March20, 1850 against John B. **Moffett**. Executive File.

Tuesday, March 25, 1851 – Springfield, IL
Defendants' motion in Watson & **Moffett** v. Gardner et al. is overruled. **Lincoln** & Herndon's motion for new trial in People v. McHenry & Graves is denied and McHenry is fined $50 and costs. Representing complainants in Gilman et al v. Hamilton et al. v. Hamilton et al., **Lincoln** and Smith file Supreme Court order remanding case. Enos v. Wright et al. is continued. Record.

Lincoln writes, has sworn and files separate answers of several defendants in Enos v. Wright et al. Herndon-Weik Collection, Library of Congress, Washington, DC.

For Dewitt County case, Twining v. Cundiff, he writes and signs, for plaintiff, bill and process, and files by mail in Clinton. Photocopy.

Thursday, June 26, 1851 – Springfield, IL
Lincoln writes and files in Sangamon Circuit Court mortgage foreclosure bill Baker v. **Moffett** & Allen, and fills out summons form. Herndon-Weik Collection, Library of Congress, Washington, DC.

Saturday, July 5, 1851 – Springfield, IL
Lincoln writes sheriff's return in Baker v. **Moffett** & Allen. Herndon-Weik Collection, Library of Congress, Washington, DC.

Thursday, November 20, 1851 – Springfield, IL
Lincoln writes and files summons in Baker v. Moffett & Allen. Herndon-Weik Collection, Library of Congress, Washington, DC.
His bank account is debited $5 for "Subscription." Irwin Journal.

Friday, March 26, 1852 – Springfield, IL
Representing E. D. Baker, Lincoln & Herndon secure decree of foreclosure against Moffett and Allen to recover debt of $2,175.56. They lose dower case, win appeal from justice's court and settle fourth case by agreement. Defendant in Johnson v. McMullen moves for new trial. Record.

Friday, June 4, 1852 – Decatur, IL
In Edwards for use of Edwards v. Florey, appeal, jury is waived and court affirms judgment of justice's court awarding plaintiff $77.65 and costs. Lincoln and Post are attorneys for defendant. **Lincoln** files declaration in Trustees of Township 16N, Range 1E v. Prather, ejectment suit. Taylor v. **Moffett**, also ejectment, is continued. Kuffman for use of Thorpe v. Edwards & Edwards, appeal from justice court, is dismissed by Post and Lincoln for plaintiff. Smith, administrator of Smith v. Prather, note suit, Lincoln for William Prather, defendant is continued. Record.

Saturday, November 13, 1852 – Decatur, IL

Lincoln writes, signs, and files defendant's plea in **Moffett** et al. v. **Moffett**, ejectment suit. In Peck v. Froman, in which nonsuit with leave to reinstate was entered November 12, 1852, he joins issue on defendant's plea. **Lincoln** loses Hanks v. Hanks, trespass, when plaintiff, John Hanks, dismisses case. He also loses Taylor v. Rea, sheriff, when court upholds plea that Sheriff Rea owes plaintiff $167.27 due on execution against John B. **Moffett**'s real estate. Two cases, Brown v. Peck & Peck, and John G. Taylor v. John B. **Moffett**, in which **Lincoln** represents defendants, are continued. Record; Herndon-Weik Collection, Library of Congress, Washington, DC.

Monday, March 28, 1853 – Springfield, IL

In Allen v. Chicago & Mississippi RR, appeal from assessment for right of way, jury assesses plaintiff's damages at $2,100. **Lincoln** & Herndon represent railroad. Record.

Lincoln writes case record in **Moffett** v. Warren, chancery concerning land, and writes replication in Johnson v. McMullen. Herndon-Weik Collection, Library of Congress, Washington, DC.

Lincoln writes to Henry E. Dummer of Beardstown: "Inclosed please find three dollars – the smallest sum I could send by mail for the $2.50 you kindly advanced for me; which please accept, together with my thanks, and offer to reciprocate." Abraham **Lincoln** to Henry E. Dummer, 28 March 1853, CW, 2:192.

Thursday, October 26, 1854 – Decatur, IL

Taylor v. **Moffett**, ejectment, **Lincoln** for defense, is continued by agreement. Record.

Agreement with John Hutchinson[1]

September 3, 1859

We, the undersigned, proprietors of lots in Hutchinsons Cemetery, in the City of Springfield, Illinois, constitute and appoint John Hutchinson our agent to take charge, and general superintendence of said Cemetery, until February 1st, 1861 - - - - which agent is assured any expenses which he, in his discretion, may incur, in such superintendence, we bind ourselves to pay.

Sept. 3, 1859

A. Lincoln   Absalom Kalb   ⋁ J.G. Loose   Thos. Moffett   George Leggott
D. Sherman   E. B. Hawley   Isaac A. Hawley   James C. Conling
Asahel Stone   Phinias H.   Sanford Bell   J. H. Kent
Willard & Zimmerman   J. S. Hough   Isaac Lindsay   J. Bunn   D. Wickersham
Francis Springer

[1]From Photostat of handwritten document, The Abraham Lincoln Association, Springfield, Illinois

ABOVE: 1860 photo of Abraham Lincoln's home in Springfield, Illinois. Lincoln himself, and his son, are visible behind the front fence, just below the nearest, front, ground floor window. In the lower right, wagon tracks in the street's mud are visible. Also note the planks put down for stepping over the streets' gutters.

BELOW: The same Lincoln family home as it appeared at the turn to the 21st

Appendix 7
The Moffetts in the American Civil War
Military Service and Family Slave Holdings[1]

Most members of the family who remained in Kentucky did own slaves. William Moffett, the immigrant, had one slave when his household was enumerated in what was then part of Montgomery County, Kentucky in 1810. In 1820, the Moffett home was now within Bath County, which had been formed from Montgomery County in 1811. William had three slaves, and his son James, who now had established his own household, had two.

As the various southern (slave) states opted to secede, four of them chose to remain in the Union. These "border states" were joined by the western one-third of the counties of Virginia, which refused to secede, and were admitted to the Union as West Virginia in 1863. These five states played a critical role during the war. Kentucky was one of these loyal border states. Still, those Moffetts (and everyone else) who resided in Kentucky had their loyalties tested by both sides. Many Kentuckians joined Confederate military units, and many joined Union units. All of the Kentucky Moffetts of this family who served in military units were Union men.[2]

In 1830, William Moffett, the immigrant, had died, but his son James still resided in Bath County, and owned four slaves. His widow, Rebecca was still a household head in that county, and she owned seven slaves. By 1840, James was the only household head named Moffett in Bath County and he owned three slaves. The census of 1850 indicates that James owned seven slaves, and in 1860 he owned eight.

William Crain, who married Rebecca Robinson Moffett (a daughter of William and Rebecca Moffett) in Bath County, Kentucky in December of 1826 also owned slaves – four in 1850 and six in 1860. Two sons of this couple served in Union Army units:

> *Simeon Lewis Crain* was just a month shy of his twenty-sixth birthday when Fort Sumter fell to inaugurate the War. He served in the Union Army, first as a Lieutenant, later promoted to Captain in Company M, 7th Kentucky Cavalry. He died from disease on December 1, 1863. This Regiment lost 147 men during its service, from August 16, 1862 to July 10, 1865. Of these, 24 were killed or mortally wounded in battle, and 123 died from disease.

---

[1]Information about slave holdings is taken entirely from the U.S. censuses.

[2]Samuel Eliot Morison, Henry Steele Commager, and William E. Leuchtenburg, *The Growth of the American Republic* (New York, 1980, vol. 1, pp. 620-621.

Moffett Lineage
Service in the Civil War

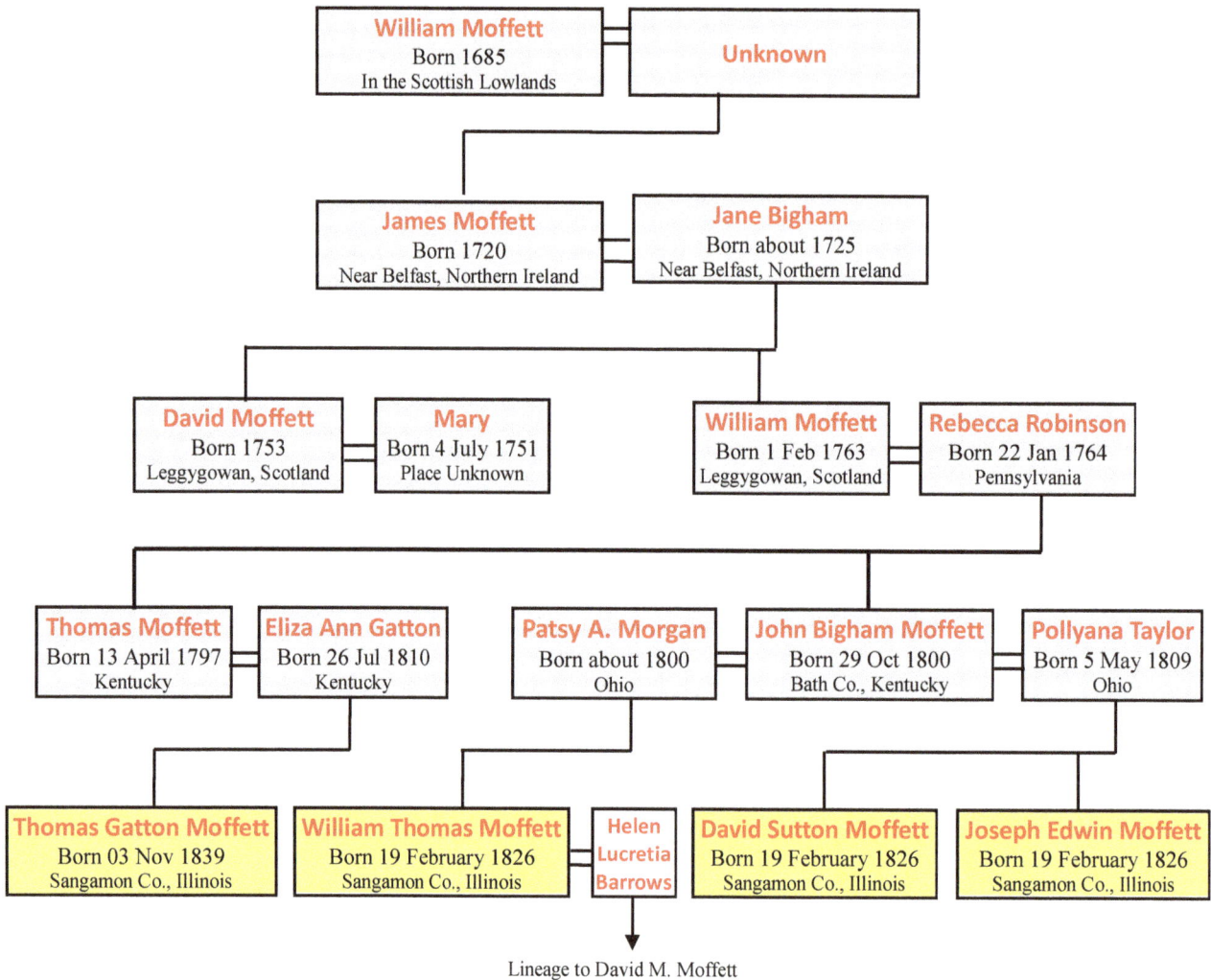

William Moffett	Unknown
Born 1685	
In the Scottish Lowlands	

James Moffett	Jane Bigham
Born 1720	Born about 1725
Near Belfast, Northern Ireland	Near Belfast, Northern Ireland

David Moffett	Mary	William Moffett	Rebecca Robinson
Born 1753	Born 4 July 1751	Born 1 Feb 1763	Born 22 Jan 1764
Leggygowan, Scotland	Place Unknown	Leggygowan, Scotland	Pennsylvania

Thomas Moffett	Eliza Ann Gatton	Patsy A. Morgan	John Bigham Moffett	Pollyana Taylor
Born 13 April 1797	Born 26 Jul 1810	Born about 1800	Born 29 Oct 1800	Born 5 May 1809
Kentucky	Kentucky	Ohio	Bath Co., Kentucky	Ohio

Thomas Gatton Moffett	William Thomas Moffett	Helen Lucretia Barrows	David Sutton Moffett	Joseph Edwin Moffett
Born 03 Nov 1839	Born 19 February 1826		Born 19 February 1826	Born 19 February 1826
Sangamon Co., Illinois	Sangamon Co., Illinois		Sangamon Co., Illinois	Sangamon Co., Illinois

Lineage to David M. Moffett

John Henry Crain, 2$^{1/2}$ years younger than his brother Simeon, was a hospital steward with Company A of the 10th Kentucky Cavalry. He attained the rank of sergeant. The history of this unit says they lost a total of 75 men in its service which ran from Sept. 8, 1862 through September 17, 1863. Of those, 13 were killed or mortally wounded in battle; the other 62 died from disease.[3]

These two Crain men were the only members of the extended Moffett family of Bath County, Kentucky who saw military service in the war. None of those who bore the Moffett name did so.

Another of the children of William and Rebecca Moffett was Jane Bigham who married Samuel Crain and lived in Fleming County, Kentucky. In 1850, she was a widow. The census indicates that she owned eight slaves, and that her spinster sister, Mary Moffett, owned three.

William Moffett was another son of William and Rebecca Moffett – a brother of John Bigham Moffett and the James Moffett who stayed in Bath County, Kentucky. William went into Missouri, which was a slave state, but he owned no slaves. Of course, John Bigham Moffett and his sons, who went to the free state of Illinois, owned no slaves during their adult lives. The other two of the five sons of William and Rebecca Moffett were Thomas and Willis G., both of whom also settled in Illinois at an early date, and never did own slaves.

As discussed in the main text, four other family members, all from central Illinois, served in the military during the War. All were grandsons of William Moffett, the immigrant Ulster Scot, and his wife, Rebecca Robinson. The first listed below was the son of Thomas Moffett of Springfield. The remaining three were sons of John Bigham Moffett of Blue Mound Township, Macon County.

Thomas G. Moffett of Springfield served as adjutant on the staff of the 7th Illinois infantry, which unit saw three months of service in 1861. At the age of 21 years, he enlisted at the organization of the unit at Camp Yates, in Springfield, Illinois, on April 25, 1861, as a first lieutenant in Company I. Six days later, he was transferred to the field and staff, was mustered in on May 1, and out on July 24 of that year. The unit saw no combat but served duty at Alton (where a military prison was established), Cairo, and Mound City in Illinois, and St. Louis, Missouri. None in the unit were casualties of battle, but five men died from disease.

On August 13, 1862, in Macon County, Illinois, David S. Moffett joined Company E. of the 115th Illinois Infantry at the regiment's formation. He was assigned the rank of first lieutenant and was to serve for a period of three years. The record shows that he was 24 years old, born in Sangamon County, Illinois, was 6 feet tall, and had light hair, blue eyes, and a light complexion. It further stated that he was married and a farmer. He and the regiment mustered in at Camp Butler, in Springfield, Illinois on September 13, 1862.

3 "Soldiers Names and Records of Union and Confederate Troops," *Civil War Soldiers and Sailors System*, National Park Service. November 7, 2006 <http://www.itd.nps.gov/cwss/soldiers.cvm>.

On October 4, the regiment proceeded to Cincinnati, where they were assigned to the Army of Kentucky. On October 6, they moved on to Covington, Kentucky, where they remained until October 20. From the 20th to the 25th they marched to Richmond, Kentucky and remained there until December, when they moved to Danville, Kentucky, arriving December 21. They remained on duty at Danville until January 26, 1863. From December 26-31, the unit pursued the cavalry units under legendary raider, Gen. John Hunt Morgan, but to no avail.

On January 26, they set out for Louisville, Kentucky, arriving there January 31, and then were assigned to move to Nashville, Tennessee. En route, at Fort Donelson in Tennessee, about 65 miles northwest of Nashville, they saw their first combat on February 4, when they were engaged in the successful repulse of an attack on the fort by the very savvy General Joseph ("Fightin' Joe") Wheeler. They arrived in Nashville February 8, and remained there until March 5, at which time they set out for Franklin, Tennessee, about 20 miles south of Nashville, to pursue General Earl Van Dorn. While still stationed at Franklin, on March 25, 1863, Lieutenant David S. Moffett resigned from his unit for disability. The records do not specify the nature of the disability, but the regimental history indicates that they lost some 200 men, "either dead or permanently disabled ... by reason of exposure on marches and scouting expeditions in the very severe winter of 1862-63...." In any case, he only lived another five years.

Joseph E. Moffett first enlisted at Decatur Illinois on February 1, 1864, with company A of the 116th Illinois Infantry, at which time he was aged 18 years, and a resident of Decatur. At this time, and for the duration of the war, this regiment was assigned to the Army of the Tennessee. With this unit, he would participate in some of the most dramatic engagements in the war.

On March 27, 1864, he was mustered in, presumably at Larkinsville, Alabama, where the 116th was then stationed, coordinating with the tt, preparing for the campaign against Atlanta. This hamlet is about 2 ½ miles west of Scottsboro in northeastern Alabama, very near the Tennessee River.

He and his unit moved into Georgia in early May, and on May 14 and 15 saw action in the Battle of Resaca (Georgia), about 75 miles north-northwest of Atlanta. They advanced on Dallas, Georgia, about 30 miles west-northwest of Atlanta, and fought battles at and around Dallas from May 25 - June 5. From here they moved east for operations around Marietta and Kenesaw Mountain, undertaking an assault on Kenesaw on June 27. They moved along Nickajack Creek in early July and along the Chattahoochie River from the 5th to the 17th of July. They were now within striking distance of Atlanta.

The 116th participated in the Battle of Atlanta on July 22, and from then through August 25, in the siege of that city. Subsequently, they were involved in the Battle of Jonesboro August 31 and September 1. From September 29 through November 3, they were occupied with operations against General Hood in northern Georgia and northern Alabama. From November 15 through December 10, they participated in the legendary "March to the Sea" under General William T. Sherman, and in the siege of Savannah from the 10th through the 21st of December.

From January through April of 1865, the 116th participated in the Campaign of the Carolinas. They arrived at Columbia on February 16, were involved in the Battle of Bentonville (North Carolina) on March 20 and 21, and initiated the occupation of Goldsboro on March 24. On April 9, Lee surrendered to Grant at Appomattox Court House in Virginia, and on the next day, the 116th began their advance on Raleigh. They initiated the occupation of Raleigh on April 14, and General Sherman set up headquarters there. That night, President Lincoln was shot in Washington, and he died the next morning.

Gen. Joseph Johnston

Gen. William T. Sherman

Sherman's Confederate adversary, General Johnston, set up headquarters in Goldsboro and asked to negotiate with Sherman for terms of surrender. The negotiations were carried out at the farm house of James and Nancy Bennitt, along the Hillsborough Road (now U.S. Route 70), about 5½ miles northwest of downtown Durham. The two armies waited for twelve days as the negotiations dragged on. On the 26th of April, after Sherman consulted with General Grant and Johnston with President Jefferson Davis, the surrender took place. It was the largest troop surrender of the war.

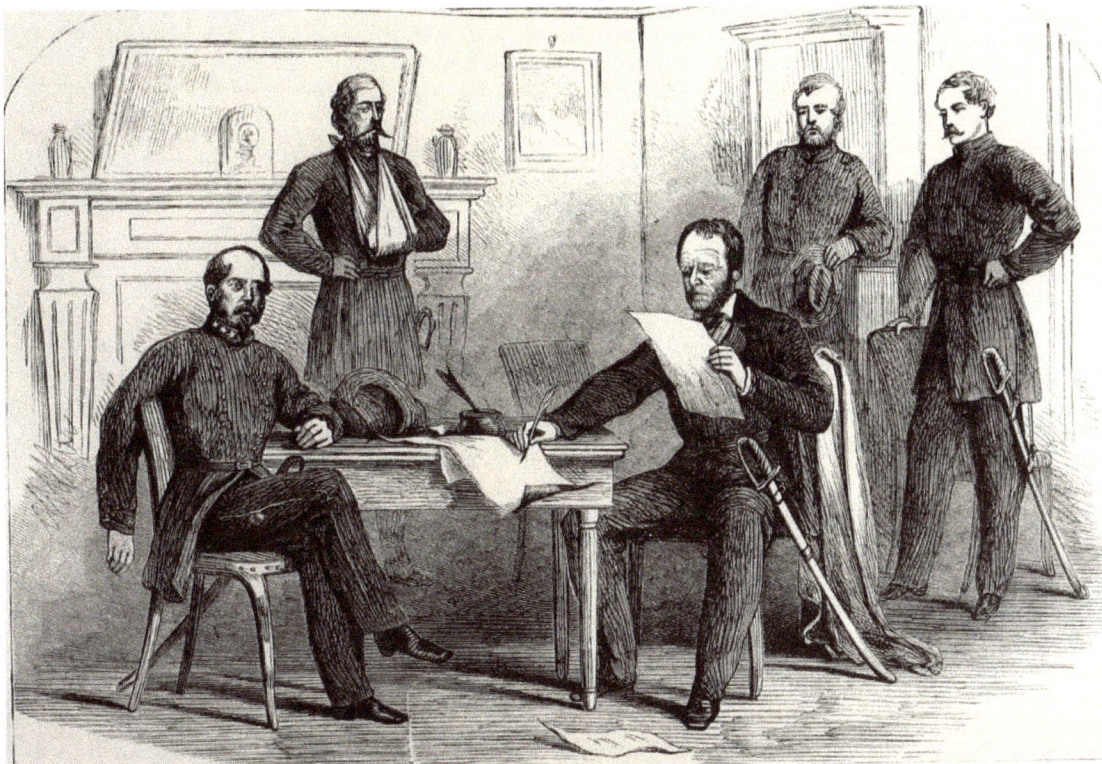

Generals Johnston and Sherman negotiating.

On April 29, the 116th commenced a march which would take them through Richmond, arriving in Washington on the 19th of May, where they prepared to participate in the "Grand Review of the Army". On May 24, the Army of Georgia paraded. Either as they were arriving in Washington, or not long thereafter, Joseph E. Moffett was transferred to Company H of the 55th Illinois infantry.

The 55th Infantry left Washington shortly after the Grand Review and went to Louisville, Ky., arriving there June 2. From June 30 to July 6, they went on to Little Rock, Arkansas, by way of Memphis, Tenn., and Duvall's Bluff, Arkansas. At Little Rock, Joseph E. Moffett was mustered out on Monday, August 14, 1865.

During the course of the war, the 116th Illinois Infantry Regiment lost 7 officers and 49 enlisted men killed and mortally wounded, and 7 officers and 232 enlisted men died from disease. (Total 295) The 55th Illinois Infantry Regiment lost 9 officers and 149 enlisted men killed and mortally wounded and 2 officers and 127 enlisted men by disease. (Total 286)

William Thomas Moffett accompanied his brother, David S. Moffett, to join the 115th Illinois Infantry when it was being formed in August of 1862. As the time for muster drew near in September, their father, John Bigham Moffett had become seriously ill, and it was apparent that his life was in jeopardy. Being the oldest son, William remained on the home front to deal with his father's worsening condition. The 115th mustered in at Camp Butler on September 13, 1862, and it was two days later that John Bigham Moffett died.

In the months after his father's death, William T. Moffett remained in Macon County and was preoccupied with his duties as executor of his father's estate. As is described in the main text, he later served as captain of a company of volunteer home guards under commission from Governor Richard Yates. Their mission was to deal with southern sympathizers in Illinois, and in particular in Macon County. No specific official records of this unit's soldiers, dates and activities appear to be extant.

History of the 115th Illinois Infantry

The Regiment was ordered into the field from Camp Butler, Ill., on the 4th day of October 1862. They Reported to Major General Wright, at Cincinnati, Ohio, on the 6th day of October, and on the same day crossed over into Kentucky and reported to Brigadier General A. J. Smith. They were assigned to the Second Brigade, Second Division, Army of Kentucky.

While in the Army of Kentucky, the Brigade commanders were: Colonel Cochran, of the Fourteenth Kentucky Volunteer Infantry; Colonel P. B. Swayne of the Regular Army; Colonel Smith D. Atkins, Ninety-second Illinois Infantry; Division commander General A. Baird. All served under General Gordon Granger, who commanded the Army of Kentucky.

Marched about the 20th October by the way of Falmouth, Cynthiana, Paris and Lexington, Ky., to Richmond, Ky. Here the Colonel of the Regiment took command of the post, and remained about two months, scouting frequently through the exposed region lying between that post and the gaps through the Cumberland Mountains.

About 21st December 1862, marched to Danville, Ky. and joined main portion of the Army of Kentucky. Remained in Danville till the 26th day of January 1863. On that day marched toward Louisville, Ky. On the 1st day of February 1863, took transports at Louisville with Army of Kentucky and moved by the Ohio and Cumberland Rivers to Nashville, Tenn. Landed at Nashville, and went into camp three miles south, on the 10th of February. Remained there till about the 1st of March. Moved thence to Franklin, Tenn. and went into camp.

Up to this time, no casualties from the battle. But, by reason of exposure on marches and scouting expeditions, during the severe winter of 1862 and 1863, the Regiment had lost about 200 men, either dead or permanently disabled. While in camp at Franklin, Tenn., the Army of Kentucky was reorganized and became the Reserve Corps, Department of the Cumberland; General Rosecrans commanding Department; General Granger, the Corps; General A. Baird, Division; Colonel S. D. Atkins, Ninety-second Illinois, Brigade. During the month of March, under Baird and Atkins, marched against Van Dorn, and drove him across Duck River. Returned to camp, and remained there, occasionally skirmishing with the enemy, till June 1st. Then marched to Triune, Tenn. Remained in camp till June 24th. On that day, marched, with Army of Cumberland, against the Confederate Army, under General Bragg, and drove it across the Tennessee.

Brigade went into camp at Wartrace, Tenn. Thence, Regiment moved to Tullahoma, Tenn., and held that post until the 5th of September, when joining the Reserve Corps, marched toward Chattanooga, by way of Stevenson and Bridgeport, Alabama. On the 14th day of September, by a forced march across the Cumberland Mountains, reached Rossville, Georgia, 5 miles south of Chattanooga. Remained 4 days. On the 19th September, engaged the enemy on the extreme left, upon the field of Chickamauga, Previously, General W. C. Whitaker of Kentucky, had assumed the command of the Brigade, and General Steadman, of Ohio, the command of the Division. In this engagement the Regiment lost 6 men.

September 20th, crossed to the support of General Tho9mas, on the extreme right, leaving camp at sunrise. Engaged the enemy, on Thomas' right, at 1 o'clock P.M., with Steadman's Division, 19 Regiments Reserve Corps. After a most fearful struggle, held the ground till night. Half the entire command was cut down. The Colonel and his Regiment were commended in orders.

Participated in all the engagements around Chattanooga and Mission Ridge. The Regiment lost, in killed, wounded and captured, in the campaign about Chattanooga, in the fall of 1863, about 235 men and 10 officers, among whom was Lieutenant Colonel Kinman, of Jacksonville, Ill., a very brave and efficient officer. The Army of the Cumberland being reorganized after the battle of Chickamauga, the Regiment became attached to Second Brigade, First Division, Fourth Army Corps, Department of the Cumberland; General Whitaker commanding Brigade; Stanley, the Division; Granger the corps; Thomas the Department.

About the 21st of February, marched, with a detachment of the Department of the Cumberland, under General Palmer, against Dalton, Ga. Spent 10 days feeling the enemy, and returned to camp, near Cleveland, Tenn. The Regiment lost 6 men. Remained here till 3d of May, when, with Sherman's Grand Army, started on the Atlanta Campaign. General Howard had previously assumed command of the Fourth Army Corps. The Regiment on 7th May, led the charge upon Tunnel Hill, Ga., driving the enemy through Buzzard Roost Gap. 15th and 16th May, engaged in battle at Resaca, Ga. Sustained, stubbornly, a charge upon the left flank, for which the Regiment was commended in orders. Lost, in this contest, about 30 men and 1 officer.

Inscribed, by orders, upon the Regimental banner all the principal engagements of the Military Division of the Mississippi, which resulted in the fall of Atlanta. Lost, during Atlanta Campaign, about 100 men. When, in October 1864, Hood threw himself on Sherman's rear, and was marching on Chattanooga, Company D, One Hundred and Fifteenth Illinois, occupied a block house in Buzzard Roost Gap, and held in check Hood's Army for 10 hours, and fighting stubbornly, refused to surrender the Gap, till the block house was rendered untenable and nearly demolished, by the enemy's artillery. One-third of the company, of 41 in the aggregate, was killed and wounded; the remainder surrendered. For this special act of gallantry, the Captain was brevetted Major, and has since been made a Captain in the regular army. This officer was Samuel Hymer, of the county of Schuyler, Ill. He mustered in as Second Lieutenant of Company D, One Hundred and Fifteenth Illinois Volunteer Infantry.

When Sherman had determined to march to the sea, the Fourth Army Corps, now commanded by Major General Stanley, together with the Twenty third Corps – all under command of Major General Thomas – were detached from the Military Division of the Mississippi and ordered back to Tennessee, to watch the detached movements of General Hood, now near Florence, Ala., on the Tennessee river, and threatening Nashville, Tenn. The One Hundred and Fifteenth Illinois still belonged to the Second Brigade, First Division, Fourth Army Corps – Generals Whitaker, Kimball and Stanley commanding respectively, Brigade, Division and Corps. The regiment took an active part in the engagements which, in November and December 1864, resulted in the destruction of Bragg's old veteran army, known as the Army of the Tennessee, and then commanded by the rebel General Hood. The Brigade to which the One Hundred and Fifteenth Illinois was for nearly two years attached, without material alteration, was known throughout the Department as the "Iron Brigade", and was, for the most of the time, up to the 23d of December 1864, commanded by Brigadier General Walter C. Whitaker of Kentucky, who neglected no opportunity to win distinction for himself and his command.

On the 23d of December 1864, while pursuing Hood, in his retreat from Nashville, Colonel J. H. Moore, of the One Hundred and Fifteenth Illinois, took command of this splendid Brigade, and continued in command until it was mustered out of the service, at the close of the war. Colonel Moore was brevetted Brigadier General, before leaving the army. Hood having been driven, with the remains of a broken army, across the Tennessee, the Regiment, with the Fourth Army Corps, marched for Huntsville, Ala., and went into camp on the 5th day of January 1865. Marched thence, on the 14th of March, into East Tennessee, thence expecting to move by the way of Lynchburg, Va., to assist in the capture of Richmond. But while in the vicinity of Greenville, Tenn., Richmond fell, and the rebel General Lee surrendered.

The Regiment then moved back, with the Fourth Army Corps, and went into camp near Nashville, Tenn., and there remained until mustered out of service, June 11, 1865. Arrived at Camp Butler, Ill., June 16, 1865, and received final pay and discharge June 23, 1865.

History of the 116th Illinois Infantry

The one-hundred-sixteenth infantry was recruited almost wholly from Macon County, numbering 980 officers and men when it started from Decatur for the front on November 8, 1862. Company F was from McLean County, Company H from Christian and Shelby counties. The Regiment, with the noble and brave Colonel Nathan W. Tupper in command, went into Camp Macon near Decatur, and was mustered into United States service September 30, 1862 by Captain Wainwright of the regular army.

The Regiment remained in Camp Macon until November 8th, when it was ordered to Memphis via Cairo to join General W. T. Sherman's Fifteenth Army Corps, and was assigned to the First Brigade, Second Division (the same which General Sherman commanded at Shiloh) and the one he selected from his whole army subsequently near Savannah, Georgia to storm Fort McAllister, *to open his cracker line*, as the General facetiously put it.

From Memphis the Regiment marched to the Tallahatchei River, reaching it on December 13, returned to Memphis and started down the Mississippi on the 20th, and on the 26th reached the Yazoo river and ascended it 15 miles.

During the following three days the Regiment received its first baptism of fire, engaging in the battle of Chickasaw Bayou, the officers and men fighting so gallantly as to receive the highest compliments from the veterans of the older regiments in the Brigade. General Morgan L Smith was wounded in this engagement.

On January 1, 1863, passed down the Yazoo to the Mississippi River, and up that and the Arkansas River to Arkansas Post, where on the 10th and 11th of January it fought its second battle, sustaining very heavy losses. Here Captain Lewis Eyman, of Company E, and Lieutenant John S. Taylor, of Company B, were killed. The casualties in Company B were particularly severe, the company coming out of the battle with but 25 men, in command of Fifth Sergeant, afterward Lieutenant and Captain Christian Riebsame.

In the month of March the One Hundred and Sixteenth went up the Black Bayou and Deer Creek in company with the Eighth Missouri, to save Admiral Porter's fleet and gunboats worth $3,000,000 from the clutches of the rebels which was done after a hard fight. General Sherman in person and on foot with his own Regiment, the Thirteenth Regulars, coming up at a critical moment to assist in accomplishing the object.

The Regiment engaged in the battles of Champion Hills and Black River Bridge and in the bloody charges on May 18th and 22nd and lost very heavily. Among the losses and casualties were these: Lieutenant Colonel Jas. P. Boyd was shot through the lungs and died of this would at home in Decatur, Captain Gustin F. Hardy, of Company A, was mortally wounded and died in the hospital. Lieutenant Nathan W. Wheeler, of Company K, was killed May 22d. Captain Joseph Lingle, of Company D, was wounded and died at home, and Captain William Grason, of Company A, was shot through the breast, but recovered. Captain Austin McClurg, of Company B, was wounded, recovered and promoted to Major. Then followed the long siege of Vicksburg which ended by the surrender of that stronghold on the 4th of July.

The following day started in pursuit of General Jos. E. Johnston, and chased the enemy to and beyond Jackson, Mississippi, and across Pearl river.

On July 25, went into Camp Sherman, near Black River, enjoying a season of rest until after the battle of Chickamauga, when General Grant sent for his trusty lieutenant, General Sherman, and his veterans to come to Chattanooga.

The One Hundred and Sixteenth embarked at Vicksburg in October for Memphis; from thence marched via Corinth to Chattanooga, which was reached on the 21st of November. During the night of November 23, the One Hundred and Sixteenth Illinois and Sixth Missouri Regiments, under General Giles A. Smith, floated down the Tennessee River in pontoon boats to the mouth of Chickamauga Creek, capturing the rebel pickets and holding the position until the whole Corps had crossed over.

On November 23, advanced to the foot of Missionary Ridge, after a lively skirmish, during which General Giles A. Smith was severely wounded. (The General's death after the war was the result of the wound received that day.)

The great battle of Missionary Ridge, Tunnel Hill and Lookout Mountain was fought next day, November 25. The One Hundred and Sixteenth, with the other Regiments of the brigade, formed the extreme left of General Sherman's Army, and obtained the credit of turning the enemy's right flank on that bloody day.

Colonel N. W. Tupper, after General Smith was disabled, assumed command of the Brigade, and proved that he was the right man in the right place. When disease, contracted in the service of his country, and of which he died on the 10th day of March 1864, compelled him to leave the army, every man in the One Hundred and Sixteenth felt that he had lost a friend and the nation a patriot.

After the victory of Chattanooga, and without being permitted to return to camp across the Tennessee for blankets or overcoats, the One Hundred and Sixteenth, with other of Sherman's Army, was hurried forward to Knoxville to the relief of Burnside. The winter was a very cold one, and while the boys could keep warm marching twenty-five to thirty miles during the days, they suffered greatly while camping at night. They would build big fires and hug them close, but the other side would be chilled to the marrow of the bon; rations, also were very short, and when at last the Regiment went into winter quarters on January 9, 1864, at Larkinsville, Ala., the men all felt that they have been on the hardest campaign during their service.

The march from Missionary Ridge to Knoxville, and back to Larkinsville via Tellico and Strawberry Plains and Chattanooga, will never be forgotten by Sherman's boys who were along. In May, the One Hundred and Sixteenth, with the rest of the Army of the Tennessee, moved against the enemy, and found him at Resaca, GA., when, on the 14th of May, the Regiment was hotly engaged, losing heavily, but driving the enemy across the creek and planting their colors upon the rebel works. The One Hundred and Sixteenth was repeatedly attacked, but could not be driven from the position gained. It was in this battle that Major Anderson Froman was wounded, and he died in the field hospital.

Then followed in quick succession the battles of Dallas, Big Shanty and Kenesaw Mountain. Captain Thomas White, of Company C, commanding the Regiment, was killed on the skirmish line May 26, at Dallas, and Captain James N. Gore, Company K, was wounded about the same time. The Regiment lost heavily on June 27, 1864, in the assault on Kenesaw Mountain. Among the wounded was Lieut. John Miller of Company B.

Crossing the Chattahoochie, engaged the enemy at Stone Mountain, driving him to the vicinity of Atlanta. Fought in the battle of Atlanta, July 22, where its Army Commander, General McPherson, fell, and with the Fifteenth Corps, General Logan, the hot battle of Ezra Chapel, July 28.

Captain George T. Milmine, Company D, and Lieutenant Samuel R. Riggs, Company F, were wounded before Atlanta in August 1864. August 31 and September 1 was hotly engaged with the enemy at Jonesboro.

After the fall of Atlanta, and when Hood started for General Sherman's rear, the One Hundred and Sixteenth assisted in the pursuit of the enemy as far as Gadston, when, leaving the rebels to the care of General Thomas marched back to Atlanta, and on the 15th day of November went with Uncle Sherman from Atlanta to the Sea, arriving at Fort McAllister, GA., near Savannah, December 12.

The next day, December 13, General W. B. Hazen, commanding Division, selected nine regiments, including the One Hundred and Sixteenth, to carry the fort, and within five minutes after the sound of the bugle "Forward" the Regimental colors were on the works and the garrison captured. Lieutenant Isom Simmons, of Company H, was killed in this charge.

After a few days rest in the beautiful city of Savanna, we started on the campaign of the Carolinas, hunting the enemy and finding him first near the swamps of Pocotaligo, chased him through creeks and across rivers, skirmishing constantly until nearing Columbia, S.C., where the Fifteenth Corps, the One Hundred and Sixteenth included, run short of chewing tobacco. Learning that there was an ample supply of the article in the city of Columbia, paid that city a visit on the 17th of February 1865, and replenished stock.

After a few days rest resumed march, facing home, crossing the great Pedee River at Cheraw, S.C., then to Fayetteville, N.C., and to Bentonville, where the One Hundred and Sixteenth for the last time encountered its old foe, General Jos. E. Johnston's Army, and fought its last battle. From Goldsboro, where the army was re-equipped (and it was in need of everything except the musket and forty rounds), the Regiment started picnicking for Washington via Raleigh, Richmond and Alexandria, participating in the grand review before the President in May 1865, being finally mustered out near Washington on June 7, 1865.

The history of the One Hundred and Sixteenth Infantry is identical with that of the Army of the Tennessee from Memphis, 1862, to Washington, 1865. It was never on detached service, but always with the moving column.

The Regiment was peculiarly fortunate in retaining through its eventful history the very efficient services of its medical staff, and the members had plenty of work to do. Major Ira N. Barnes, M.D., Decatur, Ill; Assistant Surgeon John A. Heckelman, M.D., St. Louis, and Assistant Surgeon J. H. Hostettler, M.D., Decatur, all served to the end of the war, and every one of the 350 survivors in 1865 had cause to feel grateful to them.

The *esprit du corps* of the Regiment, under the command of Colonel Tupper, was splendid, and under such Brigade Commanders as General Giles A. Smith, and Division Commanders as W. B. Hazen, retained it to the end of the war.

History of the 10th Kentucky Cavalry

Organized at Covington, Lexington and Crab Orchard, Ky., for one year's service, September 8 to November 11, 1862. Attached to Cavalry, 1st Division, Army of Kentucky, Dept. of the Ohio, to November, 1862. Unattached, Army of Kentucky, November, 1862. District of Central Kentucky, Dept. Ohio, to April 1863. 2nd Brigade, District Central Kentucky, Dept. Ohio, to June, 1863. 2nd Brigade, 4th Division, 23rd Army Corps, Dept. of Ohio, to July, 1863. 2nd Brigade, 1st Division, 23rd Army Corps, to August, 1863. Mt. Sterling, Ky., 1st Division, 23rd Army Corps, to September, 1863. (2nd Battalion attached to District of Eastern Kentucky to June, 1863. 1st Brigade, 4th Division, 23rd Army Corps, to August, 1863.)

SERVICE – Duty about Mt. Sterling, Ky., and in the District of Central Kentucky, scouting and operating against guerrillas and protecting that part of the State, until September, 1863. Skirmish near Florence, Ky., September 8, 1862. Expedition to East Tennessee December 24, 1862, to January 1, 1863. Parker's Mills, on Elk Fork, December 28, 1862. Operations against Cluke's forces February 18-March 5, 1863. Coomb's Ferry February 22. Slate Creek, near Mt. Sterling, and Stoner's Bridge, February 24. Slate Creek, near Mt. Sterling, March 2. Operations against Pegram March 22-April 1. Mt. Sterling March 22. Operations against Everett's Raid in Eastern Kentucky June 13-23. Triplett's Bridge, Flemming County, June 16. Operations against Scott's forces July 25 –August 6. Richmond July 28. Lancaster and Paint Creek Bridge July 31-August 1. Smith's Shoals, Cumberland River, August 1. Duty at Mt. Sterling until September. (2nddd Battalion served detached in District Eastern Kentucky. Expedition from Beaver Creek into Southwest Virginia July 3-11, 1863. Gladesville, Va., July 7.) Regiment mustered out September 17, 1863.

History of the 7th Kentucky Cavalry

Organized at large and mustered in at Paris, Ky., August 16, 1862. Attached to Army of Kentucky, unassigned, Dept. of Ohio, to November, 1862. District of Central Kentucky, Dept. Ohio, to March, 1863. 1st Brigade, 1st Division, Cavalry Corps, Army of the Cumberland, to July, 1863. 3rd Brigade, 1st Division, Cavalry Corps, Army of the Cumberland, to Nov., 1864. 3rd Brigade, 1st Division, Cavalry Corps, Military Division Mississippi, to January, 1865. 2nd Brigade, 1st Division, Cavalry Corps, M.D. M., to July, 1865.

SERVICE – Before muster participated in operations against Morgan July 4-28, 1862. Cyntiana, Ky., July 17 (Detachment). Paris July 19, Big Hill, Madison County, August 23. Richmond August 30. Moved to Tennessee December, 1862.   Harsville December 7, Scouting at Castillian Springs until March, 1863. Moved to Franklin, Tenn. Expedition from Franklin to Columbia March 8-12. Thompson's Station March 9. Rutherford Creek March 10-11. Spring Hill March 18-19. Columbia Pike April 1. Thompson's Station May 2. Moved to Triune June 2-4. Franklin June 4. Middle Tennessee or Tullahoma Campaign June 23-July 7. Expedition to Huntsville July 13-22.   Detached at Bridgeport, Caperton's Ferry and Nashville until December. Operations about Mossy Creek and Dandridge, Tenn., December 24-28. Mossy Creek Station December 24. Peck's House, near New Market, December 24, Mossy Creek December 26. Talbot's Station December 26-28. Mossy Creek December 29. Moved to Morristown. Kimbrough Cross Roads and bend of Chucky River January 16, 1864. Operations about Dandridge January 16-17. Dandridge January 17. Pigeon River, near Fair Garden, January 27. Swann's Bridge, Paris Ford. January 28. At Cleveland, Tenn., until May. Atlanta (Ga.) Campaign May to September. Guarding railroad in rear of army at Wauhatchie, Tenn., May 5 to June 18. At Lee and Gordon's Mills and Lafayette until August 4. Action at Lafayette June 24. Actions at Lost Mountain July 1-2. At Calhoun and Dalton until October 12. Pine Log Creek and near Fairmont August 14. Dalton August 14-15 (Co. "B"). Rousseau's pursuit of Wheeler September 1-8. Resaca October 12-13. Surrender of Dalton October 13 (Co. "B"). Near Summerville October 18. Little River, Ala., October 20. Leesburg October 21. Ladiga, Terrapin Creek, October 28 (Detachment). Moved to Louisville, Ky., November 3-9. McCook's pursuit of Lyon December 6-28. Hopkinsville, Ky., December 16. At Nashville, Tenn., until January 9k, 1865. Moved to Gravelly Springs, Ala., and duty there and at Waterloo until March. Wilson's raid from Chickasaw, Ala., to Macon, Ga., March 22-April 24. Selma April 2. Montgomery Aril 12. Columbus Road, near Tuskegee, April 14. Fort Tyler, West Point, April 16. Capture of Macon April 20. Duty at Macon until June and at Nashville, Tenn., until July. Mustered out July 10, 1865.

Appendix 8
Genealogical Tables

(1) William Moffat[1], born in Scotland in 1685[2]. His specific birthplace in that country is not known, but at the time of his birth the significant majority of Moffats resided in what were the shires of Dumfries, Lanark and Midlothian. All of these three are close together and the original location of the Clan Moffat's home was in and around what became the Town and Parish of Moffat, situated on the River Annan and bounded on the north by Lanarkshire.[3] We do not know exactly when William removed to Ireland, but it was before 1720 in which year his son James was born there. Neither do we know the name of his wife or wives, nor when he married, nor the total number of children he had. From records of men who served in the militia during the American Revolution, we do know that William1685 had at least three sons – James, from the lines of those who are discussed in this book, an older brother named William and yet another brother whose name and relative age we do not know:

(1-1) William, born in a year close to 1715, and very probably near Belfast in Ireland. He had at least one child:

(1-1-1) James Moffat, likely born in Ireland in the 1740s, but is not known to have children or to have married.

(1-2) James, born about 1720 in Ireland, very near Belfast. *See more.*

(1-3) A son whose name and year of birth are unknown.

(1-4) There may well have been a fourth son of William1685, but that is not certain.

---

[1]Moffat was the original spelling of the names of the parish and town in Scotland which are located in what was the shire of Dumfries until 1975 – now part of the shire of Dumfries and Galloway. It is not clear whether the name was first applied to the locality or to the clan, but the former is thought to be more likely. In Scotland, the surname is mostly spelled the same as the town and parish, but in America and other countries to which the families relocated the spelling can be found in several variations, although pronounced virtually the same. In the years prior to the early-middle 19th century, precision in spelling whether involving surnames or words in general, was not common. In this book's specific family line, in records involving the family in Ireland and America, the spelling was of course originally varied – Moffat, Moffet, Maffett etc., but for the most part, the first generation born here settled on Moffett and remained so for the most part in other branches here.

[2]The family tradition has long believed/understood that this was the year in which the said William was born. At that time, in most of the branches of Great Britain, a year still began on the 25th of March. In 1600 however, Scotland decided to go along with the tide in most of Europe by joining the movement of the year's first day to January 1. We can therefore be reasonably sure the year was merely 1685, and not $16^{84}/_{85}$ or $16^{85}/_{86}$.

[3]In fact, a small part of the Moffat Parish is in the Lanark side of the boundary.

(1-2) James Moffett, born about 1720 near Belfast in Ireland; married Jane Bigham in about 1748, the place being understood simply as one mile from Belfast; subsequently resided in Saintfield, County Down, all their children were born there and both parents died there in 1789. The couple had at least nine children, all born in the Townland of Leggygowan:

(1-2-1) James Moffet, born in 1750. *See More.*

(1-2-2) David Moffett, born in 1753. *See More.*

(1-2-3) Jennett Moffett, born in 1755.

(1-2-3) Mary Moffett, born in 1758.

(1-2-5) Elinor Moffett, born in 1760.

(1-2-6) William Moffett, born in 1763. *See More.*

(1-2-7) Samuel Moffett, born in 1765, died in Saintfield in 1814, leaving a will. He appears to have had at least one son, Samuel.

(1-2-8) Thomas Moffett, born in 1767; emigrated to North America in 1784 with brother William; died accidentally in Lexington, Kentucky in 1793, unmarried.

(1-2-9) Jane Moffett, born in 1769; married Robert Cole.

(1-2-1) James Moffett, married Isabella McMullen in about 1786; she was born in 1769 and died January 6, 1830 in Leggygowan. James died there April 19, 1813. Both are buried in the Church of Ireland graveyard in the parish of Saintfield. The couple had three children, all born in Leggygowan:

(1-2-1-1) James, born in about 1787, died in infancy.

(1-2-1-2) Jane, born in about 1788 and died in infancy.

(1-2-1-3) Jane, born in about 1790 in Leggygowan. *See more.*

(1-2-1-3) Jane Moffett was born in about 1790 as indicated above. In about 1808 she married Christopher Morrow of Ballynagarrick, in the parish of Drumbo, County Down. Christopher Morrow was born about 1780 and died at Ballynagarrick, October 10, 1858; Jane died there February 14, 1864. The couple had at least six children:

(1-2-1-3-1) a daughter who married.

(1-2-1-3-2) a daughter who married.

(1-2-1-3-3) Jane Morrow, born about 1814 at Ballynagarrick; died there from fever Jan. 6, 1831, aged 16 years.

(1-2-1-3-4) Agnes D. Morrow, born at Ballynagarrick 1818, died there March 21, 1885.

(1-2-1-3-5) James T. Morrow, born about 1828 at Ballynagarrick, died there February 21, 1890

(1-2-1-3-6) William D. Morrow, born about 1833 at Ballynagarrick, died there November 21, 1885.

(1-2-6) William Moffett, born February 1, 1763 at Leggygowan, Parish of Saintfield, County Down; emigrated to North America in 1784; married Rebecca Robinson, February 4, 1787 in Dauphin County, Pennsylvania; removed to Kentucky in 1787; died April 22, 1826 in Bath County, Kentucky. Rebecca Robinson was born in Dauphin County, Pennsylvania, January 22, 1764, daughter of William Robinson and Margaret Trimble, and Rebecca died July 2, 1843 in Sharpsburg, Bath County, Kentucky. William and Rebecca had ten children:

1-2-6-1) James Moffett, born October 18, 1787 in Fayette County, Kentucky; married Nancy Ratliff and had twelve children; died August 25, 1881 in Sharpsburg, Bath County, Kentucky.

(1-2-6-2) Margaret Trimble Moffett, born May 12, 1789 in Fayette County, Kentucky; married Edwin Young July 12, 1812 in Bath County, Kentucky and had children; died August 25, 1835 in Bath County.

(1-2-6-3) Jane Bigham Moffett, born March 2, 1791 in Fayette County, Kentucky; married Samuel Crain, November 25, 1819 in Bath County, Kentucky and had children; died December 24, 1861 in Fleming County, Kentucky.

(1-2-6-4) Polly (Mary) Moffett, born December 19, 1792 in Fayette County, Kentucky, and died there unmarried, June 28, 1873.

(1-2-6-5) William Moffett, born November 17, 1794 probably in Fayette County, Kentucky; married Edy (surname unknown) in about 1825 and had children; died April 19, 1852 in Linn County, Missouri.

(1-2-6-6) Thomas Moffett, born April 13, 1797 in Fayette or Bath County, Kentucky; lawyer and county judge in Sangamon County, Illinois; well acquainted with Abraham Lincoln; married (1) Eliza A. (surname unknown) in about 1833 in Illinois and had eight children, all of whom died young and unmarried; Eliza died November 11, 1867; he married (2) Nancy Spencer Grider, March 7, 1877; he died in Springfield, Sangamon County, Illinois, June 23, 1877.

(1-2-6-7) Rebecca Robinson Moffett, born March 25, 1799 in Bath County, Kentucky; married William Crain December 21, 1826 in Bath County, Kentucky and had children; died March 20, 1855 in Fleming County, Kentucky.

(1-2-6-8) John Bigham Moffett, born October 29, 1800 in Bath County, Kentucky. *See more.*

(1-2-6-9) Elizabeth Moffett, born September 29, 1802 in Bath County, Kentucky; married William Kendall in May 17, 1831 in Sangamon County, Illinois and had children; died in Hancock County Illinois after 1879.

(1-2-6-10) Willis Green Moffett, born June 9, 1804 in Bath County, Kentucky; married Caroline Stone, January 4, 1825; removed to Illinois and had seven children; removed to Hennepin County, Minnesota and died there 1870-1880.

(1-2-6-8) John Bigham Moffett, born October 29, 1800, Bath County, Kentucky; married (1) Patsy A. Morgan (born in Ohio in about 1800), July 26, 1821 in Bath County; removed to central Illinois, had three children; she died March 28, 1826 in Sangamon County, Illinois; married (2) on May 17, 1827, Sangamon County Illinois, Pollyanna Taylor and had eleven children; she was born May 5, 1809 in Kentucky, daughter of David Sutton Taylor and Sarah Young; married (3) on September 26, 1850, Nancy Spencer Grider, widow of Rev. Abner McDowell; Nancy was born in Warren County, Kentucky, about 1810, daughter of Captain Henry Grider and Elizabeth Smith; no children; John Bigham Moffett died September 15, 1862 in Macon County Illinois; Nancy died March 11, 1892 in Blue Mound Township, Macon County.

Children by Patsy A. Morgan:

(1-2-6-8-1) Rebecca Jane Moffett, born July 30, 1822 in Sangamon County, Illinois; married Lewis Robertson June 15, 1841 in Sangamon County, Illinois, and they had two children; Lewis was born in Kentucky in about 1811; Rebecca died September 22, 1845 in Illinois.

(1-2-6-8-2) Elizabeth Ann Moffett, born January 29, 1824 in Sangamon County, Illinois; married James Y. Taylor, March 19, 1846 in Illinois, and they had seven children; James was born in Illinois in about 1819, brother of Pollyana Taylor (John Bigham Moffett's second wife), both were children of David Sutton Taylor, native of New Jersey, and of Sarah Young, a native of Virginia; Elizabeth died in Madison, Madison County, Illinois, October 1, 1887.

(1-2-6-8-3) William Thomas Moffett, Born February 19, 1826, Sangamon County. *See More*.

Children by Pollyana Taylor:

(1-2-6-8-4) David Sutton Moffett, born February 14, 1828 in Sangamon County, Illinois; married Melissa Brockway May 19, 1857 in Macon County, Illinois, and they had five children; Melissa was born April 13, 1841 in Bourbon County, Kentucky, the daughter of David Brockway and Eliza Goodall; he served as a 1ˢᵗ Lt. in the 115ᵗʰ Illinois Infantry in the Civil War; he died in Macon County, Illinois May 19, 1868; she died September 13, 1912 in Jacksonville, Morgan County, Illinois.

(1-2-6-8-5) Sarah Taylor Moffett, born December 23, 1829 in Sangamon County, Illinois; married Charles Fisher in Christian County, Illinois, October 28, 1850 and they had two children; Charles was born in Quincy Township, Franklin County, Pennsylvania, December 24, 1822, the son of Samuel Fisher, and Hannah Beaver; Sarah died in Sangamon County, Illinois, February 16, 1854, and Charles died July 1, 1911 in Springfield, Sangamon County, Illinois.

(1-2-6-8-6) Mary Eliza Moffett, born March 15, 1832 in Rushville, Schuyler County, Illinois, and died there June 28, 1832.

(1-2-6-8-7) Ann Eliza Moffett, born in Rushville, Schuyler County, Illinois May 29, 1833, and died in Christian County, Illinois, August 8, 1846.

(1-2-6-8-8) Robert Moffett, born in Rushville, Schuyler County, Illinois December 7, 1835, and died in the same month.

(1-2-6-8-9) John McDowell Moffett, born in Illinois December 14, 1836; married Elizabeth Jane McDonald January 26, 1860 in Macon County, Illinois, and they had eight children; Elizabeth was born in Pennsylvania in February of 1839 and died January 18, 1923 in Macon County, Illinois; John died in Boody, Macon County, Illinois October 14, 1914.

(1-2-6-8-10) James Milton Moffett, born August 10, 1839 in Schuyler County, Illinois; died in Christian County, Illinois, May 31, 1851.

(1-2-6-8-11) Caroline Moffett, born August 6, 1842 in Illinois, and died the same day.

(1-2-6-8-12) Louisa Catherine Moffett, born September 12, 1843 in Illinois, died there July11, 1845.

(1-2-6-8-13) Joseph Edwin Moffett, born September 25, 1845 in Illinois; served as a Private in the 116th Illinois Infantry Regiment in the Civil War, February 1, 1864 to May 18, 1865, and the 55th Illinois Infantry from May 18 to August 14, 1865; married (1) Sarah M. Adams, September 1867 in Macon County, Illinois, and they had three children; Sarah was born about 1848 in Indiana, a daughter of Henry Adams, a native of Kentucky, and she died in Decatur, Macon County, Illinois May 24, 1882. (2) Nettie Hoyt, May 13, 1883 in De Witt County, Illinois, but they had no children; Nettie was born about 1865 in Illinois, a daughter of Orin A. and Eunice Hoyt, natives of Indiana, and she died in De Witt County, Illinois, and they had one child; Amanda was born in May of 1855 in Kentucky. Joseph died in Chicago, Cook County, Illinois October 13, 1918.

(1-2-6-8-14) Laura Amanda Moffett, born February 10, 1849 in Christian County, Illinois; married William Thomas Evans August 29, 1866 in Blue Mound Township, Macon County, Illinois, but they had no children; William was born in Illinois in about 1845; Laura died probably sometime in 1867.

(1-2-6-8-3) William Thomas Moffett, born in Sangamon County, Illinois, February 19, 1826; married Helen Lucretia Barrows October 15, 1856, Bridport, in Addison County, Vermont; they had eight children; Helen Barrows was born in Bridport , February 1, 1832, the daughter of Josiah Barrows and his second wife, Susan R. Walker; William organized and led a home guard unit in Macon County during the Civil War; he died October 12, 1901 in Blue Mound Township, Macon County, Illinois; Helen died August 2, 1913 in Harristown, Macon County. Their eight children:

(1-2-6-8-3-1) Edward A. Moffett, born and died July 11, 1857 in Macon County, Illinois.

(1-2-6-8-3-2) Edward Raymond Moffett, born October 11, 1859 in Macon County, Illinois; married Juliette A. Warnick in Macon County, Illinois September 27, 1882, and they had seven children; Juliette was the daughter of Ira G. Warnick and Juliette Priscilla Burke; Juliette died in Macon County, Octobver 25, 1940; Edward died there September 2, 1926.

(1-2-6-8-3-3) John Bigham Moffett, born in Macon County, Illinois, July 13, 1861. He removed to Kansas and married (1) Eva Denny, March 30, 1887 in Cimarron, Gray County, Kansas; Eva was born in St. Louis County, Missouri, August 18, 1868, the daughter of James J. Denny and his first wife, Mary Sullivan; they resided in Kansas, then removed to Oklahoma, and then returned to Macon County, Illinois; Eva died June 26, 1906 in Decatur, Macon County, Illinois; the family removed to Laurens County, Georgia; John married (2) Susan A., in 1909. John Bigham Moffett died June 27, 1926 in Jacksonville, Duval County, Florida. He and Eva Denny had three children.

(1-2-6-8-3-4) William David Moffett, born in Macon County, Illinois, January 24, 1863; married Anna M. Cottle February 2, 1894 in Macon County, and they had four children; William died in Decautr, Macon County, September 18, 1944.

(1-2-6-8-3-5) Harry Josiah Moffett, born February 5, 1865 in Macon County, Illinois; died October 21, 1866 in Macon County.

(1-2-6-8-3-6) Leonora Antoinette Moffett, born April 18, 1867 in Macon County, Illinois; married Edwin Preston Hall (born Illinois, in May of 1864, and died in Springfield, Illinois, January 3, 1937), Octobver 10, 1888 in Macon County, and they had three children; she died April 3, 1952 in Springfield, Illinois.

(1-2-6-8-3-7) Mary Helen Moffett, born in Macon County Illinois, December 28, 1868; married Wright Edwin Allen, September 1, 1887 in Macon County, Illinois, and they had 4 children; she died August 17, 1921.

(1-2-6-8-3-8) Elizabeth Ann Mofett, born November 18, 1871 in Macon County, Illinois; married William Nesbitt Rugh, April 7, 1894 in Macon County, Illinois, and they had two children; William was bornin Pennsylvania in February 1871, son of Samuel Rugh and Margaret Truby; Elizabeth died January 21, 1954 in Arcola, Douglas County, Illinois; William died May 16, 1956.

Appendix 9
Text of the Will of John Bigham Moffett[1]

<u>Last Will & Testament of John B. Moffat</u>

In the name of God Amen. I John B. Maffett of the County of Hennepin and State of Minnesota, being of sound mind and memory but in feeble health, yet considering the uncertanties of this life, do make, ordain, and publish this my last will and testament, hereby revoking all former Wills by me made or Codicils whatever.

Item 1st   After my decease I wish my body to have a decent Christian burial according according (sic) to the wish of my dear surviving relations and a neat set of marble gravestones furnished with suitable engravings on them and set at the head and foot of my grave. And if not sooner done I also wish similar graves stones furnished for the grave of my dear departed wife Polly Ann and my deceased daughter Ann, and also for my present wife Nancy S. Moffett; And I also wish to have a plat of ground at the place of my and their burial enclosed with a good substantial fence about ten by twenty feet square and all the expenses thereof as well as all other funeral expenses not then paid, to be paid out of my Personal Estate.

Item 2nd   It is my wish that all my just debts be paid out of my personal estate if sufficient there be after meeting all other provisions of this Will, but if not then I wish my Executor hereinafter named to sell so much of my Real Estate not otherwise disposed of by this will in such manner as he may think best, as will be sufficient to pay all my just debts.

Item 3rd   To my beloved wife Nancy S. Moffett I hereby give bequeath and devise in lieu of dower in my estate and during her natural life only, and in the purpose of her own comfortable support and as a home for my younger children during their minority, my homestead or home farm so called in Macon County State of Illinois, and all its appurtenances and improvements Houses, out Houses &c, situated on the following described tracts of land in which I give her a life estate only, and for the purposes above mentioned to wit

The North East quarter and the East half of the North west quarter of Section No Five (5) in

---

[1]Transcribed from pages 134-141, Will Book B, Macon County Court, Macon County,

Township No Fifteen (15) North, of Range No one (1) East of the Third Principal Meridian of Prarie lands and containing in all Two Hundred and fifty five $^{16}/_{100}$ Acres. I also give to my said wife for and during her natural life The South West of Section No Thirty one (31) in Township No sixteen (16) North of Range No one (1) East of the Third Principal Meridian containing Two Hundred forty Acres of timber land, the same to be for her use and occupation during her natural life and no greater or other than a life Estate is meant by me to be bequeathed to her, and in lieu of any dower in or claim upon my other real Estate of which I may die seized of. I further give bequeath and devise to my said wife, in addition to what is allowed by the law of the State of Illinois at the present time, to the widows of intestates, one good span of Horses, one good Cow, and all the Household and kitchen furniture which I may have at the time of my decease which may be over and above her allowances by the laws of Illinois. I also give to her all the said Statutes allow her as the widow of an intestate out of my personal property. It is my wish and desire that my two youngest Children, Joseph Edwin and Laura Amanda shall have during their minority or until they marry; if under their mature age find a home at my present homestead farm in the said State of Illinois or at such other place as she my said wife may reside, as I have made herin such provisions for her my said wife and said childrens comfort and support including necessary board, clothing, lodging medical attendance and schooling all of which I wish my said wife to provide at such place as her said home may be. And if the foregoing provisions shall prove insufficient for these purposes or if either or both of my said youngest children shall choose to live elsewhere I herin make other provisions for their support. But either or both of them shall cease to reside with my said wife, then and in that case I enjoin it upon her to furnish them or either of them, that so depart, with a good bedstead, bed, bedding, or fifty dollars in money, in lieu thereof when they or either of them shall so leave as aforesaid, and if this provision should should fail I wish my said two youngest children to have each a good Bedstead and Bedding, or fifty dollars in lieu thereof, And I also desire that they each may have one good horse apiece, or the sums of seventy five dollars in lieu thereof, the same to be furnished to them by my executor out of any means in his hands of my Estate, real or personal undisposed of by me in this will or otherwise.

Item 4th   After the decease of my said wife Nancy S. Moffett, I hereby give bequeath and devise to my two youngest children Joseph Edwin, and Laura Amanda, that part of the Real Estate herein bequeathed to my said wife Nancy during her life time, the timbered tract described to wit The East half of the South West quarter of Section No Thirty two (32) Township No Sixteen (16) North, of Range No one (1) East of the third Principal Meridian. I wish to have divided between them as follows viz

Beginning at the South East corner of said half quarter thence west four and one half rods. Thence North westerly to a large Red Elm tree about two rods East of a Spring known as the green Spring in the branch Thence from said Elm on the same course across said branch to a point where said line will cross said branch the second time. The west side thereof according to this division I hereby give and bequeath to Joseph Edwin, and the East Side thereof I hereby give and devise to Laura Amanda to be to them and their heirs and assigns forever after my said wifes decease. The three tracts of Prairie land embracing the Homestead also give to my said wife during her life time, I divide as follows viz

The North East Fraction a quarter of section N° Five (t) containing 169^{25}/$_{100}$ acres, and the East half of the North West quarter of same section containing 86 ^{1}/$_{100}$ acres Commencing at a stone planted as the half mile corner between Township N° Sixteen (16) Range One East, Thence from said corner (illegible word) South Easterly to a large red Elm tree on the west side of the branch (illegible word) Twenty four or Twenty five rods from said corner. Thence up said Branch on its west bank twenty five rods to a stake, Thence to the south (illegible word) said so as to divide them as nearly equal as can be the (two illegible words) or portion I give and devise to my son Joseph Edwin and the (illegible word) their heirs (several illegible words) from and after the decease of my said wife.

Item 5th My son William T. Moffett has now in his possession and occupancy By Deed of conveyance, The South East quarter of section N° Thirty two (32) Township N° sixteen (16) North of Range N° one (1) East of the Third Principal Meridian. Although not Deeded to him by me, yet it was by him obtained through my means, and by my approbation, and I do hereby give bequeath and devise said tract to him and his heirs and assigns forever as his specific devise of my Real Estate.

Item 6th I have heretofore made a deed of conveyance to my son David S. Moffett of the west half of the south west quarter, and the west half of the North West quarter of Section N° Thirty three (33) Township N° Sixteen (16) North, of range one (1) East of the Third Principal Meridian containing One Hundred and Sixty acres, I now give bequeath and devise to my said son David S. Moffett, as hereafter set forth, out of my personal property, One pair of Horses described as follows vis. One small Mare called Kit, One roan Horse called Bill, now in the hands of my son William T. Moffett, in the County of Macon State of Illinois; Also one thimble Skeined double or two Horse wagon now owned by me and a set of harness for said Horses. It is my intention only to bequeath the right to use the said property named for the comfort of my said son David S. Moffett and family, as long as the same may last, and the title to said property shall be in my son William T. Moffett to be held by him in trust for my said son David S. Moffett. Also one milch cow and calf, the above described personal property bequeathed by me to my said son David S. Moffett is all of my personal property that intend to give to my said son or his heirs. I further give and bequeath and devise to my said son William T. My executor as hereinafter named in trust to convey the lands hereinafter mentioned to the children of my said son David S. When they become of age, of if my said Trustee shall think that at some time before the said children shall all become of age that the land would not be in jeopardy in the possession of my son David S. Moffett hen (sic) I hereby authorize and empower my trustee to convey the title to said real estate to my son David S. Moffett during his lifetime and to his children at his Decease in fee simple. The said lands so devised are described as follows viz The West half of the South East quarter of Section No Thirty Three (33) in Township No Sixteen (16) North, of Range one (1) East of the Third Principal Meridian. I also give bequeath and devise in trust to my said Executor to be by him held and disposed of as the aforesaid described piece,. Twenty acres of timber land off from the west side of the West half of the North West quarter of Section Thirty four in Township and range last aforesaid, the aforesaid Eighty acres, and twenty acres bequeathed as aforesaid, herby the full amount of real Estate by me intended to be given to my son David S. Moffett or to his heirs or either of them.

Item 7th   I have made a deed of conveyance to my son in law Lewis Robertson for life remainder to his two children John L. And Mary Elizabeth Robertson and their heirs forever in fee, as their specific portion or devise, (illegible writing, possibly two words) off from the South end of the East half of the South West quarter and sixty acres off from the South end of the west half of the South East quarter of Section No Five (5) in Township No Fifteen (15) North, of Range one (1) East of the Third Principal Meridian, also one other tract of land amounting in all to one hundred and forty acres as per a deed of conveyance dated March 20th A.D. 1856.

Item 8th   I give bequeath devise to my son in law James Taylor and to his wife my daughter Elizabeth Ann Taylor for and during the lifetime of said Elizabeth Ann Taylor and after her decease to all of her children equally and if any of the said children shall die without issue then the whole to go to the survivors of them forever conveying fifty Eight and $^{50}/_{100}$ acres off from the west side of the North East quarter of Section No Four (4) in Township No Fifteen (15) North, of Range one (1) East, also two other tracts amounting in all to One hundred and thirty four acres, and described as follows viz Fifty four and 50/100 acres from the East Side of the North West quarter of said Section four and range; also twenty (20) acres of timber land bounded as follows vis. Beginning twenty rods west from the South East corner of the west half of the North West quarter of Section No Thirty four (34) Township No Sixteen (16) North, of Range one (1) East of the Third Principal Meridian, Thence running west twenty rods with the south line of said half quarter, Thence North parallel with the East line of said half quarter, one hundred and sixty poles to the North line of said half quarter, Thence East with said last named line twenty rods. Thence South parallel with the East line of said half quarter to the beginning. The above described three tracts amount to the said (134) acres, the above described land is the full amount of specific devises to the said James Y Taylor & wife and heirs by me made, Excepting and reserving from the first described piece of land in this Item, the following parcel commencing at the North East corner of said piece, Thence South one hundred and Eighty feet, Thence West one hundred and sixty feet, Thence North one hundred and Eighty feet, Thence one hundred and sixty feet to the place of beginning which reserved piece I give and bequeath to School district Nᵒ (3) in Towns (15) and (16) of the aforesaid Range when said district shall have paid to me or my Executor the sum of One hundred and thirty one dollars with interest as the same becomes due.

Item 9th   I have heretofore made a Deed of conveyance to my son in law Charles Fisher for his life remains in fee simple to his two Children, George and   Fisher equally conveying one hundred and thirty four acres as per Deed of conveyance thereof dated March 20th 1856 which said Land so Deeded by me was intended by me as their specific portion or share in my real Estate.

Item 10th   I hereby give and bequeath to my son John McDowal Moffett and to his heirs forever, the following described real Estate viz, the west half of the South West quarter of Section Nᵒ Thirty four (34) and the East half of the South East quarter of Section Nᵒ Thirty three (33) in Township Nᵒ Sixteen (16) North of Range one (1) East of the Third Principal Meridian being one hundred and twenty acres. Also twenty acres of timber bounded as follows viz beginning forty poles west of the South East corner of the west half of the Northwest quarter of Section Nᵒ thirty four in Township Nᵒ Sixteen (16) North, of Range one (1) East of the Third Principal Meridian. Thence with the South line of said half quarter section west twenty poles Thence North parallel with the west line of said half quarter 160 poles to the North line of said half quarter, Thence East with the North line of said half quarter twenty poles Thence South 160 poles to the place of beginning, as his specific devise or share.

Item 11th   I hereby authorize and empower my said Executor to sell and convey so much of my Real Estate not deeded or devised as expressed in this Will and the Deeds therein refered to as may remain undisposed of by me at my decease and as may be necessary for the payment of my debts and all the expenses of settling my business and satisfying all the provisions of this my Will. As the quantity of land I have given to each of my children is not equal, having given to some more than to others, I wish and devise that enough shall first be given to those who have had the smallest portions (except to my son David S. Moffett and his heirs) to make them equal to those that received the larger portions; and the remainder of my Estate both real and personal if any there be, and wherever situated after satisfying all my specific desires and bequests I desire to have divided into Seven equal parts of which I give and bequeath one of the seven equal parts to each of the following children to wit, Lewis Robertson, Charles Fisher, James Y. Taylor, William T. Moffett, John McDowell Moffett,

Joseph Edwin Moffett and Laura Amanda Moffett, being seven of my proper heirs or their representatives, the said property to be conveyed to them by my Executor in accordance with the provisions of this will and of said Deeds of conveyance already made by me to some of them. But if the real Estate in the best judgment of my executor which may rem which may remain (sic) after the specific devises have been carried out according to the provisions of this will cannot be divided as is contemplated in this Item without prejudice to the heirs mentioned in this Item then I authorize my Said Executor to sell such Real Estate in such manner as he may think best, and so to use the proceeds thereof, as first to make all of my children mentioned in this Item, or to the heirs of those then deceased equal and then divide the residue in the same manner and in the same way by giving to each their respective portions of what it may bring, that is one seventh to each of the following named children to wit, Lewis Robertson, Charles Fisher, James Y. Taylor, William Thomas Moffett, John McDowel Moffett, Joseph Edwin Moffett and Laura Amanda Moffett, being seven of my proper heirs securing to the respective children of my daughters Rebecca deceased, Sarah Fisher deceased and Elizabeth Ann Taylor and putting the same at interest so as to be paid to them when they become of age. In the event that any one or more of my children shall die before arriving at the age required by law to convey Real Estate or personal property, I herin devise and bequeath that part of my Estate heretofore described and bequeathed to them and not consumed by them at the time of their decease to each of the heirs mentioned in this Item that then survive the same proportion of such deceased minors part as herin before bequeathed to them in the same manner and in the same way as the distributions is made of the real Estate and personal property after all the specific devises and provisions of this will are made.

Item 12th   In order that live Stock which may remain as part of my estate after all the specific bequests and provisions of my said Last Will and Testament are complied with may not be sold at a sacrifice, I hereby authorize and empower my said Executor to hold and Sell the same in such manner and at such times and on such terms as he may deem the proper for the best interests of my Estate.

Item 13th   I having laid out a plan for a barn to be built on my home place in the said State of Illinois in the County of Macon therein and having cut logs in accordance with the plan and having sent the logs to Whitley's Mill in said County to be sawed, I hereby authorize and empower my said executor to go on and build and furnish said barn in accordance with said plan, and to cover said barn with three feet boards and to pay for said barn out of my personal Estate. For the better determining what said plan for said barn is I have certified on the back of said plan that it is the plan mentioned and intended in this Item of my Will.

Item 14th   The Real Estate heretofore devised by me as specific devises and described in this will situate in the State of Illinois. the Real Estate to be divided in Seven parts as heretofore set forth is situate in the State of Illinois and Missouri.

Item 15th   I hereby appoint my son William Thomas Moffett the Executor of this my last will and Testament wishing him to faithfully execute its provisions and I also wish him to consult my Brother Thomas Moffett of Springfield Illinois in all matters in which legal advice may be desired and to pay him for such advice a reasonable compensation out of my Estate.

In witness whereof I have herento
Set my hand and seal this Sixth day of August A.D. 1862

John B. Moffett

The foregoing instrument consisting of five Sheets was at the date thereof signed, sealed, published and declared by the said John B. Moffett as and for his last Will and Testament, in presence of us who at his request, and in his presence and in the presence of each other, have subscribed our names as witnesses thereto.

The addition to items (6&7) on the margin, and the erasure of part of item (6) made before signing this instrument by the above named Testator or

as witnesses

Nathan B. Hill	Residing at Minneapolis Minnesota
Edwin S. Jones	Residing at Minneapolis Minnesota
Alfred Lindley	Residing at Minneapolis Minnesota

State of Illinois
Macon County } Ss   The People of the State of Illinois

To J. C. Williams a Justice of the Peace Greeting

We reposing Special confidence in your fidelity and provident circumspection do hereby authorize and appoint you to take the testimony in writing of Nathan B. Hill, Edwin S. Jones, and Alfred H. Lindley, whom you are authorized and required to bring before you, at such time and place as you may designate and appoint for that purpose, and that at such time and place you will proceed to examine under oath Said witnesses upon the interrogatories hereunto annexed at the instance of W. T. Moffett whose application pending to admit the last Will and Testament of John B. Moffett to Record in our County Court of Macon County Illinois.

The annexed form you (illegible) Use to be filled according to the blanks enclosed and have the said Witnesses and any two of them sign it at the bottom, at the foot thereof you will add a certificate subscribed by myself, Stating that it was sworn to and subscribed by said Witnesses and the time and place where the same is taken, when said affidavit of said Witnesses so taken with your certificate thereto attached you will send directed to our Clerk of our Said County Court and State aforesaid on or before the 3rd Monday in October next together with this writ

Witness my hand and seal of said Court at
Decatur this 22nd day of September A.D. 1862

State of Minnesota

Hennepin County   } Ss

Personally   In a Justice Court of Said County

appeared in open Court Nathan B. Hill and

Edwin S. Jones, Subscribing Witnesses to the forgoing instrument of writing purporting to be the last Will and Testament of John B. Moffett late of Hennepin County, deceased, who being duly sworn according to law, do depose and say each for himself that the foregoing is the last Will and Testament of the said John B. Moffett deceased; that they subscribed their names thereto as the attesting witnesses at the request of the said Testator, and in his presence, and in the presence of each other, on the sixth day of August A.D. 1862 that he then and there subscribed his name thereto in their presence and declared the same to be his last Will and Testament: and that the said Testator at the time of executing the same as aforesaid was of full age, of sound mind and memory and under no constraint.

Nathan B. Hill

Edwin S. Jones

Subscribed and affirmed to before me this 4th day

of October A.D. 1862   J.C. Williams

Justice of the Peace

I herby certify that on the 4th day of October A.D. 1862 at the execution of the commission issued to me by the County Court of Macon County State State of Illinois with the interrogatories annexed, in the matter of the application of William T. Moffett to prove the last Will and Testament of John B. Moffett in said Court, the said Nathan B. Hill and Edwin S. Jones residents of Hennepin County State of Minnesota personally appeared before me and being first duly affirmed made the forgoing answers to the forgoing interrogatories at the time aforesaid and Subscribed their names thereto in my presence.   Witness my hand this 4th day of October 1862

J.C. Williams   Justice of the Peace

In & for said Henepin County

Appendix 10
Considerations on the Timing of William Thomas Moffett's Participation in the California Gold Rush of 1849-1853

The timing of William Thomas Moffett's travel to and from California, as reported in the local histories of Macon County, Illinois, is very likely incorrect. Biographies in the local histories indicate that he left for California in 1849. They also indicate that he had been away from Illinois for eighteen months when he responded to his father's pleas and returned. However, due consideration makes it apparent that this seems unlikely.

The 1850 federal census includes the enumeration of William T. Moffett in Macon County, Illinois. The household where he and his brother, David, were residing (that of his sister, Elizabeth, and her husband James Taylor) was visited by the enumerator on September 21, 1850. It would therefore appear that on that date in September, William was there in Macon County. Alternatively, one could argue that William was residing in his sister's home on June 1, 1850, because technically, the enumerators were instructed to record the people who were residing in a household on that date (the "census date") regardless of when the dwelling was actually visited.

William T. Moffett would not have left Illinois until early 1849, the confirmation of the discovery of gold not becoming public until December of 1848. Few if any migrants set out from their last staging area before May, when the mud of late spring would have significantly dried up. If William Moffett had set out from western Missouri as early as May, he might have left Illinois in March or April, but certainly no earlier than January, immediately on the heels of the President's December, 1848 speech. If he decided to leave California eighteen months later, he might have done so no earlier than July of 1850. Even by the sea route he took to return, the journey back to Illinois would have taken at least four months, in which case he could not have been back in Illinois until November of 1850 at the very earliest. Yet we know that he was in fact in Illinois in September of 1850, and possibly a few months earlier than that on June 1. He therefore could not have left Illinois until after he was enumerated there in the 1850 census.

On the other hand, it seems unlikely that William Moffett left for the goldfields much later than the day on which he was enumerated in Illinois. That same 1850 census shows that his father had already had to abandon his farm in Macon County for the one in exile in Christian County.

Even so, William would probably not have left Illinois much before late winter (about February or March) in 1851. Given the eighteen months he had been away when his father's entreaties convinced him to return from California, and the additional four or more months necessary for the return trip, it seems likely that William would not have been back in Macon County before about Christmas of 1852.

SCHEDULE I.—Free Inhabitants in *Macon District* in the County of *Macon* State of *Illinois* enumerated by me, on the *21st* day of *Sept* 1850.   *C. J. Rice* Ass't Marshal

	Dwelling-houses numbered in the order of visitation.	Families numbered in the order of visitation.	The Name of every Person whose usual place of abode on the first day of June, 1850, was in this family.	Age.	Sex.	Color, (White, black, or mulatto.)	Profession, Occupation, or Trade of each Male Person over 15 years of age.	Value of Real Estate owned.	PLACE OF BIRTH. Naming the State, Territory, or Country.	Married within the year.	Attended School within the year.	Persons over 20 y'rs of age who cannot read & write	Whether deaf & dumb, blind, insane, idiotic, pauper, or convict.
1	2		3	4	5	6	7	8	9	10	11	12	13
1			Amos Hall	24	M		Laborer		Tenn			1	
2	447	447	Elisha B Randal	28	M		Farmer	500	Ky				
3			Caroline "	20	F				Ill				
4			Geo. W	4	M				"				
5			Emily	1	F				"				
6			Valentine Claywell	26	M		"	600	Ky				
7	448	448	Asa Reed	44	M		"	1000	N Carolina			1	
8			Clarisa	48	F				Ohio				
9			Sarah J "	18	F				Ill				
10			Elizabeth "	16	F				"			1	
11			Perly "	11	F				"			1	
12			Clarisa "	9	F				"			1	
13			Johnathan "	7	M				"			1	
14			Edmond "	5	M				"				
15			Jackson "	2	M				"				
16	449	449	John Watkins	43	M		"	1500	Ky			1	
17			Hannah "	40	F				"			1	
18			Wm "	16	M		Laborer		Illinois		1		
19			John F "	13	M				"		1		
20			Clarisa "	6	F				"		1		
21			John Smith	7	M				Ind		1		
22	450	450	Ambros Tway	36	M		Farmer		Ohio		1	1	
23			Elizabeth A	20	F				Virginia	1			
24			Virgil Morris	20	M		Laborer		Ohio				
25			Wm D Von	9	M				Indiana		1		
26			John Tway	24	M		"		Ohio				
27	451	451	Clayford Tway	31	M		Farmer		Ind				
28			Emma "	27	F								
29			Wm H "	72	M				Ind				
30			Martha Von	33	F				N J				
31			Sarah C "	14	F				Ind				
32			Harriet J "	9	F				Ioway				
33			Mary M "	4	F				"				
34	452	452	Joseph Farris	27	M		Laborer		Ind			1	
35			Mary "	30	F				Tenn			1	
36			Dodd L Farris	15	M				Ill				
37	453	453	Jas Taylor	31	M		Farmer		"				
38			Elizabeth	26	F				"				
39			Louisa	2	F				"				
40			Wm Moffett	24	M		Laborer		"				
41			David "	20	M				"				
42	454	454	Luther Devor	24	M		Farmer	4000	Ohio			2 9 7	

The enumeration of William T. Moffet(t) in the 1850 federal census in Macon County, Illinois. He was residing in the household of his sister, Elizabeth, and her husband, Ja(me)s Taylor. Also in the household are Elizabeth and James's daughter, "Louisa" (Rebecca Louise), as well as David, the brother of William T. and Elizabeth. The enumerator visited this household on September 21, 1850.

What might be the very latest that William Moffett may have gone to California? The gold rush tapered off significantly in 1853. Additionally, in the fall of 1856, William married Helen Lucretia Barrows at her family home in Bridport, Vermont. From what is written of the economic trials of William's father, it would seem that William might not have felt free to court and marry until after those difficulties were surmounted. The time which would have been consumed by the couple's meeting, courtship, and the organization of their marriage ceremonies (which would take place halfway across the continent) must at least have been a year, and very possibly upwards of two years. It is not clear how much time may have been consumed by the legal dealings involved in rescuing the estate of William's father, but it is not unlikely that it was at least several months.

With these factors in mind, and counting the time backwards from the marriage in October of 1856, we can see that William very probably could not have arrived back in Illinois later than about the beginning of 1855. In such case, he could possibly have been among those last sizable groups who crossed the continent for California in 1853, been called to return late in the summer of 1854, and arrived back in Macon County early in 1855.

Such would seem to be at the limits of what was probable. In fact, one would think that the prudent attention needed to right the ship of the Moffetts' estate would require more than the minimum times suggested here. We therefore might conjecture that the departure from Illinois was most likely in the spring of 1851. Such timing would have made it clearer to William that the miners were the least likely to reap benefits from the gold, and that the greatest promise inherent in the discovery lay in supplying the hordes of newcomers. By late 1852, he would have been prospering, and his father's legal and economic situation would have been reaching or passing some critical points. He would likely have arrived back in Illinois the following spring, and over the next many months could have provided the cash to save many of the land parcels which represented his father's only life savings. His father would then have returned to his own land in Macon County.

With the dawn of 1854, with the estate rescued, William would have undertaken to establish his own place in the economy of central Illinois, setting up on one of the pieces of land in Macon County, and establishing a farming and livestock business, perhaps in conjunction with that of his father. Once thus established, he would have been open to the prospect of marriage. Later in 1854, his future bride arrived from New England and began two years of teaching school in Macon and Sangamon counties.

Bibliography

Archaimbault, Delores, and Terry A. Barnhart. "Illinois Copperheads and the American Civil War." *Illinois History Teacher*, vol. 3:1, 1996. Springfield, Illinois; Illinois Historic Preservation Agency, 1996.

Bangerter, Gloria. *Super Index, A Compilation of Available Irish Will Indexes, 1270-1860.* Salt Lake City: J. & J. Limited, 2000.

Bartlett, Richard A. *The New Country, A Social History of the American Frontier, 1776-1890.* New York: Oxford University Press, 1974.

Basler, Roy P., Marion Dolores Pratt, and Lloyd A. Dunlap, eds. *The Collected Works of Abraham Lincoln*, 9 vols. Springfield, Illinois: Abraham Lincoln Association; New Brunswick, New Jersey: Rutgers University Press, 1953.

Bellesiles, Michael A. *Revolutionary Outlaws.* Charlottesville: University Press of Virginia, 1993.

Biographical Directory of the United States Congress

Black, George F. *The Surnames of Scotland.* Edinburgh: Birlinn Ltd., 1993.

Boorstin, Daniel. *The Americans, The National Experience.* New York: Random House, 1965.

Bryson, Bill. *The Mother Tongue – English and How it Got That Way* (New York, 1900), Chapter 8.

Butler, Robert N., M.D. The Wonderful World of Longevity. 1 October 2001. International Longevity Center – USA. 2004. January 2006 <http://www.ilcusa.org/_lib/pdf/wonder2001. pdf/wonder2001.pdf#search='18th%2U.S.%20life%20expectancy'>

Catton, Bruce. *The American Heritage New History of the Civil War.* New York: Viking Penguin, 1996.

Chambers, Tim. "Bedtime Prayers", 19 September 2003, Go Against the Flow, Live Life Differently, 5 January 2006, <http://home.pcisys.net/~tbe/bedpryr.htm>

Clift, G. Glenn, comp. *"Second Census" of Kentucky – 1800.* Baltimore: Genealogical Publishing Company,1966. (Originally published in Frankfort, Ky., 1954.)

Culbertson, Kendel. "Springfield Church Cemetery". *USGenWeb Archives Project, Bath County, Kentucky.* April 26, 2006. USGenWeb. May 5, 2006 <http://ftp.rootsweb.com/pub/usgenweb/ky/bath/cemeteries/>

"Fertility and Mortality: Infant Mortality Rate", *The Reader's Companion to American History*, Houghton Mifflin Company, 2006, <http://college.hmco.com/history/readerscomp/rcah/html/ah_009701_fertilityand.htm>.

Fisher, Noel C. *War at Every Door, Partisan Politics & Guerilla Violence in East Tennessee 1860-1869.* Chapel Hill, North Carolina: University of North Carolina Press, 1997.

Foster, R. F. *Modern Ireland, 1600-1972*. London: Allen Lane/The Penguin Press, 1988.

Friedman, Milton. "Panic of 1837", *Wikipedia*, June 26, 2006, Wikimedia Foundation, Inc., July 6, 2006 <http://en.wikipedia.org/wiki/Panic_of_1837>.

Goodrich, Thomas. *Black Flag, Guerilla Warfare on the Western Border, 1861-1865*. Bloomington, Indiana: Uni8versity of Indiana Press, 1995.

Gray, Wood. *The Hidden Civil War, The Story of the Copperheads*. New York: The Viking Press, 1942.

"Graphing Changes in Life Expectancy", *Positively Aging, Unit 5, Our Aging World*, The University of Texas Health Science Center at San Antonio, 2005, <http://teachhealthk-2.uthscsa.edu/pa/pa05/0502.htm>

"Gregorian Calendar", October 7, 1006, Wikipedia, December 5, 2006 <http://en.wikipedia.org/wiki/Gregorian_calendar>.

Harper, Douglas. "S", *Online Etymology*. https://www.etymonline.com.

Harrison, Henry. *Surnames of the United Kingdom: A Concise Etymological Dictionary*. Baltimore: Genealogical Publishing Company, 1969.

Henemann, Charles B., comp. *First Census of Kentucky, 1790*. Baltimore: Genealogical Publishing Company, 1965. (Originally published in Washington D.C., 1940.)

Hicken, Victor. *Illinois in the Civil War*. Urbana: University of Illinois Press, 1991.

Hickey, Donald R. *The War of 1812, a Forgotten Conflict*. Chicago: University of Illinois Press, 1989.

History of Macon County, Illinois. Philadelphia: Brink, McDonough & Co., 1880.

"Hot Weather Reveals Scotland's History." August 21, 2006. *BBC News*. November 30, 2006 <http://news.bbc.co.uk/1/hi/in_pictures/5270364.stm>.

"Infant Mortality Rates, 1950-2002", *Infoplease*. ©2000-2005 Pearson Education, publishing as Infoplease, 23 January 2006, <http://www.infoplease.com/ipa/A0779935.html>.

Jacobus, Donald Lines. "Genealogy and Chronology." *Genealogical Research: Methods and Sources*, vol. I. Washington, D.C.: The American Society of Genealogists, 1960.

Josephy, Alvin M., Jr. *500 Nations, An Illustrated History of North American Indians* (New York, 1994), pp. 259-261.

Kentucky, Commonwealth of. Bath County Court. Deed Book F.

Kentucky, Commonwealth of. Bath County Tax Assessor. Tax List, 1811.

Kentucky, Commonwealth of. Montgomery County, County Court, Deed Book 2.

Kentucky, Commonwealth of. Montgomery County, Tax Assesor. Tax List, 1797.

Klement, Frank L. *The Copperheads in the Middle West.* Chicago: The University of Chicago Press, 1960.

Kull, Irving S. and Nell M. *A Chronological Encyclopedia of American History.* New York: Popular Library, 1969. (1969 edition of *A Short Chronology of American History*, originally published by the Rutgers University Press in 1952.)

Ladurie, E. Le Roy. *Times of Feast, Times of Famine: A History of Climate since the year 1000*, (London, 1972), 66.

Larkin, Jack. *The Reshaping of Everyday Life 1790-1840.* New York: Harper Collins, 1988.

Lear, Tobias (Secretary to President Washington). "Letter of Response to Col. Clement Biddle, February 14, 1790." *Today in History: February 22.* The Library of Congress, American Memory. December 3, 2006 <http://memory.loc.gov/ammem/today/feb22.html>.

Leish, Kenneth W., editor. *The American Heritage Pictorial History of the Presidents of the United States.* New York: American Heritage Publishing Company, Incorporated, 1908.

Leyburn, James G. *The Scotch-Irish, A Social History.* Chapel Hill: University of North Carolina Press, 1962.

"Life Expectancy by Age, 1850-2003", *Infoplease.* ©000-2005 Pearson Education, publisheing as Infoplease, 23 January 2006, <http;//www.infoplease.com/ipa/A0005140.htm1#5142>.

MacLean, Fitzroy. *Scotland, A Concise History.* London and New York: Thames and Hudson, Ltd., 1993.

Macon County, Illinois. Macon County Court. *Will Book B.*

Macon County, Illinois. Cemetery Inscriptions (Decatur, Illinois, 1968), vol. I, p. 21.

McBride, Ian. *The Siege of Derry in Ulster Protestant Mythology.* Dublin: Four Courts Press, 1997.

McFeely, William S. *Grant, A Biography.* New York: W. W. Norton & Company, 1981.

McPherson, James M., and David Rubel, editors. *"To the Best of My Ability", The American Presidents.* New York: Dorling Kindersley, 2000.

Merck, Frederick. *History of the Westward Movement.* New York: Alfred A. Knopf, 1980.

Milner, Clyde A. II, Carol A. O'Connor and Martha A. Sandweiss, eds. *The Oxford History of the American West.* New York: Oxford University Press, 1994.

Moffett, John B. Address, typescript in family's possession. Moffett family reunion. Blue Mound Township, Macon County, Illinois, December 25, 1900.

Morrison, Samuel Eliot, Henry Steele Commager and William E. Leuchtenburg. *The Growth of the American Republic.* New York: Oxford University Press, 1980.

New York Public Library. *Desk Reference.* New York: Stonesong Press, 1998.

New York Public Library, *Desk Reference* (New York, 1998), p. 12.

Ostrander, Gilbert. *Republic of Letters: The American Intellectual Community, 1776-1865.* Madison, Wisconsin: Madison House, 1999.

Past and Present of the City of Decatur and Macon County, Illinois. Chicago: S. G. Clarke Publishing Co., 1903.

Power, John Carroll. *History of the Early Settlers of Sangamon County.* Springfield, Illinois: Edwin A. Wilson, 1876.

Prucha, Francis Paul. *The Sword of the Republic, the United States Army on the Frontier, 1783-1846.* New York: The Macmillan Company, 1969.

"Records of Reverend Joseph P. Howe". *USGenWeb Archives Project, Montgomery County, Kentucky.* January 2, 2006. April 24, 2006 <http://www.rootsweb.com/~usgenweb/ky/montgomery/toc.html>

Register of Deeds for Ireland, Dublin. Deed books 259, 287 and 490.

Ross, Stewart, *Monarchs of Scotland.* New York: FactsOnFile Inc., 1990.

Rosner, David. "Epidemics", 2006, *Answers.com,* <http://www.answers.com/topic/epidemics>

Rothbard, Murray N. *The Panic of 1819, Reactions and Policies.* New York: Columbia University Press, 1962.

Russell, Howard S. *A Long Deep Furrow, Three Centuries of Farming in New England* (Hanover, New Hampshire, 1976).

Schlesinger, Arthur M. *The Age of Jackson.* Boston: Little, Brown and Company, 1989.

Shapiro, Larry. *A Book of Days in American History.* New York: Charles Scribner's Sons, 1987.

Shepard, Edward Morse. *Martin Van Buren.* Boston: Houghton, Mifflin Company, 1888.

Smout, T.C. *Scottish Trade on the Eve of Union, 1660-1707*(Edinburgh, 1963), 245-253.

"Soldiers Names and Records of the Union and Confederate Troops." *Civil War Soldiers and Sailors System.* National Park Service. November 7, 2006 http://www.itd.nps.gov/cwss/soldiers.cfm.

Stampp, Kenneth M. *America in 1857, A Nation on the Brink.* New York: Oxford University Press, 1990.

Stevens, Frank E. *The Black Hawk War.* Chicago: Frank E. Stevens, 1903.

Stewart, The Rev. David. *Historical Memoirs of First Saintfield Congregation (Tonaghneave) through Three Centuries, 1658-1958.* Belfast: T. H. Jordan Ltd., 1958.

The Papers of Abraham Lincoln, The LincolnLog, http://www.stg.brown.edu/projects/lincoln.

Tindall, George Brown. *America, A Narrative History.* New York: W. W. Norton & Company, 1984.

Turnbull, W. Roberson, *History of Moffat,* Chapter 1.

United States Federal Census, 1850, Christian County, Illinois, District 22.

Walton, Gary. "A Brief History of Human Progress." *Is Capitalism Good for the Poor?* Foundation for Teaching Economics. January 2006 http://www.fte.org/capitalism/introduction/index.php

Ward, Geoffrey C., Ric Burns and Ken Burns. *The Civil War, An Illustrated History.* New York: Alfred A. Knopf, 1990.

Wikipedia, the free encyclopedia. *Moffat (town of),* <https://en.wikipedia.org/wiki/Moffat>.

Wilson, David A. *United Irishmen, United States.* Ithaca, New York: Cornell University Press, 1998.

Index to Names of Moffett Family Members
(Names in italics represent persons in the direct ancestral lines of David McKenzie Moffett)

General Index

David Moffett's Additional Research, Photos and Exhibits

The Moffats, a Brief History of the Clan

The Moffat Clan is one of the oldest families in Dumfriesshire. They were an influential and powerful family as far back as Sir William Wallace.

William de Monte Alto, progenitor of the Movats, married the youngest daughter of Andlaw (Allan) Grant who came to Scotland from Norway during the 10th Century. Over the years, the name has altered to Montealt, Movat and Movest, eventually settling at Moffat. The name Moffat means "of high mountain." Another translation is "long plain."

The brief history above is consistent with the family tradition that has always claimed the Moffats are of Norman or Norse descent. The Normans were "Northmen" or "Norsemen" who had previously moved down from Scandinavia and settled in what was to be known as Normandy. In addition, there is also heraldic evidence that indicates both Movats and Moffats descend from the same family of de Monte Alto. Movat of Buchollie in Aberdeenshire and Moffat at Wauchopegill near Langholm bore identical arms, namely a silver shield with a black lion rampant with red claws and tongue. This is a variant of the pre-1190 Bruce shield and is also shown on the two de Monte Alto seals dated about 1300s.

In addition to family tradition and heraldic evidence, the Norse origin is also supported based on the author Moffett's own extensive DNA testing and analysis. This DNA analysis suggests the original origin of the family is Germanic (Anglo Saxon and Dane), not Celtic. The DNA tracking further suggests the family migrated from northwestern Germany into southern Scandinavia. From Scandinavia, they migrated into what is Normandy and finally settled in Scotland. Further DNA study reveals a clear association with the Bourbons of French and Spanish origin. Further comparisons of the DNA sample to known descendants from Dumfriesshire also show a very favorable match. These matches are consistent the genealogical research contained in this book.

Continuing on with historical review, in the 12th Century, the family was of sufficient importance to be deemed "de Moffet," showing they were considered to be principle lairds and landowners. Of particular interest was the association with the Knights Templar. The Knights Templar founded during this same period were associated with the Moffats of Gardenholm. The Knights Templar held an orchard on their lands. In fact, during the "Third Crusade" of the 5,000 Scottish contingent, more than 1,000 were from Annandale, the ancient home of the Moffats. The Moffats were among the many families of Annandale to join the Crusaders.

On his succession to the throne, David I (1124-1153) granted the Lordship of Annandale to the Norman baron Robert the Bruce. In 1300s, the then-Lord of Annandale, Robert the Bruce, granted four charters of land to the Moffats. One was to Adam Moffat of Knock. They were also granted the "feu" of Grantoun and Reddings in 1341. Other properties which became Moffat lands later were Craigbeck and Crofthead, Altoun, Sundaywell and Urr, as well as Bodesbeck, Midknock and Garrogill. Grantoun and Reddings remained principle holdings of the family until 1628 when the lands passed to the Johnstones.

As stated earlier, the Moffats gave their allegiance to the Bruce family, which held the Lordship of Annandale for at least seven generations covering two centuries, the last being Robert the Bruce, later Robert I (1306-1329). In fact, the Moffats provided the King "40 men and 40 horses," including Adam Moffat of Knock and his brother, which made up one-fifth of

Bruce's victorious cavalry at the Battle of Bannockburn in 1314.

Even before the Battle of Bannockburn, the Moffats had been distinguished for their strong allegiance to Sir William Wallace and are said to have helped Wallace construct his famous "trench" in the Ettrick forest in 1297 and 1298. Nothing would be more natural than for the Moffats to fight for Wallace since many of them were neighbors in Moffatdale to William Wallace's older sister. For example, when Wallace came into the upper valley of the "Annan water" known as "Moffatdale" with four adherents and rode out with sixteen, it is reasonable to assume that many Moffats would be among his band of "goodly chevalier" that rode out to fight with Wallace at the Battle of Bledy Gill against the English at the garrison of Lochmaben.

Despite the Moffats' loyalty to the Scottish leaders, it was inevitable they would fall from favor at some point. This was, of course, because of the lawlessness that consumed the border territory between England and Scotland. The Moffats were among the feared group of families known as the "riding clans" or "reivers" who took their name from the time-honored custom of reviving or raiding not only their neighbors' livestock, but also their neighbors across the border in England. On the Scottish side of the border, the reivers were known as "moss troopers." These moss troopers, who were well-mounted and heavily armed, were a constant problem for both the English and Scottish authorities.

In an attempt to bring order to what was known as the "debatable lands" on both sides of the border, Alexander the 2nd of Scotland had in 1237 signed the Treaty of York, which for the first time established the Scottish border with England as a line from Solway to the Tweed. On either side of the border there were three "Marches." These areas of administration known as the West, East and Middle Marches were governed by a warden. These wardens would act as an arbitrator whose responsibility was to settle complaints during Truce Days. There was also a law passed known as the Hot Trod that granted anyone who had their livestock stolen the right to pursue the thieves and recover their property. The post of March warden was a powerful and lucrative position, with rival families vying for the position. The Marches became virtually a law unto themselves.

The West March was the ancient homeland of the Moffats, but the most dominant families were the Armstrongs, Maxwells and Johnstones. Allied to the Maxwells were the Moffats. The Moffats were described as "a particularly unpleasant bunch," and having murdered a gang of Johnstones, they proceeded to decapitate them. And after putting their heads in a sack, the Moffat Heidsman is said to have uttered, "There you are then Johnstones, ye can a' greet the gither now." The Kerrs, along with the Douglases and Elliots, held sway over the Middle March. By 1504, the Moffats appeared to still be in Royal favor, because two men were hanged in the borders for the murder of Thomas Moffet, described as one of the King's liegeman or trusted officials, despite the fact that many of his relations were still notorious reivers.

One of the Moffat's most powerful enemies was the Johnstones of the West March who in 1557 exacted a murderous retribution on the Moffat family by killing Robert Moffat, the family chief, and other Clan leaders by setting fire to a building where they were gathered. Anyone who tried to escape was murdered as they fled the burning building.

By 1583, two Moffats incurred the wrath of the authorities for crimes that included "fire raising" and murder. In the same year, a band of Moffats had also raided an enemy's land, leaving a trail of devastation in their pillaging wake.

Four years later in 1587, the Scottish Parliament declared the Moffats to be an "unruly clan" of the West March. In 1594, parliament drew up a series of harsh measures "to suppress the lawless Moffats and other border clans."

The lawless state of affairs was no better by 1608, however, when a Privy Council report graphically described how the "wild incest, adulteries, convocation of the liege, shooting, and wearing hackbuts, pistols, lances, daily bloodshed, oppression and disobedience, neither are or has been punished."

The final death knoll for the Moffats was finally sounded in 1609 when a special commission was set up by King James the 6th, which arranged that many of the lands the family had held for centuries should be sold off to their bitter enemies, the Johnstones.

Many Moffats remained in the borders, but many others were dispersed throughout the realm, including Ireland and America. Some of the lands were later repurchased by Moffat descendants in the early years of the 20th Century.

The families' proud heritage was recognized in 1983 when Major Francis Moffat of Craigbeck was recognized by Lord Lyon King of Arms of Scotland as hereditary clan chief with the designation of Moffat of that Ilk. Following his death in 1992, his daughter succeeded to the same title as Madame Jean Moffat of that Ilk.

The town of Moffat in Annandale, Dumfriesshire continues to this day as the ancestral home of the Moffat Clan.

Sources: The information contained comes from a document from Clan Moffat entitled The Moffats - A Brief History; "Moffat, the Origins of the Moffats and Their Place in History" by Ian Gray; and Y-line DNA Analysis Report prepared by Roberta Estes, DNA Explained.

Ancient map of Annandale, Scotland.

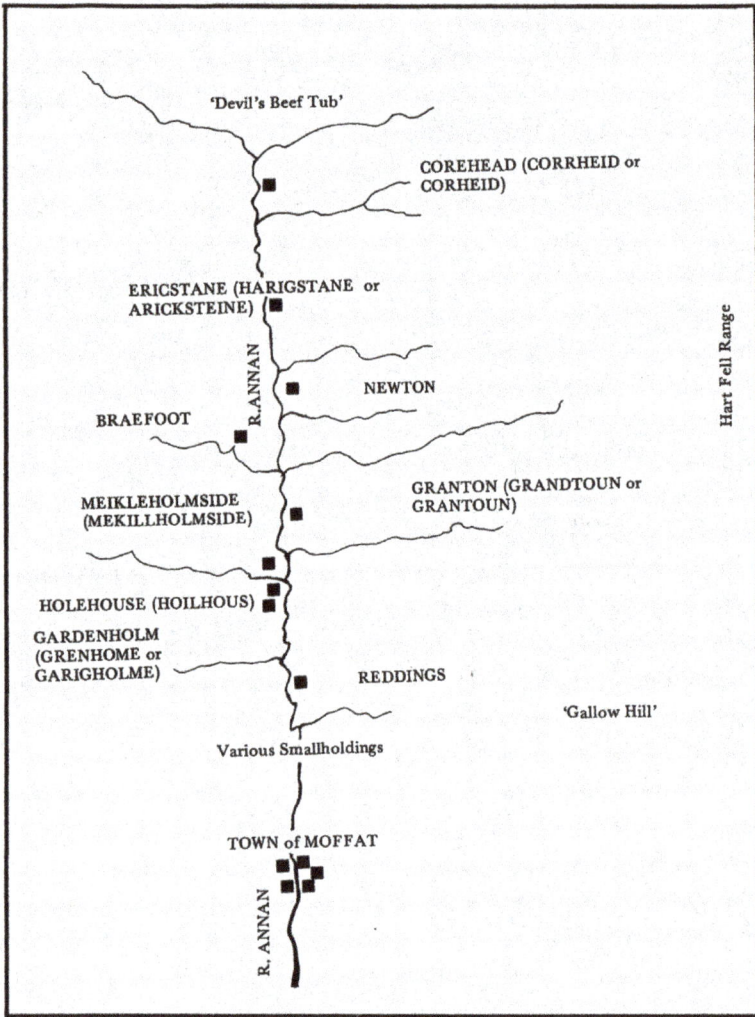

Juxtaposition of properties in the ancient Moffatdale.

Ancient map of Moffatdale, Scotland.

Map of the Scottish Marches and Associated Clans.

William Moffet, the Scotsman

There are three narratives describing the origin of William Moffet, father of James1720.

The first account of William Moffet appears in a document entitled "The Moffett Family Christmas 1900" (see Appendix 1). This document was read at a family gathering on Christmas Day 1900 in Decatur, Illinois. The gathering was held at the home of W.T. Moffett and read by John B. Moffett, son of W.T. Moffett. The only reference to William Moffet, the oldest known ancestor, was the very first paragraph.

"Somewhere in the lowlands of Scotland in the year 1685 was born William Moffet, our oldest known ancestor. At an early age he moved across the channel to the North of Ireland, where to him and his Scottish wife were born a number of children, among them James Moffet (known hereafter as James1720), our great, great grandfather".

The source of the information for this passage is unclear. There are no other family documents that research has uncovered about William1685. There are, however, two documents that by reference give us an indication of what might have been available as a source of information about William1685. First, there is a reference to "the Bible brought from Co. Down, Ireland, in 1784, by William Moffett, the son of James Moffett1720." It is clear that William1763 brought with him a Bible from County Down in 1784. Furthermore, it is clear that William's oldest son, James Moffett1787, is in possession of the Bible brought from County Down. Although research has not uncovered the "Bible from County Down," it could very well be the information in "The Moffett Family Christmas 1900" about William1685 was from that Bible. On the other hand, it could be the specifics of William1685 were simply from oral discussions that were passed down to William1763 from his father, James1720, or even perhaps from his grandfather, William1685, while in County Down. The second document entitled, "From the family Record of William & Rebecca Moffett and their immediate ancestors," lists births, marriages and deaths written by James Moffett1787 and transcribed by Thomas Moffett. This document appears to be just a record of William1763 and Rebecca's descendants.

We learn a lot about William from the first paragraph of the Christmas story about William1685. First, we know he was born in the "Lowlands of Scotland" in 1685. He had a Scottish wife, although we don't know if she came over with him or he met her in Northern Ireland. We learned he came across "at a young age." Yet we don't know at what age. We also know he and his wife had a "number of children." We know that one child's name is James. It's very curious the birth year 1685 is so precise, but the place of his birth is so vague "somewhere in the Lowlands of Scotland." This has led the author to believe the year of his birth is so certain as if it were written down or known by one of his children, but the place of his birth was never known and later generations knowing of the town of Moffat just assumed that William1685 was born in that area.

We also know from another document from Dr. William Moffett, the family genealogist, that the document states "William (born 1685) had a son William who with his wife and son came across to America before 1784," (the year James's sons, William and Thomas, came to America). In addition, we know that a letter written by James Maffet1751 in 1786 to his brother Thomas in America confirms the existence of a son, William. The letter states "P S Your Uncle William (James1720s brother) and his wife and Son is all Dead according to account out of America and the rest of your friends there is no account of them whither they are Dead or alive So I thinke you need not put yourself to any further Searchin for them." It's clear from this statement that James1751 is aware that his father, James1720, had a brother, William, who immigrated to America with his wife and son.

So, from the texts above, we learned that William, our oldest known ancestor, was born in 1685 in "the Lowlands of Scotland." He had a Scottish wife, he moved across the channel to the North of Ireland, had a number of children, two of whom were named William and James. We also know that William (son of William1685) with his wife and son sailed for America before 1784 and likely to Philadelphia, but were never heard from again.

From another branch of the William1763 family, there is a picture of a different story regarding William1685. This information comes down through James1787, oldest child of William and Rebecca Moffett, whereas the information from the first account comes down through John B. Moffett, another son of William and Rebecca. James was born in 1787 and John B. Moffett was born in 1800. Both are great grandsons of William1685. The information coming from James' line is largely material that was assembled in the 1960s. The information seems to focus on family lines of descendants and thus building out a family tree. The materials are in the possession of Cole Scott Moffett, North Conway, New Hampshire. Cole descends from James1787. There is only one file dedicated to the origin of William1685 and his son, James1720.

With regard to William1685, the record states, "William Maffet was born between 1685 and 1690 presumably in Annandale, Scotland." That is all the information I have been given other than it is believed he never left Scotland. "William was probably buried in Annandale." Notice the use of the qualifiers "presumably" and "probably." Included in the file was information regarding Moffat, Scotland. This suggests that Cole's aunt, who prepared the files, just assumed William was from the Moffat area of Annandale. In the same file, there are comments regarding William1685's son, James1720. It states, "It is believed that he (James) was born and raised in Annandale and escaped to Ireland during the religious persecutions - the Church of England against the Protestants." There were no underlying documents to support either of the claims regarding William1685 or James1720. Both statements were on a "family group record" used by family genealogists to prepare family trees.

So, at this juncture you have two conflicting histories from family documents. One states William was born in Scotland in 1685, coming across the channel, and with his Scottish wife has several children, one of whom is James, who was born in County Down. The other states William was born between 1685-1690 in Annandale, Scotland, marries and has at least one child, James, who came across the channel to Northern Ireland. The father, William1685, never leaves Annandale and is buried in Annandale.

In sorting out the differences in the two stories, the second story is questionable because of the existence of William1685's son, William. The second family history says nothing about William, son of William1685. Yet, we have a letter written in 1786 from James Maffet, son of James1720, that talks about Uncle William (brother of James1720) and his whereabouts in America. It seems likely that William, brother of James1720, was the oldest, given he had a wife and son and was not mentioned about coming over to Northern Ireland in the second history. If James1720 brother, William, stayed in Scotland and migrated to America from there, it's not likely that James1720's son would have correspondence regarding the whereabouts of William in America.

So, it seems to me the preparer of the family documents of the second history just made assumptions about William1685, his place of birth, his place of death and the birthplace of his son, James1720, and which of the two actually crossed the channel and came to Northern Ireland. Because there is no mention of William1685's son, William, in the second family history and the preparer describes his place of birth and place of burial as "presumably" and "probably" in Annandale. The use of such terms draws into question the veracity of the narrative.

The third account of William's origin comes through the line of James1787's son, oldest son of William1763. This third narrative is found in a letter written in 1890 from William Z. Moffett of Minneapolis, Minnesota to a relative, Martin Perry, of Saintfield. Martin Perry's grandmother was Jane Moffett, daughter of James1750 and wife of Christopher Morrow of Ballymagarrick. William Z. Moffett descends from James1787. In the letter dated June 23, 1890, there is a passage that describes William's origin. "The name of James Moffett's father was William Moffett, married in Scotland, settled in County Down, Ireland from about 1650 to 1660 at the solicitation of William, Prince of Orange, who was encouraging emigration of Presbyterians to settle in Ireland to oppose the Catholic (Roman) Church." The detailed records cease here, but it is related that William Moffett's parents were "shepherds in the Valley of Annan, Scotland."

The three accounts of William's origin all come from the line of William Moffett, born in 1763, in Leggygowan, son of James1720, and migrated to America in 1784. Two come from William's oldest son, James, born in 1787, and one comes from William's youngest son, John Bigham Moffett, born 1800.

The author has spent more than ten years researching and seeking to find the origin of William Moffett of Scotland. The author's research has yielded the three accounts mentioned above, but none of the accounts substantiated by documented evidence. It has occurred to the author that the accounts were handed down over time, generation to generation, and perhaps the story became altered as a result of the passage of time and circumstances. By combining the key points from all three accounts, the author proposes, as a working thesis for future research, the following scenario along the following line:

The father of James Moffett, born in 1720 in Leggygowan, County Down was William Moffett. William Moffett, James1720's father, was born in County Down in 1685 to a William Moffett who came to County Down with his wife from Scotland between 1650 and 1660. The Scottish parents of William1685 were married in Scotland, lived in the Annan River Valley, and were shepherds.

This scenario has not yet been researched at the time of this book's publication. Perhaps further research on this scenario will be included in a subsequent revised edition.

A Brief History of Saintfield and the
Townland of Leggygowan, County Down

As the family story states, William came across to the north of Ireland and there, he and his Scottish wife had several children, one of whom was named James. It is not known where William initially settled in Ulster, but eventually James settled in County Down in the parish of Saintfield in the townland of Leggygowan. That is where James and his wife, Jane, lived throughout their lives and raised their nine children. What follows is a brief history of Saint-field and the village of Leggygowan.

From the 6th Century, Saintfield was part of the larger Kingdom called "Dalaradia," later to be called Clandeboye. Clandeboye was later divided into smaller subdivisions called after the family of septs who lived in them. Saintfield was in the Slut Neales (meaning place of the family O'Neales). The Anglo-Norman invasion more or less passed the area. The English largely confined their activities to the coastline along the west of Strangford Lough. In the Middle Ages, the O'Neills of Clandeboye, based in Castlereagh, tightened their grip on the whole region and shaped the future history of Saintfield.

The beginnings of the Saintfield area is described by E.M. Griffith in his article, "An Outline of the History of Saintfield and District." "At the end of the 16th Century and the beginning of the 17th Century, English and Scottish adventurers hungry for land and social advance-ment, which its possession carried with it, swarmed into Ulster where estates could be had almost for the taking. Prominent amongst these were two Scotsman, Hugh Montgomery who settled Newtonards, and James Hamilton at Bangor. To a certain extent, these two may be regarded as the founding fathers of the Ulster Scots."

According to the "History of Saintfield and District" by Aiken McClelland, this is how the two Scotsmen gained control. "Sir Con McNeil Oge O'Neil owned property called South Clannaboy. In 1586, Sir Henry Bagenal visited South Clannaboy and described it as mostly a woodland stretching from Lagan to Killyleagh and owned by Sir Con Oge O'Neil. O'Neil lived in his castle at Castlereagh about two miles from Belfast. In 1602, Sir Con O'Neil, the last of the O'Neils to rule County Down, was falsely accused of levying war against Queen Elizabeth and fled to Scotland. There, he met Sir Hugh Montgomery, who agreed to talk to Sir James Hamilton, another Ayrshire landlord and friend of King James the First (Queen Elizabeth was now dead) to intercede on his behalf. So, in 1605, the King granted all O'Neill's lands (over two hundred townlands) to Hamilton with orders that he would divide them equally among Montgomery, O'Neill and himself. The two Scots were also ordered to plant their portions and O'Neill's with settlers of British stock. Few settlers came from England and the vast majority came from the Scotland areas of Galloway, Lanark, Dumfries, Renfrew and Ayrshire. The early settlers settled in Hollywood, Bangor, Killyleagh, Killinchy, Comb-er, Newtonards, Ballywaiter and Donaghadee."

The Reverend Andrew Stewart, who was Presbyterian minister in Donaghadee from 1646 until his death in 1671, left this unflattering description of the first settlers: "From Scotland came many, and from England few, yet all of them the seum of both nations, who for debt, or breaking and fleeing justice, or seeking shelter, came hither, hoping to be without fear of man's justice in a land where there was nothing, or but little, as yet of the fear of God. And in a few years there flocked such a multitude of people from Scotland, that these northern counties of Down, Antrim, Londonderry etc. were in good measure planted...."

The Scots did not settle in Saintfield until about the middle of the 17th Century. The 1631 Muster Roll gives the names of all the male settlers in County Down between the ages of 16 and 60 who were able to carry arms. Although over 4,000 enrolled, there is not a name from an inland parish, except a few from the parish of Dromore. Further evidence of the scantiness of the population during the early 17th Century is shown by the fact that a bishop's visit in 1622 does not even mention Saintfield.

The Hamiltons were landlords of Saintfield until it was sold in 1709 to General Nicholas Price, whose mother was a Hamilton. He bought the Saintfield estate for his third son, also named Nicholas. General Price's father, Captain Richard Price, was a Welshman who had served in Ireland during the 1640s and had been paid by a grant of land at Farranfad near Seaforde. General Price, who lived in Hollymount, near Downpatrick, and died in 1735, can truly be said to be the founder of Saintfield. He encouraged trade and opened a passable road through Saintfield from Belfast to Down. He encouraged linen manufacturers and other tradesmen to settle there and promoted the repairs of the ruinous parish church to which he gave plate and ornaments. Saintfield was early referred to as Tonaghneave – Saintfield being the literal translation of Tonaghneave.

Saintfield is located in County Down on the southern part of the Baroney of the Upper Castlereagh. The parish is bounded on the North by the parish of Drumbo and Comber; on the east by the parish of Killinchy; on the south by parish of Kilmore (the townland of Drumnaconner is located there); and on the West by Drumbo and Maghadrool (the townland of Ballynahinch is located there). The parish of Saintfield is about eight miles from Belfast. The parish is at its greatest length seven miles long, its greatest breadth is five miles, its mean length is four miles and its mean breadth is three miles. It contains 13,277 acres. It is all cultivated with the exception of a couple of small patches. The land about Saintfield is coarse and hilly. However, by drains and good husbandry, it produces plenty of rye, oats and flax, and affords pasture to sheep and black cattle.

Leggygowan is a large townland directly south and east of Saintfield. Leggygowan means "Smith's hollow." In the 1659 survey, Leggygowan was in the pre-plantation territory of Slut Kelly (Kelly's sept). The landlord was Neal Roe O'Kelly, gent. Leggygowan became part of the property allocated to Sir Con Oge O'Neill in the split between Montgomery, Hamilton and O'Neill in 1605. As a result, Leggygowan was owned by the Irish families throughout the years. For example, the survey of 1659 reports that Leggygowan has thirteen inhabitants: one is of Scottish/English origin and twelve are Irish. The names of the Irish are known because they took part in the uprising in 1641 when the Irish rebelled against the settlers. Mentioned was Brian Roe O'Kelly of Leggygowan. Also mentioned as one of the "principal Irish families" is the surname McMullen with fifteen inhabitants, one of the largest Irish families in the Barony of Castlereagh. Interestingly, James Moffett's oldest son, James, was married to Isabella McMullen. Later in 1663, a tax was levied by the new English monarch and there were only nine landowners in all of County Down to pay the tax. One was Neil O'Kelly of Leggygowan. In 1755, Sir Simon Issac, a distinguished barrister of Hollywood, County Down was landlord of Leggygowan.

Leggygowan was always associated with the Church of Ireland, Saintfield. Leggygowan was actually owned by the church of Tonaghwyn as early as 1623, which later became the Church of Ireland, Saintfield when the church moved from Tonaghwyn to Saintfield. The Church was originally built in Lisnegarric, about a half mile from Saintfield.

One interesting note: the "Annals of Saintfield" states that in 1820, James Little of Leggygowan was formerly "Seneschal" (means overseer) of the manor of Leggygowan. James Little was married to Jennet Maffet, daughter of James and Jane Bigham Maffet.

By 1837, the townland of Leggygowan was owned by Sir Bomberry (Bunberry). According to the Ordnance Survey conducted the same year, Leggygowan had 110 houses, 115 families, 289 males and 302 females. The townland had the best quality land from six to 20 acres in size. The townland had 50 farms from one acre to 80 acres, 16 being the average size. Modern day Saintfield is still a very quaint and prosperous village in County Down.

Parishes of County Down, Northern Ireland.

1659 Census of Ireland.

Church of Ireland, Saintfield Parish with author
and son William in the foreground.

Picture of the village of Saintfield, County Down around the late 1800s.

James Maffet, Son of William Moffet of Scotland and the Daughters of James and Jane Maffet

It is believed James Maffet (referred to as James1720), son of William Moffet of Scotland, was born in 1720 near Leggygowan, presumably Saintfield, County Down, Northern Ireland. In 1748, James married Jane Bigham. Where the couple were married is unknown, but presumably in the area of Belfast.

Jane Bigham was born in 1722 near Belfast, likely in County Down. Her father's name is unknown, but is likely John, given the naming convention of the Scottish families at that time. Coincidentally, there was a couple in Saintfield in 1748, John and Mary Bigham, whose daughter, Mary, was baptized December 21, 1748 at the Church of Ireland, Saintfield. Recall that James1720 and Jane were married in 1748. This John Bigham is presumed to be the brother of Jane. Also, as noted below, James1720 was a member of the Vestry of the Saintfield Church in 1749. Nothing else is known of Jane's parents. It is interesting to note that the Bigham name is rare outside Ulster in Northern Ireland and originates in both Ayrshire and Dumfriesshire in Scotland, according to the book, "The Book of Ulster Surnames," by Robert Bell. Jane's grandson, James, born in 1787 in Clark County, Kentucky, states, "My grandmother's maiden name was Jane or Jannnet Biggim. She was of a handsome, active and intelligent family; Scotch-Irish protestants and Presbyterians." From this statement, it's clear that Jane's ancestors were also of Scottish descent.

As stated above, James1720 had a strong connection to the Church of Ireland, Saintfield. The Church of Ireland, Saintfield was the Parish Church and was an adherent to the Episcopal Church of England. On March 27, 1749, according to the minutes of the Church of Ireland, Saintfield, James Maffet was selected as a "sideman (usher)" for the year. He also signed the minutes indicating he was also a member of the church's Vestry. James1720 was only 29 years old at the time he held this important position. Then again, on October 6, 1756, the church's minutes bear the signature of James Maffet. Again in 1784, the Rector of the Church comments further on the family of James1720 by stating in a Testamentary letter written for his son, William Maffet, that he comes from "Honest, Industrious, and Respectable parents." This all indicates that James Maffet and family were faithful and active members of the Church of Ireland until such time and for whatever reason they switched faiths and joined the First Presbyterian Church, Saintfield sometime after 1784 until his death in 1789. Also, keep in mind, 1784 was the year James1720's sons William and Thomas left home for America. David left in 1977-78.

The evidence of James1720 being a farmer is revealed in the 1755 "Freeholders List." It simply lists James Maffet of Leggygowan as a "Freeholder" of land in Leggygowan. The landlord is Sir Simon Issac, a barrister in Hollywood House, Hollywood, County Down. A "freeholder" held his property either "in fee" (outright ownership) or by lease for a term associated with the lives of those listed under "lives or other tenure" on the Freeholder List. There is no information listed on the "Freeholder List" naming "lives or other tenure." So, we conclude James1720 owned the land outright, likely buying the property from Sir Simon Issac. This is consistent with James1720's will, as described by Samuel, his son, in the letter of 1790 in which James1750 receives two-thirds of the land and Samuel receives about a third of the land. The location of the land owned by James1720 is believed to be lot 29 on the map of Leggygowan.

James1720 and Jane had nine children: James, born 1751; David, born 1753; Jennet, born 1756; Mary, born 1758; Elenor, born 1760; William, born 1763; Samuel, born 1765; Thomas, born 1767; and Jane, born 1771. All the children were born in Leggygowan. Of the nine children, David, William and Thomas migrated to America: David in 1777-78, William and Thomas in 1784. The rest of the children remained in Northern Ireland.

The oldest daughter, Mary, married John Thompson. In a letter dated April 29, 1790, written by Samuel in Leggygowan to his brothers in America, he states "... I let you know that Sister Mary was got Maryed to a John Thompson, son to William Thompson of Cawha_d...." In 1838, it was reported John Thompson bought a large flour and flax complex at Glasdrumman. John and Mary had a son, Alexander, who married a Mary Moffet, sister to Rev. Walter Moffat, the Presbyterian minister at the First Presbyterian Church, Saintfield.

Jennet married James Little. He was the seneschal (overseer) of the manor of Leggygowan for Sir Bonberry.

Elenor, the third oldest daughter, married a man George (surname unknown). The only other information regarding Elenor is a paragraph in the same letter cited above regarding her treatment by her father, James1720, in his will. The will states "....he left Sister Elenor nothing but the "cattle bead" which cause hir a bitter life ever since by the chiding of hir husband...."

The youngest daughter, Jane, was eighteen when both her father and mother died. She was left alone after her parents' death. Her brothers were trying to make arrangements for her to come to America, but she was too afraid to make the voyage. Jane later married Robert Cole.

Jane, wife of James1720, died on June 20, 1789, one month before James' death on July 22, 1789. They both died from a smallpox epidemic that also caused the death of son Samuel's two daughters and caused extreme illness in the family. The epidemic is described by Samuel in his letter dated April 28, 1790. The following paragraph from the letter describes James1720's and Jane's illness and respective deaths. "... our Mother and sister Jannet took fever also and remended very ill for the Space of three weeks and then our Mother expired Mutch lamented by everyone that had the smallest acquaintance of hir. She bore her Sickness with the greatest fortitude and Resignation and died calm and easy...." The passage of James1720's death follows "...our Father began then to complain with a peain in his breast and warmness and grevel but Still Keapt on foot for three weeks and then expired the 22th of July he died as he lived a very weakly man and suffered so both in body and Minde he branded his name with never inding infamy by backing brother James thrue several Scandles actions and at his death in making a very unjust will..."

James1720's will was prepared rather hastily by the Rev. Thomas Ledlie Birch, minister of the First Presbyterian Church. He was the rebellious minister who formed the Society of United Irishman. Rev. Birch was later removed from his responsibilities because of his radical political ideas and philosophy. He took an active part in the 1798 Rebellion, leading insurgents on the Sunday before the Battle of Saintfield. Both Samuel and James, sons of James1720, signed the petition in 1799 to call a new minister the Rev. Henry Simpson to lead the church upon removal of Rev. Birch.

Samuel, in his letter of April 28,1790, describes the unfortunate state of affairs brought on by their father's "miss guided Will." "...Mr. Birch was a great caus of My Fathers Making such an unjust Will for brother James went to him fore times before he got him to come and at last got his wife prayed for in meeting in order that Mr. Birch Might come to see hir altho She was sitting at the fire when Mr. Birch came our Father was unfit to settle his affairs and did as they had him.... Sister Jennet's holding lasts no longer then unmarried...." As Samuel stated in this letter of 1790, "Our Father's Will is 'unjust.' He left his oldest son James two thirds of the land with all the house, house furniture, farming utensils, stock and rope with about forty guneas in cash with all his houses and improvements.... except the Parler and cowsheeding that he left sister Jennet he left her 25 pounds to be paid by brother James.....he left his sister Elenor nothing but the cattle bead which causes hir a bitter life ever since by the chiding of hir husband....the third of the land that fell to me (Samuel) is the refues of all the farm which I get without menure or ditches or houses or any help from my father towards them except some timber and some dirt..." The will of James1720 no longer exists.

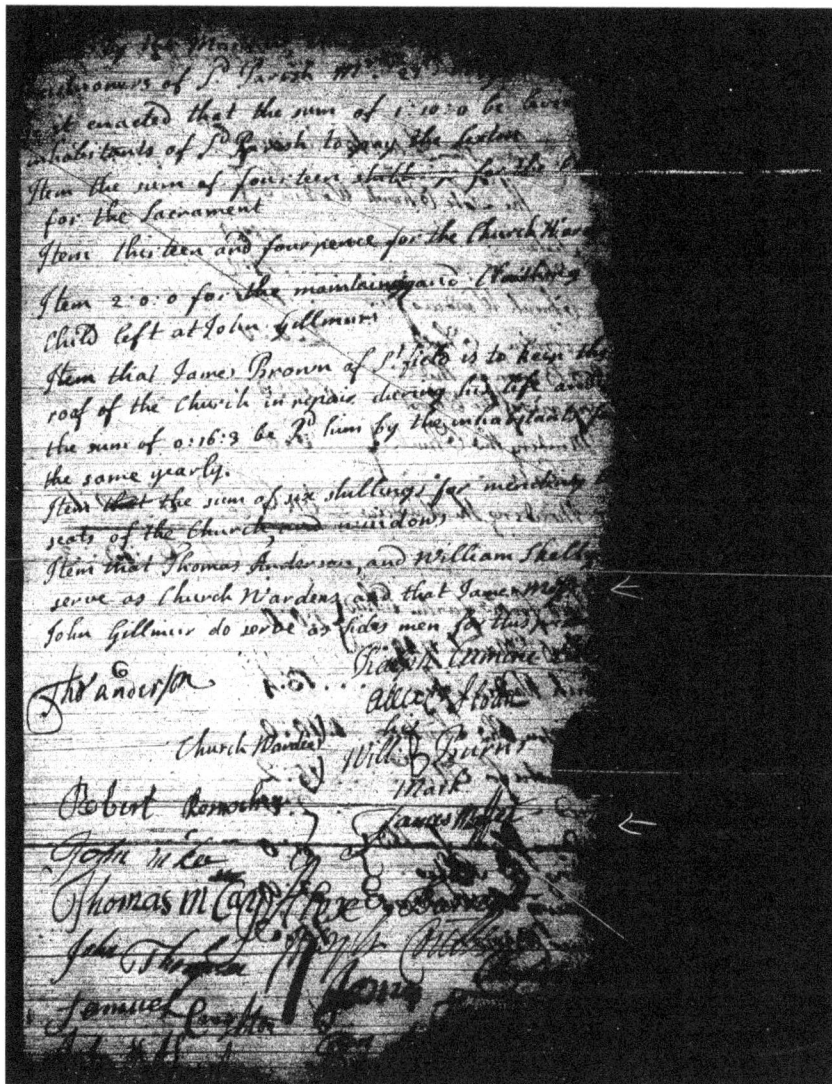

Church of Ireland, Saintfield minutes of 1749 with
signature of James Maffet1720 as a member of the
Vestry and elected as a "sideman."

Select Vestry Minutes, Saintfield Parish Church, Co. Down

MIC 1/69/1

"The Vestry Court held in the Parish Church of Saintfield by the Minister, Church Wardens and parishioners of said Parish, March 27th 1749
Be it enacted that the sum of 1 pound (£) and 10 shillings be levied of the inhabitants of said Parish to pay the sexton
Item the sum of 14 shillings for the (element?) for the sacrament
Item 13 shillings and 4 pence for the Church Wardens
Item 2 pounds (£) for the maintenance of Foundling child left at John Gillemore
Item that James Brown of Saintfield is to keep the roof of the Church in repair during his life and the sum of 16 shillings and 9 pence be paid him by the inhabitants for the same yearly
Item the sum of 6 shillings for mending the seats of the Church and windows
Item that Thomas Anderson and William Skelly do serve as Church Wardens and that James Moffet and John Gillemore do serve as sidesmen for this present year"

N.B. James Moffet also signed on 6th October 1756

Select Vestry: The Select Vestry is the business committee of a Church of Ireland Parish. It exists to manage the money and buildings as effectively as it can, so that the ministry and outreach are well resourced.

Church Warden: Church Wardens are responsible for the day-to-day functioning of the parish; not just the maintenance of the church building, but helping the smooth running of the church.

Sidesmen: A sidesman (archaic term) would have assisted the churchwardens and collected the offerings.

Sexton: A member of the church charged with the maintenance of its buildings and the surrounding graveyard.

Beverly Brown
18 August 2916

A translation of the Church of Ireland, Saintfield minutes of 1749 and a notation James Maffet signed the minutes on October 6, 1756.

Records from the family of James Moffett of Bath County, Kentucky:

From the original, an old slip of paper preserved in the Bible brought from Co. Down, Ireland, in 1784, by William Moffett, father of James Moffett.

"Parish of Saintfield and County Down, Ireland."
"We the minister and church warden of said parish Do hereby certify that William Moffett (the bearer himself) was born and brought up in said parish of Honest, Industrious and Respectable Parents, is a Protestant, and as far as we know he always behaved well; and we believe him to be a sober, Honest, and well-behaved young man. Witness our hands this 19th Day of April 1784.

James Clenlouth (?)
To Whom it may concern - William Walker Minister"

Testamentary Letter from the Church of Ireland, Saintfield for the benefit of William Maffet, son of James Maffet1720.

Leggygowan (?) Aprile 28th 1790

Loving brothers the alterations in our famely have been great Sinc
I rot Last to you which was about the first of May 1789 when i
let you know my oldest child was dead the second died also both in
the small pockes and left me childless but we expect another
Soon i let you know that sister Mary was got Maryed to a Iohn
thompson son to William thompson of cawha- d She ?
child dead at the time My oldest child Died and took the feaver
and remeaned in it for the speace of Six weekes when our parents
would have hir home to themselves again that thy Might take the
better care (of?) hir not but She was carfuly handled at home
by hir ho-(sban)dand his friends She was not long (?) till our
Mother and sister Jennet took the faver also and remened very
ill for the Speace of three weekes and then our Mother expired Mutch lemented by every one that had the smallest aquant-
ence of hir She bore hir Sickness with the greatest fortitud
and Resignation and died came (calm) and easy Sisters Mary and
Jannet got better our father began then to complain with a pesin
in his breast and warmness and grevel but Still keapt on foot for
three weekes and then expired the 22th of Iluy he died as he
lived a very weakly man and suffered So both in body and
Minde he branded his name with never inding infeamy by backing
brother James thrue several Scandles actions and at his death
in Makeing a very unjust will he left brother James t ? this
& the land with all the house house forniture farming utencils
Stock and rope with about fortie guneas in cash with all his
houses and improvements except the parler and a cowsheeting that
he left Sister Jennet he left hir 25 pounds to be payed by brother
James twenty five to Sister Mary also to be payed by James he
left Sister Elenor nothing but the cattle bead which causes hir
a bitter life ever since by the chiding of hir hosband the third
of the land that fell to Me is the refues of all the farem which
i got with out Menure or ditches or houses or any helpe from My
father towards them exsept som timber and some dirt while the
house was building Mr Birch was a great caus of My fathers
Makeing Such an unJust will for brother James went to him fore
times before he got him to came and at last got his wife prayed
for in Meeting inorder that Mr Birch Might come to see hir altho
She was sitting at the fire -- turn over (end of first page)
When Mr birch came our father was very unfit to Settle his afears
and did as they had him Sister Jannets holding lasts no longer
then unmaried James give hir neather potato nor flex ground nor
any of hir cows dung She would come to you if she could get any
trusty hand to go with alesibeth Johson came and took care of our
people when in the feaver and steas with Sister Jannet She toock
care of Me and My wife in the feaver which Lasted Seven weekes
but we got seefly thrue it and is in good health at preasent
thenkes to the father of all oure Mercys.
Deare brothers if these few lines come to your hands do not
moren as those that have no hoope but be ? ? ed to the will of
the almighty god who disposes of all things for the beast we
red your letters that you sent by Mr alinson but ? the deate
is i never saw but one glimes of them but you rite again derect
to me and to the care of Cristen ? youre letters give me the

greates pleasure to hear   that you were all in good health
and that you had a   pect of satling togither in such a find
contry brother Tom spock Somthing of coming to old Irland which
i would be glad to see for altho we are at a great distance and
long distant from each other yet you Mae belive that Sinseare
good wish is still with you i would come to you if my wife was as
willing as me but She is not and is feared that She could not
stand Such a Long Jororny i have nothing More partickeler to
rite to you Vittling is very plenty and reasonable we have had
a remarkable open winter without frost or snow of any consequence
but heas had a bad spring it is a mortal time here Deathes alexander gordan John McGibben and wife thomas Lindays wife Robert
elder James fellman Margrit Merting of the bank.
Desr brothers i beg that you will neglect no opertunety of
letting us know how you are i am vary glad to heare of brother
david beein about to go to you dear William i am glead to heare of
you beeing so well Settled in a plantation and alls of you being
so agreeably maryd and wish you Joy of youer! soon May wife
Disiers to be Remembred to you and youer wife and brother thomas
no more at preasent but remaens youer loving brother

                                        Samuel Maffet

Addressed to

        Mr. William Moffet
    on Howards Creek in Piat County
    and to the Cair of Mr. stroud at strouds station
            Canetuck
Per favour of Mr hugh Robinson

1790 letter from Samuel Maffet, Leggygowan, to his brothers in America.

Freeholders

1755 Freeholders list of Leggygowan indicating James Maffet1720 as a Freeholder.

Map of Leggygowan indicating land occupied by James Maffet, lot 29 situaed between lot 27 and lot 40.

Current day picture of Leggygowan in the approximate area of the Moffett's farm.

James Maffet, Oldest Son of James and Jane Maffet

James Maffet (referred to as James1750), oldest son of James1720, was born in Leggygowan in 1750. He was the first-born child to James1720 and his wife Jane Bigham Maffet. James1750 died on April 19, 1813 in Leggygowan. He was 63 years old when he died. James married Isabella McMullen in 1786 in Saintfield. Isabella was born in 1769 and died on January 6, 1830. She was 60 years old when she died.

James1750 and Isabella had four children. James, born 1787 (referred to as James1787) in Leggygowan, was the oldest child. Very little is known of James1787 except he is named in his brother Hugh's will dated Feb. 28, 1821. The will states "... his brother James Maffet of Saintfield ..."

Jane, the second child, was born in 1788. She died one year after her birth and is buried in the Church of Ireland, Saintfield cemetery alongside her parents James1750 and Isabella. Jane likely died from the small pox epidemic that killed her grandparents, James1720 and Jane Bigham Maffet, and several cousins.

Hugh Maffet was born in 1801 in Leggygowan. He was an assistant surgeon in the Royal Navy. He served on the HMS Frigate Topave commanded by John Richard Lumley in South Hampton. Hugh's will was executed in 1821 in the Perrogative Court of Canterbury. Executor of the Will was Christopher Morrow, husband of Hugh's youngest sister Jane. The will names his mother, Isabella, and brother James1787 in the will. Hugh died in 1821 at the age of 20. He is buried in the Church of Ireland, Saintfield cemetery.

Jane Maffet, the youngest child, was born in 1790 in Leggygowan. She died on February 14, 1864 in Ballymagarrick, in the parish of Drumbo. She was 64 years old when she died. Jane married Christopher Morrow of Ballymagarrick at the Church of Ireland parish church in Drumbo in 1808. Christopher was born in 1780 and died on October 10, 1858 in Ballymagarrick. He was 78 years old when he died. Both Christopher and his wife, Jane Maffet Morrow, are buried in the Church of Ireland, Drumbo cemetery. Christopher was a merchant in Saintfield and owned land in Leggygowan originally owned by Jane's grandfather, James1720, and inherited by her father, James1750.

Jane Maffet and Christopher Morrow had eight children: an unknown daughter who likely died at birth; another unknown daughter who also died at birth; Jane Morrow, born about 1814-15 and died January 6, 1831; Agnes D. Morrow, born about 1818 and died March 21, 1885; William D. Morrow, born in 1833 and died November 21, 1885; James T. Morrow, born in 1828 and died February 21, 1890; Jane Morrow, born 1834 and died in 1871; (She was married to Nathaniel Perry in Saintfield in 1863. They had five children.); and Susan W. Morrow, born about 1835 and died March 20, 1896.

Other than the original farm land in Leggygowan acquired by James1720, James1750 was involved with partners in other farm land in Leggygowan. For instance, in 1812, landlord Sir Simon Issac, Esquire, sold 21 acres to David Stothard of Leggygowan. David Stothard, in turn, sold to William Warren of Saintfield (wheelwright) and James Maffet1750 of Leggygowan, a farmer, a portion of the land (12 acres) for a sum of £166. James1750's signature appears at the bottom of the indenture. In 1803, James1750 is also mentioned in the Agricultural Survey as owning livestock on the farm land in Leggygowan.

Then in 1813, James1750 died. Afterward, on March 8, 1819, Christopher Morrow of Saint-field, a merchant, is added to the original lease from David Stothard to William Warren and James Maffet1750 – essentially replacing James Maffet1750 as a result of his death and hence transferred to his wife, Jane Maffet Morrow, and then to the control of her husband, Christopher Morrow. By 1833, the Title Applotment of Saintfield showed Christopher Morrow owning the 12 acres in Leggygowan. By 1863, the Griffith's valuation showed that there was neither a Morrow or Maffet in the Townland of Leggygowan.

Besides the land in Leggygowan he inherited from his father, James1720, and the land he acquired in 1812, James1750 is listed in the "Freeholder List" as a farmer owning land in the Townland of Drumnaconnor situated on the outskirts of Saintfield and adjacent to Leggygowan. The landlord of Drumnaconner was Alexander Stewart, Esquire of Newtonards, who resided at the Derry House in 1777. The Stewart family came over from Ayrshire, Scotland with James Hamilton to settle the Ulster Plantation in 1607. The Stewart family had a historic relationship to the Church of Ireland, Saintfield and the Maffets as portrayed in the following paragraph.

The story of the Townland of Drumnconnor is interesting and how it became associated with the Church of Ireland, Saintfield, the Stewart Family and the Maffet family. The book, "The Irish Roots in County Down, Stories of Family and Place," edited by Stanley R. Megraw, described the beginnings of Drumnaconnor:

"Drumnaconnor was originally held by members of the McCarten family- Phelemy McCarten and then Patrick McCarten in 1641. In 1657, Ever Magenis held 387 acres. That same year, the Commonwealth, by right of conquest and law of arms, granted Drumnaconnor (along with the Townland of Raleagh) to Lieutenant Colonel James Trail of Tullychin in Killyleagh parish who had rendered active service in the suppression of the 1641 Rebellion. According to a deed,dated May 25, 1657 and February 15, 1657, Cornelius and Samuel Rock, troopers in L.D. Fleetwood's troops of horse, sold the Townland to Lieutenant Colonel Trail for £80. After Trail's death on May 18, 1663, Drumnaconnor and Raleagh passed to his younger son Hans Trail. Hans died in Dublin in 1692, leaving his "corn-mill and tuck-mill" to his eldest son, James Trail. In 1770, Reverend Hamilton Trail of Killinchy owned the Townland. He subsequently put Drumnaconnor in the hands of Reverend James Mant, Lord Bishop of Down & Connor, and Reverend James Hamilton Clewlow (the Vicar of Church of Ireland, Saintfield) in 1775 prior to its sale to Alexander Stewart of Newtonards in December 1775 for approximately £3600."

As stated earlier, James Maffet1750 was registered as a "Freeholder" in 1789 in the Townland of Drumnaconnor owned by Alexander Stewart, Esquire of Newtonards and Kilmore. Clearly, the fact that James1750 was a member of the Church of Ireland, Saintfield and known to Vicar James Hamilton Clewlow, was helpful to James1750 in acquiring land from Mr. Stewart.

Another relationship between the Maffets and Stewarts is the marriage of Ann Moffett, daughter of Reverend Walter Moffett, minister of the Presbyterian Seceding House, to Mr. John Stewart of Saintfield. Another case of this close relationship: Mary Maffet, daughter James1720, married John Thompson, who owned a large flour and flax mill complex at Glasdrumman, and had a son, Alexander. Alexander Thompson married Miss Mary Moffett, sister of the Reverend Walter Moffett. Another Stewart relationship is through James Orr, an executor of brother Samuel's estate. James Orr was married to Helen Stewart, another member of the Stewart Family.

By 1784, three of James' brothers had left home and sailed to America, landing in Philadelphia – David and his family landing in 1777-78 and William and Thomas in the Spring of 1784. James1750 exchanged letters with his brothers often. Shortly after arriving in America, all three brothers wrote to James1750. William and Thomas wrote a letter on August 16, 1785 to James1750 and then again on November 16, 1785. James1750 wrote a letter to Thomas on April 24, 1786. Finally, upon the death of their parents in Leggygowan, Samuel wrote a scathing letter regarding their father's "unjust Will" and how James1750, their oldest brother, received most all the farm and practically everything used on the farm and left very little to the rest of his children. Samuel describes his father as "...backing James1750 thrue Scandles actions..." and pertaining to Sister Jennet "... Father give her neather potatoes nor flax ground nor any of his cows dung..."

It seems apparent that sometime between 1784 when we last have a record of the Testamentary letter presenting William Maffet and 1789 when both James1720 and Jane Bigham Maffet died, the Maffets seemed to have left the Church of Ireland and joined the First Presbyterian Church of Saintfield. It was Reverend Thomas Leslie Birch, then the Minister of the First Presbyterian Church, who wrote James1720's "unjust Will."

Upon the death of James Maffet1750 on April 19, 1813, Christopher Morrow erected a gravestone in the cemetery of the Church of Ireland, Saintfield honoring his father-in-law James1750. The gravestone states," Erected by Christopher Morrow to the memory of James Maffet of Leggygowan who departed this life April 19, 1813 age 61. Likewise, his daughter Jane age one. Also his wife Isabella Maffet departed this life January 6, 1830 age 60."

This is the last Will & Testament of me Hugh Moffet Afsistant Surgeon of His Majestys Frigate Topaze John Richard Lumley Esquire Commander now lying at Spithead in the county of Southampton made whilst in health & of sound & disposing mind memory & understanding whereby I recommend my Soul to God & dispose of my worldly Estate & Effects in manner following that is to say all & singular my ready Money Securities for Money debts due & owing to me at the time of my decease & all other my Personal Estate & Effects whatsoever & wheresoever & of what sort or nature soever the same shall or may consist at the time of my decease I do hereby give & bequeath the same & every part thereof subject to the payment of my debts funeral expences & the costs & charges attending the Probate & execution of this my Will unto my Honored Mother Isabella Moffet of Saint Field in the county of Down in the Kingdom of Ireland Widow her Executors Administrators & Afsigns absolutely & to & for her or their own use & benefit but in case my said Honored Mother shall happen to die in my life time then I do give & bequeath my said ready Money Securities for Money debts & Personal Estate unto & between my Brother James Moffet of Saint Field aforesaid Gentleman & my Sister Jane the Wife of Christopher Morrow of the same place Merchant in equal parts shares & proportions share & share alike to & for their own several & respective use & benefit & hereby revoking & making void all former & other Wills by me at any time heretofore made I publish & declare this present Writing to be & contain my last Will & Testament only & thereof I nominate constitute & appoint the said Christopher Morrow Sole Executor In Testimony whereof I the said Hugh Moffet the Testator have hereto set my hand & seal this eighth day of July in the year of our Lord 1818 — H. Moffet (LS) Signed Sealed published & declared by the said Hugh Moffet the Testator as & for his last Will & Testament on the day of the date in the presence of us who in his presence in the presence of each other & at his request have hereto subscribed our names as Witnefses W. Marshall Atty Portsea England Rich'd Knott Smith Clerk

Proved with the original
Hand a true copy of will W Pulley
J Scott

Last Will and Testament of Hugh Maffet, son of James1750 and his wife, Isabella McMullen.

pcc will

No. 2. For Executors or Administrators, with Will annexed.

IN the Goods of *Hugh Moffet* ———— deceased. } In the Prerogative Court of Canterbury.

On the *Twenty eighth day of February* 1821

Insert the Names, Residence, Titles or Professions of the Persons making the Affidavit.

Appeared personally *Christopher Morrow of Saint Field in the County of Down in Ireland the sole* ———— Executor named in the last Will

If one or more Codicils, state so.

and Testament, ———— of the said *Hugh Moffet* ———— late of *Saint Field in the County of Down* ———— deceased,

In case of Quakers, solemnly affirmed.

and *made Oath*, that the Estate and Effects of the said Deceased, for or in respect of which a Probate of the said Will is to be granted, exclusive of what the said Deceased may have been possessed of or intitled to as a Trustee, for any other Person or Persons, and not beneficially, ————

and without deducting any Thing on Account of the Debts due and owing from the said Deceased, are under the Value of *Two Hundred* Pounds, to the best of *this* Deponent's Knowledge, Information and Belief. *And he lastly made Oath that the said deceased was not possessed of or entitled to any Leasehold Estate or Estates for years either absolute or determinable on Lives to the best of this Deponents knowledge information & belief*

Sworn before me,

Christopher Morrow

Mr Morrow to sign here

Sworn *Cuss/to Vicar Gen' of Down & Connor*

G. WOODFALL, PRINTER, ANGEL COURT, SKINNER STREET, LONDON.

Executors and administrators of Hugh's will.

Townland of Leggygowan

Name	Horses	Black Cattle	Sheep	Swine	Goats
James Moffett	2	9	0	1	2
Tho.s Lindsey	2	12	2	2	1
Fre.d Lindsey	1	2	2	2	1
James Morrison	1	3	0	2	1
Henry Morrison	1	2	0	2	0
William Peake	1	6		2	1
Patrick Peake	1	3	2	3	1
Hugh Morrison	1	3		2	1
Jo.d Scott	1	4	2	1	1
Cha.s Morrison	1	2	—	4	1
Ja.s Little	2	9		2	2
Dan.l Rogan	1	2			1
Jane Bird	1	2	2	2	1
And.w Stain		2		2	
Jo.s Mc Clure	2	9	4	1	2
Anthony Stothard	1	1			1
Tho.s Boyd	1	3	—		1
Rob.t Boyd	2	1		3	1
Rob.t Robson	3	14	19	2	2
Jo.s Arundel		1	1	2	1
Fran.s Wilson	1	3		1	1
Dav.d Mahons	2	2			1
Jo.d Wilson	1	2		0	1
Rob.t Mc Mullan		2		2	
Hugh Killin		1		1	1
W.m Cammock	3	3	10	4	2
Jas Mc Alester		1			
Hugh Mc Robert	3	24	4	5	2
W.m Ferguson	1			3	1
Ja.s Swinton		1			
Jo.d Blackstock				1	
W.m Mc Cullough		2		1	
Rob.t Rowan		2		2	
Ja.s Forsythe	1	6	5	3	1
Fra.d Hamilton		5	3	2	1
Jas Donnan	1	4	3	2	1
N.o 24	(Turn over)	37	146	56	— 30

Agricultural Survey of 1803 of Leggygowan names James Maffet1750.

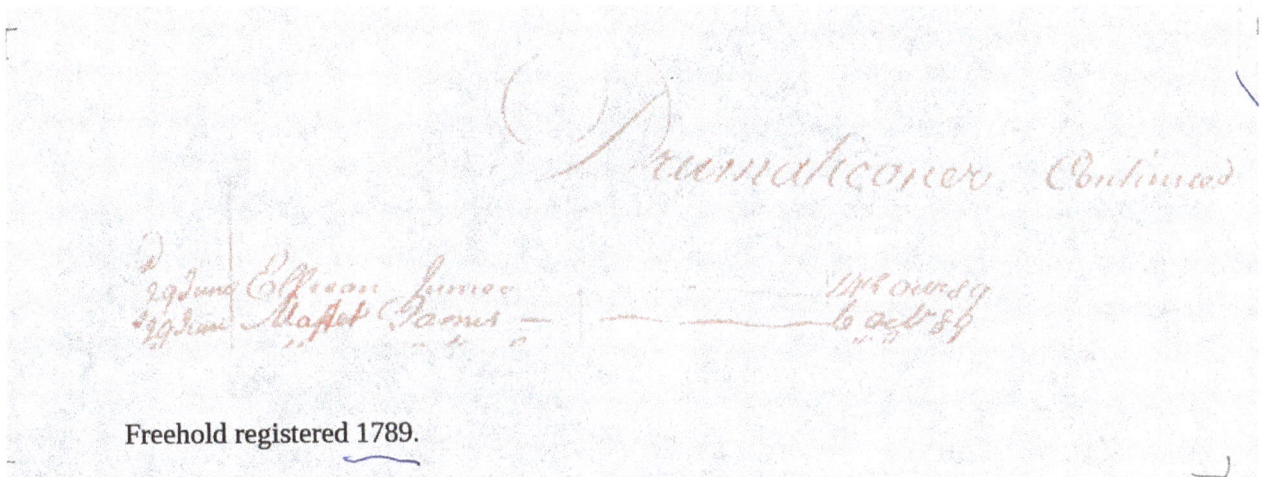

Freehold registered 1789.

Freeholder Register of 1789 in Leggygowan lists James Maffet1750.

Gravemarker of James1750 and his wife, Isabella McMullen, and daughter, Jane, in the
Church of Ireland, Saintfield graveyard.

Legygowan April 24, 1786: Loving Brother thomas, we imbrace this other
opertunity intending to let you know that we are all in good health at present
thanks to almighty God for it; hoping to hear from you all in like manner; it
grives us much to hear that you can scarce get aney account from us: and that you
are likely to charge us with ingratude; and this is the 5th letter I wrot you
  and ;3; or 4 that Brother samuel wrot; and in case that none of you should ever
get a letter from us that is none of our falts; for we intend to write ev ery
opertunity; for our ardent wish will nerve ceace towards you; we received the
letters;1; from you;1; from David and ;1; from William: of the Date August 25;
in 1784; and the ;2; you and william sent August the 16;1785 and the 2; you and
william sent Nov. ;16; in _____; which rendered us happy to heart that it pleased
God of his infinit goodings and tender mercy; to restore you and william both to
your _____ and you with the happneys of seeing brother David
and his family in that remote part of the world; Verrious are the alternations
that hath hapned in circut of your aquantances in Corce of your abstance; but as
I related every particuler worth mentioning; in the letters I wrote before I shall
not detain you aney thing but what releats some thing toward you. And first
Nancey Conltragh is married to mane James morrow from Trumbo; and Necey Cleland
is married bob gibson of Trumgiven and brother samuel is married bell Strain; and
so I quit about marriage as I hop the other letters will come to _____; and then
you will have an account both of Death and marriages So this may Sufice; ther is
a great Stagnation of traid among the _____ of this kingdom at present
owin to bad markets abroad but as brother samuel will give william an account of
these affairs; I quit our country stands on a pare at present whither it will
obtain its liberty and free traid or not we hop for this — There is a great
immegeration out of this country at present and leaceses Selling at an aminious
rate James Robinson and family and his brother john and his nancy James Willson
and Joseph morrison and his family and patrick Patterson and faimly and william
johnston of lindonan (?) and faimiy these are all gowing in a vessel called the
belfast distend for baltimore and a number out of Raphry (?) same passage
William millean James willson son of bells Diing gowing in the friendship for
pheladelphia but he intendes landing at newcastle so that we can get no bearer
but captain mcCadam (?) for our letters brother Samuel is writing to william
this minut; and is Sending a collection of tunes from john matherson to old flock;
I was in Down market either yesterday and seen john matherson; and he has his
compliments to you both and rejoice in your wellfaire Vittling is ch_____ and
                         very chape on account of the scarsity_____
good Spring cows are very Deare but all other Sorts of black cattle are verey
____Sheep and hogs are cheape unless they are fat; oatmell from ? and ;to
10 per; Cnt or ;1; and ;4; per tone wheat; of and ;2; to 10; per Cnt bent wheat
mill; 1; and ;5; course Ditto;4; and ;2; per stone rye is not sold hence and barly
is from ;4; and 10½ penney to ;6; per Cnt Butter ;2; 12; to 2; 18 and ;6; per Cnt
beef;?; and there about pr Cnt or 2⅔ and 2 4/5 per lb port ;3; per lb muttin ;3;½
and ;3; 4/5 per lb Duch flase seed; from ;7; to ;8; and 4 per pek
_____(entire line missing) _____
potatous from ;6; to ? and ;?; per bushal but we sold none this year under _____
_____ per Ditto; brother Samuel is to get the third of land; and he is writing on
other matters I will not _____and longer So adue

N B be pleased write about mary McCay and hir husband how they are Doing; and
john bell disiers to know if it is his brother; that live in your neghbourhood
that you call william bell; if God spears aney of you to write; as we hop you will
omit an opertunity be pleased to mention as many as you have aney wive in your
_____to don not to put your _____to ton much trouble; So I conclud;
m y Scronil with this remarke that it is neither too much activity nor want of
igronce that hinders me to write more complete your parents gets there health

Letter from James Maffet to his brother, Thomas, in America, dated April 14, 1786.

well bless God for it and there is no alternation among us but what is mentioned:
the Rest of the family with _____ to be _____ David and his
family and to brother william. Equal as to you: and with Due respect Remains
your loving and Sincere parents brothers and sisters uncles and ants — Adue a
second time and remaines tell death

                    James Maffet

P S Your uncle william and his wife and Son is all Dead according to account
out of america and the rest of your friends there is no account of them whither
they are Dead or alive So I thinke you need not put yourself to any further
Searchin for them

            (Addressed to)

                    To Mr. Thomas Maffet
                    hanover township
                    Langcaster County
                    to the care of Mr. Timothy Green Esq.
                    hanover township
                    Daphin County America

Received Sept. 28, 1786

        (Copied from the original — 1961)

continued...Letter from James Maffet to his brother, Thomas, in America, dated April 14, 1786.

David Maffet, Second Son of James and Jane Maffet

David was born in 1753 in Leggygowan. His wife, Mary, (surname unknown) was born on July 1, 1751, presumably in the Saintfield area. David, Mary and children came to America in either 1777 or 1778. Military records show that David was serving in the Lancaster Militia, 6th Battalion, 1st Company, as early as 1778 and saw action in Middleton, Pennsylvania. Other military records indicate he served throughout the Revolutionary War until 1783.

Interestingly, the family story read in 1900 erroneously indicated David and his family came to America in 1784 with brothers William and Thomas. In addition, recently discovered tax records of the Hanover Township, Lancaster, Pennsylvania show David as a landowner with 7.6 acres with cows and sheep as part of his farm in 1783. But later in 1786, David and now brother, William, are listed in the same tax records in the newly created Dauphin County which was created out of Lancaster County. Thomas is not listed because a person must be 21 years of age to be listed. William was not listed in the 1783 records either because he was not a resident in 1783 or because he was not yet 21. William would have been 20 in 1783. But a letter written in 1786 from James1750, the oldest brother still in Leggygowan, to Thomas, suggests David and his family traveled to America earlier than the two brothers.

The letter states "...you with the Happneys of seeing brother David and his family in that remote part of the world..." There are other indications that further suggest David and his family arrived in America before William and Thomas. For instance, normally a letter of Testamentary would have been provided to the oldest child, which in this case would have been David if all three were going to America at the same time. But the letter of Testamentary was provided to William, who was younger than David, which supports the fact that David and family came separately.

In a letter dated November 29, 1789, David wrote to Thomas and William. He indicates he and his family have settled in a place "twenty miles from hannastown and six miles from Jacobs Creek Ironworks." These coordinates suggest the family first settled in northern Fayette County. This location makes sense because Jacobs Creek Ironworks was on the Fayette County side of Jacobs Creek.

In this two-part letter, written from Ft. Pitt, David describes the family's condition: "...had a very hard winter and the early frost hurt the corn crop but have bred to Do me to spring," but goes on to say "...we are in good health at present and have a little gurl and Cali (Kelly) hur name.." David goes on to say "... in the Summer I reaped a crop of corn and then fell to the iron trade and worked cheffly at this since it is very good Imployments in these parts." He expresses his interest in coming down the river next Spring or Fall if his health permits. Twice in the letter he complains about not being paid on some debt. The letter states "... what is Due me in this settlement...and I intended to have Jeny (likely refers to Jane, youngest child in Leggygowan) this fall but was Disapointed for I could not get sum Little Debts that is due me..." He finishes by saying he "has worked for 30 days at the iron works this Spring... I had 3 shillings par day cash and pound in vitls and drink reasing chimneys." David affectionately signs off, "No mor at present but Remains your loving Brother and sister till Death."

The next year in the 1790 census, David is listed as head of household in South Huntingdon township in the county of Westmoreland, Pennsylvania with one male under 16, 2 males over age 16 and three females. This suggests David's family included himself, his wife and four children. The children's names were James, David and Cali (Kelly). The name of the fourth child is unknown.

Then in 1800, David Maffet is registered in the "List of Taxable Inhabitants" of South Huntingdon township again. Also, in the 1800 census, besides David, the household has two males under age of ten and one in the 10-15 age group, and two females, one age 16-25 and one 10-15 of age. So, by now, David and James are no longer living in David's household. Both David and James had children. James had two boys, but neither married, and David had no sons. Thus, it appears the male line of this branch of Moffetts did not continue.

We learn from an exhibit that David is working as a mason "reasing chimneys" at Jacobs Creek Ironworks. Jacobs Creek Ironworks was owned by three people: William Trumbull, a former purchasing agent and commissary for Pennsylvania soldiers during the American Revolution; John Holker, who had come to America during the Revolution as Consul General of France and as an agent for the French Navy; and Peter Marmie, who also arrived from France during the Revolution in France and managed the firm's business at the iron furnaces and lived not far away in Westmoreland County. This was the same County where David and his family lived.

The Jacob Creek Furnace was built in 1789 and was located on 301 acres at Perry Township, Fayette County, Pennsylvania. The blast furnace was located on the Fayette side of Jacobs Creek directly across from Westmoreland County. It was the very first furnace erected west of the Appalachian Mountains. The company also was known as Alliance Furnace. It was a stone structure measuring twenty-five-feet square and fifteen-feet high. It was built as a blast furnace and put in operation by 1792, but closed in 1802.

Sometime between 1810 and 1820, David died and is likely buried in the Sewickley Presbyterian Church Cemetery alongside his wife, Mary, who died on July 18, 1836. Mary is buried on row 17. Her gravestone reads, "In Memory of Mary Maffet who departed this life July this 18th 1836 aged 85 years & 14 days." The cemetery is located in Huntingdon Township, South Westmoreland County. There is another grave next to Mary's, but the gravestone is unreadable. There are no other Maffets buried in this older section. There is, however, another section in the cemetery, but paper records of the gravesites have not been gathered and published.

MAFFET, DAVID   Rank.

Lieutenancy   LANCASTER   County. Battalion   6TH

Company   1ST   Class   1ST

Remarks: SERVD MIDDELTON

Authority: C/R

Date   1778-1779   Muster Fines £   Published A(5) VII. 540-542

"Military Accounts: Militia," Records of the Comptroller General, RG-4

Revolutionary War record of David Maffet, 1778-1779.

exbt 2518

David Maffet - 1783 tax list, Hanover, Lancaster County, Pennsylvania

David Maffet, 1783 tax list, Hanover, Lancaster County, Pennsylvania.

The fourth and final page of the 1786 tax list for the township of West Hanover in (the newly established) Dauphin County, Pennsylvania

David Maffet and William Maffet listed in the tax list for the Township of West Hanover in Dauphin County, Pennsylvania.

exhibit 20

Transcription of letter from "Mr. David Maffet, November 29, 1789" to his brothers
(spellings below are those on the original letter)

Deair brothers –

I receved your letters which gave me great Satisfaction to hear of your welfair. I wrot a letter to you and one to Bro. William. If they Shuld Come to you they gave you a particular account. I live twenty mile from hanastown, Six from Jacobs Creek ironworks. I wrote thes in great herey as I met with an opertunity of sending them. I have such bad fortune in writing to you. I wrote fall and Spring Sinc I ben her(e) and onders (?) lands you have got none. I intend being hear as short time as posable I can. We have had very hard winter time then hear we had a frost in September that hurt the corn very much. I have bred to Do me to spring. I can come Down very handy. I _____ what is in Due me in this setlment and it is exceeding hard to com at for there is Very little mony amongst us hearn (turn over (Page 2) fort Pitt November the 29th 1789

So brother and Sister I received your Letters bering last March the 22nd and June 7 which gave me great Satesfaction to hearn of your Welfair and has had good fortuning in that century. I have nothing material to Writ to you. We are all in good health at present. We have got a little grill (girl) and Cali hur name and the first Sumer I reased a crop of Corn then fell to the ireson tread (trade) and his (has) worked Cheffly at that since it is very good Imployment in thes parts. I am glad to hear that you lik that Contry. I intende to have Jeny on this fall but was Disapointed for I could not get sum Little Debts that is in due me. I intend to Come Down nixt Spring or fall at fardest if health pormit.

I have no account from yr land Time (?). I lived hear no Mor at present but Remeains your afectnat and Loving Brother and Sister till Death

David and Marey Maffet

I worked 30 days at the irne Works this Spring. I had 3 shillings par Day Cash and pound in Vitls and Drink. Reasing Chimneys. No mor at present but Remains your Living Brother and Sister till Death

David and Marey Maffet

Mary is fond to Come Down the Rivor when you Writ Derect to the care of Wm turn Bol, Jacobs Crek Iron Works

Letter from David and Mary Maffet to Thomas and William Maffet on November 29, 1789.

List of a Taxable Inhabitants of South Huntington Township in the County of Westmoreland, Pennsylvania showing David Maffet as a mason.

SOUTHWESTERN CORNER OF WESTMORELAND COUNTY, PENNSYLVANIA

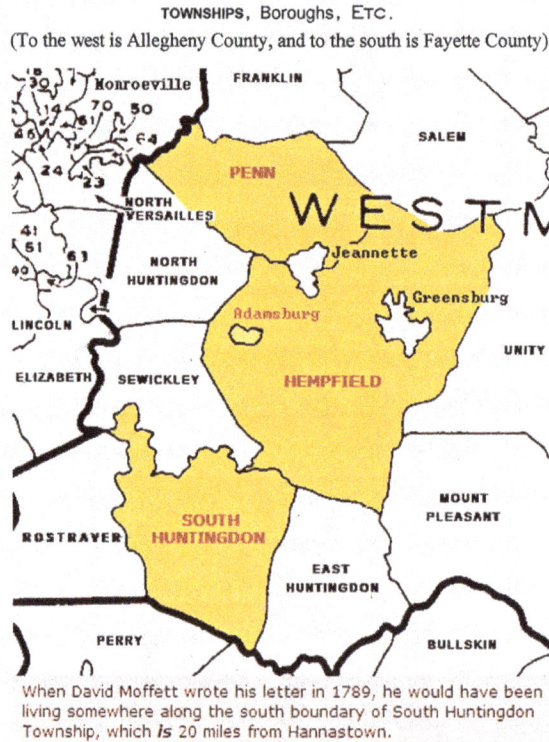

TOWNSHIPS, Boroughs, Etc.
(To the west is Allegheny County, and to the south is Fayette County)

When David Moffett wrote his letter in 1789, he would have been living somewhere along the south boundary of South Huntingdon Township, which *is* 20 miles from Hannastown.

Map of Westmoreland County indicating South Huntington and Perry Townships where Jacob Creek Ironworks was located.

Above: Alliance Furnace, Fayette County
Below: Stack of Alliance Furnace, Fayette County

Blast furnace chimney built by David Maffet for Jacob Creek Ironworks (Alliance Furnace).

William Maffet, Third Son of James and Jane Maffet

William Maffet was born February 1, 1763 in Leggygowan to James and Jane Maffet. A Testamentary provided to William by the minister and warden of the Church of Ireland, Saintfield states, "We the minister and church warden of said parish Do hereby certify that William Maffet (the bearer himself) was born and brought up in said parish." However, according to a letter from his oldest son, James S. Moffett, to Reverend E. C. Trimble in Kentucky, he states, "William was born a mile from Belfast." In those days, County Down was likely their point of reference with regard to location.

The parish of Saintfield was in County Down. County Down's northern border at this time was about a mile from the town of Belfast. Using Belfast and County Down as reference points, it would seem logical that being born in the parish of Saintfield, as stated in the Testamentary, is not inconsistent with the statement of being born about a mile from Belfast. It was likely that James S. Moffett, being born in the U.S. in 1787, had no specific experience with distances in County Down. In addition, the heading on the Letter of Testamentary is labeled "Parish of Saintfield and County Down." To James, a mile from County Down could mean the same as a mile from Saintfield parish. So, in a sense, the minister recanting that William was born and brought up in the parish of Saintfield could mean that William was born a mile from Belfast.

In the family papers, William apparently left home at a very young age for Dublin to learn the silk weavers trade. He became an expert in the business, but because of his father's failing health condition, he returned home to Leggygowan to help with the farm. He soon grew tired of his father's farm and his native land. He longed for "religious liberty" and for "civil freedom." The oppression of Ireland was at its height. Large and frequent tax levies were imposed on its people. Industrial slavery was practically the condition at that time. America offered opportunity.

American authors in "The History of Dauphin County" described the immigration of the Scotch Irish to America. Dauphin County, Pennsylvania is the location where the three Moffett brothers settled. "The Scotch Irish emigrants at New Castle and Philadelphia, save a handful who had settled on the Kennebec in Maine, and of these greater portion eventually settled into Pennsylvania." The author goes on to describe the persecutions of the Scotch Irish in Scotland, their migration to Northern Ireland and their further migration to their final settlement in Pennsylvania. "From 1660 to 1688, no less than eighteen thousand Scottish Presbyterians were put to death in various ways in defense of the solemn league and covenant and Christ's headship over the Church. It would seem what we have here (Pennsylvania) are the lineal descendants of those who loved their lives unto death, but were drowned, hanged, shot and beheaded, and their heads stuck upon poles, their bodies chopped in pieces and scattered about in the days of that human monster, Claverhouse. Through their bloodshed, in defense of religious liberty, we enjoy many and great privileges."

So, in the Spring of 1784, at the age of 21, William and Thomas set sail for Philadelphia to join their brother, David, and his family in Pennsylvania. They sailed under very stormy conditions. It was a perilous journey. There was much sickness aboard. But after a voyage of three months, the two brothers landed in Philadelphia. It's clear from recently discovered tax records that David and his family had arrived in Pennsylvania sometime in 1777-1778 and were already in Dauphin County when William and Thomas arrived in America. A note of clarification is warranted at this point. The Moffett family story read in 1900 at a family Christmas gathering says three brothers came to America in 1784. But the military records of David in Lancaster, Pennsylvania clearly demonstrate that David was already in Lancaster, Pennsylvania before 1784.

As stated above, before setting sail for Philadelphia in 1784, a letter of testimonial was provided to William by the vicar and warden of the Church of Ireland, Saintfield parish. The letter was signed by the Rector James Clewlow and witnessed on April 19, 1784 by Warden William Walker. The letter is quoted below.

Parish of Saintfield and County Down, Ireland
    "We the minister and church warden of said parish Do certify that William Moffet (the bearer himself) was born and brought up in said parish of Honest, Industrious and Respectable parents, is a Protestant, and as far as we know he always behaved well; and we believe him to be a sober, Honest and well behaved young man. Witness our hands this 19th Day of April 1784."
James Clewlow, minister
To whom it may concern- William Walker, warden

This letter of testimonial was from the records of James Moffett1787, William's oldest son born in Bath County, Kentucky. The letter was transcribed from the original slip of paper preserved in the Bible brought from County Down, Ireland in 1784 by William Moffett.

On February 4, 1787 William married Rebecca Robinson. Rebecca was born January 2, 1764 in Dauphin County, ten miles from the city of Harrisburg, Pennsylvania. Rebecca was the oldest of nine children born to William Robinson and Margaret Trimble Robinson. William Robinson's parents were James Robinson and Margaret Moody Robinson. Interestingly, in letters written to William, David and Thomas in America from their brothers in Leggygowan, the author inquired about the Robinsons in Pennsylvania. There were, at that time, the Robinson and Trimble families living in the Saintfield area and are named in the 1786 letter from James. This suggests the brothers knew the Robinson and Trimble families in Leggygowan and thus settled in Dauphin County because of the presence of those families. The Trimble and the Robinson families are also residents in Kentucky. Confirmation that William knew the them in Kentucky is evidenced in a letter of April 18, 1823 from a relative in Leggygowan addressed to James S. Moffett1787, oldest son of William Moffett. In the letter, the author recites a statement made by Samuel in Leggygowan recounting his knowledge of the people who reside in the same village in Kentucky in which James S. Moffett lives. Samuel states "....he (Samuel) informed me (the author of the letter) that he (Samuel) was acquainted with every individual in your village and that with few exceptions, the Citizens were a very honest, Industrious and Economical and that they are the right sort of folks to know how to appreciate liberty and equality...."

Shortly after the marriage of William and Rebecca in 1787, the brothers decided to part ways. William and his wife, Rebecca, and Thomas departed Dauphin County, Pennsylvania for Boonesborough, Kentucky. David and his wife departed for "his land patent" in Old Dominion (western Virginia).

William, Rebecca and Thomas arrived in Boonesbourough (then Fayette County) in the early part of 1787. They lived with Rebecca's uncle, William Trimble, on Lower Howard's Creek (then Fayette County, now Clark County). William Trimble's cabin was three miles North of Boonesbourough. Here, William and Rebecca had their first child, James S. Moffett. James was born on October 18, 1787. Two other children were born there in Clark County. Peggy Trimble Moffett was born May 12, 1789 and Jane Bigham Moffett was born March 2, 1791.

In 1791, James and Rebecca moved their family to Bald Eagle, Bath County, Kentucky (then Bourbon County, Kentucky). On April 13, 1791, William began construction of a cabin. They moved into their cabin on December 24, 1791. The house was located "one half mile a little East of North from where the Springfield Church stood. Here the seven other Moffett children were born. William founded the Kentucky stock of Moffetts."

William's oldest child, Captain James S. Moffett, once recanted a story that his father William joined a group of local settlers and pursued some Indians who had captured 19 women and children from Morgan's Station, Montgomery County, Kentucky on April 1, 1793. Morgan Station was named for Thomas Morgan, the father of Patsy Morgan, wife of John Bigham Moffett.

William and Rebecca remained in their home in Bath County, Kentucky until their deaths. William died April 22, 1826 in Sharpsburg, Bath County, Kentucky. Rebecca died July 2, 1843 in Bath County, Kentucky. William and Rebecca are buried in cemetery of the Springfield Church. In a letter written by William's son, James S. Moffett, to Reverend E. C. Trimble, he states "the late Judge Trimble of Paris, Ky. taught our first Sunday school in the Cane Breaks of our community in 1794." James was 7 years old at that time. In the fall of 1794, Reverend Joseph Howe organized the Presbyterian Church of Springfield with a few members. "My Uncle William Robinson gave a lot of the ground on which the meeting house sits and cemetery now stands." William and Rebecca and her brothers, William Robinson, Esquire, and John Robinson, were among the original founders of the church. William's will was recorded in 1826.

Versailles April 18, 1823

My Dear James

I with considerable regret red your letter of last past % T.H.C. In which you complain much your want of society. Indeed it would seem to be a matter of deep concern to a man in high life (as it is called) or of respectable birth to be thus secluded from society with which he can enjoy himself pleasantly - or to be pend up in a little village containing no inhabitants but a set of stupid clowns whose minds do not _____ information, manners, or morals - I say again that it would really appear hard to a man of respectable birth - But just at a moment when I was sympathising with you on your malancholy situation. In _____ Uncle Sam and with much gravity on his countinance informed me that he was acquainted with every individual in your village and that with very few exceptions the Citizens were very honest industrious and Econombal and that they are the very right sort of folks to know how to apreciate libery and equality and gave it as his opinion that a man ought not to be thought lightly nearly because he does not profits(?) a fortune and a few of the favourite flurishes of the rich. But says that before a man makes any remarks on the qualification of the minds of his neighbour he out (ought) to wipe the cob webs from his own brain - and agreeable to the old adage those who live in glass houses ought not to throw stones - So fare well tell I hear from you again

This from your Uncle James Youngest Nephew

(Copied from the original - 1961)

Letter from a relative in Leggygowan to James S. Moffett,
oldest son of William, dated April 18, 1823.

Springfield Church, Kentucky, founded by William and Rebecca Moffett, and the site of their graves.

Rev. E. C. Trimble -

According to promise I will endeavor to give you a short sketch of my parentage birth and life. My parents were William Moffett and Rebecca Robinson. My father was a Scotch Irishman; born a mile from Belfast, Irelan 1763. My mother was born in Dauphin County, Penn. in 1764, of Scotch-Irish parents, and all Presbyterian Protestants. After their marriage in Dauphin Co., Penn. they moved immediately to Kentucky and settled at William Trimble's on lower Howard's Creek - then Fayette County State of Virginia, now Clarke County, Ky. William Trimble was my mother's uncle. I was born at his house Oct. 18, 1787 (the first child) three miles North of Boonesboro, Ky. My father built a house on the 13 of April 1791, one half mile a little East of North from where Springfield Church now stands, and remove to it on December the twenty-fourth of the same year - then Bourbon County.

The late Judge Trimble of Paris, Ky. taught our first school in the Cane Breaks of our community, 1794. I commited the shorter Chatechism to memory in 1794, in my seventh year, which I have found of inestimable value to me in confirming me in the true doctrine and sentiment of God's Word. In the fall of 1794 Father Howe (Rev. Joseph P. Howe) organized a Presbyterian Chruch at Springfield with a few members. In what way it was organized and to what Presbytery and Synod it belonged I do not know.

My Uncle William Robinson gave the lot of ground on which the meeting-house and Cemetery now are. - and we have always held peacible and undisturbed possession of the same ever since - now seventy-six years. This Church has always adhered to the General Assembly of the United States of North America.

At thirteen years of age I heard through Jane McClure, my Aunt, of a remarkable revival of religeon at Concord Church in Nicholas County, Ky. which she had attended - a sacramental meeting, I think, then under the care of Barton W. Stone. Young men and ladies would fall and appear unconscious for an hour or two and then rise rejoicing in hope of pardoned sin and exalting all around to come to Christ. This news made a deep and powerful impression instanly on my heart and feelings, and I could but adore and wonder at the grace and mercy of God in this converting and convicting sinners by the score in so short a time. I fell in with the work of God's Spirit - this revival of religeon - most heartily and commenced holding secret prayer-meetings - morning and evening, besides ejaculatory prayer very often through the day and night season. This I kept up for more than two years, then it seemed gradually to fade away or decline and after some time I quit prayer nearly altogether., yet I took great delight in hearing religeous conversations and in singing religeous songs of that day. I attended the great meeting of Pleasant Point Church on Stoner Creek and Cane Ridge and afterward at Springfield Church - all in 1801. I partook most heartily in the wonderful religeous exercises of that day young as I was, and ought as I believe to have joined the Church - this was the imperfect beginning of my religeous course in the World - may it and better.

                                        S,
                        James Moffett

Letter from James S. Moffett to Rev. E. C. Trimble regarding his "parentage."

Bath County Kentucky
County Court
Clerk's Office
Will Book "B"

William Moffett's Will - Pg. 103

In the name of God Amen, I William Moffett Senior of the
County of Bath and State of Kentucky, being through the
abundant Mercy and Goodness of God, though week in body,
yet of sound and perfect understanding and memory Do
constitute this my last Will and Testament and desire it
to be recorded by all, as such,

Item first, I desire to have a decent burial, at the
discretion of my dear wife, the expenses of which are to
be defrayed out of my personal Estate.

Item second, I will and positively order, that all my
debts be paid out of my personal estate before any
distribution thereof shall be made.

Item third, I give to my dear and loving wife for term
of her natural life this dwelling house wherein I now
dwell together with the kitchen loom house, Barn Stables,
and other outhouses and one equal third part of my land,
to be so run off as to include the buildings aforesaid
and the Spring. I also bequeath and give to her for her
natural life all my negro slaves, except the two girls
Emily and Amanda, and after my burial expenses and other
debts are paid, one equal third part of all my personal
Estate (negro slaves excepted) forever.

Item fourth, I give to my daughter Polly my negro girl Emily.

Item fifth, I give to my daughter Rebecca my negro girl Amanda.

Item sixth, I give to my daughters Polly and Rebecca each one
Bed and Bedding, together with all their clothing and wearing
apparal.

Item seventh, My son William, had from me a conveyance of 45
acres of land, which I will to be his portion of my landed
Estate.

Item eighth, I give to my son Willis, one man horse, one cow
and calf, and one yearland, together with one-third part of
my out hogs, and one-fourth part of the crop of grain now
growing and to plant this present year, and the use of such
horses and farming utensils as are necessary for the cultivation
of the same, and one bed and bedding.

(continued).

William Moffett's Last Will and Testament.

Item ninth, I give unto my daughter Jane one young sorrel mare
two years old this fall, one cow and calf and six head of sheep.

Item tenth, I give to my son Thomas one bed and bedding.

Item eleventh, I will that the residue of my estate both real
and personal shall, after a deduction of the specifications
in the above items named, be equally divided among my children.

Item twelfth, I name and appoint my much esteemed friend Daniel
Young and my son James Moffett Executors of this my last Will
and Testament In Witness whereof I have hereunto caused my
name to be substribed, this twenty-first day of April ~~nineteen~~
eighteen hundred and twenty-six.

                              Signed: William Moffett (Seal)

John S. Hughes
Robert Moore   Attest.
Daniel Walker

Bath County June Court - 1826

Will proved in open court by oaths of John S. Hughes and Robert
Moore and ordered to be recorded on motion of Daniel Young
and James Moffett, Executors in said will named oath thereto
as the law decrees. It is ordered that probate be granted
then in one form and giving security whereupon they separatly
entered into and acknowledged Bond in the penalty of $2800. each,
the said Daniel Young with Thomas I Young and Robert Moore
his security's and the said James Moffett with Thomas Hill,
Joseph Ratliff and Caleb Ratliff his security's conditioned
for the one and faithful Administration of deceased Estate
and performance of his Will.

Whereupon the same is truly Recorded in my office as the Law
directs.

                              William M. Sudduth

(Copied by Joan Moffett - Oct. 1967
Film on file in University of Ky. Library)

continued...William Moffett's Last Will and Testament.

282

BATH COUNTY KENTUCKY
COUNTY COURT
CLERK'S Office

Wills -- Book "B" -- 1825-31

WILLIAM MOFFETT -- Amount of Sale -- Pg. 123

PURCHASERS NAMES	ARTICLES PURCHASED	
Charles Glover -	1 grindstone and bench	
Widow	1 log chain	
"	1 hoe	
Willis Moffett	2 hoes	
Olive Caldwell	------	
Willis Moffett	3 corn cutting knives	
	1 frod (?)	
Willis Moffett	1 single tree etc.	
Widow	1 cupboard and furniture	10.00
	1 folding leaf table	1.50
	1 Bureau	8.00
	1 looking glass	.50
	1 pr. scossors	.75
Polly Moffett	1 candlestand	.50
Widow	1 hackle - fine	
Mrs. Edwin Young	1 fine hackle	
Polly Moffett	Set of carpets	4.00
Widow	2 smoothing irons	1.00
"	Set of Dog irons	.50
"	seven framed chairs 1st choise - 1.75	
Willis Moffett	four framed chairs 2nd choice - 1.00	
Edwin Young	1 folding leaf table	4.00
Willis Moffett	5 weaving stays	
Widow	Steelyards (?)	
Edwin Young	Desk and bookcase	11.25
Edwin Young	Toothdrawers	.50
Widow	High Bedstead and Bed	20.00
John B. Moffett	Books - a parcel of	
Widow	Large Bible	2.00
Mrs. Jane Crain	set of Windsor chairs	6.00
Alexander Donaldson	one year old colt - Bay	30.00
Alexander Donaldson	one year old roan horse cold	30.12 &1/2
Widow	1 dark sorrel Mare	
Polly Moffett	1 Ball Sorrel Mare & Colt	38.00
Widow	1 Barshire plow and Clevis	3.00
Willis Moffett	1 shovel plow	1.00
Clabourn Fally	1 shovel plow and Clevis	
Robert Long	1 Irontooth harrow	5.00
John Groves	Mare and Colt - Bay	
Edwin Young	1 young bull spotted	4.25
James Randolph	white cow	8.00
Widow	1 pided Cow	8.00
Widow	1 brindle cow	8.00
Widow	1 speckled heifer	3.00
Sinnet Young, Jr.	1 red cow and calf	

continued...William Moffett's Last Will and Testament.

WILLIAM MOFFETT - SALE

Clayburn Fally	1 small speckled bull white back - 4	5
James Young	1 small red bull	
Elzaphen Richards	1 brindle cow and calf	
Reuben Randolph	1 haystack	
James Cook	1 haystack	
James Randolph	1 wheat stack	
Thomas C. Duvall	1 small wheat stack	
Willis Moffett	1 oat stack	
John Craig	1 rye stack	
Edwin Young	1 wheatfan	
Willis Moffett	1 dung fork	62 and 1/2
Widow	1 hayfork	" "
Clayburn Fally	1broadase (?)	
Widow	1 parcel of oats in barn	3.09
"	1 parcel of Flase	1.50
"	1 hogshead	1.00
"	2 haystacks	4.00
"	1 stack of Flase	2.25
"	10 head of sheep 1st choice	10.00
James Anderson	7 head of sheep 2nd choice	
Thomas C. Duvall	7 head of sheep 3rd choice	
Willis Moffett	spade grubbing hoe and sledge	2.00
Willis Moffett	1 handsaw	
Clayburn Fally	Tenonsaw (?)	
James Randolph	1 foot Adge	
Widow	4 Augers	2.00
Willis Moffett	4 planes	
Reliben Randolph	resp, chisel, saw, 2 planes,etc -	.50
Willis Moffett	shoe hammer and pinchers	.93 & 3/4
Claybourn Fally	spoon moulds	2.66
Widow	drawing knife, hammer Trowel, etc. -	1.(
Widow	pair stretchers and ring (or rug)	2.00
William B. Kirk	1 pr. of lsears collar, etc (?)	
Widow	ditto	2.50
Turner Anderson	1 bed and bedding	
Widow	The largest Beehive	1.00
Edwin Young	the upper Beehive	1.75
Edwin Young	1 Beehive	
Edwin Young	1 Beehive	
Clayburn Fally	1 Beehive - Lower	
Widow	1 arge kettle - 18 gals.	.75
"	2 washing tubs	.25
Willis Moffett	1 ten gallon kettle	1.00
William Smart	--------	
Thomas C. Duvall	1 ten gal. pott	
Widow	1 five fal. Pott	81 and 1/4
"	1 ten gal. Pott	1.00
"	2 pots, 2 oven and lids,etc.	
"	1 skillet and 1 teakettle, 1 bake plate	1.6*3
"	1 churn and bucket	.75
"	Vinegar barrel and Tray	.50

continued...William Moffett's Last Will and Testament.

WILLIAM MOFFETT Sale   Pg. 3

Widow	Loom	5.00
Peter R. Gill	2 barrels, churn, hogshead, can	
Sinnett Young, Jr.	1 churn and bucket	
John B. Moffett	1 plowshare and coulter	
Widow	1 Asce	1.25
Willis Moffett	1 Asce	
John B. Moffett	1 single tree and iron wedge	
Widow	2 horse shoes	12 & 1/2
Edwin Young	1 mowing Sythe, Horse shoes, etc	
Ansalum Goodman	1 Reel	
Edwin Young	1 spinning wheel	1.25
Willis Moffett	1 spinning wheel	1.814
Clayburn Fally	1 big wheel	
Widow	12 Geese	6.50
"	24 Geese	3.00
John B. Moffett	1 rifle gun	5.62 and 1/
Widow	5 Reels and Gear	1.50
"	Shovel and poker	.75
Widow	1 woman's saddle, bridle, etc.	1.00
Willis Moffett	1 Suguare Table	.75
Willis Moffett	1 pot ramble	
Widow	1 pot ramble	.62 and 1/
Polly Moffett	1 Bedstead	.75
Thomas Moffett	1 Hone	.75
John B. Moffett	2 Rasors straps and base	.62 and 1/
Daniel Young	Bar of Iron and shovel	.50
Widow	2 twilled bags	.50
Willis Moffett	2 sythes, sneads	
John B. Moffett	1 Hone	
Edwin Young	10 barrels corn	
Willis Moffett	10 barrels corn	
Edwin Young	10 barrels corn	
Willis Moffett	10 ditto	
Widow	51 barrells, 42 bushels @ 75 cts per barrel --38,920	
Edwin Young	1 lot of hogs 19 in No.	
Widow	10 large hogs	20.00
Widow	10 shoats at 16&2/3 cents each	1.66 2/
Willis Moffett	2 barrels and 2 bushels corn @814 cts. Pr. B.	
Willis Moffett	10 barrels corn @814 cts per bushel	
Willis Moffett	1 hogshead	.50

We do certify the above inventory to be a correct Bill of the Sale
made of the Personal Estate of William Moffett, deceased, so far
as we at present know, December 7th A.D. 1826.

                                          James Moffett
                                          Daniel Young --- Executors

Bath County December Court 1826

This amount of sale of the Estate of William Moffett, dec'd,
was returned approved and ordered to be Recorded whereupon the
same is truly recorded in my office as the Law directed.
            Teste William H. Sudduth C D C

continued...William Moffett's Last Will and Testament.

Samuel Maffet, Fourth Son of James and Jane Maffet

Samuel Maffet, the fourth son and seventh child of James1720 and Jane Maffet, was born in 1765 in Leggygowan. Samuel was fourteen years younger than the eldest brother, James.

Samuel was married to Isabel Strain in 1785. There are no records of their marriage, but the letter from James1750 in 1786 states the fact of the marriage of Samuel and Isabel Stain. No records of Isabel's death or burial have been located. They had two daughters. Both daughters died early in life as a result of a smallpox epidemic that swept the Townland of Leggygowan in 1789. The plight of the two daughters is described in a passage in a letter written by Samuel on April 28, 1790 to his brothers in America. "Loving brothers the alterations in our family have been great since I wrot last to you which was about the first of May 1789 when I let you know my oldest child was dead and the second died also both in the small pokes and left me childless but we expect another Soon..." It is unknown whether Samuel and his wife ever had another child.

Samuel and his family resided in the village of Saintfield. He was a merchant. In 1791, he was listed as a member of the First Presbyterian Church in Saintfield. He also was listed, along with his brother, James, as a member of the same church in 1799. He also signed the petition to call Reverend Simpson to become minister of the church to replace the Reverend Birch.

In 1811, Samuel was listed on High Street in Saintfield as a grocer. Then in 1815, Samuel was listed in the registry of the Freeholders List in Saintfield on September 29. The registry states Samuel was living in Saintfield, having property in Drumnaconnor, in the parish of Kilmore. The landlord was Francis and Nicholas Price. The names in the column "lives and other tenure" were "Their Royal Highnesses, George Prince of Wales, Prince Frederick, Bishop of Osnaburgh and Prince William Henry." Interestingly, his brother, James, is also listed in the Freeholder List in Drumnaconnor as a Freeholder farmer. The landlord was Alexander Stewart Newtonards as previously discussed in the section regarding James1750.

Samuel died on February 11, 1831, age 66. His will was probated in 1831 and 1832. His executors were Henry and William Jennings of Saintfield and Jim Orr. His place of burial is unknown, but is likely in the cemetery of the Presbyterian Church in Kilmore or the cemetery of the First Presbyterian Church in Saintfield.

Samuel was remembered fondly for his affectionate and loving expression towards his brothers. In a family letter, Samuel is remembered in the following passage: "Among our older ancestors were many farmers, tradesman and merchants. Samuel, our great, great uncle, was a merchant having a store containing clothing, wares and vittilings. He was wealthy as wealthy was counted in that day. He was learned in Latin and mathematics; wrote a good hand and was a very affectionate brother..."

His affection for his brothers was expressed in a letter written on April 28, 1790 to his brothers in America. "... Dear brothers I beg that you will neglect no opportunity of letting us know how you are. I am very glad to hear of brother David going about to go to you dear william. I am glad to hear of you being so well settled in a plantation and alls of you being so agreeably maryd and wish you Joy of youer wife. Soon my wife Disiers to be remembered to you and your wife and brother Thomas no more at present but remain your loving brother..." Later in the same letter, Samuel adds these words: "...If these few lines come to your hands do not mourn as those that have no hope but be resigned to the Will of Almighty God who disposes of all things for the best."

BARONY OF CASTLEREAGH.

12

No.	Name of Freeholders.	Place of Abode.	Situation of Freehold.	Names of Landlord.	Value of Freehold	Names of Lives and other Tenure.	Place & Date of Registry.	
172	Maxwell, Robert	Carricknevcagh	Carricknevcagh	Wills, Earl of Hillsborough,	40s	Robert, David, & James Maxwell,	Saintfield,	Sept. 29, 1815.
173	Magee, Alexander	same	same	same	40s	William Alexander & John Magee,	same	same
174	Magee, James	same	same	same	40s	John, James, and William Magee,	same	same
175	Martin, James	Cornemuck	Cornemuck	same	40s	John, Letitia, and James Martin,	same	same
176	Milliken, Edward	Carreduff	Carreduff	Mary, Marchioness of Downshire,	40s	Edward Milliken,	same	same
177	Morrison, Rainey	same	same	same	40s	Rainey Morrison,	same	same
178	Morrison, John	same	same	same	40s	John Morrison,	same	same
179	Morrow, John	Lisbane	Lisbane	same	40s	John Morrow,	same	same
180	Magown, James	Crossnacreevy	Crossnacreevy	same	40s	William Gilmore,	same	same
181	Marshall, John	Leveroge	Leveroge	same	40s	John Marshall,	same	same
182	Magee, John, jun.	Carricknevcagh	Carricknevcagh	same	40s	John Magee,	same	same
183	Martin, Hugh	Cornemuck	Cornemuck	Wills, Marquis of Downshire,	40s	William Jamison, James Martin and Prince Edward,	same	same
184	Martin, Robert	Castlereagh	Castlereagh	same	40s	John Smith, William McConnell and John McClements,	same	same
185	Malcolm, William	Hill-Hall	Hill-Hall	same	40s	Samuel Malcom, John Marshall and John McClements,	same	same
186	Murland, William	Ballycarrongannon	Ballycarrongannon	Arthur, Marquis of Downshire,	40s	Thomas Murland, Alexander Thompson and James Gibson,	same	same
187	Morrow, Thomas Birch	Lisbane	Lisbane	same	40s	Thomas Morrow, William Morrow and Martin Morrow,	same	same
188	Marshall, William	Hill-Hall	Hill-Hall	Wills, Lord Visct. Hillsborough,	40s	Samuel Marshall, Thomas Shaw and John Clarke,	same	same
189	Marshall, Samuel	same	same	same	40s	Same Lives.	same	same
190	Magibbon, William	Glasdrumond	Glasdrumond	Nicholas Price, Esq.	40s	William Magibbon, William Hoey and Francis Hoey,	same	same
191	Murray, James	Aghnadarragh	Aghnadarragh	same	40s	Matthew Forde, jun, Esq. Hon. Thos. Stewart & James Murray,	same	same
192	Murray, John	same	same	same	40s	John Murray, William Forde, Esq. and Hon. Thomas Stewart,	same	same
193	Magoean, William	Lessons	Lessons	same	40s	Nicholas Magoean,	same	same
194	Morrison, William	Saintfield	Drumaconnell	same	40s	William Morrison, Francis Hoey and Andrew McBurney,	same	same
195	Murphy, Gawin	Killinure	Killinure	same	40s	Gawan Murphy, Matthew Forde, Esq. jun. & Hon. Thos Stewart,	same	same
196	Minnis, William	Lisdoonan	Lisdoonan	same	40s	Prince of Wales, Miss Elizabeth Price and Hugh McKee,	same	same
197	Mack, James	Carsons	Carsons	same	40s	James Mack, William Forde and John Bennett,	same	same
198	Murray, Patrick	same	same	same	40s	Patrick Murray, Francis Hoey and Arthur Forde,	same	same
199	Moore, Thomas	Lisdalgon	Lisdalgon	same	40s	Thomas Moore, William Forde and Hon. Thomas Stewart,	same	same
200	Malcom, William	Killinure	Killinure	Francis Price, Esq.	40s	William Malcom, Robert Malcom and Alexander Stewart,	same	same
201	Magibbon, Francis	same	same	same	40s	James Magibbon, Francis Magibbon and Janett Magibbon,	same	same
202	Marshall, Samuel	same	same	same	40s	William Marshall, Jane his wife, and William Marshall,	same	same
203	Macarian, James	Saintfield	Drumaconnell	same	40s	Prince of Wales, Bishop of Osnaburgh and Prince William Henry,	same	same
204	Marshall, John	Drumaconal	Drumaconal	same [Esqrs.	40s	Same Duke of York and Duke of Clarence,	same	same
205	Moorhead, Robert	Saintfield	same	Francis Price and Nicholas Price,	40s	Prince of Wales, Bishop of Osnaburgh and Prince Wm. Henry,	same	same
206	Maffet, Samuel	same	same	same	40s	Robert Morrow, Flora Morrow and William Morrow,	same	same
	Morrow, Robert	Ballycairn	Melogh	Roger M. H. McNeill, Esq.	40s		same	same

Freeholders List of Barony of Castlereagh of 1815 showing Samuel Maffet as a freeholder in Drumnaconnor.

Thomas Maffet, Fifth Son of James and Jane Maffet

Thomas Maffet was born April 13, 1767 in Leggygowan, Northern Ireland. He was 17 years old in 1784 when he left his home in Leggygowan. Thomas landed with his older brother, William, in Philadelphia, Pennsylvania in the Spring of 1784. Thomas remained in Dauphin County, Pennsylvania with his brother until 1787 when he and his brother, William, and William's wife, Rebecca, departed for Boonesborough, Kentucky.

We know from a letter Thomas received from his brothers in Leggygowan on September 28, 1786 and dated April 24, 1786, that he lived in Hanover Township, Lancaster County, Pennsylvania. The letter was addressed in the care of Mr. Timothy Green, Esq. at the Hanover Township, Dauphin County, Pennsylvania. Interestingly, Timothy Green was a prominent citizen of Dauphin County. He was born in 1733 in Hanover Township and served as the first presiding judge. His father, Robert Green, was of Scottish ancestry from the North of Ireland settling initially near the Kittochtinny Mountains on Monda Creek in 1725. After arriving in Boonesborough, Thomas departed between 1791 and 1793 for Lexington, Kentucky while William and Rebecca relocated to Bald Eagle, Bourbon County (now Bath County) Kentucky, about 40 miles from Lexington.

Not long after Thomas arrived in Lexington, he died in a horse racing mishap on the streets of Lexington in 1793. He was 26 years of age when he died. Presumably, Thomas is buried somewhere in Lexington or in the Springfield church cemetery where is brother, William, and wife, Rebecca, are buried. From a transcript of a reading by Thomas' nephew, John B. Moffett, entitled "The Moffett Family Christmas 1900," the death of Thomas is described:

"It happened in this way; Thomas was riding along on horseback when two young sports contested in a horse race. Their horses were high strung and coming up behind Thomas ran against his horse. Thomas's horse jumped and in consequence he was thrown off. He landed on a stump, striking his stomach, from the effects of which he lived but a short time. Thomas never married. At the age of 17 he crossed the Atlantic with his older brothers. He had the courage at an early age to do what those of mature years would quail before. A mere boy, he bid a lasting farewell to his parents and native land, passed from under parental roof out onto a stormy ocean and was borne more than 2,000 miles away over his bosom to a land full of peril. As we contemplate the heroism, the pluck, the fortitude that animated such a boy, we might well wish he had been spared to enjoy the reward to which such sacrifice entitled him."

John Bigham Moffett, Son of William Moffett

John Bigham Moffett was born October 29, 1800 in Bath County, Kentucky. His father was William Moffett, who emigrated to America in 1784 from Leggygowan, County Down, Northern Ireland. His mother was Rebecca Robinson from Dauphin County, Pennsylvania. He was the eighth of ten children born to William and Rebecca.

In 1821, John moved to Sangamon County, Illinois and located seven miles southwest of Springfield. He worked as a wheelwright when he came to Illinois. Shortly after arriving in Sangamon County, he married Martha "Patsy" Morgan on July 26, 1821. Patsy was a school teacher. She was born March 2, 1803 in Hamilton County, Ohio.

Patsy was the daughter of Thomas Morgan and Elizabeth Bell Butler. Thomas was born about 1783 in Kentucky near Cincinnati. He married Elizabeth Bell Butler near Cincinnati. This was Elizabeth's second marriage. She was born Elizabeth Bell in 1773 in Maryland. Elizabeth and Thomas Morgan had seven children in Hamilton County, Ohio and later resettled in Sangamon County in 1821 south of Spring Creek in what was called Gardiner Township. Thomas and Elizabeth later moved to Schuyler County where they both died in 1858. Interestingly, Elizabeth's parents were Zephaniah Bell and Henrietta Ratcliff, who was related to John Bigham.

John B. Moffett and Patsy Morgan had three children: Rebecca Jane, born July 30, 1822; Elizabeth Ann (Betsy), born January 30, 1824; and William Thomas, born February 19, 1826. All were born in Sangamon County, Illinois. Shortly after William's birth, Patsy died on March 28, 1826.

After the loss of his wife, Patsy, John Bigham continued to work as a wheelwright in order to supply the needs of his children and to get a start on the new and growing state of Illinois. He was a natural mechanic and could turn his hand to almost anything in the way of the use of tools and was considered the handyman of his community. He was a cabinetmaker in Springfield and afterwards an architect and builder. John and David S. Taylor designed and built the third county courthouse in Springfield. This was the same courthouse where Abraham Lincoln became famous.

While in Springfield, he married Polly Ann Taylor on May 17, 1827 in Rushville, Illinois. Polly was the daughter of Judge David Sutton Taylor and Sarah Young in Springfield. The couple had two children born in Springfield: David Sutton, born February 14, 1828, and Sarah Taylor, born December 23, 1829. In the spring of 1831, they relocated to Rushville, Schuyler County, Illinois, where John Bigham turned his skill to the trade of millwright. There, he erected the first steam saw and flouring mill in the military district, the area lying between the Illinois and Mississippi rivers. He remained in Rushville and was employed in the milling business for ten years. While he was in Rushville, he obtained a government patent on land in Blue Mound Township, Macon County, Illinois. The land was twelve miles west of Decatur on Old Springfield Road. The property had 212 acres. The Sangamon River was a quarter-of-a-mile behind the house. This was the land on which the Moffett homestead was built. The original patent was obtained by John Bigham Moffet.

Before going further, it's worth pausing for a paragraph regarding a grandson of John Bigham. John's oldest son by Polly Taylor, as mentioned in the paragraph above, was David

Sutton Moffett. David Sutton was born February 14, 1828 in Sangamon County. On May 19, 1857, David Sutton married Melissa Brockway in Decatur, Illinois. Melissa was born April 13, 1841. The couple had a son, Dr. William Thomas Moffett (MD). Dr. William Thomas was born April 13, 1867 near Madison School, Blue Mound Township, Macon County, Illinois. Dr. Moffett not only served as the family genealogist at the time, but also was the first Clan President and as Acting Historian of "Clan Moffat in America." On October 7, 1914, the Department of State of the State of Illinois issued a certificate of incorporation as a family association to Clan Moffat in America. The location of the corporation was noted to be the City of Blue Mound in the County of Macon, Illinois. The organization was the forerunner of what today is known as "Clan Moffat Society." The original Board of Directors consisted of the following Moffats: John T. Moffat, attorney and district judge from Tipton, Iowa; Alvus H. Moffet, banker from Larned, Kansas; James Robert Moffatt, banker from Troy, Tennessee; Linden Byron Moffett, railroad conductor from Muncie, Indiana; Arthur Bingham Moffatt, manufacturer from St. Joseph, Michigan; and Dr. William Thomas Moffett, President, from Blue Mound, Illinois. The Clan Moffat in America held its first meeting on August 2, 1915 for a three-day convention in the Marquette Hotel, St. Louis, Missouri. The Clan focused on assembling the names and pedigree of all persons in the U.S. with the name Moffat. The Clan also published the "Moffatana Bullentin" about all things Moffat.

The Moffett house was constructed by John Bigham and his oldest son, William Thomas. It was a pretentious house for its day. The weather boards and other timbers were sawed in his sawmill. The house had ten rooms, six of them downstairs and four upstairs. The interior was trimmed in solid walnut. The house has been occupied by a Moffett since the year it was erected. William Thomas bought the house and the surrounding 212 acres when John Bigham died in 1861. The House remained in possession of WT's wife until her death in 1915. The house was then bought by William Thomas' eldest son, E. R. Moffett, who served as Deputy County Clerk of Macon County. Following the death of E.R. Moffett, the house was bought by ER's oldest son, Ira G. Moffett.

While in Rushville, John and Polly had five more children: Mary Eliza, born March 15, 1932, but died shortly thereafter on June 28, 1832; Ann Eliza, born May 29, 1833; Robert, born December 7, 1835 and died later than same month; John McDowell, born December 14, 1836; and James Milton, born August 10, 1839.

In 1842, John and Polly moved their family to his new farm in Blue Mound Township, Macon County and he spent the rest of his life as a farmer until his death in 1862. There, he and Polly had four more children: Caroline was born on August 6, 1842 and died shortly after birth; Louisa Catherine was born on September 12, 1843; Joseph Edwin was born on September 23, 1845; and Laura Amanda was born February 10, 1849. Polly died later in 1849.

Shortly after moving into his new home in Blue Mound Township in 1842, John Bigham also built the second school house in the township and first one in his settlement.

On September 26, 1850, John Bigham Moffett married his third wife, Nancy McDowell. They had no children from their marriage. Nancy was the widow of the Reverend Abner McDowell. Her maiden name was Grider. Her brother was Henry Grider, a well-known Kentucky politician who represented the Bowling Green district in the U.S. Congress for thirty years.

During the outbreak of the Blackhawk War, John Bigham served as a private in Captain Allen Whiles' Company. He served alongside his friend and attorney, Abraham Lincoln, also a private in the same company.

During his later years, John Bigham was embroiled in at least nine legal cases between June, 1852 and June, 1856 against other members of both the Moffett and Taylor families. In each case, John Bigham was the defendant and was represented by his friend and future President of the United States, Abraham Lincoln. Each of the cases was settled without a jury trial and with only monetary settlements from soured land deals.

John Bigham Moffett was described by his grandson, John Bigham II, as "a typical Moffett compared to his ancestors full 6 feet in height as a man of powerful physical build, of great force of character, much above the average in intellectual abilities and possessed a fine discriminating judgement. Long lived, strong in character, honesty and integrity. For many years, he was an elder of the Cumberland Presbyterian Church and did much in his day toward the work of evangelization. He was public-spirited, and never let an opportunity pass without encouraging all measures, having in contemplation the social, religious and educational welfare of his community. He built school houses and churches and supported them with his moral and financial ability.

John Bigham Moffett died on September 15, 1862 on his farm amongst his friends and family, loved by all as a man who loved God and his fellow man, and who lived without reproach, and whose enthusiasm inspired men to do and dare in the cause of right and public good.

John Bigham Moffett is buried in Brown Cemetery, Decatur, Illinois. His wife, Nancy, died on March 11, 1892.

The story of John Bigham would be incomplete without mentioning his brother, Judge Thomas Moffett. Judge Moffett was an important and critical public servant during the early years of Springfield, Illinois. Abraham Lincoln tried a number of lawsuits before Judge Moffett as a young Springfield lawyer. Judge Moffett's significance to Springfield is highlighted in an article printed in the Moffatana Bullentin in April, 1907. The article states, "I am sorry to say that the proud city of Springfield, Illinois has desecrated the grave of Judge Thomas Moffett and about 200 other graves by appropriating the ground, removing the stones and leaving the bodies. It is the old Hutchison buying ground in the heart of the city about three blocks northwest of the capitol buildings. The city illegally condemned the grounds, razed the monuments and turned the ground into a park. The city now proposes to sell the ground for residence sites and has asked the heirs to quit-claim which they will not do. Why did not this city remove the bodies, as is custom?"

Judge Moffett's support of the anti-slavery movement is revealed in a passage from "The Lincoln's Portrait of a Marriage" by Daniel Mark Epstein. The passage underscores the relationship between the Moffetts and the Lincolns. The passage is as follows: "Lincoln friends Judge Thomas Moffett and Orville Browning had organized an event in which abolitionist Cassius Clay would give a speech in Springfield in the State House Rotunda. At the last moment, a Illinois Democrat opposed to the fiery abolitionist's sentiments against slavery, challenged the government officials to cancel Mr. Clay's appearance at the Rotunda. Handbills were posted everywhere stating "On the Order of A. Starnes and John Moore Commissioners, the Rotunda of the State House cannot be used for Cassius M. Clay's lecture. So, with the support of Lincoln, Judge Thomas Moffett and Orville Browning reconvened the speech by constructing a makeshift platform on a hill in a grove five blocks from the square and Judge Moffett introduced the famous abolitionist and friend of the Lincolns, Cassius Clay."

THE CLAN CHARTER.

STATE OF ILLINOIS,
DEPARTMENT OF STATE.

Harry Woods...............................Secretary of State.

To all to whom these presents Shall Come, Greeting:

WHEREAS, A CERTIFICATE, duly signed and ackowledged, has been filed in the Office of the Secretary of State, on the 7th day of October, A. D., 1914, for the organization of

"THE CLAN MOFFAT IN AMERICA"

Under and in accordance with the provisions of "AN ACT CONCERNING CORPORATIONS" approved April 18, 1872, and in force July 1, 1872, and all acts amendatory thereof, a copy of which certificate is hereto attached;

Now, Therefore, I, HARRY WOODS, Secretary of State of the State of Illinois, by virtue of the powers and duties vested in me by law, do hereby certify that the said "THE CLAN MOFFAT IN AMERICA," is a legally organized corporation under the laws of this state.

In Testimony Whereof, I hereto set my hand and cause to be affixed the Great Seal of State.

[SEAL]

Done at the City of Springfield this Seventh day of October, A. D., 1914, and of the Independence of the United States the one hundred and 39th.

HARRY WOODS,
Secretary of State.

STATE OF ILLINOIS, } ss.   Fee, $10.00
MACON COUNTY,

To Harry Woods, Secretary of State:

We, the undersigned William Thomas Moffett, William David Moffett and Walter Alexander Moffett, citizens of the United States, propose to form a corporation under an Act of the General Assembly of the State of Illinois, entitled, "AN ACT concerning Corporations," approved April 18, 1872, and all acts amendatory thereof; and for the purpose of such organization we hereby state as follows, to-wit:

1. The name of such corporation is "THE CLAN MOFFAT IN AMERICA".

2. The object for which it is formed is to maintain a family or clan association, to hold family or clan reunions and to purchase real estate suitable for such clan and family reunions or for clan settlement, to publish clan bulletins and a clan history and genealogy and to gather data for such publications.

3. The management of the aforesaid "The Clan Moffat in America," shall be vested in a board of Six Directors, who are to be elected annually.

4. The following persons are hereby selected as the Directors to control and manage said corporation for the first year of its corporate existence, viz: John T. Moffit, Alvus H. Moffet, James Robert Moffatt, Linden Byron Moffett, Arthur Bingham Moffatt and William Thomas Moffett.

5. The location is in the city of Blue Mound, Illinois in the county of Macon in the State of Illinois, and the postoffice address of its business office is at No. X Street in the said city of Blue Mound, Illinois.

(SIGNED).

WILLIAM THOMAS MOFFETT,
WILLIAM DAVID MOFFETT,
WALTER ALEXANDER MOFFETT

STATE OF ILLINOIS, } ss.
COUNTY OF MACON,

I, J. E. VanCleve, a Notary Public in and for the County and State aforesaid, do hereby certify that on this fifth day of October, A. D., 1914, personally appeared before me William Thomas Moffett, William David Moffett and Walter Alexander Moffett, to me personally known to be the same persons who executed the foregoing certificate, and severally acknowledged that they had executed the same for the purpose therein set forth.

IN WITNESS WHEREOF, I have hereunto set my hand and seal the day and year above written.

(SEAL)

J. E. VANCLEVE,
Notary Public.

Charter issued by the State of Illinois to
incorporate Clan Moffat in America.

The following excerpts are from a book entitled <u>ABRAHAM LINCOLN IN DECATUR</u> by Otto R. Kyle (Editor of the <u>Decatur Review</u> editorial page) published by Vantage Press, New York, 1957.

The cases are found in the APPENDIX, entitled Lincoln Law Cases in Decatur, pages 127 through 138, and include the years: 1838-1859.

"1852 . . . <u>June 4</u>. John G. Taylor vs. John B. Moffett, ejection. Lincoln representing Moffett. Plaintiff files declaration and defendant is to appear and plead within 20 days.

<u>Nov. 13</u>. Thomas J. Moffett. Rebecca Moffett, William Moffett, Elizabeth Moffett, Eliza Ann Moffett, Francis J. Moffett, Edy Moffett, James H. Moffett, Caroline Moffett and Mary J. Moffett vs. John B. Moffett, ejection. Lincoln files defendant's plea.

<u>Nov. 13</u>. John G. Taylor vs. John B. Moffett, Lincoln for defendant with Emerson and Wait for plaintiff. Case continued. (In a Taylor vs. Moffett ejection case filed June 4, 1852, the defendant did not appear on Nov. 12, 1852 and award was made to plaintiff of $349.37 and costs.)

"1853 . . . <u>May 27</u>. John G. Taylor vs. John B. Moffett, ejection. Lincoln for defendant. Emerson and Wait for the plaintiff. Case is submitted to court without a jury. Find for the defendant. Plaintiff asks for a new trial.

<u>May 27</u>. Thomas J. Moffett and others vs. John B. Moffett. Lincoln for the defendant; Emerson and Wait for plaintiff. Case continued.

<u>Oct. 24</u>. Thomas J. Moffett and others vs. John B. Moffett (Nov. 13, 1852, May 27, 1853). Post and Lincoln for defendant. Case dismissed by agreement, the defendant to pay all costs.

<u>Oct. 25</u>. Taylor vs. Moffett, ejection (May 27, 1853). Lincoln for defendant. Continued by agreement to be tried by some attorney to be agreed upon by parties at next term of court.

"1854 . . . <u>Oct. 26</u>. Taylor vs. Moffett, ejection (May 27, 1853) continued by consent. (In Oct. 1853, there was agreement that this case be tried by some attorney to be agreed upon at next term of court.)

"1956 . . . <u>June 2</u>. Taylor vs. Moffett, ejection (May 27, 1853, Oct. 25, 1853, Oct. 26, 1854. Lincoln for defendant. Change of venue to Sangamon County.

Excerpts from "Abraham Lincoln in Decatur" regarding Lincoln's role as attorney for John B. Moffett against the Taylor family lawsuits.

John B. Moffett

Portrait of John Bigham Moffett.

294

William Thomas Moffett, Son of John Bigham Moffett

William Thomas Moffett was born February 19, 1826 in a log house in Sangamon County, Illinois to John Bigham Moffett and Martha (Patsy) Morgan. He was the third child and the only boy born to the couple. William's Mother, Patsy, died just six weeks after his birth, leaving his father to care for the three children: Rebecca, Elizabeth and William Thomas.

In 1836 at the age of 10, the family moved to Springfield, Illinois where William Thomas attended school for two years and then moved to Rushville, Schuyler County where he lived for three years attending school where his father, John Bigham, worked as a carpenter and wheelwright. William was an exceptional student, especially in mathematics.

John Bigham was now remarried to Polly A. Taylor, daughter of Judge Taylor of Springfield. He remained in Rushville, employed in the milling business for ten years. At the same time, John Bigham worked with William Thomas to improve his farm in Blue Mound Township, an investment he made while living in Springfield.

In 1841, John Bigham moved his family to the south side of the Sangamon River in what was later called Blue Mound Township. In 1842, William's father built a home on a site located on a hill across the river and a half-mile west of where Abraham Lincoln lived ten years earlier. Here, the well-known "Moffett settlement" was made, and where William lived until his marriage in 1856. His father, John Bigham, remained on the farm until his death in 1862.

By 1847, at the age of 21, William considered himself equal to any task. He was enthralled with the spirit of adventure spurred by the discovery of gold in California. So, in 1849, he crossed the Great Plains in charge of a division of wagon trains headed for Sacramento. They arrived the same year and commenced panning for gold in the rivers outside Sacramento.

For a short time, William was engaged in placer mining, but soon turned his attention to "freighting" and trading. William Thomas' adventure was highly lucrative and he was loath to abandon it, but after an absence of eighteen months, at the earnest and repeated requests of his ailing father, he sailed home. His journey home took him through the Isthmus of Panama to Havana, Cuba and then to New Orleans.

In returning from California, William Thomas found his father's business affairs in an unsatisfactory condition. The large farm was encumbered, family expenses were very high and a general financial crisis was approaching. So, using the money he earned in California, which was considerable, he set about willingly and with unremitting toil, to restore his father's estate. Afterward, he was then able to turn his attention to his own interests.

Before William Thomas left for California, he had purchased a quarter-section in Blue Mound Township. He focused his time on making improvements to his land, which later became one of the most substantial estates of its kind in Macon County.

On October 14, 1856, William Thomas married Helen Lucretia Barrows of Bridgeport, Vermont. They married in Bridgeport (Addison County). Helen was born on February 1, 1832 in Bridgeport. She was the daughter of Josiah Barrow and Susan Walker. Helen grew up in Bridgeport. Her childhood home sat on the summit of a hill looking eastward toward the Green Mountains and westward toward the towering Adirondacks. Early in her life, Helen prepared herself to become a school teacher. She attended public schools and qualified to become a teacher. She furthered her education by entering Castleton Seminary at Castleton, Vermont. She graduated with honors in 1852. Upon graduation, she pursued job opportunities. At that time, there was a significant demand for teachers with her qualifications. Wages for New England teachers were higher out West than in the East. So, in 1854, Helen Barrows, traveled out West with her sister, Susan, who herself was on her way to accept a teaching position in Mississippi.

Helen had been invited by her cousin, Erastus Wright, a noted abolitionist in Springfield, Illinois, with the intention of getting her to accept a teaching position in Springfield. After making her way out West, she was delighted with the school and accepted the job to teach. She taught for two years before her marriage to William Thomas and for many years taught in Sangamon County and Macon County schools.

Helen's mother, Susan R. Walker Barrow, at some unknown time, moved to Blue Mound to be with her daughter, Helen, and William Thomas. Susan Barrow died on August 10, 1881. She is buried in Brown Cemetery, Mount Auburn Road, Macon County, Illinois. Her gravestone is erected near the gravestones of Helen and William Thomas Moffett. The inscription on the gravestone reads: Susan R., wife of Josiah Barrow, born in Hubberton, Vermont. Died August 10, 1881.

As an aside, Susan Barrow's Uncle was Artemus Ward, Commander of the Continental Army before General George Washington. Artimus Ward lived between 1727 and 1800.

At an early age, William Thomas took an interest in politics. When he was 14, he took a lively interest in the 1840 U.S. Presidential campaign. He urged the election of Benjamin Harrison for President. William was an ardent Whig and supported the party as long as it had a candidate in the field. He attended political rallies and his voice was often heard shouting "Tippecanoe and Tyler Too." In 1856, he cast his vote for Millard Fillmore for President because he was a Whig. Henry Clay was his political ideal and the American system protection his shibboleth.

William Thomas's opinions, in part, came from his father, John Bigham Moffett, who was native born and a revered citizen of Kentucky and a devotee of the "Great Commoner," and in part from his own independent thoughts. For William it was a short step from the Whig to the Republican Party. But his reason for joining the Republican Party was the preservation of the Union. He had a personal acquaintance with Abraham Lincoln as both a man, friend and lawyer and had formed a good opinion of his ability and character and as a standard bearer of the party in 1860.

While William never became a soldier in active service during the Civil War, he did serve as a volunteer and went to Camp Butler to engage in military service. After a short absence to care for his father, he was commissioned by Governor Gates as captain of a company of volunteer home guards and in that capacity rendered valiant service to the Union cause.

In the 1860s, William's interest in politics moved to public service. In 1861, he represented Blue Mound Township on the Board of Supervisors of Macon County. He filled this position again in 1864 and for the next five succeeding years in 1876 and 1894, serving a total of nine years as a representative on the Board of Supervisors.

William was elected to serve as a representative in the Illinois General Assembly. He was a member of the twenty-seventh and twenty-eighth General Assemblies for the State of Illinois.

In 1876, he was elected to be a member of the State Board of Equalization and after serving two years, he resigned to take a vacated seat in the Senate of the State of Illinois. He served in the Senate for four years, continuing on and serving a second term as Chairman, Committee for Agriculture, where his knowledge of farming enabled him to suggest many measures to expand industry and commerce in the West.

In his later years, William was on the Board of Trustees of Milliken University in Decatur and donated much of the land on which the college now stands. He attended board meetings until his health failed. He was a faithful and dedicated supporter of the university and felt deeply about the necessity of education.

On October 11, 1901 at 8:35 p.m. at the age of 75, William Thomas Moffett died after years of declining health from stomach cancer. He died at his home in Blue Mound Township. He is buried next to his wife, Helen, in the Brown Cemetery in Macon County, Illinois. Services were held at the Madison Cumberland Presbyterian Church in Blue Mound.

Children of William Thomas and Helen Lucretia Barrows Moffett are:

1) Edward A. Moffett was born on July 11, 1857 in Madison, Illinois. He died at birth. He was buried in Brown Cemetery.

2) Edward Raymond Moffett was born on October 11, 1859 in Madison, Illinois. He died September 13, 1926 in Decatur, Illinois at age 67. Edward Raymond was considered by most to have been better-schooled than most boys reared on a farm. After he completed his school work in the rural schools, he attended Lincoln University at Lincoln, Illinois. Afterward, he completed a business course at Valparaiso, Indiana. He was engaged in farming, and during his time in Blue Mound Township, he served as a member of the Board of Supervisors. In 1902, he was elected County Treasurer by the Republicans. After that term expired, he served as Deputy County Clerk and for a number of years served as Chief Clerk for the Decatur Township Assessor. Edward was a member of the Westminister Presbyterian Church, the Masonic Fraternity and a member of Beaumanior Commandery No. 9 Knights Templar. He was considered a kindly man, devoted to his home and family and left many friends.

3) John Bigham Moffett was born on July 13, 1861. John Bigham Moffett II is covered in Book 2, "John Bigham Moffett and Descendants: The Southern Moffetts."

4) William David Moffett was born on January 24, 1863 in Macon County, Illinois. He died on September 18, 1944 in Decatur, Macon County, Illinois. He was buried in Brown County Cemetery. He was married to Anna Martha Cottle in Macon County on February 1, 1894. Anna was born October 15, 1868 in a log house across the Sangamon River and the home of Abraham Lincoln. Anna was the daughter of George Cottle and Susan Browning. The couple were married for 50 years. William David graduated from the University of Illinois as a civil engineer. He was the Macon County Surveyor from 1924-1942. He also performed custom surveying and farm drainage work in Macon and adjoining coun-

ties and completed the plats of the four major Decatur cemeteries and twenty-two others in the county. He also was employed as a surveyor for a number of railroad companies, as well as a mining company in Denver, Colorado in 1891. From 1893 to 1912, William David was employed by the Rio Grande Railroad as a field worker. He was a member of the Westminister Presbyterian Church and also served as an Elder. Interestingly, in 1887, William David and his brother, John Bigham Moffett II, both acquired land in Dodge City, Kansas. John Bigham was a lawyer serving as Justice of the Peace and William David was serving as Deputy County Surveyor for Ford County and was also Assistant City Engineer for Dodge City.

5) Harry Josiah Moffett was born on February 5, 1856 in Macon County. He died eight months later on October 21, 1865.

6) Leonara Antoinette Moffett was born on April 18, 1867 in Springfield, Sangamon County, Illinois. On October 10, 1888, she married Edwin Preston Hall in Springfield. Leonara and Preston had three children: Lucille Moffett Hall; David Stevenson Hall; and Edwina Mildred Hall. Edwina died on April 3, 1867 in Springfield.

7) Mary Helen (Minnie) Moffett was born on December 28, 1868 in Madison County, Illinois. On September 1, 1887, she married Edwin Wright Allen. Mary and Edwin had four children: Leonara Antoinette Allen; David Skilman Allen II; Marie Amanda Allen; and Moffett Barrows Allen. Mary Helen died on August 17, 1921 in Macon County.

8) Elizabeth Ann (Betty) Moffett was born on November 18, 1871 in Madison, Illinois. She married William Nesbit Rugh on February 7, 1894. Elizabeth and William had two children: Lucian Edgar Rugh and Samuel Truby Rugh. Elizabeth died on January 21, 1954 in Arcola, Illinois and is buried in the Arcola Cemetery.

Portrait of William Thomas Moffett.

Portrait of Helen Lucretia Barrow Moffett,
wife of William Thomas Moffett.

Portrait of Susan Walker Barrow and three generations of Moffett-related women. From left to right, Helen Lucretia Barrow Moffett; Leanora Moffett Hall; Lucille Hall Chapman; and Susan Walker Barrow.

William Thomas Moffett and family in the early years of Decatur. From left to right, Mary Helen (standing); Helen Lucretia Barrow Moffett (seated); John Bigham II (standing); Edward Raymond (seated); William David (standing); Elizabeth Ann (seated); William Thomas (seated); and Leanora Antoinette (standing).

www.ingramcontent.com/pod-product-compliance
Lightning Source LLC
Chambersburg PA
CBHW040319100426
42811CB00012B/1482